BLOOD IN THE ARENA

 UNIVERSITY OF TEXAS PRESS   AUSTIN

ALISON FUTRELL

BLOOD
in the
ARENA

The Spectacle of Roman Power

First paperback printing, 2000

Requests for permission to reproduce material from this work should be sent to
Permissions, University of Texas Press, Box 7819, Austin, TX 78713–7819.

⊗ The paper used in this publication meets the minimum requirements of American
National Standard for Information Sciences—Permanence of Paper for Printed
Library Materials, ANSI Z39.48–1984.

Library of Congress Cataloging-in-Publication Data

Futrell, Alison, date
    Blood in the arena : the spectacle of Roman power / Alison
Futrell. — 1st ed.
        p.   cm.
    Includes bibliographical references and index.
    ISBN 0-292-72504-3 (alk. paper)
    ISBN 0-292-72523-x (pbk.)
    1. Gladiators—Rome.   2. Games—Social aspects—Rome.   3. Rome—
Civilization.   4. Amphitheaters—Rome.   5. Human sacrifice—Rome.   I. Title.
GV35.F88   1997
796'.0937—dc21   97-4693

Quotation on page 1 reprinted with the permission of Scribner, a Division of Simon
& Schuster, from THE PERSECUTION AND ASSASSINATION OF JEAN-PAUL MARAT AS PER-
FORMED BY THE INMATES OF THE ASYLUM OF CHARENTON UNDER THE DIRECTION OF THE
MARQUIS DE SADE by Peter Weiss. Copyright © 1965 John Calder, Ltd. Copyright
© 1981 Atheneum Publishers. British and Commonwealth rights courtesy Marion
Boyars Publishers Ltd.

CONTENTS

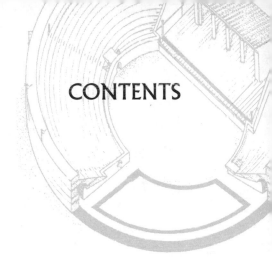

ILLUSTRATIONS

FIGURES

MAPS

ABBREVIATIONS

A Arch Hung	*Acta Archaeologica Academiae Scientiarum Hungaricae*
AE	*L'Année Epigraphique*
AJA	*American Journal of Archaeology*
AJAH	*American Journal of Ancient History*
AJP	*American Journal of Philology*
ANRW	*Aufstieg und Niedergang der römischen Welt*
BAR	*British Archaeological Reports*
BCAR	*Bollettino della Commissione archeologica comunale in Roma*
BCH	*Bulletin de Correspondance Hellénique*
BICS	*Bulletin of the Institute of Classical Studies of the University of London*
BJ	*Bonner Jahrbücher*
BMC	*Coins of the Roman Empire in the British Museum*
CAH	*Cambridge Ancient History*
CIL	*Corpus Inscriptionum Latinarum*
CLPA	*Cahiers Ligures de Préhistoire et d'Archéologie*
CQ	*Classical Quarterly*
CSSH	*Comparative Studies in Society and History*
HSCP	*Harvard Studies in Classical Philology*
ILTG	*Inscriptiones Latinae Trium Galliarum et Germaniarum*
JDAI	*Jahrbuch des deutschen archäologischen Instituts*
JDAI(AA)	*Jahrbuch des deutschen archäologischen Instituts (Archäologischer Anzeiger)*
JRA	*Journal of Roman Archaeology*
JRS	*Journal of Roman Studies*

LIMC	Lexicon Iconographicum Mythologiae Classicae
MDAI(R)	Mitteilungen des deutschen archäologischen Instituts (Römische Abteilung)
MEFRA	Mélanges d'archéologie et d'histoire de l'École française de Rome, Antiquité
NC	Numismatic Chronicle
NSA	Notizie degli scavi di antichità
OLD	Oxford Latin Dictionary
PBSR	Papers of the British School at Rome
PECS	Princeton Encyclopedia of Classical Sites
RA	Revue Archéologique
RAAN	Rendiconti dell'Accademia di Archeologia, Lettere e Belle Arti di Napoli
RE	Paulys Real-Encyclopädie der klassischen Altertumwissenschaft
REA	Revue des Études Anciennes
REG	Revue des Études Grecques
REL	Revue des Études Latines
Revista CIADAM	Revista del Centro de Investigaciones Andinas de Alta Montaña
RhMus	Rheinisches Museum
RIA	Rivista dell'Istituto Nazionale di Archeologia e Storia dell'Arte
RIB	Roman Inscriptions of Britain
TAPA	Transactions of the American Philological Association
ZPE	Zeitschrift für Papyrologie und Epigraphik

ACKNOWLEDGMENTS

A MONOGRAPH CAN NEVER truly be the work of just one person. Without the kind participation of the following people and groups of people, this work would never have been possible.

I would first like to express my appreciation for the generosity of those institutions that provided financial backing during the creation of this manuscript. The University of Arizona provided me with a Social and Behavioral Sciences Research Grant and assistance from the Provost's Author Support Fund, which were key to the revision process. The MaBelle McLeod Lewis Fellowship Fund gave generous support during the writing of the dissertation in 1990–1991, following the Pritchett Fellowship Fund, which honored me as Pritchett Fellow, 1988–1990.

Much gratitude goes to the scholarly assistance of a number of people. Particular thanks are due to Robert C. Knapp and to Erich S. Gruen, both long-term mentors, for the many hours of wrestling with my tortured prose and feeble arguments and for remorseless encouragement and support at moments of lassitude. Other scholars gave helpful assistance during the writing stage, in particular Thomas N. Habinek, Ronald S. Stroud, and John K. Anderson. Keith Hopkins and Oliver Nicholson offered suggestions on proto-versions of the first chapter. Ruth Tringham provided welcome suggestions and frank advice. The students in Tom Habinek's Arena Seminar and the Celtic Colloquium, both at the University of California Berkeley, offered useful comments on various portions of the work. David Ortiz, Laura Tabili, and Susan Crane made sage suggestions at a critical moment, and Jim Millward had helpful insights and provoked renewed efforts on numerous occasions. Matt Redekop and Brian Atkinson provided cartographic assistance. Many thanks as well to the University of Texas Press, especially Nancy Moore, Carolyn Wylie,

and Ali Hossaini, and a number of anonymous readers whose specific recommendations helped shape the final manuscript. Any errors should be
attributed to my own stubborn capriciousness, as all these did their best
to guide my efforts.

A list of personal thanks to friends would be extremely long and detailed, filled with cryptic references and inside jokes. Most of you know
who you are. I want to take this opportunity to express my sincere gratitude for bearing with me throughout the effort and for attempting to
keep me relatively sane. Particular thanks to Martha Jenks, Judy Gaughan,
Lisa Zemelman, Susan Crane, David Ortiz, Jim Millward, Kathy Morris-
sey, Molly Richardson, Eric and Kathy Orlin, Pamela Vaughn, Jeannie
Marchand, Haley Way, Girish Bhat, Sharon Steadman, Joan Gruen, Jane
Edwards, Jenni Sheridan, and Peter Wyetzner and to the faculty, staff,
and students of the Department of History at the University of Arizona.

Finally, much gratitude to my family for support and distraction
throughout the effort, indeed, throughout my life: my mother Earlene,
my father Jean, my brother Craig, and my stepmother Anne Graham. It is
to them that I dedicate this work.

BLOOD IN THE ARENA

INTRODUCTION

We only show these people massacred
because this indisputably occurred
Please calmly watch these barbarous displays
which could not happen nowadays
The men of that time mostly now demised
were primitive we are more civilized.

PETER WEISS, *Marat/Sade*,
ACT 1, SCENE 2

THE YEAR OF 42 B.C. was troubled by disturbing evidence of divine disquiet, warning the Romans of violent disruption awaiting them, of the utter transformation of heaven and earth.[1] The signs were, quite literally, unearthly. The sun would shine both day and night, its orb growing to enormous proportions, three times its usual size, and then shrinking dramatically, to the merest pinpoint of light. The boundary between the cosmic and terrestrial realm was ruptured, as bolts of lightning and meteorites rained down from above. Roman sleep was broken by eerie sounds: the call of trumpets, the clash of weapons, and the clamor of phantom men in arms came from the gardens near the Tiber. One dog buried the corpse of another, killed in a canine coup, beside the Temple of Ceres. Prodigies were born, whose mutations spoke of excess and discord.[2] Most dreadful portent for the unity of the Roman State, those gathered on the Alban Mount for the festival of Latiaris saw the statue of Jupiter gush blood from its right arm. Warnings appeared in other areas of Roman activity: in Macedonia, where Brutus and Cassius, the assassin liberators, had their headquarters, rivers dried up or ran backward. Bees swarmed threateningly outside the legionary camp. A boy carrying the statue of Victory in procession fell down, and that hallowed symbol of Roman solidarity and achievement plummeted to the dust. Overhead, vultures and other carrion-eaters gathered, shrieking in warning and in anticipation of carnage to come.

Thoroughly alarmed by these marvels, men sought to avert misfortune through ritual expiation, taking extraordinary measures to assure the gods of Roman piety and devotion. The urban praefect took on the duty of holding the *Feriae Latinae*, the Latin festival, which was meant to be a celebration of the unified Latin people and a ritual expression of the state's success in expansion.[3] Normally this task fell to the consuls, but they were not available to fulfill their obligation. The plebeian aediles decided that the circus races usually held in honor of Ceres were inadequate tribute to the goddess; instead, gladiatorial combats were presented. This too was an innovation and not only for the festival of Ceres. Gladiatorial games had never before been held as part of the official spectacle of the Roman State. Despite their increasing prominence as a means of political persuasion, the *munera*, or gladiatorial games, were traditionally presented on a private basis, in loose association with the public funerals of eminent citizens.[4] Now the power and grandeur of this ritualized exhibition would be harnessed to serve the state in its hour of need; the *munera* would be part of the formal interaction between Rome and the cosmic forces that determined its fate.

Despite these frenzied efforts by the Roman people and their leaders, the peace of the gods was not to be restored. Ambiguous success, at best, was the result of all the pious attempts made in 42 to avert the portended cataclysm. The Battle of Philippi followed shortly thereafter, and the victory of Antony and Octavian over the assassins of Julius Caesar guaranteed the failure of the oligarchy, thus transforming the Republic forever.

The choice of gladiatorial combats as an innovative means of expiation in this context can be interpreted as an encapsulation, in symbolic form, of the changes taking place in the Roman world. Just as would soon happen at Philippi, opponents drawn from the same group battled at the *Cerialia*, in a contrived combat whose power was in what it represented rather than in what it achieved. The gladiatorial battles accomplished no strategic gain, led to no diplomatic arrangements. Their meaning and significance was as a means of communicating the message of Imperial authority; the medium of spectacular death was a persuasive piece of performative rhetoric. The reading of this message is hardly straightforward: the *munera* had become endowed with a number of meanings in the public sphere, which form the subtext to Dio Cassius' text.

Gladiatorial combats in Rome had always been surrounded with the miasma of death. This was due not merely to the bloodshed involved but to their origin in the ceremonies of the public funeral. The choice of formalized combats as funeral performances was a directed one: the heirs of the deceased had a *munus*, or duty, to ease the transition between the world of the dead and the world of the living by providing the lubrication or sustenance of blood as a rite of passage. The blood spilt in ritualized combat guaranteed the community's continuity despite the passage of its leaders. Thus death is not an end but a transition, just as the empire itself does not end but continuously recreates itself anew. With this in mind, we can see that the *munera* of 42 retain their association with death; there is, however, no funeral as such for the death of the Republic. We can view these as the last of the funereal games; henceforth, *munera* would be presented as part of the official calendar of public spectacles, meant to ensure the continuity of the state through regular acknowledgment of its protective forces. The gladiatorial games were thus disassociated from the death of the individual, held, rather, in celebration of the continued life of the Roman State.

Death to ensure life, bloodshed to guarantee safety, the paradox of the arena extends to its political context as well. The games of 42 can be interpreted as the logical fulfillment of Republican competition. Politics during the Roman Revolution had become increasingly violent, in terms of methods and goals. From the early civil discord that resulted in the deaths of the Gracchi to the mayhem committed on the Roman citizenry by officially sanctioned proscriptions and unofficial gangs of thugs, Rome was stained with its own blood. The civic bloodshed occasioned by Rome's leaders was deliberately paralleled in their presentation of Roman spectacle, where the expression of violence in representational form increased in scale and in production values. Rome committed a vast amount of energy, resources, and attention to the extravaganza of destruction, a celebration of the violence turned inward. Rome in the arena consumed itself in grand style, as Rome watched from bleachers in the Forum.

Dio's description of the events of 42 also highlights the cataclysmic, almost performative nature of the conflict and its larger meaning. Philippi was a battle surpassing all others, not in the number of troops involved or the physical scale of the destruction but because of what it represented, because of the political impact of the outcome. Philippi has been seen as the last stand of Roman liberty, the final clash between tyranny and self-government. Liberty was doomed to fail at Philippi. We can read the seeds of failure in the institutionalization of gladiatorial combat at the expiatory games of the same year; the *munera* have often been portrayed as the ultimate expression of an autocratic régime and its ability to compel extraordinary services, extraordinary sacrifices.

Yet Dio admits that the issues were not so clearly drawn, that Philippi was not a stark conflict between good and evil but a civil war. In such circumstances, victory could never be unambiguous, as "the people at one and the same time triumphed over and were vanquished by themselves, inflicted defeat and were themselves defeated."[5] The amphitheater partakes of a similar dualism; the arena contained the force inherent in a totalitarian system, replicating the brutality of empire in a controlled environment, which dramatized the cost of empire paid not only by Rome's opponents but by Rome as well, a cost that was gladly paid.

Far more than merely an architectural construct, the amphitheater is saturated with the dynamism of Roman politics and society. To study the spread of the amphitheater throughout the empire is to reveal the process of Romanization itself, as seen in the imposition of an institution and its accompanying set of values on the people of western Europe, where the amphitheater is most prevalent.[6]

Why did the Romans take so much pleasure in watching gladiatorial combats? What sparked this grotesque, albeit fascinating, pastime? Was the kernel of the *munera* purely Roman, or did some alien culture induce the gladiatorial habit? We begin with an examination of the rise and development of the amphitheater, in terms of both the architectural construct and the events that it housed, which predated and inspired the building form. The origins of gladiatorial contests are a much-debated question, this interest heightened by the importance of the role played by the games in the development of an image for Rome that could be useful in the Mediterranean political dialogue.

The mid-third century B.C. gave rise to gladiatorial combats in the Roman context. This was a time of radical change in Rome, set in motion by the expansion of Rome beyond the confines of Italy and Roman participation in contemporary world politics. The increased interaction with non-Roman peoples would have heightened the need for self-definition. Public spectacle would have provided that: it not only entertained, it served the purposes of Roman hegemony as a means of bringing together the Roman community to commemorate its shared past and to invoke an ideal of a group future.

The placement of amphitheaters in the landscape of the western provinces must be considered in relation to Roman urbanization. Although the arena functioned as a key component in the Roman concept of the city, its distribution in the empire complements the process of imposing an urban network on the countryside as well. The amphitheater held a unique and independent status, one obscured by the standard interpretation of the amphitheater as a fairly superficial part of a typical Roman city. This oversimplification cannot stand, once the true importance of the imperial amphitheater becomes clear. There is, for example, no real one-to-one correspondence between major urban centers and the placement of amphitheaters. Other factors were more important in determining the construction of an amphitheater, such as the presence of a military frontier in Britannia and on the Rhine and Danube. In Gaul we find the phenomenon of the rural amphitheater, where construction of arenas was mandated despite their complete isolation from any habitation center. Gaul demonstrates that the mere size and urban setting of the potential audience were not determining factors in planning an amphitheater; greater weight was given to the projected sociopolitical impact, either in quelling potential unrest or in incorporating non-Roman peoples into the Roman worldview.

The Imperial goal of assimilating provincials made use of the arena as a sacred space. When religion is understood as a functional means of unifying a community and providing the individual with a sense of corporate identity, we can view the amphitheater as a setting for public ritual for the provincial populace. In three cultic practices, the Imperial Cult, Celtic ritual, and the cult of Nemesis, the amphitheater served as a backdrop for sacred performance and thereby served a public purpose desirable to the center of Roman power. By defining the worshipper's place within the subgroup of the cult, the individual has a basis for interaction with the larger society; more than that, he has an intellectual construct for this interaction, provided by the cult.

Augustus made clearest use of the amphitheater as an integral part of the Imperial Cult, in the earliest phase of emperor-worship. The amphitheater encouraged a large number of participants to join in the celebration of the central authority, thereby confirming the divine status of the emperor and legitimizing his rule. The establishment of this sort of corporate identity in the provinces was a more important goal in the early Principate, when a new series of social relationships was being established, running vertically and horizontally, between center and periphery, on many levels and involving many social groups. The amphitheater accommodated and fostered the formation of such communal bonds.

Celtic group identity was incorporated into Romanized forms, not merely providing continuity in the midst of political transformation but causing a new and dynamic creation, born from the combination of traditions. The amphitheater became an integral, functional part of the Celtic sanctuary complex. The images of the amphitheater are closely connected with certain issues key to the Celtic worldview, such as the concepts of liminality and the struggle for balance that liminality implies;[7] the amphitheater, as a building type, epitomizes human conflict, the universal struggle played out on a human scale. The Romano-Celtic amphitheatrical games were therefore not merely entertaining; they were representative of the essence of human existence as understood in Celtic society.

Nemesis appears in the amphitheatrical context most often of all the Mediterranean pantheon, worshipped by lowly gladiators yet also solemnly acknowledged by Imperial magistrates. She was seen as the distributor of good and evil and was related to the basic concept of the *munera* as *munus*: obligatory distribution for the benefit of the deceased and the living. In the ritual surrounding Nemesis, therefore, the arena becomes a metaphor for life itself, for the struggle of the individual to survive against the potential hostile forces of chance and fortune.

Understanding the specific planning process behind the construction of amphitheaters can show us how the center actually wielded this tool of Romanization. These structures were a special part of the public building process in the Roman world, played out against the backdrop of local and regional politics. Public works were a vital part of the interaction between Romans; more importantly, public works often left tangible evidence of this interaction, which remains today in the archaeological record. Who built the amphitheaters? Did private or public funds finance their construction? Was the sponsorship of an amphitheater, like giving games, considered a political coup, but, considering the expense and the permanence of the structures, much more important as an appeal to the electorate? If the funding were municipal as opposed to private, to what extent could the Imperial government be involved in the decision-making process? Pliny the Younger, writing of provincial administration in Bithynia, suggests that approval of public works by Rome became standard policy. By the Severan period, this approval was mandatory for amphitheaters and other spectacle buildings. Was it simply to cut down on fiscal waste in the provinces, or was there some greater risk in these structures that necessitated tighter control over the process?

Amphitheaters can also be analyzed according to conceptual design, which is related to what economic and material resources were available in the vicinity. The policy of controlled access to the amphitheaters, by means of reserved seating and purchased tickets, is another important issue. The stratification of Roman society was expressed in the amphitheatrical *maeniana*, or levels of seating, where the targeted audience was exposed to the spectacle according to the desired impact, mandated largely by the central government but varying according to the local social system. The better seats went to those who were better connected to the center of power or to those whose support was the most useful to the local representatives of Rome.

Having concentrated on peripheries and externals of the amphitheater, from the origins of the building type and the fabric of its construction to the distribution pattern in the West and its association with local and regional cult, we turn to the issue central to our study: how to reconcile the bloodiness of the arena and the events it sheltered with the arena's centrality in Roman society. The determination of the current trend in scholarship to secularize the arena, to make its events into mere "entertainment" or "sport," does not sufficiently address the fascination it held for the Romans and the avid support it enjoyed from the Roman State. We must look elsewhere for elucidation. One explanation of this phenomenon focuses on gladiatorial combat in its larger interpretation as mass slaughter of human beings, that is, the *munera* as human sacrifice. Human immolation, as a rule, takes place as a drastic response to a crisis situation, which demands a reevaluation and renewal of the bonds of society through the performance of the highest, and yet most vile, sacrifice.

This pattern for human immolation has existed in a variety of societies whose practices in many ways mirror those of the Romans. The motivation for human sacrifice is often associated with the maintenance of an absolutist power structure. This basic pattern is detected in both the New World and the Old, in the empires of the Aztec and Inca, in China's Shang period and in early Sumeria, in the twilight years of Carthage and of Dahomey. Vestiges of other types of human sacrifice can be found in the Roman context, and the prior disposition toward this sort of activity in Roman society may have influenced the form taken by the amphitheatrical complex during the Roman Empire.

Understanding gladiatorial combat as a form of commuted human sacrifice affects our assumptions about the social institution symbolized by the amphitheater. The amphitheater was a political temple that housed the mythic reenactment of the cult of Roman statehood. The struggle of the gladiator embodied an idealized and distilled version of the military ethic of *Romanitas*. His passion was the foundation sacrifice, which answered the crisis of empire, validating the Roman struggle for power and offering a model for understanding the basis of that power.

The Roman amphitheater is a mighty thing. Redolent of Roman authority, it dominates the landscape like no other ruin. The façade curves endlessly, limitlessly, symbolic of tradition while defying the limitations of both post-and-lintel architecture and time. From the outside, one sees a continuous series of columned archways, an architectural motif that resonates of the stoa and shelter provided for the citizen in pursuit of his public responsibilities. From within, there still arises, however faintly, the muffled roar of the crowd's reaction, most alive at the moment of death. *This* stoa is only a façade, a false openness that lures one inside, a cage surrounding the encapsulation of Imperial power. Yet the fact that the lure was taken, that the citizens of Rome's empire eagerly collaborated in the spectacles of the amphitheater, suggests that the "stoa" of the colonnade was not entirely a lie but did indeed represent a mediation between the interior and exterior, between the real world and the manufactured image. The amphitheater was more than a striking Roman architectural type; it was a venue for the enactment of the ritual of power. The *munera* were a means of persuasion, through the use of symbols and actions from Rome's traditional repertory, of the validity and continuity of Roman order. The amphitheater was a sociopolitical arena for interaction between the institution and its participants, between the Imperial mind-set and the provincial lifestyle, between the center and the periphery, between Rome and Europe.

I. BEGINNINGS

... to feed on human blood while the people cheer.

PETRONIUS, *Satyricon* 119.18

ALL ROADS LEAD TO ROME and seemingly converge on the Colosseum as the navel of Rome. The Flavian Amphitheater is set apart from the rest of the city, dwarfing all other buildings. In the same way, the Colosseum, and the bloody games it housed, has become emblematic of both the glory and the doom of the Roman Empire.

The amphitheater as a building took on several forms, variations on the basic theme of an elliptical arena surrounded by a podium on which were built raised tiers to seat a multitude of spectators. It resembled the fusion of two theaters, a resemblance that gave rise to the term "amphitheater," which literally means "theater on both sides." It was as if the two orchestral areas had been turned back to back to form the arena, the stage building or backdrop being discarded in the process.[1] Decorative refinements of the amphitheater drew on the tradition of classical architecture, with the outward façade recreating the prestigious Greek orders in engaged columns and the lavish use of elaborate stone and sculpture masking the more utilitarian building material typical of Roman architecture. The seating was supported by a series of vaults radiating outward from the center and sloping upward to enable the maximum number of spectators while still allowing for good visibility. The arena was surrounded by a podium wall, which points to a key distinction between the function of the amphitheater and that of the theater. The amphitheater housed dangerous games, which could potentially pose a risk to the audience as well as the participant; this podium wall was necessary to protect the spectators from the violence of the spectacle.[2] And the spectacle was indeed violent; the amphitheater housed the most notorious celebrations of blood sport known: the *venationes* and the *munera*.

Venationes were "wild animal hunts," in which the thrill of the chase was elaborated and institutionalized in exaltation of the dominance of civilized man over the realm of beasts.[3] But the distinction between man as hunter and animal as victim was blurred in the Roman arena. Human beings were often hunted by animals, as the arena housed the execution of Roman law in the literal execution of those who transgressed the dictates of the state. This was the Roman way of commemorating the triumph of civilization over a bestiality identified, in the arena, with a challenge to the hegemony of Rome. The *munera*, the gladiatorial combats, are the most infamous of Rome's blood sports. The term literally means "duties" or "obligations," originally defined in terms of the duty owed the deceased by his survivors but eventually identified with the duty owed the people of Rome by its leaders.

The amphitheater as a building type was developed in the Late Republic, a creation of the political context and the need to enhance the spectacles used in the furtherance of a political agenda. The achievement of power in Roman politics involved increasingly violent forms of persuasion, both real force and its representation. The developed amphitheater heightened the impact of the representations while allowing the producer of the games to retain his control over the audience's reaction. The usefulness of the amphitheater in achieving this effect, the transmission of a particular message to a particular group with maximum regulation of the outcome, ensured its adoption for political purposes.

The amphitheater as an Imperial concept was more than just a fancy building, more than a place for expensive, bloody games; it represented a social and political institution central to the Roman Empire. The basic function of the amphitheater was as a tool of Romanization, not merely in terms of its outward form, specific to the Roman world, but as pertains to ideas, concepts, and overall impact. The amphitheater must be viewed in association with Roman Imperialism as a conscious means of persuasion of the legitimacy, supremacy, and potential for violence of the Roman State. The amphitheater was an arena of social and political control that took shape, literally and ideologically, during the Late Republic, achieving maturity in the Early Empire and becoming established throughout the Roman sphere in the late first and early second centuries after Christ.

To understand the fundamental concept of the amphitheater, it is important to study certain basic elements, which combined to create the Imperial institution. In the study of architecture, it has become axiomatic that "form follows function"; the hackneyed nature of this cliché does not, however, undermine its essential validity. We will therefore first examine the origin and development in the Roman sphere of the events most closely associated with the amphitheater, the *munera* and *venationes*. Turning next to the location of these events, we will consider the development of the amphitheatrical ambience, that is, the early arenas that housed *munera*, and how the arena was gradually modified to suit the requirements of the event. This eventually led to the creation of the amphitheater as a specialized building type in which the practical needs of the games were met in an environment imbued with the sophistication and glamour of classical architectural forms. We will then address the context of amphitheater construction in Roman society and the function of the arena as a sociopolitical institution.

Gladiatorial combats, identified so closely with the essence of the Roman Empire, may not have been Roman in origin. Several suggestions as to the source of the *munera* have been debated by scholars of the last two centuries.[4] The main discussion has centered on whether a taste for bloody combats came to Rome from its northern neighbors or its southern ones. Most recently, the Campanian source has been accepted with little apparent dissension. The question deserves a closer examination.

CAMPANIAN GLADIATORS

A Campanian, or specifically an Osco-Samnite, origin for gladiatorial combat has found a strong advocate in Georges Ville, who dates this innovation to the beginning of the fourth century B.C. in southern Italy.[5] This theory suggests, in brief, that a rustic armed competition of these Italic peoples was later organized and made formulaic by the Etruscans in the late fourth and early third centuries; still later this custom was exported to Rome as the *munera*.

The literary evidence for the "Campanian" theory is fairly meager, depending solely on references in Livy, Strabo, and Silius Italicus.[6] All three cite the use of gladiatorial combat as entertainment at Campanian dinner parties, their descriptions meant to point up the difference between Campanian or Capuan customs and Roman mores. All emphasize the negative aspect of these events, how cruel, arrogant, decadent, and frivolous the Campanians were to arrange them, while, in sharp contrast, contemporary Romans were serious, simple, pious people, surely better suited for leadership. The construction of this Capuan/Roman dichotomy had relevance for the narrative of the Second Punic War, acting as an explanation for the Campanian betrayal of Rome for Hannibal and as justification for the subsequent harsh treatment of the traitorous Campanians at Roman hands.[7] Most importantly, none of the sources cited in support of the Campanian theory actually says anything about gladiatorial combat in the fourth century, let alone the origins of the practice.[8]

The material evidence for early Campanian *munera*, however, is more extensive and more important, involving representations of what may be gladiatorial combat in Osco-Samnite tombs and South Italian vase paintings, all dating to roughly the second half of the fourth century B.C.[9] The tomb paintings tend to be formulaic and somewhat static, showing pairs of men fighting it out using either spears or very long swords (see Fig. 1). The combat scenes are sometimes associated with representations of other events, such as boxing matches and chariot races. Sometimes an additional figure, identified by posture and costume as a judge, is present (see Fig. 2).[10] The vase paintings likewise depict the occasional presence of noncombatant armed men, apparently awaiting the outcome of the duel, suggesting that these may not, in fact, represent scenes of warfare.[11]

The literary and material evidence for an Osco-Samnite origin for the *munera* is suggestive rather than conclusive. Additional problems of a more theoretical nature in this reconstruction concern particularly the chronology of and motivation for the transferral of the *munera* from Campania to Etruria to Rome.

The Etruscans were indeed interested in Campania and worked to expand their southern connection from early trade links to actual occupation of some sites possibly as early as the eighth century B.C. and definitely by the seventh.[12] The penetration of Etruscan hegemony is less clear, despite some outright declarations by ancient sources that Campania was ruled by an Etruscan federation.[13]

Although Etruscan presence in Campania is verified by the archaeological record, Etruscan cultural influence in the long run was not very

Top: FIGURE 1. Duel scene in fresco on northern wall from Tomb 10, Laghetto (Paestum). *Bottom:* FIGURE 2. Duel scene, with judges, in fresco on southern wall from Tomb from 1937, Andriuolo (Paestum). Both originally published in A. Pontrandolfo and A. Rouveret, *Le tombe dipinte di Paestum* (Modena: Franco Cosimo Panini, 1992), p. 202, pl. 1, and p. 210, pl. 2.

strong. This is particularly true for the areas already familiar with the Greek style of urban civilization. The Etruscan "occupation" of Campania may have been limited to a few aristocratic families, perhaps originally with commercial interests, who lingered on to become local elites.[14]

Contact between Campania and Etruria proper was disrupted by the upheavals of the late sixth and fifth centuries. The overland connection between north and south was broken by the migrations of Italic tribes. The increasing threat from the Greek cities to Etruscan expansion in the western Mediterranean proved an unfortunate distraction, one unsuccessfully countered by Etruscan military forces in critical clashes at Cumae.

By the end of the fifth century, Etruscan presence and influence in Campania, never very strong, was drastically diminished.[15]

There is thus a chronological gap of some one hundred years between the end of "Etruscan Campania" and the transferral of the *munera*, in Ville's scheme, from Campania to Etruria. One must therefore wonder about the mechanism of transferral, given the lack of proximity between the Etruscans and the alleged original Osco-Samnite developers of *munera*. Furthermore, what sort of motivation was there for them to add this ritual to their funeral panoply?[16] Why ape the Campanians? The Osco-Samnites were no doubt fearsome warriors, a power to be reckoned with in Southern Italy. But by Etruscan standards, they were crude barbarians who dwelled in scruffy little huts in squalid villages.[17] There was hardly the glamour worthy of emulation that the Etruscans had found in the Greeks and in the sophisticated cultures of the eastern Mediterranean.[18]

ETRUSCAN GLADIATORS

The strongest literary evidence for an Etruscan source comes from Nicolaus of Damascus, writing in the late first century B.C., who made reference to gladiatorial combat as a practice the Romans took over from the Tyrrhenians, whom the Romans called the Etruscans.[19] Nicolaus does not explore the history of the custom among the Etruscans. Nevertheless, the statement indicates that, during the Roman period, there were traditions current that saw the *munera* as previously Etruscan. The Augustan period may also have seen the introduction of Charun, the Etruscan hammer-wielding demon, as a regular character among the arena personnel, with the particular duty of carrying away the bodies of dead gladiators.[20] Isidorus of Seville provides another connection between the *munera* and Etruria, explaining that the word *lanista*, the technical term for a dealer in gladiators, derives from the Etruscan language.[21] Skeptics may point out that commerce in gladiators has no bearing on the ultimate source of that type of combat and that *lanistae* would have appeared with the spread of such combat through Italy.[22] Yet Late Republican commerce in gladiators was located to a large extent in Campania, where noted Romans kept schools of fighters available for hire and sale.[23] It is thus puzzling and seemingly significant that an Etruscan word would be associated with a "Campanian" trade.

A fragment attributed to Suetonius states that Tarquinius Priscus, the first of Rome's legendary Etruscan kings, initiated the presentation of paired gladiators to the Romans, an establishment that continued for twenty-six years.[24] Although the existence of official games, held annually as part of the Roman calendar, at so early a date would be most unusual, the Suetonian fragment may provide a mechanism for the transferral of the gladiatorial combats. The Etruscan domination of Rome was a period during which many such transfers were allegedly made, particularly those related to statecraft and religion.[25]

The literary sources for Etruscan *munera* are thus hardly proof positive of a northern gladiatorial origin, although they do actually refer to the custom as coming from outside Rome; the *munera* are Etruscan, both in a general sense and in terms of specific details. Better evidence for bloody competition in the arena is available from paintings on the walls of Etruscan tombs.[26] These depictions can be divided into two groups: representations of "Pyrrhicists," whose alleged connection with armed or Pyrrhic dancing should, perhaps, be shifted to the arena, and a particular scene with the character "Phersu," who is involved in a wild animal combat reminiscent of later *venationes*.

A figure labeled "Phersu" is depicted in several paintings at Tarquinia.[27] Dressed only in a multicolored shirt, topped off with a striped conical hat, Phersu is masked and bearded. In the Tomb of the Augurs, Phersu stands holding the leash of a vicious dog or large cat that attacks a man dressed in a loincloth with a voluminous hood or sack over his head (see Figs. 3 and 4).[28] Even though his vision is obscured by his headgear, the hooded man holds a club.

This scene may be some sort of combination *venatio-munus*, with Phersu present as beast-master. Ville disagrees, claiming that the thong at the hooded man's genitals is that of an athlete rather than a prisoner, that Phersu is watching with a slackened leash, which makes it difficult for him to control the animal and direct him in his attack, and that the alleged *venatio* seems to be a draw. The lack of excessive blood and hostility that Ville perceives in this representation has been taken as an indication of the event's true nature: this must be a footrace, taking place as part of the funeral games.

Ville's identification of this scene as track and field competition is strained, to say the least; a *venatio* interpretation is surely preferable. The

Top: FIGURE 3. Phersu and hooded *venator*, fresco from Tomb of the Augurs, Tarquinia; photograph courtesy Deutsches Archäologisches Institut in Rome. *Bottom:* FIGURE 4. Line drawing of Phersu scene, by author.

lack of detail in the fresco as preserved does not allow one to say whether the hooded man's outfit is specific to athletic competition. Despite Ville's claims, the scene is loaded with carnage, as the hooded man bleeds profusely from several wounds opened by the animal. The allegedly slackened leash wraps around his arm and leg, surely hampering any efforts at running a race course. If this is a footrace, it is certainly a most peculiar one and quite unlike any other representations of such from antiquity.

A group of tomb paintings, dating mostly to the fifth and sixth centuries B.C.,[29] includes the depictions of so-called pyrrhic dancers, that is,

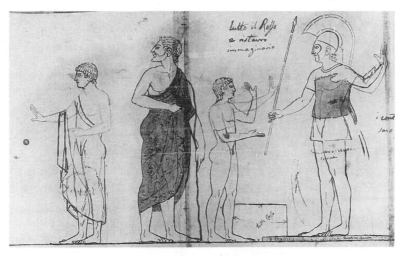

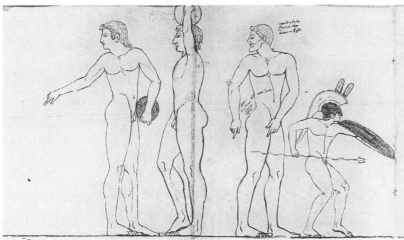

FIGURES 5 and 6. Two images of Pyrrhic dancer and other performers at funeral games. Frescoes from Tomb of the Bigae, Tarquinia; drawings courtesy Deutsches Archäologisches Institut in Rome.

armed men who are not obviously soldiers, usually interpreted as non-combatants, performers in the *Pyrrhica* (see Figs. 5 and 6).[30] Pyrrhic dances were actually not very much like a dance at all but rather a sort of parade-like display of flashy military maneuvers, done to music.[31] Roman exhibitions of *Pyrrhica* were a dramatic event, with performers often acting out episodes from the legendary past. Under the emperors, *Pyrrhica* took place in the amphitheaters alongside the bloodier events.[32]

The figures identified as Pyrrhicists in the Etruscan tombs are men armed with helmet, shield, often a cuirass and sword or lance. They stand with no obvious opponent, although some assume potentially hostile stances. There is nothing, in fact, to prevent their reidentification as gladiators. Indeed, the depictions of the Pyrrhicists in the Tomb of the Bigae seem to argue for such an interpretation (see Figs. 5 and 6). The left wall of the tomb shows a series of nude performers of various types, all waiting to go "on-stage." In clumps between the nudes are men in more formal garments carrying staffs or *lituus*. One Pyrrhicist, drawn to a smaller scale than his naked coperformers, stands at the end of a group, shield and spear in position. A man in robes faces him, hand lifted in a gesture that suggests waiting. A second Pyrrhicist, garbed in a different armature, stands upright behind another man in robes and a nude youth. The distinction here made in the armature may imply an early use of the traditional heterogeneity in technique, which was customary within a combative pair in the later Roman *munera*; pyrrhic dancers would be more uniform. The Tomb of the Bigae is therefore best understood as a realistic representation of the ambience of funeral games; the Pyrrhicists are depicted as part of a series of performers/competitors waiting to enter the event.[33] These armed men could in fact be gladiators, of a type more conventional than Phersu.

ORIGINES GLADIATORUM

The whole controversy surrounding the origins of gladiatorial combat assumes that the early Roman *munera* were, in fact, a non-Roman anomaly. This may be a rash assumption to make. In the tremendous variety of human endeavor, surely the idea of dueling as performance, whether for the living or for the honored dead, is not such a bizarre concept. It may well be that the Roman version of gladiatorial combat was the systematization of a practice common to Italic peoples and not an import at all. This possibility must be considered, especially given the fairly tenuous nature of the arguments on both sides of the question of origins.

No straightforward, utterly unquestionable ultimate source for gladiatorial combat can be determined on the basis of the Etruscan and Campanian material and literary evidence. Artistic representations of bloody combat can be found in both areas, seemingly in connection with funeral games, a connection analogous to the known historical context of *munera* in the Roman Republic. The physical remains from Etruria, however, are earlier by a century or more. When the surviving written records from the Roman period mention early *munera*, which, admittedly, they rarely do, it is given an Etruscan flavor. If one, therefore, pushes this evidence, an Etruscan source, or at least the existence of *munera*-like activity in Etruria at an early date, seems the stronger argument. It may also be that this sort of event was presented in Campania from at least the late fourth century. But in terms of influence on the Roman adoption of gladiatorial combat, I find an Etruscan source more persuasive, not only because of the material and literary evidence but also on a theoretical level. As with the alleged Etruscan-Campanian connection above, it is unlikely that Romans of the third century would have appropriated an Osco-Samnite institution, given the history of recent hostility, given the relatively unsophisticated nature of Samnite culture as a unit, and given the lack of comparable "borrowings."

EARLY SPECTACLE IN ROME
Munera

The date generally accepted for the earliest *munera* in Rome proper is 264 B.C., but there are some indications that gladiatorial combats were held there prior to this time.[34] The most straightforward of these comes from Suetonius, who attributes the establishment of regular, state-sponsored *munera* to Tarquinius Priscus (traditionally 616–579 B.C.).[35]

The Tarquins are generally credited with the early development of Rome as an urban entity and the establishment of institutions typical of a "civilized" lifestyle.[36] Under Tarquin rule, the Forum was drained and planned, the Capitoline Temple was built, and Rome took on many of the accoutrements of high culture. More pertinent to the current study is the supposed Tarquin influence on religion and the symbols of state. The Roman emphasis on maintaining a highly formalized relationship with divine powers, as well as the particular forms that relationship assumed, has been attributed to the lasting prestige of Etruscan practice. The markers of political status, such as the curule chair, the toga, the *fasces*, and the triumph, were adopted by Rome under Etruscan hegemony. It may be that the *munera*, a quasi-religious commemorative institution of uncertain antiquity but with definite political overtones, were later assumed to have come to Rome in the general context of the "civilizing" process of the

Etruscan kings. Such an interpretation parallels the habit in Roman sources of constructing an Etruscan derivation of the practice as a whole.

Potentially important as well to the background of the early Roman *munera* is the ongoing development of the Games. The Roman *Ludi* in general were closely identified with the religious ceremonies of the Roman State, the oldest being the *Equirria* and *Consualia* for Mars and Consus respectively. Votive games, promised, usually to Jupiter, in exchange for military success, came to be regularized as the *Ludi Magni*, to be held on an annual basis. Great *Ludi*, including the *Floralia* and *Cerialia*, were added to the Roman calendar particularly during the third century, a period of critical importance to the expansion of Roman influence beyond central Italy, a time when divine assistance was especially needed and lavishly acknowledged upon receipt.[37] Surely it is no coincidence that the specific date assigned to the first *munera* is in the middle of the third century. But can we accept this date as absolute? Or might Romans have enjoyed gladiatorial spectacles prior to 264 B.C.?

Indirect evidence for earlier *munera* comes from the activities of one C. Maenius and the specific term that came to be given the seating of amphitheaters: *maeniana*. Maenius, censor in 338 B.C., constructed a column in the Forum west of the Comitium and south of the Carcer.[38] Festus explains that the *maeniana* were named after Maenius because he was the first to enlarge the seating capacity of the Forum for the viewing of spectacles.[39] The identification of Maenius with the seats for the particular purpose of watching gladiatorial combat suggests that such combat took place during the later fourth century.

Further evidence hinting at the pre-third-century presence of gladiatorial combat in Rome may be the introduction of the "Samnite" type of gladiatorial armature. It is presumed that the "foreign national" types of gladiators originated in the induction of prisoners of war as gladiators.[40] Based on this assumption, the most logical time period for the Romans to codify the Samnitic type would, of course, be during the Samnite Wars, which took place off and on between 343 and 290 B.C., that is, prior to the earliest known presentation of *munera*.[41]

The canonical date given for the introduction of gladiatorial combat to Rome is 264 B.C., at the funeral games of Junius Brutus Pera, when, as Livy puts it, "Decimus Junius Brutus was the first to put on a gladiatorial combat in honor of his deceased father."[42] Livy's assertion is reiterated by

Valerius Maximus, who specifies that the *editores* were Decimus and his brother Marcus and that the combat took place in the Forum Boarium.[43] Ausonius provides further detail in terms of armature and the presentation of the *munera*, claiming that there were three pairs of gladiators, fighting in consecutive combats in the Thracian style.[44] Servius speculates on the early nature of the whole institution and the practice of sending captives as some sort of obligation owed the deceased. There is an implication of the high status of the dead person who warranted such treatment, but Servius contributes few other specifics about the Junian celebration.[45] A variety of sources thus do agree that the commemoration of 264 represents the first gladiatorial combat to take place in Rome. Who was this Junius Brutus Pera, to merit such innovation at his funeral?

The *gens Iunia* is associated in Rome's legendary past with the Etruscan presence in Rome.[46] The earliest known possessor of the name was one Marcus, who married the sister of Tarquinius Superbus, thereby acquiring most intimate ties with Etruria. The son of this union, Lucius Junius Brutus, was the celebrated liberator of the Roman people, the founder of the Roman Republic and its first consul. The actual historicity of this character, as is generally true for individuals of Rome's remote past, is questionable, as is his connection with the historical Junian clan. For one thing, L. Junius Brutus was a patrician, while the later *gens* was plebeian.[47] Another problem to be explained away was Brutus' execution of his two sons, which would have limited his direct descendants, to say the least.[48] Nevertheless, the Republican possessors of the Junius name claimed and stoutly defended their connection to the famed liberator of the Roman people.

A notable oddity, in conjunction with the first *munera* honoree, is the double *cognomen* of the deceased. Brutus and Pera are both known *cognomina* of the Junii but do not otherwise appear together, these two branches of the family having diverged at some early date.[49] This "Brutus Pera" *cognomen* need not invalidate the report, as uniqueness does not necessarily prove lack of historicity.[50]

Livy and Servius do not use the Pera *cognomen*, an omission that makes possible identification of the specific individual slightly easier. He may have been D. Junius Brutus Scaeva, who was consul in 292 B.C.[51] Under his auspices the Faliscans were conquered, which offers a context for a more recent link to Rome's northern neighbors and thus, perhaps, access to alternative, non-Roman funerary traditions. The Faliscan victory would also mean that he might have had war captives within reach, in keeping with the tradition preserved in Servius; after some three decades, however, the Faliscan war prisoners may have been slightly hoary.

If the *cognomen* Brutus has been mistakenly assigned by the sources to the first gladiatorial honoree, then the deceased may have been the father of D. Junius Pera, consul of 266 with N. Fabius Pictor.[52] This consul triumphed twice in 266, over Sassinates, Sollentini, and Messapii. It may be that Italic captives, brought to Rome for the triumphal celebrations, were forced to perform in these *ludi funebres*. Again, access to war captives would be an advantage to the *editores* of these games, although with only three pairs of men recorded for the *munera*, surely the acquisition of enough fighters would not be too excessive a burden.

The location of the *munera* is variously given. Valerius Maximus specifies the Forum Boarium, while Ausonius places the combats at the tomb itself, presumably near a major thoroughfare outside the city walls.[53]

Ausonius also adds the detail that these were gladiators of Thracian type, an armature that utilized a small, round shield, sword, and greaves. The date for the introduction of this particular type is debatable. One argument suggests that Thracian mercenaries were taken captive during the war against Perseus (171–167 B.C.), then were removed to Rome and forced to compete as gladiators.[54] Another line of reasoning places their introduction in the age of Sulla, following the Mithridatic war of the mid-eighties.[55] Both theories put Thracian-style combat considerably later than 264 B.C., and it seems likely that Ausonius here uses some anachronistic poetic license in his description.[56]

The first *munus* was followed by others, with increasing frequency. The next to appear in the historical record took place in 216 B.C., when, as Livy tells us, "the three sons, Lucius, Marcus, and Quintus, gave funeral games for three days and twenty-two pairs of gladiators in the forum for [their father] M. Aemilius Lepidus, who had been consul twice and augur."[57] The context for these *munera* is still funereal, but the lavishness of the entertainment has been considerably heightened, soaring from three pairs of gladiators to twenty-two.[58]

The Lepidus branch of the patrician *gens Aemilia* first appeared in the early third century with M. Aemilius Lepidus, consul of 285 and presumed grandfather of the honoree of 216.[59] From this inception, the Aemilii Lepidi became quite a potent political force, with consuls in nearly every generation. This particular Lepidus had twice been consul, as Livy says, in 232 and probably again in 220 B.C.[60] He led troops against the Sardinians during his first consulship. Lucius and Quintus, his sons, are known only from this passage, but Marcus was praetor in Sicily in 218 and possibly held office in Rome the next year.[61] Livy refers to his unsuccessful candidacy for the consulship of 216. This first known association between the giving of *munera* and electioneering for the highest offices would establish a key pattern for the politicization of the gladiatorial combats in the later Republic. A further hint at the public nature of the games is in the historiographical placement of the *munera*.

Livy is the most important source for these earliest attested combats, and an understanding of the Livian context is basic to our interpretation of these events. The notice of the Aemilian combats is sandwiched between accounts of the dedication of the Temple of Venus Erycina and the celebration of the Roman and Plebeian Games, all major state events of the year. Livy is probably presenting a close replica of the abbreviated public records he used as the basis of his history. The inclusion of gladiatorial combats in such documents would imply that, even at this early date, the *munera* were perceived as public celebrations that were important to the Roman people and state as a whole.

The cultic significance of these funeral rituals can also be extracted from the Livian context, specifically with reference to the dates of the Iunian and Aemilian *munera*. The year 264 saw the beginning of the First Punic War. The year of the Battle at Cannae was 216. The chronology of the *munera* is surely no coincidence; these ritual combats, as they appear in the sources, should be understood as part of the morale-boosting social and religious innovations and reforms made to deal with the threat from Carthage. Was there in fact a gap of nearly fifty years between the "first" and "second" *munera* in Rome, or does the reportage of these events say something about the historical context? Other *munera* given in the third century may have gone unreported because there was no crisis to attach them to, to make them noteworthy in Roman eyes. It may be that this distinctive type of funeral commemoration, steeped in Etruscan ritualistic trappings, was deemed more appropriate in times of crisis for the state. The fact that Livy places them alongside the dedication of the Temple of Venus Erycina and the celebration of the *Ludi Romani* and the *Ludi Plebeii*, religious measures meant to assuage divine displeasure, is hardly coincidental.[62]

The *munera* continue to appear sporadically in the literary sources, revealing great advances in terms of scale and, presumably, elaborateness of the production. From twenty-two pairs at the Aemilian games, to twenty-five pairs at the funeral of M. Valerius Laevinus in 200, to sixty pairs in 183 and seventy-four pairs in 174, the numbers involved increased consistently.[63] The enhancement of public spectacle took place within the context of Late Republican politics, when the utility of such presentations in furthering one's magisterial career was made apparent. This was true especially of the *munera* but also of other equally lavish, equally exploitable forms of spectacle, such as the wild animal hunts.

Venationes

Alongside the performances of men, animals were used for entertainment purposes in Rome in a variety of ways. The simplest form was the exhibition of wild or unusual animals. Once captured, many animals were capable of being trained to do interesting tricks, which were a source of amusement to the Roman crowds. Eventually, however, the Roman taste for bloody exotica overshadowed the milder types of animal exhibitions, as thousands of animals met their deaths in combat during the Imperial period. To be included as part of the *venatio* blood bath were the executions of those *damnati ad bestias*, condemned to the beasts.

In contrast to the gladiatorial combats, *venationes* have not been perceived as stereotypically Roman. The struggle between human beings and the other inhabitants of the planet is surely one of the most basic of conflicts, and the mastery of one or several odd or dangerous animals must be one of the earliest forms of interactive entertainment.

There are two reconstructions of the origin of *venationes* as spectacular entertainment in Rome. They are not necessarily mutually exclusive. Indeed, it is likely that both suggested motivations shaped the presentation of spectacle during the middle Republic.

The first theory emphasizes the use of animals in ritual not merely as sacrificial victims but as active participants. Three holidays are of particular interest here: the *Ludi Taurei*, the *Cerialia*, and the *Floralia*.

Ludi Taurei were not part of the series of *Ludi Magni*, but were more similar to the *Ludi Saeculares*, held on an infrequent basis. Like those games, they were held in honor of chthonic rather than celestial deities and were meant to turn aside pestilence, as Servius makes clear: "Thus these *ludi* are called *Taurei*, which were instituted in perpetuity by King Tarquinius Superbus at the instigation of the Books of Fate, because all the women who had given birth were doing poorly, while others say the Taurean Games were instituted by the Sabines because of a pestilence, in order to transfer the disease to the sacrificial victims."[64] Interesting in light of the gladiatorial evidence is Servius' attribution of these games to Tarquinius Superbus, that is, to an Etruscan source. Additional evidence from Festus could suggest that bulls themselves were let loose and hunted in the Circus; indeed, these bulls may have been set on fire, an impressive spectacle, surely, if rather unkind.[65]

The *Cerialia* honored the goddess of Italian agriculture on April 19. During the event, as Ovid describes it, foxes were sent running with backs ignited by torches tied to them.[66] Ovid goes on to explain that once in Carseoli, a fox that had made off with many hens was finally captured and set on fire in punishment. The vixen escaped and ran through the fields of wheat, the stalks blazing up in her wake. Thus ever after, a representative fox was burned annually just as the crops had been burned long ago. The adequacy of Ovid's explanation for such an odd and nasty ritual is somewhat lacking, but most scholars agree that the practice originated in the dim mists of archaic Italy.

It may be that the fox was meant to represent the wheat spirit, who took the form of a fox in some agricultural societies.[67] The *Cerialia* ritual would thus symbolize the release of a divine force to permeate the fields, imparting some essential fertility to them. The eventual incineration of the fox in the Circus, however, seems to negate this theory, as surely some sort of disrespect to the wheat spirit is implied by the destruction of her agent. The fox may be just that, a fox, the bane of agriculturalists everywhere, whose ritualized death was meant to work some sort of sympathetic magic on all such pests.[68]

The *Floralia* were celebrated from April 28 to May 3, a festival during which hares and roebucks were hunted in the Circus. Ovid questions the honored goddess as to the choice of animals, asking why she prefers the killing of soft and fuzzy deer and scared little rabbits to that of, say,

Lybian lionesses. Flora responds that the woods are not her domain but rather the gardens and cultivated lands, where one does not find such dangerous animals.[69] Notable here is the cultic distinction drawn between these herbivores and "fighting animals," the *pugnaci*, a distinction also drawn with reference to animals of the arena. Rabbits and deer are victims of the arena, necessary to the performance of blood spectacle but hardly professional participants.

Ovid had asserted previously that the *Floralia* were instituted in 240 B.C., in commemoration of greater control over public lands. A temple was then built for the goddess in 238, on the advice of the Sibylline Books.[70] The *Floralia* were changed from occasional to annual games in 173 B.C., in Ovid's account. They were apparently notorious for their intemperate conviviality.[71]

The second theory regarding the origins of the *venationes* sees it as an effect of the spread of Roman hegemony, suggesting that during the third century and after, success in battle against foreign foes opened up areas abundant in exotic animal resources, now exploitable by Romans. They displayed these new wonders in spectacles. After the initial excitement generated simply by their appearance wore off, the Romans sought novel sensations by making the animals fight.[72] This theory assumes that only exotic animals could be utilized in spectacular games; the "exotic" label could hardly be applied to bulls, foxes, bunnies, and deer. Elephants, however, were the fantastic beast *par excellence* in Roman estimation and by definition were endlessly fascinating.

Elephants were first brought to Rome in triumph by M'. Curius Dentatus in 275 B.C., having been taken from Pyrrhus in the south of Italy.[73] The elephants were apparently displayed as part of the war booty, as the sources associate the elephants with the triumph of the consul rather than with games of any sort. A much more elaborate exhibition, showcasing 142 of the beasts, was mounted in 252 B.C. by L. Caecilius Metellus. Pliny gives a lengthy description, with some doubt as to the ultimate fate of the animals.

Rome, five years later, saw elephants in a triumph; she saw them again in great numbers in 502 A.U.C. (252 B.C.) captured from the Carthaginians in Sicily in the victory of L. Metellus the pontifex.

There were 142 or, according to others, 140 elephants who made the crossing on the rafts that Metellus put on top of ranges of storage jars. Verrius says that they were made to fight in the circus and were killed with javelins, because no one knew what to do with them, since no one wanted them either to be fed [at public expense] or be given to the kings. L. Piso says that the producers were satisfied simply with bringing the elephants into the circus and, in order to increase contempt for them, made them be chased across the arena by laborers armed with blunted spears. The authors who think that they were not put to death do not say what did happen to them afterward.[74]

Animals from overseas were presented at votive games in 186, arranged by M. Fulvius Nobilior who had vowed them years previously at the capture of Ambracia, as part of the *Magni Ludi* for Jupiter Optimus Maximus. Livy tells us that a hunt of lions and panthers was greatly appreciated, as contemporaries wallowed in the excess and variety typical of the period.[75] In the Livian account, Nobilior's ten days of games followed immediately after two days of *Ludi Taurei*, given for religious reasons. It seems fortuitous that all sorts of animal shows should be lumped together in the celebrations, both the more regularized "religious" ones of the *Ludi Taurei* and the supposedly more secular ones offered by Nobilior.

In 169 B.C., as part of the growing extravagance in games, Scipio Nasica and Cornelius Lentulus exhibited, as part of the official aedilician games, sixty-three African cats and forty bears and elephants.[76] Whether they fought is unclear. The debate rages around Livy's use of the term *lusisse*, which has been taken to indicate that the elephants did not fight, but perhaps the other animals did.[77] It seems more likely that *lusisse* should be taken as referring to all the animals, in the absence of another verb. In fact, this passage in its entirety has been used to define *ludere* as "to take part in a public spectacle or show," which participation could take a variety of forms, playful and deadly.[78]

The Nasica referred to in this passage must be P. Cornelius Scipio Nasica Corculum, who became consul (briefly) in 162 and again in 155, having been censor in the interim since 159. He was known as a firm upholder of the *mos maiorum*, staunchly opposed to all forms of cultural innovation. He opposed the destruction of Carthage, in that its survival would prove an object lesson in the dangers of licentiousness. His presence here, in a passage Livy introduces as an example of the prodigality of the times, is odd and may reflect the hostile attitude of Livy's source.

Nowhere does Livy say that the events of 186 and 169 represented some novelty at the time. This is especially striking in the games of Nobilior because the historian does specifically state that this was the first time Greek athletics were part of the games. Surely other innovations would have been noted as well. In the absence of such a notice, we must assume that animal spectacles were well established in the Roman program of official productions.

In 170, the Senate apparently acted to bar the importation of African beasts to Italy, a measure countered by a *plebiscitum* sponsored by Cn. Aufidius, the tribune of the plebs in that year.[79] The motives of the Senate are unclear but may be related either to the fear of an enriched Carthage or to the fear of demagogues currying political favor as *editores* of fabulous *venationes*.[80] Pliny's description of the *plebiscitum* suggests that it was designed to provide an exception to the law, specifically for the import of animals destined for venations; this would argue against the association of the law with political in-fighting. The presence of large numbers of animals for the aedilician games of 169 also argues against the applicability of the law to spectacular entertainment.

Damnatio ad Bestias

The use of exotic animals for public executions is first known from 167 B.C., when Aemilius Paullus had army deserters crushed by elephants after his victory over Perseus. A precedent was thus set for Roman commanders abroad. The act was done publicly, a harsh object lesson for those challenging Roman authority. This unusual method is highly touted by Valerius Maximus, who perceives the spectacular element as encouraging greater discipline out of the fear of the greater humiliation involved.[81] It is also significant that the deserters were not Romans but soldiers of foreign origin, more deserving, by definition, of such deadly degradation.[82] From the outset, then, it seems that the *damnatio ad bestias* was strongly linked to the goals of Roman Imperialism in the guise of "military discipline." It has been suggested, moreover, that these executions were part of Paullus' victory games. This combination of spectacular celebration of Roman conquest and public execution would set a pattern to be followed for centuries.

Scipio Aemilianus brought the display to Rome in 146 B.C., making *damnatio ad bestias* an integral part of his triumphal games instead of, nominally, a military execution. "Once the Punic hegemony had been overturned, [Aemilianus] threw the deserters of foreign origin to the wild beasts, in a spectacle put on for the People."[83] Note that the executions here are connected with the triumph, that venerable institution meant to commemorate Roman Imperialism.[84] As with Paullus, the victims are not Romans but rather auxiliaries who revealed their inherent barbarism and inferiority by their treacherous behavior.[85] There also may be some sense of retribution motivating this demonstration, a payback for the atrocities committed on Romans by the Carthaginians during the course of the war.[86]

Animal shows were housed in the Circus until the Early Principate when *venationes* were combined with gladiatorial combats and *ludi meridiani* to become the *munus legitimum*, at which time they were definitively located in the amphitheater. On occasion under the empire, mostly in the first century, animal shows would again be located in the Circus Maximus, but these were events at which a huge number of very large animals would be displayed all at once. These were special occasions, triumphs and anniversaries, or specific events that called for room to fight in crowds (*ad gregatim*) or otherwise needed excessive amounts of space.[87] The influence, therefore, of the animal shows on the earliest accommodations for *spectacula* was minimal. Such inspiration came, rather, from the *munera*.

THE LATE REPUBLIC: SPECTACLE AND POLITICAL MANIPULATION

The last century of the Republic saw many changes in the process of Roman politics. The changes in Roman society resulting from the spread of Roman hegemony had provided a catalyst for changes in the methodology of public discourse. The traditional political forum was circumvented more and more, as new groups demanded the attention of ambitious Roman politicians, who saw in these groups the potential for achievement independent of the conservative framework of civic management. Yet the demonstrative nature of Roman politics would shape the urban inter-action of the Late Republic; public spectacle replaced the usual political assemblies as the crucial venue for establishing and legitimizing the new leaders. The public shows provided a backdrop and a ritualized structure for public discourse, discourse sparked by the nature of the spectacle as well as by the proximity of key players in the political game.[88]

The public funerals of important Romans became increasingly poli-ticized. These had always been opportunities for the expression of the Roman value system and the exaltation of virtues perceived as vital to the success of Rome. Polybius' discussion of the character of the Roman people, the articulation of the reason behind Roman greatness, showcases an extensive description of the public funeral as both the embodiment of the national strengths and the best means used to inculcate the young with the appropriate ethics and civic priorities.[89]

Public funerals in the Late Republic gave occasion for political manip-ulation and dissension. The impact of these events had been intensified through the heightened display of elaborate symbolism, a by-product of increasing sophistication in the use of spectacle forms to direct audience participation. The manipulative techniques involved could evoke a pow-erful response, as happened at Sulla's funeral in 78 B.C., when the Roman people were numbed by ambivalent feelings of fear, amazement, and a genuine sense of loss.[90] The response could turn violent as well, with long-range effects beyond, perhaps, the original calculations of the fu-neral arranger. The riots associated with the funerals of Clodius and of Caesar led directly to the outbreak of civil war.

Despite the increasing politicization of the public funeral, the *munera* were gradually dissociated from these events. The *munera* had much to offer as an implement of public persuasion, and one could not count on a death occurring at the optimal moment. The temporal connection be-tween the death of a noted individual and the production of *munera* was therefore stretched quite thin.[91] The gladiatorial games were so appealing to those in public life and to their constituency for many reasons. There was the entertainment aspect, the display of spendthrift liberality by the *editor* in providing flashy and striking shows.[92] This, too, was manipula-ble: the *editor* had the ability to direct the movement and attention of the target audience through the presentation of cohesive representations.

There was also the "extraordinary" character of the *munera*: unlike other Roman games, the *munera* had never needed to receive official sanction, had never based their legitimacy on the official structure of the state religion. Yet the *munera* still had a strong religious resonance, which would enhance the effect by providing an element of *sollemnitas*.

The contemporary ambience of civic disorder also favored the use of the *munera*; the violence in the arena replicated in many ways the faction fighting among the gangs of political thugs in Rome's streets.[93] The arena, however, had certain advantages: the impact and outcome of the mayhem could be controlled by its organizers. This was idealized violence, violence in support of order instead of disorder. The tendency to make use of gladiatorial games as a means of furthering one's political career gained real impetus in the last decades of the Roman Republic, when the propagandistic dimension of *munera* was openly exploited.

The value in *munera* for ambitious leaders lay not just in the spectacle itself but in the provisions for the spectacle; the interaction between audience and *editor* was the essence of its political meaning. This interaction need not have been confined to the day of the games. An early incident in which the potential impact of the arrangements for the arena was felt featured Gaius Gracchus.[94] The populist politician staged a piece of political theater in 122 B.C., when he tore down the boxes of the nobles taking up prime spectating space around a temporary arena in the Forum, blocking the view of Rome's common folk, the plebs.[95] In so doing, he annoyed many people, particularly the magistrates who had constructed the seating. Gaius' action against the gladiatorial bleachers was a demonstration of his preference for the Roman plebs as his political constituency at the expense of the wealthy oligarchs. Even more intriguing is the clear connection Plutarch draws between Gracchus' "antisponsorship" or deconstruction (literally) of the *munera* and his failure at the elections and, ultimately, his doom. This is an indication of the power the spectacles held as a venue for politically charged performances by Rome's potentates.

The Gracchus incident also points up particular features of the *munera* in terms of their role in manipulating popular behavior and expressing public opinion. The "insiders" of the games of 122, those who promoted and produced them and lost by their destruction, were opponents of Gracchus, identified by Plutarch with the conservative element in the ruling class. The antipopulist sympathies housed by the arena are detectable as well in the writings of Cicero, who values the expressions of public opinion manifested at the games very highly, specifically for this very reason. The "popular" leaders were not popular at the shows, in direct contrast to the assemblies. Cicero therefore sees the audiences at public spectacles as a truer representation of the Populus Romanus, as being less vulnerable to demagogic manipulation and as more closely replicating Roman society as a whole, the segregated seating allowing for the presence of a cross-section of the public.[96] Cicero, of course, has his own political agenda, tending to favor conservative policy as less damaging to the Roman State and as more likely to foster his own dream of a consensus among "good men." Likewise, the audience of the spectacles could be manipulated by the *editores* as well; admission to public games was determined on the basis of who had access to the sponsors of the shows. The suggestion, however, that public shows were produced predominantly by nonpopulists is intriguing, with implications for the development of the institution of the amphitheater as an important tool of the Imperial machine.

The popularity of these events lent itself to exploitation by a variety of politicians who sought to curry favor with their constituency. Eventually, this quality led the Senate to attempt to exercise some sort of restraint over the *munera* in the mid-first century, when laws were formulated, or at least interpreted, in such a way as to affect specifically the presentation of gladiatorial spectacles.[97] The *lex Calpurnia de ambitu* of 67 imposed fines, removal from office, and loss of the *ius imaginum* on those convicted of electoral bribery. Cicero apparently promoted an interpretation of this law which was an attempt to control the political use of the *munera* by limiting candidates' distribution of seats at these spectacles.[98] In 65 a measure was passed by the Senate to limit the number of gladiators an *editor* could house in the City while *munera* were in production.[99] Cicero involved himself further in the regulation of *munera* by sponsoring the *lex Tullia de ambitu* of 63, which proscribed the presentation of gladiatorial games within two years of candidacy for office.[100]

The force of these measures seems largely to have been circumvented, as *editores* continued to offer this sort of spectacle as a powerful donative for the Roman people. Whether these laws were ever intended to be true and solid deterrents to the production of *munera* is another question. It was standard practice for Roman senators, like Cicero, to use this sort of legislation as a weapon in factional wrangling, as part of the general effort to inhibit the electioneering of one's political opponents. It may be, however, that these measures were also motivated by some genuine concern for public safety. The scale of *munera* had continued its phenomenal growth from the previous century; Julius Caesar in 65 planned to exhibit 320 pairs of gladiators.[101] The decision to restrict the number of gladiators in the City may have been a response to the danger represented by huge numbers of armed and trained fighters in a city without a police force, without a home guard, at a time when ambitious politicians were all too willing to resort to violence to achieve their ends.

The force employed by Rome's leaders, both the "spontaneous" thuggery and the carefully planned *munera*, was most effective when most visible.[102] A proper backdrop was required.

The Setting

The preponderance of material evidence associated with early *munera* points to a relationship with death, not just in terms of the risk taken by the individual contestants but, more importantly, in the commemoration of a deceased person by the holding of funeral games. The Etruscan tomb paintings are generally assumed to depict events surrounding the interment of the dead, as may have also been the case in Campania. Italic vases also have funerary motifs in conjunction with presumed archaic gladiatorial combat.[103] What impact did this context have on pragmatic considerations for the presentation of the *munera*? What part did these funeral games play in the actual disposal of the body?

If we ponder these questions in terms of what is known about Roman funerary ritual, it seems that there are three locations in which *munera* may have taken place, if part of the actual funeral. The first potential locale is the private home of the deceased. The primary drawback to this location would be the limitation on space, but this need not have been an insurmountable barrier. In terms of the current study, however, the accommodation of *munera* in the private home must be considered of little relevance, as gladiatorial combat was hardly the primary purpose of the dwelling and thus had little impact on residential architectural design, nor did domestic architecture affect the design of spectacle building types.

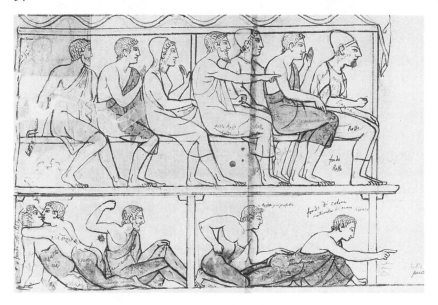

FIGURES 7 and 8. Temporary bleachers set up for spectators at Etruscan funeral games. Frescoes from Tomb of the Bigae, Tarquinia; drawings courtesy Deutsches Archäologisches Institut in Rome.

The second and perhaps the most obvious location for early *munera* is the vicinity of the tomb itself. A level area may have been paced off, and spectators could stand around this simplest of arenas. As this would have been outside the city walls, no limitations could have been imposed by urban structures and planning. Tertullian suggests a sepulchral setting, as "then on the appointed day they put those whom they trained . . . to use before the tombs of the dead." [104] Servius addresses the issue of location indirectly. When considering the derivation of *bustuarius*, he claims that "truly it was the custom to put captives to death at the graves of strong men, which later seemed a bit cruel, so it was decided to have gladiators fight at the tombs. . . ." [105] Thus from Servius and Tertullian we gain more informative detail as to the rationale behind early funereal *munera* but little specifics as to seating and performance arrangements in the necropolis area. Neither author makes any specific reference as to *which* originators, be they Etruscan or Campanian or even Roman, located their *munera* in this way.[106]

Basic accommodations around the tomb may be reconstructed using material evidence from Etruria. An urn from Perugia depicts a wooden barrier, presumably to separate the audience from the spectacle and to keep the crowd under control.[107] Even more can be extrapolated from the cycle of scenes at the Tomb of the Bigae in Tarquinia (see Figs. 7 and 8). Here, the contestants and spectators are shown at different levels, which may suggest a podium of some sort providing support. The spectators are seated on wooden seats, propped up by a wooden substructure. Spectators appear on either side of the performers, which may be meant to represent seating on at least two sides of an arena.

So far the evidence for location has referred to very early spectacle, still in the Etruscan ambience. In the specifically Roman sphere, we are presented with the third, and typically Roman, setting for the *munera*. Gladiatorial combat in Rome cannot be viewed separately from the increasing publicization and politicization of the *funus publicum* of the illustrious dead.[108] Indeed, the earliest references to Roman *munera* are all associated with the most public of spaces: the Forum. It is in the Forum that design modifications were tested and standardized to maximize the impact of the *munera*. These modifications were later to be incorporated and enhanced in the construction of the amphitheater.[109]

The Republican Forum was a multipurpose civic center, serving as governmental headquarters, agricultural market, focus of public cult, and a fine place to meet, exchange goods and ideas, and be entertained. In fact, Vitruvius specifies that the *fora* of Italian towns were devised to house *spectacula*, the elongated form being especially optimal for gladiatorial combat.[110] Vitruvius' design specifications call for a length:width ratio of 3:2, those being the best for the purpose. While it is true that the primary function of the forum was political or commercial, Vitruvius' statement implies that the requirements of the *munera* to be held there were most important in the planning stage and perhaps took precedence over the less demanding or restrictive needs of politics and commerce, whose activities could be accommodated in a varied range of settings.

The third century was a crucial one, during which the *munera* were established as an integral part of Roman society. Can we see this reflected, as Vitruvius suggests, in the *fora* of Italian *coloniae* established in this period?[111] Later overbuilding usually allows only the simplest analysis of the general features of earlier plans, but there are notable exceptions.

What came to be the urban centers of Paestum and Cosa had no earlier construction to distract city planners, so the *fora* there were very regularly laid-out rectangles. Cosa measures 140 by 60 meters, a ratio of 2.33:1,[112] very similar to Paestum's 150 by 57, with the ratio 2.63:1.[113] The forum at Luna in northwest Italy, founded in 177 B.C., is likewise longer and narrower than Vitruvius would have recommended, possessing the proportions 1.75:1.[114] Older city centers, such as those at Pompeii and Rome, tended to be more trapezoidal in shape, a distortion caused by their role as a junction of roads. These *fora* measured, respectively, some 110 by 38 meters (2.89:1) and 118 by 67 meters (1.76:1).[115] Although these all tended toward the Vitruvian rectangle, the proportions are not the prescribed 3:2. Thus here, as elsewhere in his work, Vitruvius presents a theoretical ideal rather than a pragmatic representation of an architectural norm.

The pragmatic demands made by the Roman spectacles on architecture, the actual requirements that inspired Vitruvius' ratio, can be best understood by extrapolating the primary focus of the performance area of the entertainment building types of the Roman world: theater, odeum, stadium, and circus.[116] Certain basic aspects of the main spectacle for each building type were key in determining the form each building took. Theaters housed dramatic works; an appreciation of theatrics relied on good acoustics so that the audience could understand what the actors were saying.[117] The odeum featured music and poetry rather than dramatics, and the demands made on the acoustics were even more stringent.[118] Track and field events were the focus in stadia. The emphasis of the design specifications was thus on movement rather than acoustics. A flat, straight track of a certain length and width was needed for the track events; the visual perception of the audience was secondary.[119] Circuses also were centered on the movement of the performers, but here the participants required a great deal of space to accommodate the speed and size of the chariots. Particular aspects of chariot racing required modifications in what would otherwise resemble an overgrown stadium track: the *carceres* were offset to compensate for the shorter length of the inside track, and a *spina* ran down the center to allow for the continual motion of the race.[120]

What were the aspects of the *munera* most important in terms of design?[121] Priority was probably given to a combination of visual perception and movement. The audience had to see the action in the arena with some clarity in order to appreciate fully the lavishness of the sets, costume, and armature and to feel the full psychological impact of the danger, blood, and death. The nearer the spectator was to the combat, the greater the involvement and the greater the enjoyment.[122] In terms of movement, a large, open space was needed to accommodate the multidirectionality of the combat.

The Roman Forum may have been used for the *munera* as early as the fourth century B.C., when literary sources note modifications made to suit *spectacula*.[123] As Rome's importance in the Italian sphere grew, the Forum was renovated to reflect Rome's increasingly prestigious status. The flammability of Rome's increasingly crowded downtown also was the occasion of frequent construction.[124] The Basilica Porcia was built by Cato in 184, on the former site of some public *atria*, one of which was owned by a Maenius, the presumed descendant of the column- and seat-builder discussed earlier. Cato was able to purchase this lot only on the condition that Maenius and his descendants would have the right to claim a specific column of the basilica as a reserved area for seating on the occasion of *munera*.[125]

Granting access to preferred areas of the Forum, season tickets, as it were, to *munera*, was apparently a cherished privilege, which could be bestowed upon worthy civil servants. Such was the case for Ser. Sulpicius, "since so excellent a man met his death while an ambassador on behalf of the state, it was decided by the Senate that a bronze standing statue be set up at the Rostra at their expense and that around this statue a space of five feet in all directions be reserved for his children and his posterity at *ludi* and gladiatorial combats, because he had died in the service of the state."[126] One should thus imagine that the best vantage points were "owned" by Roman magistrates and their families, for their exclusive use at the gladiatorial games.

By around 170, the Forum had assumed the general proportions it would have during the great developments in spectacle of the Late Republic. The Basilica Aemilia and the Basilica Porcia were to the north, the Basilica Sempronia to the south, surrounding the relatively open area in the center of the Forum and setting the civic center apart from the rest of the city. The colonnades on the long sides of the basilicas provided seating for spectators.[127] The open central area had tribunals at either end, whose curvature may have transformed the Forum, visually, into a small, stadiumlike arena, bounded by the basilicas and the Regia.[128]

With some renovations, the Forum retained this same basic form until the fire of 52 B.C. cleared the way for Julius Caesar's reconstruction of the area as something of a monument to himself, one with decreased emphasis on traditional forms of political participation.[129] The new Forum was a showcase for the Roman heritage, a place to be admired by the spectator, and a place designed for spectacle. The Basilica Sempronia was razed to allow for its larger replacement, the Basilica Julia, and Caesar restored the Basilica Aemilia at the same time.[130] The Comitium, which had served as a primary location for popular assembly, was removed, and its functions were largely transferred to the Saepta Julia in the Campus Martius, away from the civic center.[131] The Rostra, ancient monument to Roman naval victory, was remodeled and realigned, its curvature immortalized on ancient coins.[132]

Most interesting was the order of Caesar to install subterranean passages in the Forum, clearly special arrangements made specifically for the *spectacula* he planned.[133] They included a long trunk gallery, paralleling the Basilica Julia. Subsidiary branches of this gallery carefully respected earlier monuments, such as the Cloaca Maxima and the Lacus Curtius. Vertical service passages to the surface would allow for the rapid transferral of sets and participants from a storage area to the arena.

Further Caesarean innovations, in connection with accommodations for spectacles, were made outside the confines of the Forum. For his quadruple triumph in 46, he built something called a hunting theater, a *kynegetikon theatron*. This was a temporary structure of wood, which Dio says was even "called an amphitheater . . . because it had seating on all sides without a stage structure."[134] Ville sees this structure as of little distinction, something more along the lines of bleachers set up in the Forum, but Dio clearly distinguishes between the *kynegetikon theatron* and what Caesar did in the Forum. Furthermore, the structure was not entirely unprecedented.[135]

The hunting theater, as described by Dio, may indicate Caesar's familiarity with the amphitheater building type, and indeed, the earliest amphitheaters predate Caesar's Forum by several decades. The first steps toward the Colosseum came with revolutionary advances in Roman architectural achievement, including their development of concrete and of a theater building that was specifically Roman.

Although mortar of various types had been around perhaps for millennia, it was under the auspices of Rome that *opus caementicum* or concrete was introduced, a material composed of chunks of aggregate (*caementa*) in a high-quality mortar made of lime, water, and a special kind of volcanic ash known as pozzolana.[136] It was this mortar that made the combination so different. The pozzolana had a high silica content, which enabled it to set under water. It needed less lime than other "sands" and thus bonded more completely within its matrix. It was considerably stronger than other mortars, a quality of which Roman architects took advantage. The ready availability of the basic ingredients in Roman concrete made it much cheaper to work with than traditional building materials, and its adaptability to curved shapes laid the foundation for experimentation and innovation in the use of vaulted structural forms, which, more than anything else, exemplified what is known as the Roman Architectural Revolution.[137]

Early experimentation in *opus caementicum* can be seen in the town walls of Cosa, from the early third century. In Rome, the Porticus Aemilia, a warehouse built near the Tiber in 174 B.C., combined concrete with barrel vaulting. But the combination of *opus caementicum* and the curvilinear forms of the vaults are set off to best advantage in two new building types conceptualized in the second century B.C.: the Roman theater and the amphitheater.

The Roman theater is distinct from the Greek in its independence from hillsides. The Roman theater is thus a freestanding entity, self-supported by means of vaulted galleries radiating perpendicular to the line of the seating. Constraints imposed by a flat terrain could now be ignored as Roman architects built theaters at will. This freestanding characteristic was crucial to the development of the Roman amphitheater and preceded such development by only a few years. The oldest extant Roman theater, dating to the last half of the second century, is in Campania, at Teanum.[138] The earliest amphitheaters were also built in Campania.[139]

The dominant role Campania played in the early innovations of Roman architecture can be explained in several ways.[140] In terms of material systems, Campania was fortunate in possessing an abundance of pozzolana, spewed forth by Mt. Vesuvius over the centuries. The Bay of Naples possessed one of Italy's few good harbors, allowing for the trade activity that would generate commercial prosperity. The fertility of the *ager Campanus* made Campanian agriculture a most profitable venture. Much of the wealth generated in this way was redistributed at home in public building programs.[141] Of the 310 public buildings known from all of Republican Italy, 128 are from this region.[142]

Key to the distribution of public building may be the challenge to Rome presented by Campania in the Social War (90–88 B.C.). The backlash to the Italian rebellion was Roman colonization, Sulla's forced "reconstruction" of the area. Roman colonization, by its very nature, involved the subjugation and control of those opposed to Roman interests.[143] Colonies were set up to punish local resistance and to guarantee the security of the area.[144] Colonies also can be seen as a tool of cultural imperialism, in the establishment of a set of civic standards that were Roman, not Italian, at base. We can, in the case of Sulla, detect perhaps even more specific ideological motivation for the imposition of specific Roman institutions as a form of political discourse. Sulla's restructuring of the Roman distribution of power was directed toward reinforcing and maintaining the senatorial class, as rebuilt by Sulla's supporters. Sulla took action to suppress popular politics, the perceived license of the mob, most particularly through undermining the role of the tribune as chief rabble-rouser. Likewise, Sulla's colonization plan was intended to undermine Italian popular authority through the establishment of a new Roman elite and Roman institutions in newly subdued areas. The dictator was willing to use force to achieve his aims. It may be that Sulla was willing to use symbolic force as well: the incorporation of the amphitheater into the Sullan policy of domination in Italy. This practice may furthermore have important implications for the development of the amphitheater in the decades succeeding the Sullan dictatorship. Sulla's innovative use of the amphitheater on behalf of conservative politics may have set a precedent for the Roman arena, seen in the noted preference for *munera* by anti-populist partisans of the later Republic.

Of the known Republican amphitheaters, the majority are located in Roman colonies, including the Sullan colonies of Pompeii, Abella, and Telesia.[145] Evidence from Pompeii is especially instructive, as the dedicatory inscription for the amphitheater has been preserved.[146] In it, the quinquennial duumvirs specify the beneficiary of their civic expenditure as the colony, that is, the colony of Sullan veterans. They further guarantee the right of those colonists to reserved seating in the amphitheater in perpetuity. No mention is made of the precolonial residents of the city, who may, in fact, have been excluded from the political process and may even have had their personal mobility constrained.[147] Here is an indication of the inspiration for Campanian architectural achievement in the Late Republic. The Roman-style structures were not merely the luxurious by-products of Roman peace and prosperity, they were not simply persuasive examples of the "good life" now sponsored by Rome. These buildings housed Roman institutions, intended as permanent reminders of the Roman hegemony, a point driven home in the inscriptions put up by the Roman colonists. The violent means by which that hegemony was achieved would be reenacted on a regular basis in the *munera* produced by Pompeii's magistrates.[148]

Campania was an area with great material advantages for architecture in general and innovative public architecture specifically. We should not, however, consider the amphitheater building type as part of "Campanian architecture," as distinct from Roman architecture. It is only under Roman hegemony and impetus that these developments in materials and styles are made, developments typologically paralleled in the city of Rome proper.

The new architecture in the capital city postdates, generally speaking, its appearance to the south. While some might interpret this situation as another example of Romans being stylistically imitative rather than innovative, to suggest some sort of retardation in architectural development in Rome is surely misleading. The overbuilding especially apparent in Rome must skew the picture, with Republican buildings, however original at the time of construction, being overshadowed by the brilliant architecture of the Imperial period. Rome had, nevertheless, no permanent theater building until fairly late in the Republic. The reasons behind this delay are not related to lack of technical sophistication or financial resources but rather to the special situation in Rome, a situation politically charged and relevant to the social function of the amphitheater.[149]

The first mention of a Roman theater in the sources refers to events of 154 B.C., when C. Cassius Longinus wanted to build a stone theater on the side of the Palatine but was opposed by, among others, Scipio Nasica.[150] The monument was destroyed and future construction of permanent monumental seating was forbidden within a mile of Rome.[151] Various reasons for this situation are given: Nasica found theaters "useless" and "likely to be injurious to public morals" or it was more appropriate to Roman virility and character to stand at public shows.[152]

This squabble has been interpreted as part of the pro-Hellene/anti-Hellene confrontation, with the implication lurking in the subtext of Valerius Maximus that *virilitas* is not *propria* to the Greek race.[153] Others rightly emphasize the role of theaters in democratic disturbances, analyzing the antitheater stance as a measure against popular agitation.[154] The theater represented a danger to oligarchic control of the urban constituency. The possibility of a permanent facility specifically designed for mass meetings, with acoustics to facilitate vocal exchange, was far too threatening to the conservative element of Rome's ruling elite. It was in their best interests to maintain their control over the public sphere by maintaining their control over the setting of public assemblies of all kinds.[155] Rome saw no stone theater until 55 B.C., when Pompey built an enormous theater complex as part of the sanctuary of his Temple of Venus Victrix, justifying such a menace to public safety in the name of pious fervor.[156]

The ban on building permanent theater seating within Rome's city limits may have been applied to amphitheaters too, particularly given the volatile political ambience of the *munera* during the later Republic. Perhaps the alternative was more attractive: politicians may have been eager to exploit the mob's preference for gladiators on a more frequent and varied basis by building short-lived wooden arenas. By avoiding a commitment to a permanent structure, *editores* could overawe the public with novel and lavish temporary surroundings. Surely the structure built by C. Scribonius Curio should be understood in this way.

In 52 B.C., Curio, perhaps in anticipation of his candidacy for the aedileship, commissioned the building of two large wooden theaters, placed on revolving pivots in a back-to-back position. Scenic performances were scheduled for the morning's entertainment, then in midday, while the spectators remained in their seats, the theaters were spun around to face each other, the combination of a theater on each side creating, literally, an *amphitheatrum*, that is, a "theater on both sides."[157] Whatever the historicity of Pliny's anecdote, the story suggests that novelties were the norm in the presentation of games for the masses.[158]

It was not until Augustus' hegemony that the first stone amphitheater was built in Rome by Statilius Taurus, located in the southern part of the Campus Martius.[159] It may be that Statilius' structure had seats of wood atop a stone substructure, representing therefore a transitional status between a permanent building and the more temporary venues provided by Republican *editores*. For the next eighty-odd years, however, *munera* were still housed in other facilities, suggesting that Statilius' structure was insufficient in some way. Caligula, after housing a series of spectacles in lavish temporary structures, started the construction of an amphitheater near the Saepta on the Campus Martius, which required the destruction of part of the Aqua Virgo to clear space for it.[160] Nero in A.D. 58 built an extremely lavish, immense wooden arena northwest of the Pantheon, a description of which, according to Tacitus, would fill useless volumes.[161] At any rate, the Statilian amphitheater was destroyed during the fire of A.D. 64.[162] Augustus apparently planned to build another amphitheater in the city center, in the area later exploited by the Flavians.[163] It was the reign of that dynasty that saw the full architectural development of the amphitheater, exemplified by the Colosseum, with its complex network of tunnels and chambers under the arena and its provision for the rapid and efficient entrance and exit of spectators contained within an extremely sophisticated support system, combined with a decorative canon that adapted Greek architectural elements to Roman utilitarianism. The Flavian Amphitheater set a standard that spread throughout the empire, proliferating especially in the late first and early second centuries after Christ.[164]

THE IMPERIAL GAMES

Livy told the story of Corbis and Orsua, Iberian participants in *munera* organized by Scipio in Carthago Nova. Corbis and Orsua were local politicians who decided to resolve their long-term rivalry by a final duel in Scipio's arena: the winner would dominate local government, the loser would be beyond politics, or any other earthly concerns, entirely. For Livy, this was a cautionary tale, a morality fable that resonated strongly for a survivor of the Civil Wars. The personal combat of Corbis and Orsua, fought to the death before a screaming crowd, was the logical extension of all such heedless political competition. "Since they could not be dissuaded from their great madness, the spectacle they provided . . . was a lesson on how great an evil for mankind was the desire for power."[165] Such competition left unrestrained must lead inexorably to death and disaster. The Empire would provide the necessary restraint; the arena would be subject to state control.

In the months prior to the death of Julius Caesar, as part of the sycophantic and fatal series of honors granted the dictator, the Senate decreed that henceforth all *munera* given in Rome and all of Italy should have one day set aside in honor of Caesar.[166] This was the first official participation in the scheduling of gladiatorial games, but it should be remembered that the private status of *munera* was left untouched by this *senatus consultum*. The impetus to provide such games was still left to the individual.

A few years later, in 42, gladiatorial combats joined the official roster of publicly sponsored games. At the celebration of the *Cerialia*, the aediles offered armed combats in place of the usual circus events. The context in which these first *munera legitima* are placed is provocative.[167] Dio Cassius clearly sees the provision of these spectacles as connected to the omens surrounding Philippi. They were presented apparently as a means of propitiating the gods in the wake of a series of unpleasant portents, but the innovative nature of their scheduling suggests to Dio that they should be interpreted as ominous themselves.[168] Despite the menacing cast laid on the games of 42, their presence at one of the regular holidays set a precedent for the inclusion of gladiatorial combats on the roster of public games.

Augustus recognized the good public relations value of bloody *spectacula* and proudly declared for posterity his provision of eight gladiatorial shows in which ten thousand men participated.[169] His *munera* were thus the largest ever seen, far more splendid than anything offered by the politicians of the Late Republic. This was to be expected. Augustus had vast financial resources to support such presentations; more important, he had the authority to dominate all such spectacles. By 22 B.C. he had transferred control of the Roman Games to the center of power, and the ordinary *munera* came under Imperial auspices. Limitations were set on the frequency and size of the official games; the praetors were granted access to public funding to give *munera*, subject to senatorial license, twice a year, using 120 men total.[170] The amount of money the praetors could spend on public games was also subject to limitation by the emperor.[171] All other gladiatorial games would be produced by the emperor and his family; henceforth, it was to them that the plebs would owe their gratitude for the lavish spectacles. There would be no wastage of resources in spectacular competition; Rome would foster no Corbis and Orsua. The spectacles would thus serve the purpose deemed appropriate by the *princeps*: the demonstration of the proper use of Roman *imperium* in a carefully orchestrated form, rife with symbols meaningful to the Roman heritage. The ritual of the arena manipulated traditional symbols and events as an instrument of power, rearranged by Augustus to distinguish himself and his successors from the previous *editores* of the games. In the hands of the emperor, the amphitheatrical performances became potent political rhetoric.[172]

The political importance of these games in the Empire can be analyzed on several levels, the first of which is an extension of a notorious quote from Juvenal: "There was a time when the People bestowed every honor—the governance of provinces, civic leadership, military command—but now they hold themselves back, now two things only do they ardently desire: bread and games."[173] Juvenal carefully contrasts Republican political activity and public entertainment, which is significant in itself. The games have been seen as a surrogate political assembly.[174] Deprived of any voice in government during the Principate, the plebs exchanged their traditional forum for a form of expression in the amphitheater. They formed claques to chant about whatever was on their minds. The issues could be relatively simple ones, characterized by the chant "*Iugula! Iugula!*" (accompanied by a graphic throat-slashing gesture), or touch on more standard political areas, such as demands for cheaper bread or changes in taxation. This chanting sometimes assumed a rather more ominous tone. Dio gives us a firsthand example from the reign of Commodus, "the Gladiator," when senators were forced to chant: "You are lord, and you are first, and you are most fortunate of all men! You conquer! You will conquer! Unto eternity, Amazonian, do you conquer!" [175]

One may question how effectual this sort of activity was as a means of expressing popular desires. In the long run, it makes little difference. The main point is that they were making themselves heard, directly, face to face with the emperor. [176] They had a unique opportunity for immediate vocal contact with their heads of state, and they used it. The image of direct communication was more important than the communication itself. And it could be fairly effective, particularly when the granting of their chanted objective added to the spectacle. An emperor could, for example, make a splashy display out of pardoning and setting free favorite gladiators. Claudius in particular seems to have made a show of fawning on the amphitheater crowds, calling them "*Domini*" and acceding to their every wish. [177]

This leads us to another aspect of the political function of the games: the support of the establishment or the maintenance of the *status quo*. The audiences in the stands participated freely in the display of authority over the masses, much as the crowds do today in St. Peter's Square. Romans could see the emperor, he could see the Roman people, they all sat together and enjoyed the spectacle. This rubbing of elbows with the common herd was deemed necessary for the emperor's public relations because it partially dissolved social and political barriers. For this moment or day or week, the government was not an impersonal and impervious body, distanced from the average person, but a fellow-spectator, practically within reach, one with the Populus Romanus. [178]

Thus far the utility of the *munera* has been that of any such assemblage of people or large gathering. One cannot, however, ignore what was going on in the arena at the same time: people were killing each other. Any analysis has to take into account the inherent violence and death. One ethnographic parallel is public execution in later European history.

People were sentenced to the games or to the gladiatorial schools, and so for the most part, the people dying in the arena were criminals.[179] Foucault discusses the political nature of capital punishment, which he says was not merely righting an injustice.[180] The criminal had not only wronged his victim, he had attacked the people who abide by the law, society at large and the sovereign, who was the force of the law. Crime thus placed the ruler in contempt. Public execution restored the law through the destruction of the criminal, the threat to the system. It reestablished the sovereign, who made a display of his strength by his contempt for the life of the criminal. More than that, public execution was an exercise in terror. By making a spectacle out of the suffering and death of the individual, the ruler emphasized his own power and his own superiority. It was meant to be cruel and unusual. To maintain order, the emperor provided an object lesson for the Roman people, a warning about the fate of those who dared to offend the state. Public execution was a tool of a totalitarian government, a public statement about power.

The export of the gladiatorial games seems to have started very early. In 206 B.C., Scipio held games at Carthago Nova, to honor the *di manes*, or departed spirits, of his father and uncle, who had died some five years previously.[181] The competitors, unlike at Rome, were largely made up of volunteer Spaniards, fighting out of local pride, a wish to please Scipio, joy in competition, or an alternative to legal measures, that is, trial by combat.[182] In this particular instance, the holding of *munera* may be considered an object lesson for the enemies of Rome, as was much of Scipio's activity in Spain. The gladiatorial games are bracketed in Livy's account by the capture of Iliturgi, at which men and women, the aged, the infirm, and the infantile, were all put to the sword, and by the siege at Astapa, at which the inhabitants killed themselves rather than fall into Roman hands. It was a time in which desperate measures were taken on both sides. The Romans had to show themselves as enemies to be reckoned with, for whom death and slaughter were a form of entertainment and an obligation owed the worthy dead. The *munera* were part of the Imperial package of propaganda, in which a local audience was indirectly threatened by the might of Rome.

Regardless of how well the games served the purposes of Imperial rhetoric, they would have been nothing had not the Romans wanted the games, enjoyed watching gladiatorial combat, and clung to the *munera* throughout numerous coups d'état and massive governmental turmoil. What was behind this enthusiasm, this bottomless lust for blood?

Violence in sports has been approached from several different angles, one of which emphasizes compensatory violence.[183] Lack of political power acted in conjunction with an increasingly controlled society, which also clung stubbornly to restrictive traditions. One such was the concept of the *paterfamilias*. Legally, the male head of the house had complete mastery over his clan: financially, socially, even in matters of life and death.[184] The options of the individual in Roman society grew more limited as time passed. This combination of private and public forced submissiveness may have led, in some, to feelings of helplessness and frustration, of being manipulated by forces beyond one's control. A tendency toward compensatory violence was the result. Some modern analysts have seen this as a pathological condition, relating compensatory violence to sadism and seeing the Colosseum, in which "thousands of impotent people got their greatest pleasure by seeing men devoured by beasts, or killing each other" as an extravagant monument to such impulses.[185]

Spectator sports provide an opportunity for vicarious expression of aggressive drives and thereby may act as a "safety valve" in society. Konrad Lorenz popularized this "catharsis" interpretation in 1966, and many people, particularly those involved in professional sports, still support it as valid.[186] The theory suggests that people work out all their frustrations screaming for their favorites, then come home placid, peaceful, and filled with the milk of human kindness. Lorenz was moved by the sportsman's absolute dedication to ideals of chivalry and fair play.

The practical application of the catharsis theory, unfortunately, is not so straightforward. This is readily apparent in the modern world, where sports are increasingly surrounded with an atmosphere of violence. Comparable situations are known from antiquity. Tacitus relates that in A.D. 59 a terrible riot broke out among the audience at a gladiatorial spectacle held at Pompeii, between the local inhabitants and their neighboring rivals of Nuceria (see Fig. 30). From the improvised arsenal of rocks and sticks, the carnage progressed to the point where real weapons were used to inflict permanent damage.[187] So dreadful was the resulting bloodshed that the Roman central government took a hand; a *senatus consultum* banned all such events at Pompeii for ten years to come.[188] Another example comes from Suetonius, who relates that the empress Poppaea was kicked to death by Nero because she complained that he was home late from the games.[189] Watching violence runs the risk of drawing the spectator into the action, transforming him from a vicarious participant to an agent of violence himself.[190]

The narrative form of the violent performance may direct the audience reaction to it. The different contexts of performative violence affect response more than the simple presence of "gratuitous" acts of bloodshed. Theatrical performances provide an analogy. "Tragic" violence, in which the spectators sympathize with the victims of unjust, unrelieved violence, may evoke a cathartic reaction, while "melodramatic" violence, with a simplistic portrayal of victims as deserving of their fate, is likely to promote a very different response, to serve as a catalyst for the audience's bloodlust. When the victim is demonized or alienated from the empathy of the audience, the viewers identify instead with the perpetrators of violence, gaining an intense feeling of satisfaction, even joy, in their vicarious "revenge" upon the victim.[191] Seen in this way, the arena spectators were meant to participate in the "punishment" of the performer; they were his judges, inflicting the fate he merited, both by his marginal status and by his actions in the arena. The possibility of this bloodlust extending beyond the controlled environment of the amphitheater was something that greatly concerned the Roman state, as indicated by the prompt and severe official response to the riot in Pompeii.

As explained earlier, the *munera* achieved special prominence in the Late Republic, when Roman political competition reached new levels of ferocity and violence. The gladiatorial games can be interpreted as replication of this turmoil, with a crucial distinction: the violence of the *munera* was stylized, purposeful, highly ordered, and under the strict control of the *editor* of the games. Over time, as the *munera* came under Imperial auspices, the central government clearly indicated its intention to control all aspects of the gladiatorial complex; the structure imposed on the arena was symbolic, on a number of levels, of the order imposed on the Roman Empire. The shedding of blood was done in an orderly fashion, placed in a ritualized context, with all participants, spectators, performers, and producers, playing out their expected roles.[192] The form taken by the performance was significant as well; the structured gladiatorial combats evoked certain basic elements of Roman ideology.

Channeling one's aggressive feelings into exuberant spectating has been interpreted as a substitution for warfare.[193] Rome was, in its origins, a militaristic society. The expected participation of the individual Roman evolved over the years, and by the Imperial period, Rome had a professional army, made up largely of units recruited from outside Rome proper. The Roman urbanite was no longer required to serve on the front lines. He could perhaps now find the emotional equivalent of actual warfare at the arena. The blood, the dust, the death, the gladiators dressed like foreign nationals: the games were war at its best and offered no real risk to the individual spectator. The utility of the blood-spattered example in promoting discipline for the common good seems to have been consciously realized by the Romans themselves.[194]

Not that Roman militarism was an atavistic urge simply to inflict death, to which the arena offered cathartic release. This is clarified by the ethical value of the amphitheater: a reading of the relevant ancient sources suggests that the Roman upper class found a moral value in gladiatorial combat.[195] The slaves and criminals were not real men. They were less human than their social superiors and therefore their deaths, as individuals, were of lesser significance, caused no real loss to the community.[196] Yet in the arena they fought bravely and with glory and died with honor like men, like heroes; if such men could die admirably, surely real Romans could do no less.[197] The didactic purpose of watching the *munera* is articulated by Pliny the Younger when he calls gladiatorial combat "nothing enervating nor weak, nor anything that would soften and break the manly spirit, but something that awakens contempt for death and indifference to wounds, since even in the bodies of slaves and criminals a love of glory and desire for victory can be seen."[198] In this too there was political utility: the public in the stands was expected to emulate and surpass the gladiator in qualities highly appropriate to the imperialist goal. On the one hand, the gladiator displays stoic indifference to bloodshed, even when the blood is his own; this suggests the willingness to inflict and suffer death, if necessary. Then too there is the positive aspect of the performance, the zeal for *laus* and *victoria* instilled in the audience. Personal glory and success in Rome was evaluated by public achievement, by efforts on behalf of the greater community. Pliny thus reads gladiatorial combat as instruction in selflessness, in the endurance of mortal violence in exchange for Imperial victory. Indeed, this was not weakness, this was not softening of the manly spirit: far from it. This was the discipline and self-sacrificing obedience of the battlefield being demonstrated to the spectators in the stands, involving them in the reenactment of the process of empire.[199]

The extra-Roman origins of the *munera* are elusive. The evidence itself is inconclusive, with perhaps slightly more weight on the Etruscan side of the scale. The lack of clarity itself is provocative. Perhaps the issue has been overemphasized by scholars, since the *munera* were certainly Roman by the historical period. The early gladiatorial combats were linked with the public funerals of great men and thus were carried out in the Forum area, a location traditionally used for events that concerned the city as a whole. Indeed, the design of the Roman and Italian forum was standardized to accommodate these spectacles.

Several influences were brought to bear on the development of the *venationes*. The more or less elaborated ritual action of animals in certain of the festivals predisposed the Romans toward the presence of animals in spectacle. The major impetus was Rome's gradual conquest of the Mediterranean and the exotic animals that were acquired as booty. The use of animals as a means of public execution increased concurrently; the heightened sense of spectacle that the animals brought to such proceedings magnified the dire consequences of challenging Roman authority.

The *venationes* and the *munera* came together as the *munus legitimum* under Augustus and were housed in what would become their standard venue, the amphitheater. The influence of Augustus in this process should not be underestimated. As canonizer and controller of Games, he linked the *munera* permanently to the emperor and his deliberate beneficence.

II. A SCATTER OF CIRCLES

Every effort yields to Caesar's amphitheater;
let this one work bring fame to all of them.

MARTIAL, *De Spectaculis* 1.7–8

IN THE POPULAR IMAGINATION, ancient Rome is inextricably linked to the games of the amphitheater. In the scholarly imagination, the amphitheater is bound to Romanization of the most visible sort: the spread of Mediterranean-style buildings throughout the lands under Roman hegemony.

Rome is often credited with the urbanization of the European West. Urbanization should be understood as more than simply putting up structures of masonry, brick, and concrete; it is the imposition of a set of political and social institutions, the establishment of a set of relationships, with certain beliefs and expectations on both sides. The importance of this process can be taken still further, as the Roman conceptualization of "the city" was infused with religious significance. The act of founding a city was essentially the imposition of cosmic structure on the landscape; the ritual of inauguration, key to the formal establishment of a Roman town, was intended to transfer the divinely ordered pattern of the universe into the physical setting of the new settlement. Not only the building of civic structures but also the alignment of roads, the placement of sanctuaries, and the division of cultivable fields were determined according to the Roman understanding of the pattern of creation. The adoption of the urban model, therefore, was more than simply the adoption of

Roman technical standards and style of ornamentation; it demanded a fundamental acceptance of, quite literally, a new world order, based on the Roman ability to control and manipulate the environment. The spread of Roman urban forms was the spread of Roman Imperium.[1]

Any Romanized public building, then, is far more than fired brick and concrete, joined with the sophisticated technique so typical of Roman efficiency. Each implies the penetration of the Roman hegemony, political, social, and natural. The particular types of buildings fostered under Roman control extended this hegemony to the daily life of the individual, shaping the ways in which he would interact with other individuals, with the community, and with the Roman overlords through the imposition of specific methods, priorities, and settings. The old ways would be changed forever, as the goal of political and cultural unity was sought using the outward physical expression of the Roman process of control.[2]

The amphitheater has a particular role to play in that process. This was not merely a distinctive building type but an institution saturated with social significance. It was a monumental and grandiose stage set for the enactment of very bloody games. But the performance was not restricted to the arena; the spectators were also participants, carefully arranged according to the level of their participation in the local expression of the Roman power structure. How are we to understand the spread of this phenomenon regionally? Was the amphitheater simply one aspect of urbanization? Close analysis suggests that the decision to build a provincial amphitheater did not rely solely on the presence of an urban center; not all amphitheaters are located in cities. The diffusion of amphitheaters involved processes that reflected rather a complex course of imposition, interaction, and adaptation, as did, indeed, the dynamic of Roman Imperialism as a whole.

By comparing the placement of cities with the placement of amphitheaters, and the relative density of each in the landscape of the Roman West, it becomes clear that the distribution of amphitheaters was determined by local needs and circumstances, which did not necessarily coincide with the basic demands of urban development.[3] This runs counter to traditional wisdom, which tends to interpret the placement of amphitheaters along exactly those lines, namely, that a regional center of a certain economic and political status was expected to have an amphitheater as an appropriate marker of its urban prestige and level of Romanization.[4]

How, and how far, the amphitheater departs from this assumption can be demonstrated by considering the scatter of amphitheaters region by region.

THE IBERIAN PENINSULA

The Spains and Lusitania were home to twenty-two amphitheaters, hardly what one would call a dense scatter but comparable to the spread of urban centers found in the peninsula (see Map 1).[5] The relative scarcity of cities in Iberia can be explained in several ways. It could represent continued influence exercised by powerful pre-Roman tribes, which became large *civitates* after the absorption of the peninsula into the Roman realm by the first century B.C. People dwelt in only a few population centers but each was densely inhabited.[6] More likely factors in the Iberian case are the effects of geographical fragmentation and the specific needs of pastoralism, as opposed to more sedentary agricultural practices. Cities in Roman Spain, like amphitheaters, were located on the coastline and along the river valleys, as the ruggedness of the terrain prevented a more even spread of the urbanized zones. The highlands were, and still are, good for herds, the inherent mobility of which demands vast amounts of unpopulated areas. The combination of the inhospitable landscape, which was difficult to make conform to urban constructions, and the disincentive for permanent settlement fostered by pastoral economics would tend to focus cities, and their accompanying amphitheaters, into a small, select group of sites.[7]

Even so, there are few amphitheaters in Roman Hispania and Lusitania, in comparison to the rest of the West. Indeed, of the twenty-two amphitheaters used in my statistical calculations, the physical existence of only twelve is actually vouchsafed.[8] This paucity of monuments seems peculiar, especially given the Iberian bent for amphitheatrical spectacle at an early date. We know, for example, that Scipio gave *munera* in honor of his father and uncle in 206 B.C. at Carthago Nova, funeral games held five years after the decease of the honorees.[9] The enthusiasm with which Scipio's local adherents entered the ranks of the performers would suggest they were receptive to this new custom.[10] More than just the gladiatorial combats, wild animal hunts were adopted by the residents; indeed, the *corrida de toros*, or bullfight, is popularly acknowledged to be the vestigial remnant of the *venationes*. The modern bullring at Cartagena (ancient

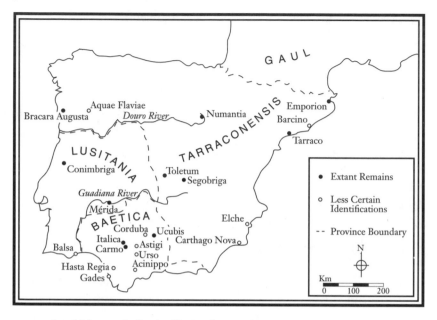

MAP 1. Amphitheaters in Iberian Peninsula.

Carthago Nova) is located above the ruins of the amphitheater; even now, every August sees the Roman theater at Sagunto housing the fiestas of *toros embolados*, in which the bulls run with balls of flaming tar on their horns.[11] This hints at continuous celebration of the amphitheatrical events for more than two thousand years.

Gladiatorial combat and animal fights, the amphitheatrical events, do appear in the archaeological record of Hispania, glorified in surviving epigraphy and pictorial representation.[12] Amphitheaters themselves were constructed here from an early date. Indeed, it is in Spain that we find two of the eleven total Republican amphitheaters that survive to us, those being the structures at Carmo and Ucubis. The other datable examples also tend to be earlier than in the other provinces, two of them being Augustan and three Julio-Claudian.[13] The generally early date of the Spanish arenas may be a clue as to why Spain has relatively few amphitheaters, relatively widely dispersed.

We have already considered the role of the Republican forum as a venue for gladiatorial events and the strong functional link postulated by Vitruvius between forum design and the accommodation of these spectacles.[14] The early interest shown by Hispania in arena events may have

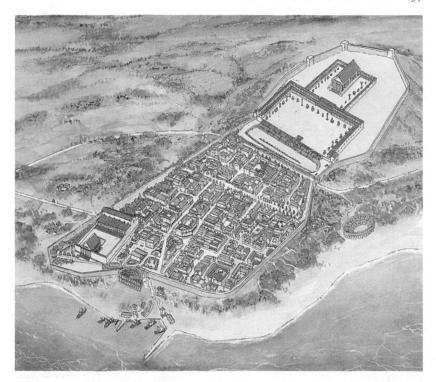

FIGURE 9. Reconstruction of Roman Tarraco (first–second century A.D.), with provincial forum in inland quarter and amphitheater on the beach, drawing © X. Dupré and J. G. Sempere.

biased them towards the earlier venue for the *munera*: the forum.[15] The Romanization of the Iberian peninsula was comparatively early as well, with architectural norms established prior to the full development of amphitheatrical design.[16] It may be that Hispanic requirements for such events were more on the conservative side and could normally be satisfied with the "traditional" surroundings provided by the Italianate forum.[17]

The scatter of amphitheaters follows that of the cities, clustering, as the urban centers do, in Baetica's Guadalquivir valley and along the Mediterranean coast.[18] Arenas do not appear in the central Celtiberian area nor in Galicia to the northwest, which is intriguing, given the apparent interest in the institution shown by Celtic neighbors to the north. The relationship between population and amphitheater size also presents some contradictions, as more than half of the Spanish amphitheaters seat more than twenty thousand spectators. The cities themselves, in apparent contrast, seem to have been rather small, in comparison to those in the more urbanized sections of Gaul.[19] The latest and largest amphitheater in Spain was the Hadrianic monster at Italica, which seated some thirty-four thousand spectators.[20]

The association between a large-scale, Hadrianic amphitheater and Italica, the emperor's home town, leads us to a key feature of provincial amphitheaters, that being the link between the placement of amphitheaters and the ostentatious expression of loyalty to the emperor. This relationship seems clear at Tarraco (modern Tarragona), the seat of the provincial administration (see Fig. 9). The Augustan period saw the monumentalization of Tarraco's administrative facilities with the building of a grand provincial forum graced with cult accommodations for Roma and Augustus. Although located outside the immediate civic center, the amphitheater should be linked to this program.[21]

BRITANNIA

The province of Britannia held some nineteen amphitheatrical structures (see Map 2). If the presence of an amphitheater were the mark of a "true" city, the urban scatter of Britain would be denser, certainly, than we saw in Hispania but still characteristically provincial, a spread not to be found in long-urbanized Italy.[22] Again as in Spain, this urban scatter may represent some degree of continuity from the pre-Roman organization of habitation zones by tribal rather than by central authority. The centers are spaced beyond half a day's travel, far enough away from outlying districts to discourage frequent journeys to and from the urban units. Some would suggest that the heroic Celtic society described by Caesar in the Gallic War would have had such a system of placement, with the elite of a wide area meeting for a few weeks out of the year for governmental, judicial, or diplomatic reasons.

In and of itself, this is not an unreasonable picture of Roman Britannia. It is frequently acknowledged that the Mediterranean urbanized lifestyle had relatively little impact on the Britons in general.[23] A more reasonable explanation, however, lies elsewhere. Romano-British amphitheaters have strong military associations; almost half the examples can be linked to the legions in some way. Although military centers often gave rise to urban ones, their placement depends on criteria wholly different from that of the civilian centers.

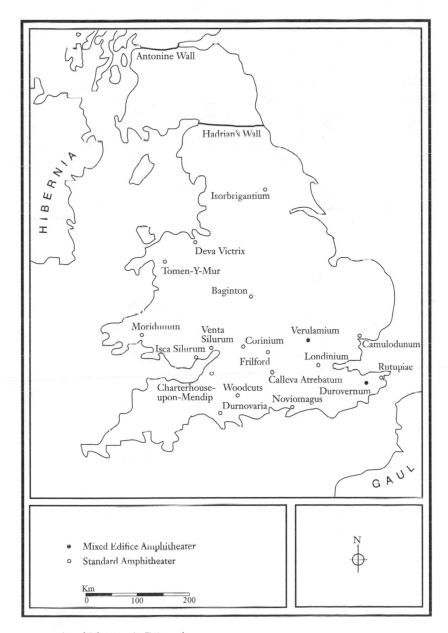

Antonine Wall

HIBERNIA

Hadrian's Wall

Isorbrigantium

Deva Victrix

Tomen-Y-Mur

Baginton

Moridunum   Venta   Verulamium
         Silurum   Corinium   Camulodunum
Isca Silurum   Londinium
        Frilford   Rutupiae

Charterhouse-   Woodcuts   Calleva Atrebatum
upon-Mendip   Durovernum
          Durnovaria   Noviomagus

GAUL

•   Mixed Edifice Amphitheater
○   Standard Amphitheater

Km
0   100   200

N

MAP 2. Amphitheaters in Britannia.

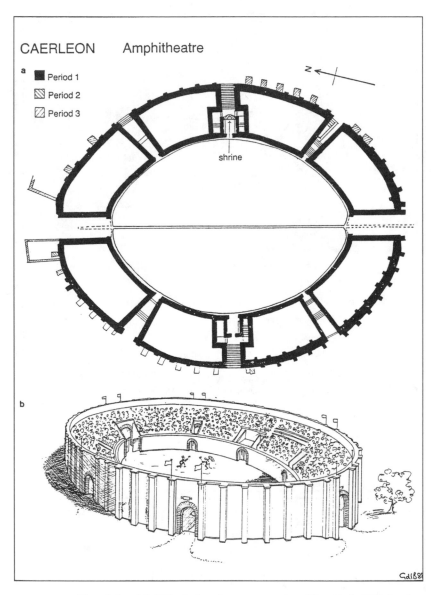

CAERLEON   Amphitheatre

a

■ Period 1
▨ Period 2
▧ Period 3

shrine

b

FIGURE 10. Plan (after M. Wheeler) and reconstruction (after J. A. Wright, but adapted) of amphitheater at Isca Silurum (Caerleon), showing retained earthwork construction and relatively simple superstructure, by G. de la Bédoyère, *The Buildings of Roman Britain* (London: B. T. Batsford, 1991), fig. 47.

Britannia's legionary bases at Deva Victrix (Chester) and Isca Silurum (Caerleon [see Fig. 10]) supported amphitheaters; it is generally acknowledged that the remaining legionary headquarters at Eboracum (York) likewise had an amphitheater, although none has yet been uncovered.[24] Further evidence for the connection between the Roman army and amphitheaters can be found at the minor fortresses at Baginton and Tomen-y-Mur.[25] Indeed, even indirect links are suggested by the amphitheaters at towns that started out as military installations and may have kept some of the military flavor after the centurions marched off.[26] The amphitheater in Londinium (London) was built adjacent to the fortress housing the garrison established there under the Flavians.[27] Even the construction technique used in Britannia, in which the superstructure is supported by earthworks, is more typical of the military amphitheaters elsewhere, and the vital role in their construction played by military architects, engineers, and sheer manpower is attested epigraphically in Britannia.[28]

Military amphitheaters were multifunctional. The amphitheaters contributed to morale by keeping the troops well entertained, vital to maintaining order among a standing army not always in the field. The performance need not be provided by professionals of the arena; the military amphitheaters would provide an excellent venue for parade and military spectacle, also crucial to the maintenance of standards and morale for a standing army.[29] Arenas could further the Roman agenda in a very practical sense; a setting designed for the visual enhancement of combat would also be suitable for weapons training and military exercises, for cavalry display and drill.[30] But practice for the soldiers was not the whole story. Part of the Imperial mandate given military personnel was the keeping of the Roman peace through assimilation to Roman customs and habits and promotion of an identification with Roman interests. The content of these spectacles, in the militaristic support of the Roman hierarchy and celebration of Imperial conquest and control, would promote the proper attitude among the legionaries, whose fidelity to the aims of Rome should be above question. Amphitheaters also provided a stylish setting for graphic examples of what happened to those who challenged Roman authority, a warning to be understood both by the army and by residents of the frontier.[31]

Even among the nonmilitary sites, the placement of amphitheaters is linked to motivations beyond simple urbanization.[32] Canterbury (Durovernum Cantiacorum), Frilford, Verulamium, and possibly Woodcuts as

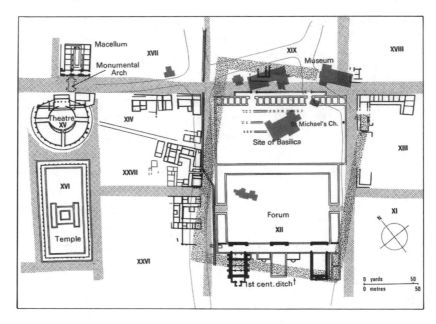

FIGURE 11. Plan of central Roman Verulamium, showing relation of mixed edifice and Romano-Celtic sanctuary, by J. Flower, published in M. I. Finley, *Atlas of Classical Archaeology* (New York: McGraw-Hill, 1977), p. 27.

well are all combination theater-amphitheaters, like the many examples to be found in Gaul (see Figs. 11 and 12).[33] Here, arenas are built in connection with a sanctuary site, possibly one of pre-Roman significance, and may have been the venues for rituals of local derivation.

British amphitheaters more or less fall into two periods: the decades immediately following the Roman conquest (A.D. 43) and the Trajanic/ Hadrianic period (A.D. 98–138). Many of these must fall within the Flavian stimulation of amphitheater construction, inspired by the dynastic focus on the Colosseum.[34] Indeed, some of this inspiration may have been more or less direct, as part of the official recognition of the long-term relationship between Rome and Cogidubnus, a strong support of Roman, and specifically Flavian, interests in a time of duress.[35] Cogidubnus' city, Noviomagus Regnensium, has an amphitheater datable to A.D. 80, the year the Flavian Amphitheater was dedicated.

THE NORTHEASTERN FRONTIER

The twenty-eight amphitheaters found on Rome's European frontier do not fit the pattern of urban distribution. A statistical comparison of the

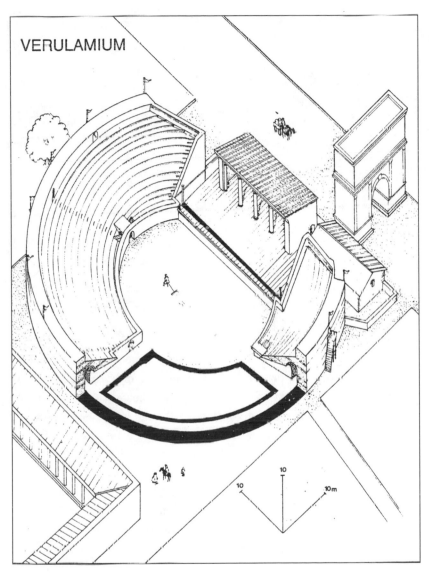

VERULAMIUM

FIGURE 12. Reconstruction of mixed edifice at Verulamium showing combination of podium wall and stage building, by G. de la Bédoyère, *The Buildings of Roman Britain* (London: B. T. Batsford, 1991), fig. 79.

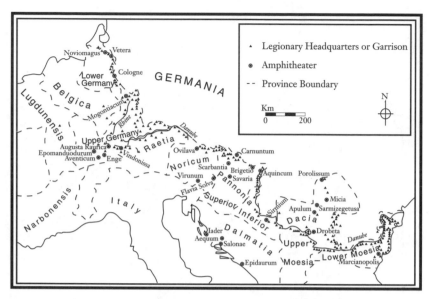

MAP 3. Northeastern Frontier: military and amphitheater coincidence.

spread of amphitheaters with that of cities made little sense in this region. It seems clear from the maps alone, even more than in the case of militarized Britannia, that amphitheaters and settlements follow the line of the *limes*, rather than spreading out across the landscape (see Map 3).[36] Fully two-thirds of these amphitheaters thus have primarily military associations and can be seen as providing a front line for the Romanization process.[37]

Typical of this function are the constructions at Carnuntum and Aquincum, both located along the Pannonian Danube.[38] A military installation appeared on each site during the reign of Tiberius, the period of early Roman expansion in the area. The earliest amphitheater at Carnuntum was built of wood during the Julio-Claudian era, then was rebuilt in stone by a veteran under the Antonines.[39] The emperor Hadrian visited Carnuntum in A.D. 124 and promoted the *vicus* to the rank of *municipium*. It was at this time that a much larger civilian amphitheater was built to supplement the wooden military one, perhaps to accommodate the swollen population of the newly acknowledged regional center (see Fig. 13). A similar sequence of events can be traced at Aquincum, whose municipal status was achieved under Trajan and celebrated by the building of a civic amphitheater. There was, presumably, an earlier wooden military amphitheater, which was renovated in stone during the reign of Antoninus Pius.[40]

The multipurpose role of the amphitheater on the military frontier is demonstrated by its presence at Colonia Agrippinensis.[41] The settlement was founded as Oppidum Ubiorum in 38 B.C. as a new location for the Ubii tribe. These were the early years of the Roman presence across the Rhine, and the new settlement had two legions headquartered in the vicinity. An Imperial altar and its appropriate structures were set up, and, it is likely, an amphitheater as well, forming a complex analogous to those at Lugdunum (modern Lyon) and Tarraco, functioning both as a focus for Roman loyalty and a warning against possible dissidence in a vulnerable area.

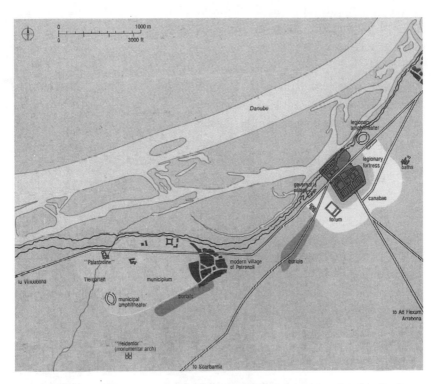

FIGURE 13. Plan of Roman Carnuntum, showing relative locations of civil and military amphitheaters, by J. Brennan, published in T. J. Cornell and J. Matthews, *Atlas of the Roman World* (New York: Facts on File, 1982), p. 142. Courtesy Andromeda Oxford Ltd.

These strong military associations suggest that amphitheaters were part of the standard operating procedure for the Roman army on the frontier.[42] Even in the frontier zone, however, there are seemingly civilian amphitheaters, places that supported the presence of an amphitheater, despite the lack of a clearly military context. There are four such sites along the Illyrian coast, far from the formal frontier of the empire: Iader, Epidaurum, Salonae, and Aequum.[43] All had settlement prior to the Roman presence, and all received colonial status fairly early.[44] Why were these amphitheaters built? Aequum and Iader, in fact, had an indirect military link, in that their colonial status was due to the settlement of veterans there by Claudius and Octavian. Salonae was the capital of Dalmatia, which may account for its possession of the largest amphitheater in the area, and had a population of some sixty thousand by the time the arena was built.[45]

Other amphitheaters in the frontier provinces were built at towns along Roman roads, which had strategic significance if no actual military outposts.[46] Epomanduodurum was the site of a sanctuary with a theater and baths, possibly akin to the similar Gallic rural phenomenon. As our evidence for an amphitheater there is epigraphic, it may be that we should reexamine the known theater as a potential example of the "mixed edifice" known from Gaul and Britain. Should this prove to be the case, Epomanduodurum's amphitheater would be the result of Celtic adaptation of Roman architecture to local traditional practices.[47]

THE GALLIAE

With Gaul, we return to the comparison between amphitheater and city distribution, with some interesting results.[48] All Gaul held seventy-two amphitheaters. Lugdunensis was the most blessed with amphitheaters, with thirty examples dotting the Lyonnaise landscape (see Map 4). Bekker-Nielsen's analysis of Gaul's urban scatter more or less matches that of the amphitheater spread and by implication conforms to the "tribal" pattern of urban density much more closely than Britannia does.

Gallic centers, as marked by associated amphitheaters, were located within a two-day round-trip journey, which would be undertaken to participate in political or religious functions or fulfill state-required obligations, like the census or taxes. The seeming correspondence between the scatter of Gallic amphitheaters and the pattern of urbanization as a whole

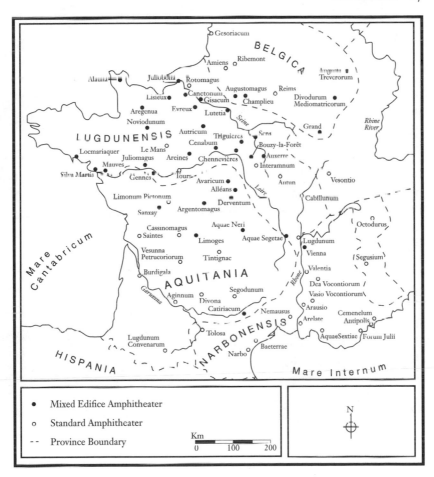

MAP 4. Amphitheaters in Gaul.

is, however, misleading, as becomes clear when one pays particular attention to the phenomena of rural amphitheaters and mixed edifices. A comparison between population density as suggested by seating capacity of
the amphitheaters and that suggested by the extent of urban spread in the
archaeological record is also enlightening.

The concept that the seating capacity of amphitheaters should bear
some relation to the population of the city seems only sensible.[49] Amphitheaters were expensive objects to construct, requiring not only a great
deal of money for materials and manpower but also community organization dedicated for some years to the completion of the project. These

MAP 5. Seating capacity of amphitheaters in Gaul.

needs are greatly intensified for the larger amphitheaters, which rank among the largest buildings in antiquity. It seems only reasonable to look for such resources in greater population centers, which would be expected to have surplus funds and labor for public works of this nature. Seating capacity need not, therefore, be taken simply as a one-to-one correlate of a given town's adult population but rather as a possible indicator of the excess wealth and administrative energy to be found in highly Romanized centers. I have therefore plotted amphitheaters onto the Gallo-Roman landscape according to their capacity and compared the results

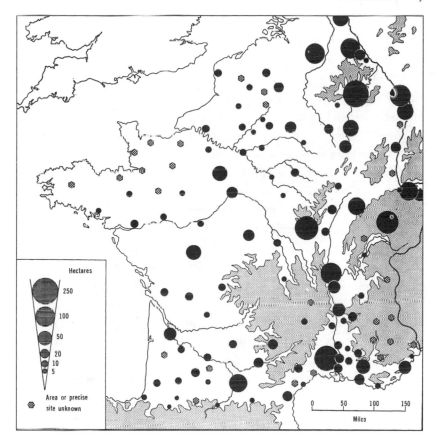

MAP 6. Populations of Roman cities in Gaul as determined by seating capacity of amphitheaters, from N. J. G. Pounds, "The Urbanization of the Classical World," *Annals of the Association of American Geographers,* 59 (1969): 135–157.

with studies of provincial population density calculated by other means (see Maps 5 and 6).[50]

The outcome of the analysis was surprising. Although there are sizable amphitheaters in areas of known density of urban settlement, such as the Rhône valley and the Mediterranean seacoast, the amphitheater scatter would lead us to believe the western and north-central parts of Gaul shared in this urbanization, Roman style. The archaeological record, however, does not support this, pointing instead to a rural population pattern, with urban centers relatively few and on the small side at that. Part of this discrepancy may be due to a peculiar preference of Roman Gaul for the so-called theater-amphitheater, or mixed edifice.[51] One could even say that the mixed edifice is the standard type of amphitheater in Gallia Lugdunensis, home to twenty-one such structures.[52]

There are two types of mixed edifices: the semiamphitheater and the theater-amphitheater, distinguished by their conformity to the typical amphitheater and theater as building types. The semiamphitheater, like a "normal" amphitheater, possesses an elliptical arena, but, unlike the standard, it also has a stage, however small.[53] The proportions of the *cavea*, or seating area, vary substantially, from a third the size of the usual ellipse, as found at Chennevières, to more than half, as at Lutetia (see Fig. 14).

The theater-amphitheaters closely resemble a standard theater but have a small arena defined by a podium wall in place of an orchestra. The identification of a ruined theater as a theater-amphitheater is, however, problematic. It is possible that many more of this type of mixed edifice once existed but have unfortunately lost their distinguishing characteristics and thus have been misidentified as theaters by modern scholars. The stage of the theater-amphitheater tends to be smaller than that of a theater, averaging twelve by four meters in size. The tininess of the area would severely limit the performance of dramatic works. The arena is also much smaller than in the more amphitheatrical buildings. Can the specifications of these structures be linked to developments in theatrical display? Scholars have described, with some distaste, the increasingly

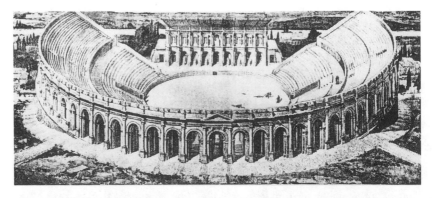

FIGURE 14. Reconstruction of mixed edifice at Lutetia, drawing by J. Formigé, originally published in *Procès-Verbaux de la Commission du Vieux Paris*, January 12, 1918. Courtesy Commission du Vieux Paris.

graphic and violent nature of Roman drama during the Principate. Since, however, this would involve increasing spectacle as well, one cannot explain the small-scale performance areas in the mixed edifices as part of that wide-scale Roman phenomenon of dramatic "degradation."[54]

The mixed edifice may have been built as a multipurpose entertainment center, its hybrid nature making it far more economical, in terms of construction costs, than the standard amphitheater.[55] Since the *cavea* was reduced in size by as much as two-thirds, the builders could use a nearby hill to support the seating, as was done with Greek theaters, instead of having to assemble some costly artificial substructure. Given the generally rural location of the mixed edifices, it is very likely that fewer financial resources were available to the builders and that this proposal, to some extent, is correct.[56]

The placement of mixed edifices in the rural landscape, however, was a deliberate decision made in accordance with local goals; it is probable that economic factors per se were not paramount among the motivations. The Gauls could, after all, instead have built relatively inexpensive earthwork structures with wooden retaining walls, as did the doubtlessly pragmatic military architects on the frontiers of Britannia and the northeastern *limes*. It is clear that function, not cost, was of primary concern in Gaul. Mixed edifices tended to be located near a small habitation center, often one predating the conquest, or an important sanctuary, as at Grand and Chennevières, which would also be of pre-Roman origin. With the smaller area for performance, these were not settings for classical theater in the grand tradition nor for elaborately staged gladiatorial combats. The roughly semicircular nature of the seating may indicate a concern for acoustics, which one might not expect among predominantly gladiatorial aficionados.[57] Apparently, Gallo-Romans, particularly in the North, had a liking for spectacles, possibly religious, which combined dramatic performance with some sort of combat.[58]

These mixed edifices were, however, on the small side, the largest being the nearly 18,000-capacity building in Lutetia. This was an extreme case, as the average capacity of these constructions was about 7,000 people.[59] There still remains the question of population density and the six huge amphitheaters of west-central Gaul, planted in an area not only lacking the larger cities of the south but also not overly endowed with

Gallo-Roman sites of any scale. Where and what were these amphitheaters? The cities involved are today known as Bordeaux, Saintes, Tours, Périgueux, Poitiers, and Limoges.[60] All were *civitas* capitals, the Romanized tribal administrative centers. Bordeaux became, eventually, the capital of Aquitania, which may explain its inclusion in this group. I will examine in greater detail four of these: Poitiers, Saintes, Périgueux, and Limoges, and the construction of amphitheaters in a more historical context.

Poitiers, Saintes, and Périgueux are not only among the largest Gallic amphitheaters, they are quite early, predating the dazzling Flavian constructions of Narbonensis by some decades.[61]

Poitiers was the chief city of the Pictones or Pictavenses, whose capital was known as Pictavis from the fourth century B.C. It boasted the largest amphitheater of the six, as well as one of the earliest, and shows architectural similarities to the amphitheaters of Saintes and Périgueux.[62] It is dated to the Julio-Claudian period because of an architectural characteristic common to the three: it lacks a peripheral gallery on the ground floor, which became characteristic of the monumental amphitheater in the Flavian period, with the Colosseum providing the Imperial model.[63]

The amphitheater at Saintes is dated to the Claudian period by epigraphic evidence as well as by the architectural indications noted at Poitiers (see Fig. 15).[64] It was built inside the city limits, less than 500 meters from the forum itself, as part of the building program begun under Tiberius.[65] It is notable for its excellent state of preservation as well as for the high standard followed in its construction. The superimposed *fornices* of the façade provide a link between the great Roman theaters of the Late Republic and Early Empire and the amphitheatrical masterpieces to come in the Flavian period and later.

The *oppidum* of the tribe of the Petrucorii, later known as Périgueux, continued to be an administrative and religious center for the region during the Roman period, although its actual location was moved down the hillside from its former strategic placement, as sometimes happened to those who sided against Caesar in his Gallic campaigns.[66] The amphitheater's dedicatory inscription gives the name of the builder, A. Pompeius Dumnom(otus), a military tribune and prefect of public works under

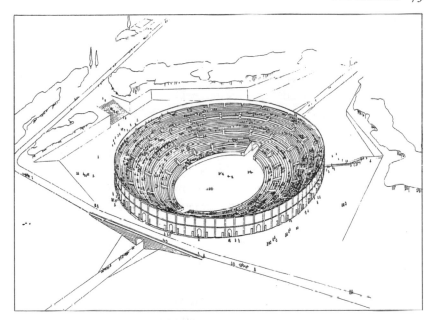

FIGURE 15. Reconstruction of amphitheater at Saintes as viewed from the west, originally published in *L'Amphithéâtre Gallo-Romain de Saintes* by J. Doreau, J.-C. Golvin, and L. Maurin, Editions du CNRS, Paris, 1982.

Tiberius.[67] The structure at Périgueux is located near the sanctuary complex of Vesunna Tutela, with a characteristically Gallic round temple located south of the arena.[68]

The Julio-Claudian period was a time of some unrest in Gaul, possibly connected with increased taxation to pay for campaigns elsewhere in the empire.[69] Dissension reached a head in a failed rebellion led by Iulius Sacrovir and Iulius Florus in A.D. 21, born to the Aeduan and Treviran tribes respectively. This period can be seen as part of a series of Gallic revolts, beginning in 38 B.C. and recurring at intervals until the Flavian period.[70] The immediate causes varied, but most can be traced to forced Romanization of the nastiest type: the imposition of financial demands on Roman subjects, including the census and its concomitant efficient system of taxation. The earlier establishment of the altar and amphitheater of the Three Gauls at Lugdunum has been linked to Gallic disquiet.[71] The amphitheaters in western Aquitania may likewise have been erected in response to native resistance, an expression of Rome's concern to foster appropriate interaction with her subjects, the amphitheaters offered as a venue and catalyst for engagement in Imperial discourse.

The middle of the first century also saw apparent subversive activity by other Gallic nationals, specifically the Druids.[72] Pliny refers to the suppression of the Druids by Tiberius, which may point to a religious subtext underlying the Sacrovir rebellion. The Druids could have been involved in either motivating the revolt because of local resentment of Roman intolerance of native religion or serving as a means of uniting and organizing the rebellious Gauls.[73] Suetonius refers to the abolition of Druidism by Claudius; whether this is continued activity against subversive Druids or a doubling of the Tiberian episode is not clear.[74] The construction of amphitheaters can be linked to anti-Druid sentiment in that amphitheatrical games may have been considered an acceptable, Roman alternative to the blood sacrifice attested for the Gallic cult.[75]

Limoges was the capital of the Lemovices, located on a crossing of the Vienne river. The amphitheater has been dated to either the Flavian period or the early second century. Early excavations uncovered Hadrianic medallions in the interior, but this can only provide a *terminus ante quem*. Its structural material, being simple *opus vittatum* without brick, may indicate an earlier date.[76]

The years since the building of the Julio-Claudian amphitheaters in Aquitania were most significant in terms of Gallo-Roman interaction, particularly during the revolt of Vindex in 68, a revolt that found support among a number of tribes and local leaders who had previously been cooperative with the Roman center of power.[77] The same period saw anti-Roman sentiments expressed by locals in the destruction of Augusta Convenarum, with particular vehemence directed against the trophy of Augustus. Vindex himself was a descendant of an Aquitanian royal house and apparently first sought support for his insurrection there.[78] Whether the revolt of Vindex and the general havoc in Gaul during A.D. 68–69 were the immediate catalysts for the proliferation of Flavian amphitheaters in general and at Limoges in specific is not easily demonstrable, but at least eleven amphitheaters, possibly more, were built in Gaul under the Flavians.[79] The political message of the Colosseum was thus translated in this particularly sensitive province as an amphitheatrical harbinger of enforced peace and prosperity, entertainment courtesy of the Imperial dynasty, calculated to cater to Gallic habits.[80]

The importance of the urbanization process is generally underrated, with too little attention given the implications of mandating fundamental changes in the living environment. Architecture and urban forms, however, are not passive, they are not merely decorative; they embody a system of assumptions about how society works and what is expected of the individual. The nuancing of those assumptions through negotiation on the local level is the essence of the change wrought by Rome in Europe. But change *was* demanded, a widespread, deep, profound change from the lifestyle that prevailed prior to Roman dominance in the West.

The cavalier treatment of the imposition of cities on the Roman provinces often goes hand in hand with casual references to amphitheater construction, as if both the whole and the part were mere "conveniences," luxurious additions to the Roman lifestyle. There is far more to the issue than this, in terms of both urbanization and the amphitheater. Not only the outward forms of Rome were adopted but also the meanings and assumptions that went along with the mandatory use of these structures as part of the process of assimilation.

The layers of meaning in building and using Roman cities complicate our understanding of the spread of amphitheaters as structures best known from an urban context. Does the presence of an amphitheater represent no more than an unusually high level of Romanization? Amphitheaters were, indeed, a typically Roman building type, one favored by those with the resources to support such an institution, which may imply a certain amount of cooperation with the center and the rewards accruing from such cooperation. But provincials imported the amphitheatrical institution on their own terms and in their own way. In Spain, an early and enduring fondness for the Games may have lessened the urgency to monumentalize their setting. Thus Iberian amphitheaters were relatively rare. In the northeastern militarized zone, and to some extent in Britannia, amphitheaters followed the army and performed a function specific to the legions on active duty. Gaul seemed the likeliest candidate to demonstrate the scenario that amphitheaters were built in an urban center, which was initially proposed. Although the scatter of amphitheaters mimics that of Gallo-Roman urban centers, the strong presence of rural amphitheaters and non-Roman amphitheatrical types, as well as the discrepancy between population density and large-scale amphitheaters, indicates that here, too, an *interpretatio provincialis* was in operation. Whether the impetus came from below, on the part of the natives, or from above, with the manipulation of this building type by the Roman establishment for purposes specific to the area, clearly the provincial amphitheater was not merely superficial decoration for the new-fangled Roman town but rather served as an expression of local needs and enthusiasms.

III. ORDER AND STRUGGLE
Cult in the Amphitheater

Clouds of blood will come to you.

THE DESTRUCTION OF
DA DERGA'S HOSTEL

RELIGION IN HUMAN SOCIETY acts as a way to alleviate cognitive discomfort by offering a symbolic framework through which to categorize, reenact, and reconcile with socially perceived conflict. In other words, religion helps one feel better about his or her place in society and the cosmos by offering some sort of pattern for understanding that appeals to the heart and to the mind. Rituals and associated beliefs are organized into cult institutions, complexes unified by focus and goal, with some functional overlapping between institutions. The goal of such a religious institution can be largely defined as the inculcation of group identity values, necessary for the operation of society through the smooth interaction of its various well-integrated parts.[1] Cults and their associated rituals endow secular activity with emotion-laden meaning; links forged in so affective an environment provide strong motivation for social cooperation.

This functionalist approach is particularly pertinent to the Roman provinces. The Roman State persistently and conspicuously harnessed Roman religion for the accomplishment of Roman political aims. Romans took great pride in their piety, claiming, in Cicero's words, to be the most religious people in the world.[2] The state cult was directed toward the maintenance of proper power relationships not only between gods and men but also within the human sphere.[3] From an early period, religion governed the vertical structuring within Roman society, but the state gods also were responsible for Rome's position of authority in its world; the expansion of the Roman State was sacralized. The official rites of the Roman State included regular prayers for the increase of empire.[4] The conduct and outcome of war were seen as a direct manifestation of divine will, and the Romans were meticulous in their efforts to ensure divine support at every step, from the declaration of war by the fetial priests, to the taking of the auspices at the start of the campaign, to the *evocatio* of the enemy's gods before the taking of a city.[5] Preservation of the *pax deorum* gave state actions divine sanction: keeping peace with the gods legitimized war against others. The result of Roman religiosity was world empire, a causal connection acknowledged as early as Polybius.[6] The development and maintenance of that empire, its reconciliation within the Roman conceptualization of power, would likewise utilize religion.

Roman central authority found it highly desirable that provincials perceive themselves as politically unified and part of corporate Rome: such an attitude was conducive to the Imperial goals of peace and prosperity. This was the function fulfilled by the Imperial Cult, which, particularly in its earliest phase, can be demonstrably linked to the construction of amphitheaters. The arena was not merely a backdrop for the performance of "patriotic" rituals; the message implicit in the Imperial Cult made an impact by being delivered through the local amphitheater and audience.

The official encouragement of Roman political unity did not, however, exclude promotion of group identity on a local level. The flexibility of *interpretatio Romana* allowed provincials largely to retain their own traditions, fostered and maintained by particular cult practice. We see this attitude manifest in the amphitheaters at rural sanctuaries in Gaul, where Celtic belief was to some extent syncretized with Roman forms to create a cult complex meaningful in the new sociopolitical dynamic. That this effort was largely successful is surely implied by the number and continued use of these mixed edifices in the Celtic landscape.

Yet change is an inherent aspect of human existence; success or failure of the individual is ultimately unpredictable, being largely dependent on the whims of fortune. The dynamism of the Roman Empire, although potentially highly adaptable, could also be too unstable for comfort. In the cult of Nemesis, the worshipper implicitly acknowledged his inability to control his destiny. Striking a bargain with Nemesis, the custodian of

Fortune and thus of the outcome of the arena games, relieved the individual of the anxiety of personal responsibility and allowed him to maximize his performance in critical moments. Nemesis thus offered a means of control, which, in the context of the amphitheater, was linked to scenarios designed to demonstrate the use of discipline and domination. Nemesis' presence in the amphitheater was not only as the representative of divine justification for the dictates of destiny; her close affiliation with the sponsors of the event, the local representative of Roman power, would serve to validate the dominion of Rome and to endow the performances in the arena with cosmic significance.

The amphitheater was part of the ritual complex of three aspects of the religious system of the Roman Empire: the Imperial Cult, Celtic cult practices, and the cult of Nemesis. The arena, as backdrop to particular events, was pertinent to these cults; the "message" of the amphitheater was enhanced through a connection with religious practice. The amphitheater presented the argument of empire as a ritual embodying a set of tensions; the discourse of empire was a formalized symbolic exchange imbued with the power of the supernatural, drenched, as we shall see, with the blood of sacrifice.

IMPERIAL CULT

Actions of 30/29 B.C. caused ripples that reverberated throughout Imperial history.[7] Octavian was approached by local dignitaries from Ephesus and Nicaea, Pergamum and Nicomedia, who wanted to demonstrate their loyalty to him by establishing his cult.[8] Octavian was faced with something of a problem. To refuse such worship, which had been part of standard political and diplomatic dialogue in the Greek East for some time, would be gauche, setting an awkward precedent for future interaction. On the other hand, Octavian was well aware of the ill luck that had recently befallen other Roman worthies, such as Caesar, Pompey, and Antony, who had perhaps hubristically overindulged in theistic playacting in the East. In other words, Octavian was concerned about the negative impact the presence of such a cult would have closer to home; he wanted to maintain his public image as a highly ethical and traditional man, who sought to serve and glorify Rome, not himself. Octavian gave in to their demand, but only on the condition that this Imperial Cult be centered on himself *and* Roma. Roma had long been an acknowledged goddess in the Greek sphere, where her worship developed as a means of validating Graeco-Roman diplomatic interaction through the symbols of ritual.[9] Her partnership with Octavian offered non-Romans the opportunity to show their fidelity both to the abstract notion of Rome as a sociopolitical entity and to Octavian as *the* Roman authority figure, *Romanitas* incarnate: worship thus enshrined the ruler and the rule.[10]

It was at Lugdunum that the Imperial Cult of the western empire was first established, setting a standard, formally and ideologically, for centuries to come.[11] The major historical sources take notice of this momentous event, including Livy, a contemporary who described it as the "altar of deified Caesar, set up at the confluence of the Saône and Rhône, with the elected Aeduan *sacerdos* C. Julius Vercondaridubnus."[12] Preserved among the paraphrased events of 12 B.C., Livy's notice raises some questions, among which is the issue of the object of cult at Lugdunum.[13] The fragment names *divus Caesar*, which would seem to suggest Augustus' adopted parent, C. Julius Caesar. The adjective *divus* came to be associated with deceased emperors, and indeed, the former dictator had been dead for some years by the time of the altar's foundation. Most important for our purposes, however, is the formal precedent described by Livy, that is, worship conducted by a *sacerdos* at an altar. Also notable is the use of the term *creatus*, which has been interpreted as meaning that the *sacerdos* was elected by the newly legitimized Concilium of the Three Gauls.

Additional notices of the establishment of the altar can be found in Dio Cassius and Suetonius, with further clarification to be had. Dio tells us that "he sent for the leaders of the territory, giving the excuse of the festival, which even now they hold at the altar of Augustus at Lugdunum."[14] Like Livy, Dio locates the cult at an altar, a *bomon*, this time one that commemorated Augustus specifically. Dio's ambiguous "even now" may simply be a reference to the festivals involving Imperial Cult celebrated continuously through the early third century, or, as we will see, it may allude to pre-Roman cult activity later acknowledged in a Roman adaptation, possibly independent of the *ara Augusti*.

The Imperial Cult in the West seems to have been conceived as a means of pacification in an unruly period. A census had been set up in Gaul to allow for taxation in support of Roman expansion on the German frontier. When some resistance was encountered, action was taken to counter it, including the formation at Lugdunum of the Concilium of the Three Gauls, a body that was to play an important role in provincial relations. Building on pre-Roman tradition, this was a participatory, albeit nonpolitical and nonadvisory, assembly that met annually to demonstrate loyalty to the regime and to elect the revolving priesthood of the Imperial Cult, an office that held status in the local provincial *cursus* possibly equivalent to that of the Roman censorship.[15] The Concilium also sent embassies to Rome, providing a direct communication link to the emperor independent of the official bureaucracy. It may further have served as a means of unifying disparate elements in the Gauls, in a "civilized" structure reminiscent of the Senate but with strong foundations in Celtic tradition as well. Caesar describes a number of such tribal assemblies, for example, the one held at Bibracte in 52 B.C., and the religious authority surrounding the delegates and their decisions.[16] Caesar was to call such assemblies himself, finding them a useful mechanism in fostering a working relationship between Gallic and Roman interests in the area. The utility of this tradition was recognized by Augustus and incorporated into the Imperial agenda.

Celtic tradition may also have played a part in selecting the location for the Imperial Cult center. Dio's wording points to the existence of a pre-Roman festival in the area, and indeed, the first of August marked Lughnasa, the feast of the Celtic deity Lug.[17] One of the most frequent toponyms in the Celtic world, Lug is known from the vernacular sources as a powerful member of the Tuatha dé Danaan dynasty of gods and is notable for his wide expertise in warfare and craft, possibly hinting at a polyvalence verging on omnipotence.[18] Lug was often syncretized with Roman Mercury, whom Caesar recognized as the most commonly worshipped of all Celtic deities.[19] It has been suggested that the confluence of the Rhône and Saône rivers was home to an Iron Age sanctuary of Lug, possibly with a cult center on the peak of Fourvière near the later Imperial site (see Fig. 16).[20] The ritual significance of water in Celtic belief may explain the connection between the Imperial Cult here and infrequent instances of immersion practices in the vicinity.[21]

The first of August had particular meaning in the Roman sphere as well, being the "natal day" or dedication festival of the temples of Victoria and Victoria Virgo on the Palatine.[22] Victory had been associated with ruler cult since Hellenistic times. The king was presented as more than human, as a man gifted with extraordinary success and good fortune by merit not only of his unique qualifications but also of his divine favor.

Imagery and ideology combined in a "Theology of Victory," in which victory in battle was clear proof of the gods' choice, thus legitimizing imperialist expansion as a kind of manifest destiny.[23] Ambitious Romans during the Republican period promoted similar claims, in which Victoria, originally the achievement of the Senate and People of Rome, became a personal companion of the individual commander.[24] Caesar, in particular, subscribed to this concept, adding the *ludi* of Victoria Caesaris to the calendar of ordinary games. Caesar's viewpoint is further clarified by the sculptural representation of the dictator set up in 46 B.C. on the Capitolium: like Victoria, *Invictus* Caesar's foot rests on the globe.[25]

Augustus also adopted victory as a major motif of his program for mass persuasion.[26] Avoiding the now unlucky epithet *invictus*, he nevertheless suggested the characteristic by gaining the right to wear the laurel in public from 29 B.C., a right that became his alone thirteen years later.[27] Victory was not only a sign of personal divine favor but a prerequisite for Pax Augusta, a theme driven home notably on the Ara Pacis.[28] Victory was the primary rhetorical referent for the decorative program of the Lugdunum altar, on which laurel trees flanked a central oak crown, trees flanked in turn by laurel wreaths, the altar as a whole set off by twin

FIGURE 16. Model of Roman Lugdunum showing position of Imperial Cult sanctuary across the river from city proper. Copyright © Paul MacKendrick 1972. From: *Roman France*. By: Paul MacKendrick. Reprinted with permission of St. Martin's Press, Incorporated.

Victories atop pillars on either side, holding crowns of laurel triumphantly aloft (see Fig. 17).[29]

So the stage is set for the amphitheater at Lugdunum, the backdrop both literal and ideological for its construction; a combined stone and wood construction predated the more monumental phase of the amphitheater at Lugdunum, whose later remains are now visible. C. Julius Rufus, *sacerdos* of Roma and Augustus, claimed responsibility for the construction in stone of its arena and podium during Tiberius' reign.[30] This same individual had set up an arch at Saintes in honor of Tiberius, Drusus, and Germanicus, the inscription of which dates his election to the priesthood to A.D. 19 and thus his work at Lugdunum to the following year.[31] The most interesting feature of the amphitheater, and the key to its cultic significance, lies in the seating arrangements. The remains suggest that originally seating was extremely limited, with only two or three tiers above the podium (see Fig. 18). Traces of inscriptions giving tribal affiliations were found, which would suggest that the seating was in fact reserved for tribal representatives, specifically for the delegates of the Concilium of the Three Gauls. This would link the meeting of the Concilium to the activity inside the amphitheater, making the arena an integral part of the Imperial festal day each year in August. Further support for a close connection between the Imperial Cult at Lugdunum and the amphitheater is in the location of the building at the west end of the sanctuary. Axially aligned with the other cult structures, the amphitheater shares the sacred space.[32]

FIGURE 18. Substructure of seating at amphitheater in Imperial Cult sanctuary of Lugdunum, photograph by author.

Indirect evidence for the incorporation of the amphitheatrical *specta-cula* in ritual performance comes from the earliest representations of the altar on coins. Objects appear on top of the altar proper, indistinct blobs in the later renderings but clearly intended as busts and statuettes inside baldaquins in the first issues.[33] We know that the Imperial Cult in the East paraded busts in *pompa*, or sacred processions, and western examples of this activity are hinted at in the Charter of Narbonensis.[34] The ramps on either side of the altar would have accommodated such processions. We know further that these ritual processions regularly inaugurated the Games, with the gods of the state, their priests, the presiding magistrates, and the competitors all marching to their places accompanied by the cheers of the spectators. Might not the altar and amphitheater of the Three Gauls (see Fig. 19) have served as origin and endpoint for an annual *pompa* in celebration of Augustus and his house?

The connection between altar, regional assembly, and amphitheater is clearest at Lugdunum, but traces of similar complexes can be found elsewhere in the empire. At some point, the Imperial Cult was extended to the German frontier, with the construction of a federal center at Ara

Ubiorum (Cologne).[35] The main evidence for the existence of such a sanctuary comes from Tacitus' description of the rebellions on the frontier immediately after Augustus' death, where he mentions that legates from the Senate met with Germanicus at the Altar of the Ubii.[36] He goes on to say that the first and twentieth legions were headquartered there for the winter. Hence we have some indication of an altar located in an area noted for its strategic importance to Roman interests yet affiliated with a local tribe. Tacitus later refers to Segimundus, a member of the Cherusci tribe, as a *sacerdos* elected at the altar of the Ubii, which provides us with still more parallels to Lugdunum; the use of the term *sacerdos* for the chief priest of the cult, evidence for at least a second tribe (the Cherusci), the presence of more than one tribe and the use of *creatus*, implying an elected priesthood, all support a projected similarity to Lugdunum.[37]

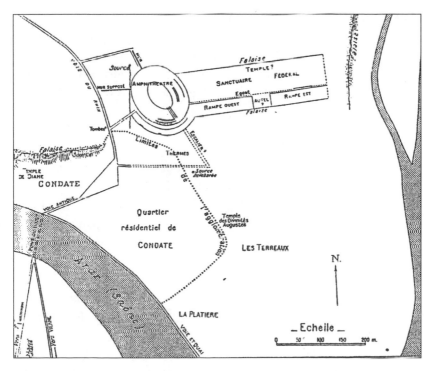

FIGURE 19. Plan of Imperial Cult complex at Lugdunum, from A. Audin, *Essai sur la topographie de Lugdunum* (Lyon: Revue de Geographie de Lyon, 1964), fig. 7.

The date of the altar's establishment is uncertain, but may have been, like Lugdunum, under the auspices of Drusus, who was in the area from 12 to 9 B.C., or, alternatively, those of Tiberius, present in 8–7 B.C. and in A.D. 5. There is, unfortunately, no archaeological trace of the altar, and evidence for the amphitheater is likewise meager: sadly, little is known other than its location on the north side of the ancient city.[38] The establishment of the Imperial Cult here at Ara Ubiorum, with the suggestion of some sort of regional assembly as well, implies that the town was intended as the religious and political center of Roman Germany. The disaster in the Teutoberg forest in A.D. 9, the *Clades Variana*, in which three legions were destroyed, may have shifted the focus from the city, which continued to be referred to as Ara but has no further trace of emperor-worship on the provincial level.

The literature preserves some allusion to the elusive *arae Sestianae*, the "Sestian altars" of an early Imperial Cult center in northwestern Spain, about which the sources themselves are confused.[39] Pomponius Mela puts these three altars on the Asturian coast, while Pliny claims the coast involved was the west of Callaecia; Ptolemy simply locates them on an unspecified coastal promontory.[40] The eponymous Sestius, too, is a shadowy figure, possibly to be identified as L. Sestius Quirinalis Albinianus, who was in all likelihood the Roman governor of Hither Spain from 16–14 B.C. when there is a gap in the *Fasti*.[41] If so, the altars may have been built in association with Augustus' stay in Spain during the same years. There are probably three altars either because three legions were stationed there at the time of Pomponius Mela and Pliny or due to some sort of parallel to the *conventus* districts of Lucus Augusti, Bracara Augusta, and Asturica Augusta. Later inscriptions, from the Flavian period, mention a *sacerdos Romae et Aug(usti)*, which provides a match, in object and agent of cult, for the Imperial complex at Lugdunum.[42] The as-yet-unknown location of the altar itself, and the relative silence of the sources, precludes the clear association here between altar, *sacerdos*, provincial assembly, and amphitheater. An amphitheater nearby at Bracara Augusta was still visible in the eighteenth century but has never been excavated.[43]

Fishwick suggests that this first, Augustan phase of the Imperial Cult was concentrated specifically in the newly pacified territories of the West, that is, Gaul, Germany, and northwestern Spain, where altars to Roma and Augustus were planted by members of the Imperial House, to be serviced by elected *sacerdotes*.[44] This is an attractive perspective and seems especially applicable to the perceived function of the Imperial Cult as a mechanism for the integration of worshippers into the group identity. But the link between Imperial Cult and amphitheaters is more dependent on the assumed presence of a provincial assembly to both service the cult and provide an audience for the *spectacula*.[45] Despite Fishwick's claim that this sort of cult-cum-spectacle was less appropriate to the more Romanized and more demonstrably loyal provinces of the West, there is some evidence for such worship in Hither Spain, specifically at Tarraco.

Quintilian refers to an altar to Augustus at Tarraco as being in existence during the emperor's lifetime, an assertion supported indirectly by numismatic evidence, with later coins from Tarraco depicting some sort of monumental altar to be associated with the emperor cult.[46] An inscription from the lower forum has been restored as *flam[ini] [Romae] et August[i]*, which links the worship of Augustus, appropriately, to that of Roma.[47] The amphitheater at Tarraco is not datable with any specificity other than "Julio-Claudian," although it is generally understood to be Augustan in date.[48] The controversy here centers on whether this cult is municipal or provincial, the distinction based on which entity set up the cult in the first place. Fishwick plumps for "municipal," seeing the beginning of the provincial cult at Tarraco under Tiberius, when the cult took on its post-Augustan format of temple, *flamen*, and deified dead emperor. I am swayed, however, by the coincidence of altar, Roma and Augustus, provincial assembly, and amphitheater and would like to see the establishment at Tarraco as being part of the same Augustan policy that began with the altar at Lugdunum.[49]

The second phase of the Imperial Cult was triggered by the death of Augustus. Within days, the Senate met to declare him an official god of the Roman State, with cult appropriate to such an exalted status. No longer sharing worship with Roma, *divus* Augustus was honored at a temple by a *flamen*, by definition a high priest of the state cult. Tiberius, as Augustus had before him, could now call himself *divi filius* and gain the prestige of such a status. Indeed, the entire Imperial House was now divine. The precedent of the emperor's heir encouraging the official deification of his predecessor was thus set for all future worthy emperors.

Fishwick sees two lines of development in the provinces during the Julio-Claudian period, drawing a distinction between whether or not the cult, established from above, was directed toward the reigning emperor or the deceased Augustus and his deified house. The former, with its emphasis on immediate loyalty toward the current regime, would be more appropriate to the frontier and to potentially disruptive areas, while the latter would serve the more Romanized and sedate areas.[50] Although the differentiation between target areas is not so simple and straightforward as Fishwick suggests, the separation between cult of the living and of the (dead) deified emperor is clear, and it is to the former that the amphitheater has been attached.

The members of the Flavian dynasty, upstart imperials from outside the traditional ruling class, saw the need to utilize the Imperial Cult to legitimize their seizure of authority. This incentive sparked innovation in terms of cult and signaled another major period of development of provincial worship, analogous to that of Augustus. Having swept the East in his quest for the purple, Vespasian now concentrated on the West, specifically on those areas perceived as potential sources of trouble. Africa had supported Otho, and Spain and Gaul had provided the means for the advancement of Galba and Vitellius respectively, in A.D. 69, the so-called Year of the Four Emperors.[51]

The Flavian version of the Imperial Cult emphasized the construction of temples, serviced by a *flamen divorum*. Whom these *divi* would have included is another matter. If only the deceased deified emperors were meant, as would be the obvious interpretation of *divi*, this would limit the object of worship solely to the Julio-Claudian dynasty, which would do the new ruling family little good. It is thought, therefore, that the living emperor now came to be incorporated into the state pantheon proper at this time, thus elevating his status even above that implied previously by "Roma and Augustus."[52]

Narbo provides an idealized version of how the new, Flavian model of the Imperial Cult was put into practice in a provincial center.[53] Constructed at the edge of the urban build-up, the Imperial Cult complex was allotted space to develop along desired lines, incorporating a portico and amphitheater into the sacred space of the sanctuary. The cult center is also the findspot for the charter of the capital of Gallia Narbonensis, which gives us details relevant to the management of the Imperial Cult.[54] The charter mentions sacrifice and *spectacula*, and we can perhaps reconstruct Narbo's ritual activity as similar to that at Lugdunum, with the ritual procession of the *pompa* as the connection between the amphitheater and the temple. One difference between this location and Lugdunum is in the seating; at least fifteen thousand spectators could be accommodated at Narbo from the outset. The projected audience of participants for emperor-worship at Narbo was not, therefore, limited to the leaders of Gallic ethnic groups but had a much more general character. The expansion of the targeted audience may be related to the different background of the Imperial dynasties and the expanded social group among whom power could be shared during the later period. By broadening the range of potential seekers of the purple to admit the equestrian class, the number of rivals was increased. The corresponding need to broaden the dynastic support system may be reflected in the structural expansion of the amphitheater at Narbo.

Narbo is the best example of open Flavian utilization of the amphitheater as part of the loyalty cult. Elsewhere in the West, the two phenomena are not so closely linked. The Imperial Cult was standardized as worship of the living emperor in a temple by a *flamen* and concentrated in areas relatively neglected by the Julio-Claudians, notably in the Iberian peninsula and North Africa. Amphitheater construction under the Flavians was not limited to the cult centers of the Imperial dynasty. This was the time in which the amphitheater reached an apex of technical sophistication, embodied in the construction of the Colosseum in Rome, whose glory and utility transformed a location previously devoted to Nero's refined private needs. The rhetorical value of the amphitheater was exploited in Rome proper as well as abroad. The example of the Colosseum was followed in the western provinces, and between thirteen and thirty-five amphitheaters went up in the Flavian period. Even when not specifically linked to official Imperial Cult, the amphitheater had solid political resonance as a continual reminder both of the potential force backing the Roman State and of its concern for the well-being of individual citizens. The amphitheater was threateningly entertaining, a potent combination indeed.

The potency of the amphitheater in Imperial imagery of the Trajanic period is clarified by its appearance on what is surely the most elaborate piece of artistic mass persuasion: the Column of Trajan, erected in A.D. 113 as part of the Ulpian Forum in downtown Rome. Two amphitheaters are depicted in the course of the narrative of the Dacian campaigns [55] The first instance is in scenes 81–82 in the fifth spiral from the bottom, where

FIGURE 20. Scenes 81–82 from Trajan's Column, amphitheater in background, pl. xxv from F. Lepper and S. Frere, *Trajan's Column* (Gloucester: Alan Sutton, 1988).

barbarians besiege a river town of some importance on the Danube (see Fig. 20). This amphitheater appears to be simply an image from Rome's expanding frontier. As we know, construction of amphitheaters seems to have been a standard part of troop management in the militarized zone, which became civilianized with the settlement of the frontier. Here the amphitheater is arranged alongside an arch topped by a quadriga, another potent symbol of triumphal Roman authority. The meaning is clear: although sorely beset by barbarity, Rome's frontiers hold firm and will eventually prove victorious.

The second usage of the amphitheater on Trajan's column is scene 263 in the fifteenth spiral, much of which is taken up with Apollodorus' triumph of engineering: the bridge over the Danube (see Fig. 21). The amphitheater is in the fortress town of Drobeta, settled by Trajan's veterans on the banks of the river. A meeting is taking place before the amphitheater; Trajan and his companions, properly clad in togas with appropriate Roman accoutrements, have reached accord with a motley group of barbarians, identifiable by their clothing as various tribes of northeast Europe. All figures, on both sides, are depicted with dignity, faces smoothly classicized. The amphitheater in the background reminds us, however,

FIGURE 21. Scene 263 from Trajan's Column, arena in background, pl. lxxiii from F. Lepper and S. Frere, *Trajan's Column* (Gloucester: Alan Sutton, 1988).

who has the upper hand. The arena is a powerful symbol of authority in its own right, and the Roman audience could hardly fail to be reminded of Trajan's Games celebrating the Dacian triumph in A.D. 110, in which ten thousand combatants, many of them Dacian prisoners, faced death.

A few traces linger of Trajanic Imperial Cult activity in the Danube area, with some evidence for amphitheatrical connections.[56] Here the focus seems to be entirely on the living emperor, an emphasis appropriate for a newly conquered area now expected to be loyal to a new line in the Imperial succession. Roma does not share in the cult, which again implies that fidelity toward the Imperial Person, rather than the government as a whole, is the goal. An *ara Augusti*, serviced by a *sacerdos*, was located at Sarmizegetusa, now reorganized as Ulpia Traiana.[57] Sarmizegetusa also had an amphitheater from the earliest days of the city, indicating the strong connection between this construction and the expansion and maintenance of empire.[58] Upper Pannonia was administered from its newly established capital at Savaria, complete with *ara Augusti* and *sacerdotes*.[59] Savaria's amphitheater cannot be dated with any precision but was built between the reign of Domitian and A.D. 188, possibly contemporary with the institution of a Trajanic Imperial Cult.[60]

Evidence for Imperial Cult machinations by Trajan can be found at other regional centers. Inscriptions from Troesmis mention a *sacerdos* for Moesia.[61] Scardona in Dalmatia has a Trajanic-looking regional *ara Augusti Liburnorum*.[62] At Gorsium, in Lower Pannonia, a group of ceremonial buildings, including an altar and Concilium house, may date from the Trajanic period.[63] None of these have been connected as yet with any arenas.[64] Instead, other frontier amphitheaters seem to be linked to *limes* consolidation, particularly in the second century, rather than with the Imperial Cult per se.[65] One would not necessarily expect a connection in this area. The Imperial Cult as a whole seems to be much more of a civilian phenomenon; the frontier amphitheaters were military constructions.[66]

The use of the amphitheater as an integral part of the Imperial Cult seems clearest in the earliest phase of emperor-worship, under Augustus. The association between the basic elements of the cult (*ara*, Augustus and Roma, *sacerdos*, assembly) and the amphitheater is present from the beginning at Lugdunum and can be traced at several early Imperial sanctuaries. The integration of the amphitheater into post-Augustan phases of the Imperial Cult is more problematic but arguable under the Flavians at Narbo and during Trajan's rule on the Danube frontier.

Granted, the sites where one finds unequivocal physical connection between amphitheaters and the Imperial Cult are relatively few and far between. Some would claim that this infrequency argues against the association in terms of cult. I would downplay the proximity objection, for reasons mentioned earlier: amphitheaters were very large and cumbersome objects to construct. To erect an amphitheater from scratch in the civic center would necessitate a good deal of demolition and clearing before work on the building itself could even begin. The increased cost of such preparation was no doubt the prime motivation for building amphitheaters away from the traditional town centers. Standard cult structures, whether altar or temple, were far less trouble to construct, and so they could be more easily accommodated in a central location. We should, therefore, give greater weight to the example provided by "model" Imperial Cult centers, such as Lugdunum and Narbo. Here, where the congeniality of the terrain allowed the construction of an ideal sanctuary, the ultimate impact of the Imperial Cult could be achieved in the combination of cult building, assembly, and amphitheater.

The function of the amphitheater in the ritual of loyalty can be reconstructed only hypothetically, but it draws upon the public nature of Roman state cult, its need for an audience to witness the *pompa* and *munera*.[67] The political utility of games, particularly gladiatorial combats, had been recognized for many years. It was Augustus' doing to link the provision of spectacular entertainment with the Imperial House; the appropriate and expected response on the part of the audience was not merely gratitude but also continued loyalty to the state and to the emperor in particular. Such fidelity was expressed in the provinces through the Imperial Cult, which from the outset was closely connected to public *munera* and *ludi*. The amphitheater allowed a very large group of spectators to share in the affirmation of loyalty to the central authority, the confirmation of the ruler's divine nature and his concomitant justification as ruler, and the identification of the individual with the rest of the community. All those present shared a specific relationship to the emperor and were thus all part of the Imperial congregation of the Roman State.[68] The establishment of this sort of corporate identity in the provinces was a more important goal in the early Principate, when a whole series of such relationships, on many levels and involving many social groups, was first being established and codified. This may have been especially the case in Gaul, where civic tension and threat of revolt mandated the formation of social and political bonds between Romans and provincials. The amphitheater accommodated and contributed to the establishment of the stable hierarchy necessary for maintaining order in the provinces.

CELTIC CULT

Planted in the green, wooded landscape of the Gallo-Roman countryside, isolated even from the modest bustle of the preindustrial provincial centers, were fabrications of stone and cement suddenly thrusting into the peaceful pastoralism of sylvan Gaul. These were the Romano-Celtic rural sanctuaries, which incorporated amphitheaters and baths, structures bred in an urban nursery, into a Celtic cult complex, polished with a thin veneer of Roman-ness. But these were not standard amphitheaters either, being instead mixed edifices, which combined characteristics of theaters and amphitheaters in a building type peculiar to the northwestern provinces. Of the thirty-five examples of the mixed amphitheatrical type, at least twenty-four belong to the category of rural sanctuaries, and at least half of these were in sanctuaries seemingly specific to a Celtic water cult. An examination of what is known about the Celtic belief system and cult practice, on the basis of Graeco-Roman and Celtic literary sources as well as from archaeology, is fundamental to our consideration of the amphitheater as an integral functional part of the Celtic sanctuary complex. The rural amphitheaters in Gaul can be seen as a monumental crossroads of the Celtic and Roman civilizations; in them, the cultic motifs of water and combat represent, metaphorically, the interaction between the Celts and the Mediterranean world. Both issues bear directly on our understanding of the rural amphitheaters in Gaul.[69]

Graeco-Roman sources can be divided into two schools of thought in terms of attitude toward the Celts, dread marauders from the North. One group staunchly disapproves, painting the Celts along the lines of howling, lime-bleached barbarians with fingers smeared with red by the blood of human sacrificial victims.[70] The other school of thought, the "Alexandrian" group, acknowledges the Celts as merely different rather than as fiends from beyond civilization's pale, even lending them something of a "noble savage" stature.[71] The slant of the sources, as well as questions about their accessibility to information about contemporary Celtic society, makes them somewhat problematic.[72]

A further problem lies in the general purpose for which the Graeco-Roman writers conceived their work. They were not interested in producing a comprehensive ethnography of the Celts but rather drew thumbnail sketches of the folk, concentrating specifically on aspects of their lifestyle that provided a sharp contrast to Mediterranean ways.[73] The Celts were "the Other," their customs only interesting insofar as they were quaint and/or disgusting. Because of the sharply drawn distinction prevalent in the ancient sources, we may be wholly unaware of large slices of Celtic culture that were *not* dramatically different from the Graeco-Roman culture and thus not worth mentioning. We, too, know the Celts largely as "the Other."[74]

The Celtic vernacular tradition may offer one way to compensate for the skewed perspective of the Mediterranean literature. The Celtic sources consist of two basic groups, as defined by geographical origin; using the testimony from either group as evidence has drawbacks. The literature of these two groups, the Irish and the Welsh, postdate the Roman period by centuries, but they are generally acknowledged to be codified versions of myths and legends transmitted orally for some time, with the originals dating as early as the second century B.C.[75]

The Irish tales from the Ulster cycle form the older group, and they were first written down in the early eighth century.[76] One of the problems with this group can also be seen as an advantage, that being its very Irishness. Ireland was not conquered by Rome. The Irish tradition may thus represent a more purely Celtic society, untainted by Roman civilization.[77] The society depicted in the tales is polytheistic, with some parallels to the Iron Age Britain and Gaul described by Caesar.[78] Christianity, when it does appear, seems a superficial imposition and does not mesh with the mythic action.[79]

The Welsh group of tales, known collectively as the *Mabinogion*, was set down in written form between the eleventh and thirteenth centuries, allowing for at least three additional centuries of accumulated late clutter to obscure the Celtic kernel.[80] Christianity has more thoroughly infiltrated the Welsh texts, with priests replacing Druids entirely and the Celtic deities almost completely made mortal by a process of euhemerism.

What then can we learn of Celtic religion from the ancient texts of both the Graeco-Roman and Celtic vernacular?[81] There are only a few passages in the Graeco-Roman sources that discuss the Celtic gods in specific terms. Caesar is typical in taking a syncretist approach, identifying the divinities by their Roman analogs, as he perceived them.[82] Mercury, in his role as road guide, merchant extraordinaire, and the inventor of all arts, is hailed as the recipient of the widest cult among the Celts. Next in priority comes a healing divinity (whom Caesar identifies as Apollo), followed by a war god (Mars), a sky god (Jupiter), and a patroness of arts and crafts (Minerva). Further, Gauls claimed descent from *Dis pater*, who, in his association with night and death, in this context may be some sort of chthonic patriarch.[83]

Few descriptions of Celtic religious sanctuaries appear in the Graeco-Roman sources, and these passages are rather vague and ambiguous. Generally, however, the sites can be classified as either formal, urban sanctuaries or simple, rural sacred areas. This perceived distinction has been linked to an alleged historical deterioration in the prestige of specifically Celtic religious sites.[84] The earlier sources describe sanctuaries organized along familiar Mediterranean lines, with defined limits and structures, like those on islands described by Strabo as holy to Dionysus, Demeter, and Kore. The post-conquest writers, such as Tacitus, Pliny, Pomponius Mela, and Lucan, emphasize groves and forests as sacred areas of the Celts, which may suggest that Roman discouragement of native worship forced it into the remote, nonarchitectural rusticity of the woods. One should not, however, make too much of this supposed decline, given the acknowledged rural locations of sanctuaries in the preconquest sources, the lack of detail in the sources overall, and the continuity in cult evident in the archaeological record.

The vernacular sources, being retellings of myth as distinct from the expository Graeco-Roman literature, do not lend themselves easily to definition of divinity and cult practice. Different groups of gods can be discerned, none mutually or temporally exclusive. The closest parallel to the Olympian pantheon is the Irish Tuatha dé Danaan, the people of the goddess Danu, a divine society that ruled prior to the coming of mortal men. Some gods are distinguished by function, such as Dían Cecht, the divine healer, and Gobniu, the smith, but the more powerful of the Tuatha are multipurpose gods, such as Echu Ollathair, also known as the Dagda, who is the father of all and the king of the Tuatha, and Lug Samildánach, the divine expert in all kinds of warfare, all kinds of crafts. The largest group of Irish divinities, however, is that of the tutelary goddesses, who are expressly tied to the land, which they protect, administrate, and make fertile.[85]

Heroes are prominent in the vernacular, beings who straddle the line dividing mortal and immortal. Foremost among them is the Hound of Culann, Cú Chulainn, son of the Irish god, Lug. Heroes were gifted with superhuman powers, especially in terms of martial achievement, and seem to act as agents or instruments of patron deities.[86]

Religious sites, ambiguously defined in the Graeco-Roman sources, are even less noticeable in the vernacular tradition. The Celtic sources seem to revere the liminal, to hold sacred the boundaries between tribal territories, between one type of landscape and another, between the water and the land, between the world and the underworld, and between the natural realm and the supernatural.[87] Boundaries were the meeting places of divinities as well as of their mortal followers, and significant mythic events took place at these borders, reestablishing the distinction proper and necessary to the natural order. For our purposes, the most significant liminal events are those requiring some sort of combat; many such battles are fought at the thresholds between water and dry land. Pwyll, for example, gains mastery over the Otherworld of Annwvyn by defeating Havgan at a riverford.[88] Cú Chulainn, at the age of seven, begins his heroic career at a river, where he challenges the sons of Nechta Scéne. One of them, Fannall, who can tread on water as lightly as a swan or swallow, meets him at the ford. Cú Chulainn defeats him, taking his head and his weapons.[89]

Cú Chulainn becomes something of a specialist in fighting within streams: indeed, one of Cú Chulainn's most feared weapons is the *gáe bolga*, which seems to have been designed for use in a running stream.[90] He uses this skill in combat against his foster brother, Fer Diad mac Damáin. The two engage in elaborate reviling before their epic battle. Fer Diad taunts Cú Chulainn at length, referring to the public, spectacular nature of the combat: "I have come . . . before warriors, before troops, before hundreds, to thrust you beneath the waters of the pool."[91]

Water and combat appear repeatedly in the tale of *Bricriu's Feast*, which centers on the contest between three heroic figures for the champion's portion, the *curadmír*, from Conchubur mac Nessa, the king of Ulster.[92] One episode involves a mysterious figure named Úath, and another involves a lake monster. Úath is called a shape-changer, a Druid, and a specter. The three contestants go to Úath's lake to appeal to him as an authority figure and judge. Úath sets the competition as a mutual beheading, offering to be decapitated that day and to act as headsman the following day. Conall Cernach and Lóegure Búadach refuse the challenge, but Cú Chulainn snatches up a sword and promptly removes Úath's head. Úath takes his head back to his lake, returning the next day to complete the contest. Úath's sword, however, three times rebounds from Cú Chulainn's neck. Cú Chulainn thus proves that a true hero always keeps his head under pressure. The final competition, where Cú Chulainn becomes not only victor but even the savior of his rivals, involves a lake monster, where the lake itself at times seems to be incarnate as the monster.[93] Cú Chulainn tears out its heart, chops it up into tiny bits, and puts its head in his collection.

Where did these divinities make contact with the world of men? One scholar has estimated that there is evidence for at least 760 cult places where the religion of the indigenous people was being practiced in the Romano-Celtic period.[94] Many were small shrines or altars, incorporated into the urban or rural landscape with little fuss. Others were more monumental, taking advantage of Roman technical expertise in masonry to formalize ancient and syncretized sacred space with the architectural innovations brought in by the conquerers. The sacredness and inviolability of boundaries in the Celtic vernacular were now reinforced in the real world by the erection of cult centers that made use of Roman concepts of construction, design, and symmetry, the stone architecture of the Roman period leaving a more lasting impression in the archaeological record. However simple or monumental, the most frequent focus of the Celtic sanctuary was the sacred boundary represented by bodies of water or springs. It is at these very locations that the Celtic type of amphitheater, the mixed edifice, appeared in the Roman period. The rural amphitheater is concentrated particularly in the Loire valley of east-central France.[95] The presence of mixed edifices has frequently obscured the properly cultic ambience of these complexes, as the excavators, excited and distracted by the appearance of genuine amphitheaters, have largely ignored the cult buildings proper. Still, the scatter of these complexes seems fairly dense, even today, separated from each other sometimes by only a few kilometers.

A typical rural sanctuary includes a mixed edifice, a bath complex, and a Romano-Celtic type temple or *fanum*, which consists of a central *cella*, surrounded by an enclosed gallery. Although these structures are usually quadrangular, at times they assume a multifaceted shape in plan, which may be reminiscent of round wooden structures used in the pre-Roman period.[96] The gallery is believed to have a cultic function, providing both a distinct delimitation of the sacred space and a specific area for ritual circumambulation. The provision of public baths may relate to the cult of sacred waters frequently evidenced at these centers. The amphitheaters may also have served to mark the ritually liminal waters, given the connection made in Celtic myth between combat and sacred springs, rivers and lakes. The following examples of rural sanctuaries are generally typical of this under-studied phenomenon.

The sanctuary at Sanxay, located some thirty kilometers from Poitiers, occupied an area of about sixteen hectares in its heyday (see Figs. 22 and 23). The mixed edifice was located in a forest clearing on one side of the

Vonne river. Across the river were the baths, on the far side of a court-
yard from the temple, which was on a large rectangular terrace surrounded by a portico. The plan of the temple can be described as octagonal, in which four sides of the octagon have been pushed outward to give
the building an ornate cruciform appearance in plan.[97]

The complex at Chassenon, located on the Peutinger Table as a stop
on the road from Saintes to Limoges, has similarities to that at Sanxay,
particularly in the shape of the temple. The temple, in addition, has pits
or shafts inside, cutting into the bedrock below. One shaft has the remains of animal sacrifice; the function for the other shafts is not so clear.
It is possible that they had something to do with the water cult at Chassenon and were used ritually in conjunction with the basins inside the
temple, also cut into the rock.[98] It should be noted, however, that pits and
shafts played a part in Celtic chthonic practice, functioning continuously
from the pre-Roman period to foster fertility. Of course, in Celtic religious belief, water and chthonic deities were not necessarily distinct from
each other, healing and fecundity both being aspects of the earthy well-
being offered by the gods. Other water monuments at Chassenon included
baths and cisterns. The ruins of the mixed edifice were located some hundred meters north of the temple and may date to the Hadrianic period.

Included as part of the Gallo-Roman sanctuary to Gisacus, the local
god, is a theater-amphitheater at Tintignac. Tintignac's mixed edifice is

FIGURE 22. Aerial photo-
graph of the Romano-Celtic
rural water sanctuary at
Sanxay. Copyright © Paul
MacKendrick 1972. From:
Roman France. By: Paul
MacKendrick. Reprinted
with permission of St. Martin's Press, Incorporated.

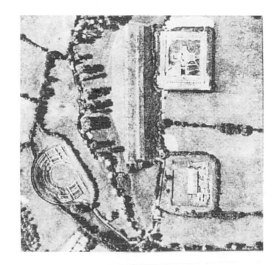

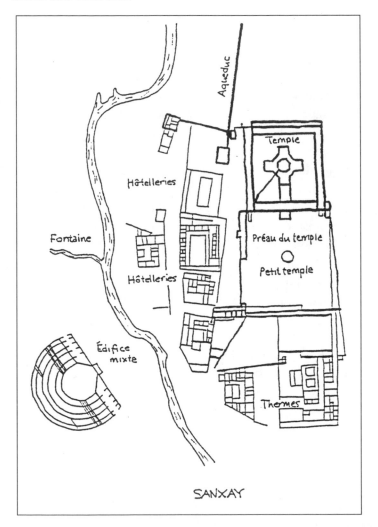

FIGURE 23. Plan of sanctuary at Sanxay, from G. Coulon, *Les Gallo-Romains: Au carrefour de deux civilisations* (Paris: Armand Colin, 1985), pp. 67–68.

unconventional, even for such a nontraditional building type. The back wall of the *cavea* has been modified drastically to allow for the attachment of another semicircular construction, paralleling the curvature of the *cavea*, with curved niches flanking squared ones articulating the rear wall of this additional unit.[99] It appears that Gisacus was revered at Vieil-Evreux as well, the site known as Gisacum in antiquity.[100] At Vieil-Evreux,

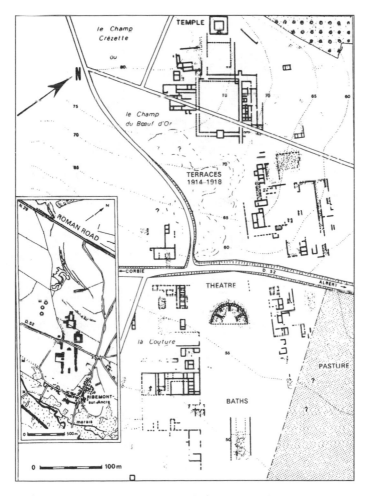

FIGURE 24. Plan of sanctuary at Ribemont-sur-Ancre, from J.-L. Brunaux, *The Celtic Gauls: Gods, Rites and Sanctuaries* (London: Seaby, 1988), p. 18.

the pre-Roman population was moved some seven kilometers to a new capital at Mediolanum Aulercorum, the old habitation site surviving as a sanctuary.[101]

Chennevières' sanctuary was located near a spring, captured and monumentalized in a series of basins. The temple building, like those at Sanxay and Chassenon, is octagonal in plan, with a large basin or pool in the center. A spring rises in the center of the pool, and steps around the edge of the pool allow access to the water. Other pools, seemingly cold

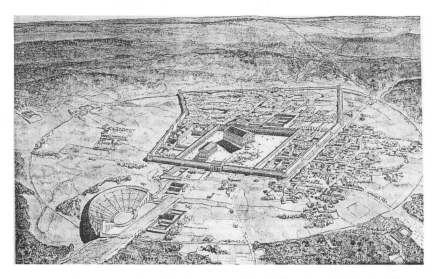

FIGURE 25. Reconstruction of Roman Aquae Granni (Grand), with mixed edifice in foreground, Romano-Celtic sanctuary at center, from J.-Cl. Golvin, "A propos de la visualisation des édifices de spectacle dans leur contexte urbain (en Gaule)," in *La ciutat en el món romà*, vol. 2 (Tarragona: Institut d'Estudis Catalans, 1994), pp. 174–175.

plunge baths, can also be found in the sanctuary. The arena is located at the base of a small nearby hill, upon which it relies for the support of the seating area.[102]

Triguières' sanctuary is located a scant fifteen kilometers northeast of Chennevières, near the confluence of the Dardenne and the Ouanne and near the Fontaine Sainte-Alpais spring, surely a location abounding in healing waters and liminality. The temple, slightly south of the mixed edifice, is built hypaethrally around a menhir, suggesting continuity with pre-Roman cult practices. Another small temple, which, as the ex-votos suggest, was dedicated to a female divinity, shares the sanctity of the locale.[103]

Ribemont-sur-Ancre showed some Roman concern for symmetry in the design of the complex, with monuments arranged along an axis defined by the temple located on a rise at one end (see Fig. 24). The heart of the site, however, is the mixed edifice several hundred meters east of the temple, mistakenly identified as a simple theater in most plans of Ribemont. Especially intriguing is the presence of a pre-Roman ossuary located in the temple's vicinity, where human bones offer evidence for cult practice at the original *fanum*.[104]

Unlike the others, Aquae Granni (modern Grand) was a habitation center of some note (see Fig. 25).[105] Indeed, Aquae Granni was a famed sanctuary and place of pilgrimage in the Roman period; it was here in A.D. 309 that Constantine had his first (and perhaps only) vision.[106] The local deity was named Grannus and was syncretized with Apollo in his healing and oracular aspects. Located originally on the boundary of two cantons, near the source of the Ornain, the city grew up around the sanctuary. Aquae Granni's mixed edifice was fairly large, measuring 133 meters across at its greatest expanse. Its relative lavishness was due, no doubt, to the fame of the sanctuary and the material advantages derived from the pilgrim trade.

As suggested above, the mixed edifices seem to have had a significance and purpose peculiar to the Romano-Celtic experience. The function of these structures, like the form of the structures, may have involved a combination of Roman and Celtic customs. The Celtic community was predisposed toward the arena; the performance of ritualized combat played an important role in Celtic religious practice and constituted a "tournament of value" in the Celtic social economy, even prior to the coming of the Romans. Into this environment Rome introduced the amphitheater, an institution charged with meaning in Roman politics and cult but also an institution readily susceptible to a Celtic interpretation of authority and the sacred. The Celtic rural amphitheaters could thus serve as a venue for the symbolic reconstitution of the status quo on the mortal and the cosmic level, a syncretization of Celtic and Roman symbolic systems.[107]

Grenier took a step in this direction by suggesting that the Celtic arena housed the reenactment of myth, basing his assertion on the depictions of Hercules on a pair of Graufesenque vases dating to the first century after Christ (see Fig. 26).[108] The hero is represented fighting against the Erymanthian Boar, the Nemean Lion, and the Hydra of Lerna, but these are not the standard images of Hercules familiar from Graeco-Roman sculpture and painting. Nor does the hero use the accepted weaponry from myth but rather the arms of a *bestiarius*. The unusual weaponry and tableaux of the hero indicate that the model for the vases is not an artistic one but rather an amphitheatrical one. The vases depict scenic reenactments of the Labors of Hercules, combining dramatic mythological narrative with depictions of combat performance in the mixed edifices of Celtic architecture.[109]

FIGURE 26. Herculean amphitheatrical feats depicted on fragments from two Graufe-senque vases, fragment 1 (above) from vase in Demaison collection, fragment 2 from vase in Hermet collection. Drawings by J. Evrard in F. Hermet, *La Graufesenque* (Paris: E. Leroux, 1934), pls. 109.1 and 109.2.

Celtic significance, however, is our primary consideration here. Combats performed in the mixed edifices may actually have been reenactments of battles in Celtic myth or syncretized Romano-Celtic legends. Some legends lend themselves to this sort of performance more than others, such as the story of the battle for the hand of Creiddylad, the daughter of Lludd Silver Hand.[110] To keep the peace, Arthur ordained that her suitors, Gwyn, son of Nudd, and Gwythyr, son of Greidyawl, should fight each other every year on the first of May, until Doomsday. Thus one mythic battle, at least, was reenacted each year on the date of Beltane, one of the major festivals in the Celtic religious calendar.[111]

Further evidence of such practice can be extracted from Irish historical ethnography, in conjunction with festivals celebrated in honor of Lug, more or less depaganized over the centuries but still, theoretically, retaining vestiges of ancient Celtic ritual.[112] First, there is the frequent association between lakes, rivers, and wells with locations sacred to the festival of Lughnasa, or Lammas-tide. Here horses and cattle were led through the water, to bless and purify them for another year. Here, too, was the ceremonial gleaning of "first fruits," commemorated by reaping some wheat or digging a potato, which was then either ritually eaten or offered to the "fairies," surely to be identified as remnants of pre-Christian deities. Garlands of flowers decorated the vicinity and the people, there was dancing, and there are vestiges of the previous sacrifice of a sacred bull or a sacred youth at Lammas-tide. These festivals are often connected in legend with a struggle between heroes, or heroized divinities, in which Lug achieves superiority.

More germane to our purposes, however, is the practice of faction fighting, or party fighting, recorded at several Lughnasa sites.[113] In this custom, groups of men from "opposing" towns armed themselves with shillelaghs and tried to beat the other group to some sort of conclusion. One eyewitness account says that the fight lasted some ten minutes, that some five or six people were injured (although not seriously), and that this rivalry did not extend beyond the festival, nor, indeed, beyond the fighting ground itself.[114] A folksong collected from Mám Éan in the early nineteenth century refers to this tradition as possessing some antiquity.

> For I was not a man to put myself forward
> Although I had done nothing to bring me shame
> Beyond striking a blow with a stick on Donach a'Mhama
> For that was ever the custom of the country,
> And with no thought of it on the morrow
> But to have a return bout that day next year.[115]

This faction fighting was often connected with a mythic origin, which varied by location. At Caher Roe's Den and at Arderin, ritualized dancing led to the fight, while elsewhere the fighting seems to be connected to legends about battles waged by the fairies in the Otherworld. This may be a reflection of the original mythic tale of Lug, in which the god is the key to the victory of the Tuatha dé Danaan pantheon over the Fir Bolg and the Fomoiri, the previous generation of divine monsters. If the faction fighting at Lammas-tide is recognized as the reenactment of mythic combat, the seeming lack of interest in actual victory would be explained. It was the observance of custom that was important, not whether one side was soundly defeated. The theme of struggle, which keeps reappearing in the rituals surviving for Lammas-tide, may reflect a cosmos perceived as a balance between dual forces. The periodic mimetic performance of mythic struggle reestablishes the balance and results in an active release of the power of divinity: at Lammas-tide Lug forces his divine opponent to give up his "treasure" of prosperity, fertility, and health.[116]

An interpretation of performative combat as reenactment of myth does not, however, tell the whole story. To understand the role played by the amphitheater in Celtic cult, we must draw together different aspects of Celtic society, the religious and the more secular. Combat was central to Celtic group identity, as a means of negotiating power relationships within the community and as a regular alternative to peaceful intertribal exchange and between Celts and Mediterranean outsiders.

As we have seen, the Celtic peoples of Europe were regularly "Otherized" in the Graeco-Roman ethnographic tradition, which saw the Celts as notable especially for their warlike and aggressive nature. Even the earliest sources offer this portrayal, with Polybius claiming that the only Celtic pursuits were war and agriculture, especially war, as the Celtic habit of mass migration would sharply limit their agrarian role.[117] Fortune, said Polybius, had afflicted the whole race with the epidemic of aggression.[118] Strabo echoes this view, characterizing the entire nation as war-mad, quick for battle.[119] But so are all barbarians, he claims. All are likewise passionate, disinclined toward self-control and the rules of "civilized" behavior espoused by the Greeks and Romans. Strabo, especially, emphasizes the Celtic inclusion in the barbaric normative, repeatedly referring to them as such.[120]

Alongside this alienating ethnographic tendency, however, is a strain of admiration for the Celts, whose fearlessness and contempt for death was reminiscent of the heroes of Greek and Roman legend.[121] Polybius admits the real threat to Roman interests that came from Celtic audacity and courage, a threat still present in the time of Caesar, who was impressed by Celtic persistence in warfare.[122] This aspect combined with stubborn tenacity in matters of honor on the battlefield; because defeat was so distasteful to Celts, they would prefer death to capture.[123]

This Celtic characterization was captured in the Hellenistic statuary groups of Gallic figures.[124] These representations portray Mediterranean expectations of "typical" Celts, with the hairstyle and personal effects described by the classical writers. They suggest the Celtic spirit as well, with its passion and fierce determination to fight to the death against dishonor (see Fig. 27). The baroque style of the High Hellenistic is particularly suited to the depiction of the stereotypical Gaul, with its penchant for physical and emotional extremes. Indeed, during this time the Gaul joined the Amazon and the Giant as a fixture in the iconographical repertoire of barbarism.[125]

Thus conduct in warfare was basic to the external identification of the Celtic nation. Militarism was, however, also a vital part of internal Celtic perceptions. The vernacular tales seem to view warfare as a normal state of affairs, even a desirable one.[126] Archaeologically, martial elements dominate the material culture of Iron Age Europe. The defensible settlements and the weaponry found as grave goods in prestigious burials both point to a connection between sociopolitical authority and military might. The way of the warrior provided a mechanism for the stratification of society.[127]

The reconstruction of Celtic social organization is a tricky matter, as was the case with Celtic religion. Little information is available from the primary texts, and extrapolation of societal specifics from material remains is likewise difficult. The Graeco-Roman sources describe Celtic society as a warrior aristocracy, with the king preeminent and noblemen, warriors, and priest-scholars making up the elite.[128] Networks of social obligation spread vertically through the Celtic tribes in a clientage system not unlike that found in Rome.[129] This hierarchy bears a resemblance to the society reflected in the Irish vernacular and in archaic Irish legal tracts, in which the mutual responsibilities of patron and client are spelled out.[130] The leaders of Celtic society initiated the distribution of status markers through social exchange, reifying the stratification through public activities.

Regulated feasting occasions served a "potlatch" function among the Celts, an occasion for community participation in the distribution of status and of food.[131] Held at times of religious significance, these feasts represented an opportunity to verify the current hierarchy or to inaugurate new leaders.[132] The feast was thus an articulation and performance of one's place in the Celtic world and cosmos; it also was a dynamic venue for the resolution of tensions within the group, not only through

FIGURE 27. Ludovisi or Suicidal Gaul, original dating to late third century B.C., at Museo Nazionale Romano delle Terme, Rome, courtesy Alinari/Art Resource, NY.

differential access to food items but also through spatial relations. Each rank was accorded its appropriate meat: the king was given a leg of pork, the haunch went to the queen, the charioteer got a boar's head, and so forth.[133] Athenaeus describes the stratified seating arrangements at Celtic feasts, as they sat grouped "in a circle, with the most powerful in the middle, the one who is the foremost leader of the land, outshining the others whether in martial skill, in lineage, or in wealth . . . [the others] successively on either side, according to the level of excellence."[134]

It was at these feasts that single combats would break out among the warriors, as these junior elites competed for the choice cut of meat.[135] The Graeco-Roman authors generally present the Celtic habit of fighting at feasts as demonstrative of their high-strung, uncivilized temperament, a habit that could prove detrimental to their long-term success in the battlefield.[136] A close reading of the texts, however, supports an interpretation of this sort of duel as a much more ordered event. The single combat can be seen as a public demonstration of strength, not only the power of brute force, but the standing of the participant within the warrior elite.[137] It was a public performance governed by strict rules, some of which survive in the Irish legal tracts, such as the concept of *fír fer* or "fair play"; this mandated that these combats be one-on-one, not, for example, five-on-one.[138] Athenaeus' description of the single combat hints at such rules as well, informing us that this custom evolved from the archaic battle to the death over the "hero's portion" to the current practice, in which the spectators ensure that no one is killed.[139] Diodorus implies a strict ordering of levels of competition, in which violation of personal space leads to verbal haranguing, then, finally, to the use of weapons.[140] Athenaeus also specifically links the custom of single combat to the distribution of status markers of other sorts, including silver, gold, and jars of wine, the material symbols of the social pledges exchanged.[141] Thus the communal feasts were the occasion and backdrop for the display of social dominance, a display inherently linked to combative prowess but driven toward the ultimate goal of order, harmony, and balance.[142]

The struggle to achieve balance takes shape in Celtic society at many levels: in myth, personified supernatural forces do battle and thereby make possible the continuity of the established order of things and of life itself in this world. Life among the Celts was also filled with conflict and decisive, even violent action. This too, however, was directed towards a clear goal, that being the establishment of right order through a keen awareness of the "fitness of things," the balance to be achieved in the human realm.[143] In the Celtic worldview, everything finds support and sustenance in the active achievement of a balance between struggling forces. The amphitheater, as a building type, is itself redolent of human conflict, the universal struggle being played out on a human scale. The Romano-Celtic amphitheatrical games were therefore not merely entertaining: they were representative of the essence of human existence as understood in Celtic society. Thus Celtic group identity was incorporated into Romanized forms. There was continuity despite the political transformation.

NEMESIS

The amphitheater, as a major political tool for Roman control and as one of the most imposing architectural frameworks of the ancient world, would be expected to attract a variety of cult expressions, which would incorporate the traditional divinities of the Mediterranean. Vitruvius recognizes the amphitheater as the appropriate location for shrines of Hercules, but significant evidence for this connection has not been forthcoming from the material remains.[144] Mars, god of war, is linked in literature to combat in the arena, but again there is little material support for cult practice in the West to give substance to the poetic affiliation.[145] It is Nemesis, of all the Graeco-Roman pantheon, who appears most often in the amphitheatrical context.

The dominance of Nemesis over the arena is unexpected; our puzzlement over the Nemesis connection is not lessened by the relative silence of the literature toward Nemesis. The traditional explanation of Roman Nemesis describes hers as a cult of desperate men, of shady characters of low repute, such as gladiators, men whose only hope for retribution lay with Nemesis, a more or less abstract personification of "vengeance," to be marshaled against competitors in the arena. More judicious analysis has broadened our perspective somewhat, pointing to Nemesis' close association with the traditional agents of Roman control, with the bureaucracy and the military.[146] Nemesis should be understood as an Imperial Fortuna, whose worship was bound to the network of obligations that linked the individual to the mechanism of the Roman Empire. Nemesis was responsible for the distribution not only of punishment but also of

benefactions; in this, she was not unlike the Roman power structure itself, which demanded taxes and exacted penalties for noncompliance but
also provided access to the benefits of Mediterranean civilization. To understand how Nemesis became the quintessential goddess of the amphitheater, we must examine her origins and her function and meaning
in myth and cult and then turn to the worship of Nemesis as the cult of
the arena.

Nemesis' earliest appearances in literature vary. At times she is a personification of a natural force, a powerful abstraction rather than an individual, personalized goddess.[147] The tales of the epic cycle depict a deity
quite different from this shadowy entity in Homer and Hesiod. Nemesis
of the *Cypria* is a strong personality in her own right, the object of Zeus'
passion and a powerful shape-changer.[148] The existence of an archaic,
deep-seated cult at Rhamnous, in addition to the extensive myth, argues
against Nemesis' original identity as "merely" a personified moral abstraction but rather as a fully individualized chthonic deity.[149]

Nemesis' chthonic quality, in the role she plays at birth and death as
major events in the human lifespan, and her preference for sexual chastity,
implied by her determined avoidance of Zeus' lustful inclinations, are
qualities the goddess shares with Artemis. The sources give evidence for
further identification with Artemis, specifying that Artemis Oupis was
worshipped at Rhamnous, where there was a statue of Artemis sculpted by
Pheidias.[150] Artemidorus even conflates the two into "Nemesis Artemis."
These links with Artemis, like the relative deficiency in personal mythology, have been used to bolster the cultic devaluation of Nemesis and to
deny her identity as a "real" deity.[151]

Part of the scholarly hesitation to credit Nemesis with full-fledged divine status, as opposed to her identity as some sort of upstart personification, seems to stem from the name "Nemesis" and its strong ethical resonance in Greek thought. The concept of nemesis was the expression of
the major form of interaction between gods and men; humans who
strayed from the norm were liable to punishment motivated by some sort
of divine indignation. How are we to reconcile the abstract concept of
nemesis with the divinity bearing that name, who seems to have been a
recipient of cult in her own right from very early times? Some attempts
have been made to resolve this by suggesting that "nemesis" was originally only the epithet of an Artemis-like chthonic goddess at Rhamnous,

whose personal name somehow dropped out of common usage. The epithet was of greater concern to that goddess' worshippers, since, more than simply expressing the goddess' aspect in the local cult, the title implied a real, personal relationship between the deity and her cultists. This high moral tone for what seems to have been in origin a vegetative chthonic entity may be somewhat unwarranted. The ethical resonance attributed to Nemesis may be more literary than cultic; "nemesis" as an object of cult may represent rather the general uncertainty of individual fate, and therefore the epithet should be interpreted as relating to "distribution," not "retribution."

Nemesis, as one of the chthonic deities of fate, has some similarity to the Erinyes, or Furies, who, like Nemesis, seem to have lacked their dreadful associations at first, being understood instead as morally ambivalent agents of fortune. Like Nemesis, they simply dispensed death, swooping down suddenly from above, wings unfurled. Of great interest for the understanding of Nemesis in the Roman period is the character of the Etruscan Erinyes, particularly Vanth. Vanth is represented as a beautiful winged woman, who is present at the death of the individual, ready to conduct his soul to the underworld. Like Nemesis, the snake is her companion. Like Artemis, she wears hunting boots and apparel.[152] Like Nemesis, she is the agent of death.

To extend the search for Nemesis to Etruria is to cross cultural barriers, and indeed, her cult was eventually dispersed throughout the Mediterranean world. The traditional reconstruction suggests that the major diffusion of the Nemesis cult took place in the pre-Hellenistic time, with her temples at Rhamnous and Smyrna providing the prime impetus for spreading into the Aegean and Asia Minor.[153] From Smyrna Nemesis was supposedly taken to Thrace and Macedonia and from there to Rome's *limes* frontier. This reconstruction, although it acknowledges the importance of soldiers and slaves in the spread of the cult, claims that evidence is lacking for Nemesis in Italy and the western provinces. By this account, Nemesis is an unimportant phenomenon in the Roman world, an obsolescent vestige of classical Greek religious practice. A closer examination of the material evidence used to support this assertion suggests a different story.[154]

The preponderance of evidence for the cult of Nemesis comes from the Roman period, more specifically, from the western empire, and must be post-Hellenistic. The inscriptions are the most important category of evidence used to prove the strength of Nemesis in the Classical Greek period. In fact, these inscriptions point to a knowledge of Nemesis as a deity of some power more than they indicate active cult practice, with concomitant sanctuary, priesthood, and sacrifice.[155] The suggestion that the Nemesis cult spread from Smyrna to Macedonia and thence to the *limes* seems unlikely, given the scantiness of pre-Roman evidence in Macedonia. The role played by soldiers and slaves was a real factor in the transmission of the Nemesis cult but dims in significance next to the association between Nemesis and the amphitheater, which was the single most important factor in the spread of the cult in the Graeco-Roman world. The amphitheater "made" Nemesis, and her link with the arena was the true cause of her rise from relative obscurity to a powerful member of the Mediterranean pantheon.

A simplistic explanation for Nemesis' importance at the amphitheaters stems from her relationship with Artemis, identified as Diana in the Roman period.[156] Diana was the goddess of the hunt, an activity transformed into spectacle as the *venatio*. Indeed, the *venatores'* guild in Philippi set up reliefs to her, honoring her as both huntress and mistress of animals, like Artemis. The Diana connection may be important for the *venationes* but does little to explain why gladiators, disassociated completely from such hunting reenactments, should be inclined to deal with Nemesis to ensure their own success.[157] Why was Nemesis linked with the *munera*?

In some sense, Nemesis came to be seen as a goddess of athletic competition. The reasoning behind this is somewhat questionable, but the usual argument claims that Nemesis was first appealed to as judge at her own games in Rhamnous and Smyrna, then, as her reputation as the goddess who balanced and punished spread in the Greek world, so did her importance at competitions of athletes and such, since success in this sphere ultimately depended on the whims of fortune.[158] After all, no victory was ever a sure thing, as games could be lost in the final moments, and over-exuberant victors invited the punishment of jealous divinities. The extension was made from athletic competitions to competitions and performances in general, and the Lady of the *agonia* in the Hellenistic period eventually became the patroness of the amphitheater.[159] The main drawback to this traditional interpretation has to do with its emphasis on

Nemesis as sinister punisher of foolish humans, an aspect of Nemesis that has more to do with literature and philosophy than with actual cult and which is based to a large extent on evidence from a Greek context.

We have seen, however, that Nemesis of the Games and amphitheaters is a creature of the Roman Empire. As such, she should be seen not as a vindictive judge and jury but as the power of changing fortune, *Nemesis id est vis quaedam Fortunae*.[160] The wheel and tiller are shown with Nemesis at Aquileia and Carnuntum, attributes usually associated with Tyche or Fortuna. Inscriptions acknowledge some sort of identity as well, addressing themselves to "the goddess Nemesis or Fortuna," *Deae Nemesi sive Fortunae*.[161] We should, then, understand our Nemesis as a Tyche/Fortuna analog, whose worship achieved some popularity during Tyche's heyday in the Hellenistic period but who really came into her own under the Roman Empire. Nemesis, as a Fortuna-like distributor of good and bad, is relevant to the basic concept of the *munera* as "*munus*," the obligatory distribution for the benefit of the deceased and the living.[162]

A broader definition of Nemesis may explain her significance to a larger segment of the population.[163] Nemesis has often been regarded as a cult of the poor, limited largely to slaves and freedmen whose livelihood depended on the arena. There is some truth in this, as gladiators and *venatores* are often found on Nemesis votive inscriptions, but this cannot be the whole picture.[164] Far more worshippers of Nemesis came from the Roman structure of control, from the army and the administration.[165] Nemesis cultists from Italica, for the most part, possess the *tria nomina*, the three names that were the mark of a free man. One even identifies himself as *sacerdos* of the colony; more than merely free, this was a gentleman of influence and prestige, a muckamuck, in fact. Similarly, an inscription from Corduba states that it was dedicated to Nemesis *ex acto flamonio*, at the behest of the official state priest. It may be that other Nemesis dedicators were local magistrates, which may hint at their particular relationship with the goddess. One of the primary duties of the annual magistrate was the presentation of games, which could be rather costly and could, in fact, bring a magistrate to the brink of fiscal disaster. Nemesis, as a Fortuna analog, would watch over those who assume such a financial risk. A dozen inscriptions, originally located in the arena of Italica's amphitheater, have, interestingly, depictions of feet on them, which

may be a reference to starting one's magistracy on the right foot by trust-
ing to Nemesis for the protection of one's fortune, both literal and figu-
rative, throughout the year of office.[166]

The epithets given Nemesis point to her wide importance in the Roman world. In Latin, *Augusta* is by far the most frequent, followed by *Ultrix*, *Regina*, and then *Sancta*; all others trail far behind.[167] The frequency
of Augusta is suggestive; not only do Dike and Tyche share this epithet
but the word is associated most frequently with people and events of political importance to Imperial Rome. The connection between Augusta
and Nemesis has been explained as indicative of the universality of
Nemesis' moral resonance, but I am more inclined to see political overtones, as Nemesis appears periodically on Roman coinage as part of the
Imperial program of propaganda using material culture.[168]

The first series for which we have extensive documentation was minted
under Claudius (see Fig. 28). Nemesis, as usual, is depicted with wings.
She advances towards the right, pointing a caduceus at a snake on the
ground before her. The legend reads *Paci Augustae*, which has been explained as indicating that Victory imbued with the spirit of righteous fear
has brought lasting peace to the Roman Empire. Supposedly, the audience would be reassured that Claudius would not abuse his triumph, not
with Nemesis keeping a close watch.[169] This interpretation is not entirely
persuasive. We know that Nemesis and Fortuna were somewhat syncretized in the Roman sphere; might not the important role played by
Chance in Claudius' ascendance be the key to Nemesis' appearance on his
coinage? In this reading, Claudius' rule, although owing much to Nemesis in the circumstances of its establishment, is nevertheless legitimized

FIGURE 28. Claudian aureus with Nemesis
reverse, winged, brandishing the caduceus at a
snake, legend commemorating "August Peace,"
dated A.D. 50–51, minted at Rome, by courtesy
of the Trustees of the British Museum.

and divinely blessed by the august peace achieved through victory. The coincidence of Claudius' birth and opportune location is thus transformed into destiny, validated by the choice of Nemesis. Claudius was, of course, born at Lugdunum, where later an amphitheater would rise in commemoration of his family's political agenda, with Nemesis celebrated in the arena's chapels.

Vespasian revived the Claudian type of Nemesis, with the legend likewise referring to Pax, which has been interpreted as appropriate to the vigorous Flavian settlement in Gaul, inciting a righteous fear of the goddess of retribution in the aftermath of Flavian victory. I would, however, construe the symbolism of the issue along the lines suggested for the Claudian Nemesis coinage, with Nemesis representing the unexpected changes of fortune as integral to the divine plan. As with Claudius, Vespasian's Pax Augusta refers to the peace of the gods, the *pax deorum*, as well as peace at home and abroad, *pax domi forisque*.[170] The association between Pax and Nemesis certainly emphasizes Nemesis' role in the Roman cult as the distributor of positive fortune, not merely as the agent of divine indignation.

Chapels that have been identified as *nemesea* appear in various locations in amphitheaters.[171] Most often such shrines are found at one end of the ellipse's shorter axis, with access both to the arena itself and to the presidential box located above the chapel. The *nemeseum* at Emerita was identified as such by a painted inscription on a wall inside. The shrine at Tarraco, dating to the third century, held at least one altar to Nemesis, while that at Carnuntum's civil amphitheater held three.[172] The military amphitheaters at Trier, Durnovaria, and Isca Silurum had *nemesea* on the short axis, and the collection of Nemesis inscriptions at Italica all came from this area as well. Other chapels in this location have been found at Puteoli, Fréjus, Aquincum, Lugdunum, Aquae Granni, and Senlis and possibly should be reconstructed at Pompeii, Cimiez, and Avenches.[173]

Less frequently, the chapel was built at the extreme end of the ellipse's long axis, either opposite the major entrance or incorporated with it. Such is the case at Deva, where the centurion Sextus Marcianus dedicated a small altar to Nemesis.[174] A statue of the goddess was found in the shrine at Carnuntum's military amphitheater, where a vestibule gave access to the main entrance of the building.[175] It is thought that *nemesea* held this position at Corinium Dobunnorum and at Aquincum's civil amphitheater.[176]

A test trench in Scarbantia's arena uncovered a stela dedicated to Nemesis, which the excavators wanted to enshrine at the south end of the long axis. At Flavia Solva and Ulpia Traiana, the *nemesea* flank the main entrance on the long axis but next to the exterior façade of the amphitheater rather than the arena.[177] An altar to Nemesis was found near the entrance to Pula's amphitheater, and we should perhaps reconstruct a *nemeseum* in the vicinity, analogous to those at Flavia Solva and Ulpia Traiana.

Thus the amphitheatrical *nemesea* are located at prominent architectural focal points; the significant positioning of the *nemesea* suggests that they were functionally linked to activity in the arena. One should recall, however, that the ritual of the *munera* involved more than just combat: there was the *pompa* as well. As we saw in the Imperial Cult, both gladiators and magistrates marched into the amphitheater as part of the *pompa*. The link between the *nemesea*, specifically those on the short axis, and the presidential seating in the boxes above may indicate that the *nemeseum* was used as the endpoint for the *pompa*. The magistrates could proceed directly to their seats while the gladiators returned to the arena for their performance. This connection between the loge for dignitaries and the *nemesea* adds further backing to the argument that Nemesis held particular meaning for local magistrates in her identification as a Fortuna analog. The deluxe accommodations made for cult in some Nemesis chapels also indicate that moneyed individuals participated in this worship, cult enthusiasm being shared by the lowly gladiators and *venatores* and the political elite of the Roman world.

Nemesis has been an underrated deity in the Roman period, often cast aside as an obscure, obsolescent goddess whose only relevance dates to the fifth century B.C. The archaeological record belies the relative silence of the contemporary literary sources, with an abundance of evidence for cult practice in the West, specifically in the amphitheaters. Nemesis seems to have much the same sort of significance as Fortuna, as the morally ambivalent distributor of good luck and bad, of success, and of death. She was connected with the state in terms of loaded epithets like Augusta and of her appearance in Imperial propaganda.

The cult of Nemesis played a role in the reconciliation of the faceless individual to the Roman world. As suggested earlier, the Roman government in the Imperial period grew increasingly autocratic, decreasing the importance of the individual in the workings of the system as a whole.

The *spectacula* offered a release for the frustration engendered by this impotence. Nemesis represents the unexplainable effects of mysterious, uncontrollable forces. By acknowledging and even embracing one's relative powerlessness, and by channeling Nemesis' power by means of ritual, the individual can accept with greater equanimity one's isolation in the face of the pervasive prevalence of the Roman state. Nemesis offered a powerful connection; she could intercede for the individual with the workings of destiny.

Yet Nemesis was herself "destiny," in a sense, and as such she was a powerful representative of the Imperial Mission. As part of the amphitheatrical institution, she offered divine legitimization for the spectacle of the arena, in many ways reflective of the nature of Roman authority. Nemesis' connection with the sponsors of the games gave tacit approval to the outcome of the combat and endowed the institution as a whole with the endorsement of the gods. The amphitheater, like the empire itself, was an instrument of fate, who, personified as Nemesis, personally supervised the spectacles of Rome.[178]

The arena as a sacred area resonated with the functional concerns of struggle and order. The cults of the amphitheater operated to ease the stress engendered by the imposition of the order of Rome, by offering the citizens of the empire a set of symbols and ritual interactions that helped define their world and their place in it. The amphitheater formed a nexus for the Imperial Cult, Celtic cult practice, and the cult of Nemesis, each of which provided a meaningful pattern to reconcile the individual and his social or political group within the desired structure. The center of power encouraged these cults as a means of achieving provincial unification under Roman rule; members of a coherent group perform more effectively as individuals and as administrative units. The Pax Romana relied on such cooperation. The amphitheater was a crucial part of this new group identity. Within amphitheaters devotees met, sat together, and shared the communal experience of the cult event. The activity associated with the Imperial Cult focused their cohesive feelings around the person of the emperor, as embodiment of the state. The particularly Gallic style of amphitheater was constructed at Celtic sacred spaces, acting as a locus for Celtic interaction within a Roman context. The mixed edifice was the catalyst for the adaptation of Celtic practices in accordance with the new political reality. *Interpretatio Romana* incorporated the Celtic notion of cosmic struggle and raised an amphitheatrical monument to it. The social transition of the rural Celt was eased by the cultic action adaptable to the amphitheater; could the cosmopolitan citizen of the empire have such recourse? The goddess Nemesis, like her cohort Fortuna, provided a means of understanding the radical changes wrought by the onslaught of Rome. She did not judge but offered a strength that the individual called on in his search for order in the chaos of human existence.

IV. THE SYSTEM OF CONSTRUCTION

I tell this tale, which is strictly true,
Just by way of convincing you
How very little, since things were made,
Things have altered in the building trade.

R. KIPLING, *A Truthful Song*

WHAT WE CAN CALL the system of construction was the whole complex of ways and means surrounding the building of an amphitheater. The system worked at times from the top down, with the leaders of Rome's social hierarchy supplying the initial impetus for construction, which then worked its way through down to the individual workman, hired perhaps on a daily basis, who depended on such building projects to support his family at the subsistence level. This social economy involved the financial networks of the Roman world, which organized the funding for what might have been the most expensive structure a Roman town would ever build. The system has a technical aspect, involving the literal methods by which the amphitheater itself was erected. One should also include the system of entry, the means by which people were given or denied access to the amphitheater and the social and financial factors that determined those means.

A third-century mosaic, found in Tunisia, offers a graphic depiction of a series of duels between venators and leopards, put on by a group of professional performers hired by Magerius, a local notable, to maximize the impact of his spectacles (see Fig. 29).[1] That Magerius was successful in doing so is the central point of the mosaic. The focus of the representation is not, as one might expect, on the life-and-death struggle of the

FIGURE 29. Magerius mosaic, with acclamation for Magerius as *editor* inscribed in center, from private home in Smirat, Tunisia, © Gian Berto Vanni, courtesy Vanni/ Art Resource, NY.

bestiarii but on the interaction between the *editor*, Magerius, and the audience. The political discourse behind every Roman spectacle is carefully articulated in this mosaic, captured in the form of an inscription, framed by the vocative "Mageri." The crowd lavishes praise on the *editor*, focusing on Magerius' ostentatious generosity, the unique quality of the spectacle, their magnificence not to be seen again. Most important is Magerius' response to all this acclaim. "This is what it is to be rich. This is what it means to be powerful."[2]

Magerius' epigram is a powerful statement that encapsulates the meaning of the arena in Roman society, the use of spectacle presentation to establish and reestablish the vertical relationships of power between rulers such as Magerius, who likely put on these games as part of holding a high magistracy, and the ruled, the members of the community, seated in the audience according to their civic status. Magerius' understanding of the interconnectedness between the arena and politics was hardly unique. Throughout the empire, Rome's leaders acknowledged their duty and found their glory in the provision of spectacle and spectacular venues. Public figures used private funds to serve the public interest and their own.

In the Roman world, membership in the civic community was a form of immortality to which even those not born to the ultimate power could aspire.[3] Although the individual passed on, his mortal remains crumbling to dust, his city could withstand the years, and membership in that collective allowed him to share in the city's timelessness. The identification of the individual with the city meant that, to a great extent, the status of the individual was defined by the status of his city. By glorifying the city, one glorified oneself, an effect enhanced by permanent commemoration of one's actions on behalf of the city, whether that commemoration took the form of epigraphical acknowledgement of one's benefactions or benefactions that were themselves permanent, with public architecture being the highest expression of public service. The more visible the benefaction, the greater glory accrued to the donor.[4] Grand gestures on behalf of one's city and fellow citizens were an essential part of being wealthy. Wealth without the public acclaim was not really wealth.[5] The amphitheater, as public architecture, is part of this whole social complex, strongly tied to these concepts of civic duty and civic immortality, public benefaction and euergetism.

In the amphitheater, public and private spheres and motivations met and overlapped. In many ways, the amphitheater was a public building.[6] This is obvious, to some extent, given the function of the structure to entertain, persuade, and control the populace. In addition to this outward direction of the established building, the originating impulse for amphitheater construction was public; the building of an amphitheater required governmental approval.[7] This is verified by evidence from the corpus of Roman law.

One piece of legislation regulating the construction of amphitheaters was prompted by a disastrous occurrence in A.D. 27. In that year a certain freedman, Atilius by name, erected an amphitheater in the town of Fidenae not far from Rome. His motivations were not those of Magerius; Atilius did not want to redistribute excessive wealth nor court the favor of fellow citizens but rather pursued this project *in sordidam mercedem*.[8] He wanted to make some money off the venture. Unfortunately, the amphitheater was built on unstable ground and collapsed, killing thousands of spectators.[9] The outcry at such a disaster prompted official action to clarify the government's stance toward such projects. The ensuing regulation highlighted the Roman viewpoint on public building in general and amphitheater construction specifically. A *senatus consultum* was passed that limited the future editorship of *munera* to those with fortunes worth 400,000 sesterces or more, adding "an amphitheater in future should not be placed anywhere except on ground of certified solidity."[10]

The legislation links the building of amphitheaters to the presentation of *munera*, suggesting that the same people would be responsible for both activities. The statute does not forbid holding *munera* for profit, but by limiting editorship to a certain sociopolitical status, it maximizes the chances that the motivations of the editor will be "legitimate," that is, that he be driven by abundance of wealth and municipal ambition.[11] In short, he will be inspired by the traditional motivations of the Roman euergete.

Aemilius Macer, a Roman jurist writing in the first half of the third century after Christ, refers to limitations placed on the construction of new buildings in general and spectacle buildings, circuses, theaters, and amphitheaters in particular.[12] The statute considers two types of construction as distinguished by financing source: private and public. Private building projects need no permits from the central government, except in certain instances: when some sort of civic rivalry is involved, when the project might be a cause of sedition, or when the project has the construction of a circus, theater, or amphitheater as its goal. Public building projects, of any type, must all be submitted for authorization to the *princeps*.[13]

The amphitheater is thus an exceptionally public "private" building. The reasoning behind the exceptions may have some bearing on our understanding of the social role of the Imperial amphitheater. There is a thematic link binding these special cases, in which the potential threat of civic turmoil is minimized by keeping a close watch on the means and venues for public interaction and rivalry. Amphitheaters, like theaters and circuses, were important areas for public assembly in the Imperial period and thus could foster discord and rioting, political or otherwise. There was also the potential for worrisome demagoguery in a man so wealthy and so concerned with his public image as to underwrite the construction of an amphitheater. Such an individual would be worth Imperial scrutiny.[14]

One should also take note of the last interdiction of the statute, which forbids the inscription of any name other than that of the person who paid for the building and the emperor himself. This explains the dearth of evidence for other professionals involved in amphitheater construction, most lamentably, the lack of evidence for architects.[15] More importantly, it seems an effort to limit the prestige to be gained from amphitheater construction to a small group of people: the wealthy and the powerful, the emperor and the euergete. The builders of amphitheaters were also the builders of the Roman Empire.

THE EARLY BUILDERS

The pattern for public construction was begun during the Republic. Responsibility for initiating individual projects fell to one of three groups: the censors, the aediles, and the triumphators. The experience of each would have an impact on amphitheater construction and public building in general during the Principate, as the mechanism developed during the Republic was adapted for empire-wide use as the focus of power gradually shifted outward. Censorial construction established the authority of leading magistrates in taking the initiative in public construction, which would have an important impact on the community and serve as a monument to his leadership. Aedilician construction, although more limited in extent than the censorial programs, provided a connection between public building and the sponsorship of games. It was the activity of the triumphators, however, that was the key to amphitheater construction under the emperors. The *viri triumphales* had the financial means to undertake expensive building projects, means not subject to even minimal senatorial control. Military victory, the source of their funds, was also the occasion for triumphators to mount lavish spectacles, extravaganzas that bespoke Roman power, managed to best effect by the skill of the *vir triumphalis*.

Censors

The censors were chosen every five years, mainly to perform a census but also to see to the maintenance of public buildings and the construction of any new edifices deemed necessary to the public good. The censors took control of public building at an early date, handling the construction of Rome's city walls in the early fourth century.[16] This concern for public welfare went hand in hand with the political agenda of the individual

censor, however; a censor could choose a project as a permanent reminder of his political vision, as did Ap. Claudius Caecus, who built the
Via Appia and the Aqua Appia as censor in 312 B.C.[17] Such a memorial
went beyond contemporary politics, as public buildings named after their
sponsors were eternal monuments to the glory of the censor and generations of his descendants. This served the purposes of Rome as well, as the
explosion of censorial building, financed by a treasury enriched by conquest, recreated the appearance of the city in accordance with her new-
found Imperial majesty.[18]

The initiative came from the individual censors themselves, for whom
new buildings would serve as a monument to their term as censor. The
Senate participated in public building only by allocating or denying
sufficient funds to undertake any given project.[19] The money came from
the *praesens pecunia*, which was the funds at hand in the *aerarium*. Any special arrangements for funding were made on an ad hoc basis every five
years.[20]

Once the decision to build had been made, the censors accepted public bids from contractors for carrying out the actual construction of the
individual projects. As the *locator*, or lessor, of the contract, the censor
would normally be responsible for the final *probatio*, or inspection, which
was requisite to the fulfillment of the contract and the final payment of
the contractor. When major building projects were underway, however,
there was no guarantee that the *probatio* could take place during the eighteen months of a censor's term.[21] Either special arrangements had to be
made or responsibility for the *probatio* was delegated to others.[22] The pe-
culiarities of Roman magistracies, particularly the limited terms, created
a system obviously not designed to handle extensive building projects.

Permanent buildings for public spectacle were relatively rare in Rome
but did occasionally touch on the censorial sphere. Gaius Flaminius
Nepos, the first plebeian censor, oversaw the construction of the Circus
Flaminius in 220 B.C., which met a favorable response from the populace.[23] Theaters may have been proposed by censors in 179 and 174. As
we have seen, the theater planned by the censors in the mid-150s met
with fierce senatorial opposition; the project was aborted and the Palatine
building site was cleared of construction.[24] This controversy has already
been discussed, but it should be emphasized here that the arguments
raised against the theater focus on the censors' mandate to act for the
public good; a permanent theater, for a variety of reasons, was contrary to

this mandate. More important than the clash with the censorial mandate, however, is the matter of chronology. There are few permanent ludic constructions in Rome proper prior to the first century B.C., by which time the censorship had been deprived of much of its energy, certainly as far as public building was concerned.[25]

Aediles

Aediles were involved with public works, as part of their responsibility for *cura urbis*. Aediles were more likely to be responsible for maintenance than for new construction, but there are some aedilician links to the latter.[26] This is particularly pertinent to the construction of amphitheaters, given the prominence of gladiatorial games in Republican campaigns for the aedileship.[27]

D. E. Strong credits the aediles with the construction of buildings to accommodate public entertainment. Since as early as the fourth century, aediles sponsored the public games of Rome during their year in office, and some sort of temporary structures would have been put up for this purpose.[28] Admittedly, temporary buildings could be quite lavish, as was Curio's construction in 52 B.C., but they are temporary. These aedilician structures probably did not long outlive the *ludi* for which they were built.[29] Although defining these temporary accommodations as public works is somewhat problematic, the ludic structures of aediles like Curio were directed toward a political goal, that being to maximize one's public image and status in the world of Roman politics.[30] The venue for the spectacles enhanced the transmission of the desired political message to the select audience, seated in the bleachers provided by Rome's aediles.

Triumphators

Extending beyond the magisterial constructions of aediles and censors, the realization of the potential of architecture as a political tool in private hands was key to the development of Imperial architecture. The agents of this development belonged to the third category of Republican builders, the triumphators, victorious generals who decided to spend a portion of their *praeda*, or booty, on public works. They acted as private citizens, although the funds were acquired in the service of Rome.[31]

The use of *manubiae*, or booty converted into cash, for public works highlights the interdependence and mutual support between military success and public works, mediated by the agency of ambitious leaders.

The profits of conquest were fed back into projects for the public good. This benefit could not be taken for granted but was due to the beneficence and ostentatious public-mindedness of the individual general. The triumphator *chose* to use his booty in this way. As military success became increasingly important to political competition, individual triumphators came to see the possibilities of manipulating both their status as victors and the funds brought by victory in creating an *ornamentum urbis*, a civic monument, which could be a potent element in the manufacture of a successful public image. In the face of declining censorial building activity, ambitious triumphators stepped up the level of architectural generosity, eventually overshadowing all official efforts.

The ornament could take a variety of forms. The permanent commemoration could be simply a sculptural monument to the triumph itself, which, although visually striking, would not have the greatest impact on the public sentiment. Better to enhance one's military reputation through the ostentatious performance of pious duty. The general in the field, who vowed a temple contingent upon his victory, would be happy to sponsor its construction as a sign of his divine favor.[32] Regular use of such a monument by the Roman public, and the name of the triumphator used as a means of identifying the temple, would add deeper resonance to the impression left by this type of victory monument on the public consciousness. Alternatively, the triumphator could express himself as a true Roman dedicated to the public good by constructing a secular building. Such a building was hardly devoid of triumphal imagery or references to divine intervention. The building projects of triumphators grew increasingly complex as their efforts to direct the response of the Roman public became increasingly sophisticated.

Acting in this tradition, Sulla devoted much of his hefty *praeda* to building in Rome. He began the reconstruction of the Capitolium, which would incorporate the huge columns he had removed from the Temple of Olympian Zeus in Athens. He also began working on plans for an overall rebuilding of the Forum, plans which were not actually carried out but which did broaden the conceptual possibilities for ambitious, civic-minded individuals.[33]

Pompey, as triumphator, indulged the Roman public with architecture, constructing the first permanent theater in Rome, sheltered from official opprobrium by the attached Temple of Venus Victrix. More than simply a theater, more than simply a temple, the complex contained gardens and places for public gathering; its polyvalent character would maximize the impact made on a broad audience.

Julius Caesar extended the plans of Sulla to envision not only a renovation of the Forum but also a comprehensive restructuring of the entire city.[34] It was in carrying out his adopted father's plans that Augustus revised the Republican system of public works in Rome.

Augustus

The limitations of the system were apparent: what Rome needed was full-time professional staff to administer and maintain Rome's construction. They would have the knowledge to oversee consistency of quality, without other leadership duties to distract them. Augustus took important steps toward providing the needed infrastructure for public works, by putting together the curatorial boards. The *curator aquarum* and, later, the *curator viarum* were appointed posts, with permanent staff to see to the maintenance of roads and aqueducts for Rome. Agrippa, Augustus' right hand, was the first *curator aquarum*, while Dio Cassius says that Augustus himself was *curator viarum*, possibly from as early as 31 B.C.[35]

Octavian wanted to expand on the use of manubial funds for public works. He was, however, concerned lest construction again become a tool for excessive political competition among Roman *generalissimos*. In the Triumvirate and Early Principate, Augustus' generals, such as Domitius Calvinus, Marcius Philippus, and Lucius Cornificius, sponsored prestigious buildings to commemorate their, and, importantly, his martial achievements. Regardless of who technically undertook each individual project, Augustus' guiding hand was always visible in the accomplishment of the task. This period saw the construction of the first permanent amphitheater in Rome, under the sponsorship of Statilius Taurus, who had led land and sea forces for both Octavian and Antony, siding, in the end, with the former. As Dio describes the situation,

> When Caesar held his fourth magistracy (29 B.C.), Statilius Taurus
> built a stone hunting theater in the Campus Martius and put on
> gladiatorial games for its dedication and for this he received the
> right to choose each year one praetor for the people.[36]

The political advantage, the right of choosing one praetor annually, which Statilius Taurus was granted despite his acting in a technically private capacity, points to the high value placed on such construction by the *princeps*. Augustus' cronies were rewarded for their support. Again, the connection between politics and public building is made clear, here highlighting that connection for the amphitheater.[37]

After Augustus, the glorious burden of new construction more and more was assumed by the emperors, funded by the Imperial purse and executed by Imperial staff. It was under Imperial auspices that the Colosseum was built. Although built with "private" funds on "private" land, this was the grandest gesture made by the emperor as an appeal to popular tastes in a traditionally Roman way.[38]

BUILDERS DURING THE EMPIRE

Thus far we have concentrated on Rome, the center of power. One major difference between Roman architecture of the Republic and of the Imperial period is in the relationship between the center and the periphery.[39] The second-century censors had engaged in some extramural projects, aqueducts and roads being such by definition.[40] During the later Republic, the resources of the empire were affected by a centripetal dynamism, in which the city of Rome was embellished and the lives of her citizens enhanced at the expense of the provinces. This tendency was redirected beginning with Augustus, who encouraged the use of local resources within the provinces themselves, setting an example by sponsoring building projects in far-flung areas of the empire.[41]

The process often began with an appeal to the center. Envoys of the city in need could request help from the emperor in person or submit a request through the local representative of the central authority.[42] The success of the appeal was helped by the emperors' strong desire to build. Architecture was a powerful tool of mass persuasion. Its size could convey the grandeur and majesty an emperor needed to impress his subjects. The dimensions also made it a highly visible part of the Romanized terrain and maximized the impact of the visual rhetoric. The regularization of a peculiarly Roman architectural style under Augustus fostered the spread of buildings that not only reeked of wealth and prestige, as would any such monument, but also of Roman-ness.[43]

Buildings meant to be used by the public were especially effective in enhancing positive feedback. The emperor thereby expressed his concern for public needs and his willingness to respond to those needs by transforming his personal wealth into the means for bettering the standard of living of his fellow man.[44] He was thus a true benefactor, one who could understand what the people wanted and who was generous enough to see that they got it.

These important justifications for the use of architecture as Imperial propaganda were recognized in antiquity as essential motivational factors and were emphasized by agents for provincials in their efforts to persuade the center to sponsor building. Examples of this can be found in the correspondence of Pliny the Younger, in his repetitious attempts to convince Trajan to give his indulgent blessing to favored building projects, which he describes as *tuo saeculo . . . dignissimam*, most worthy of your age, or *aeternitate tua . . . digna*, worthy of your immortality, or *dignum . . . nomine tuo*, deserving of your name.[45] Pliny thus participates in the same sort of discourse found in the stands at Magerius' spectacle.

Some involvement of the emperor in construction was indirect. He could encourage construction in the *leges datae* handed down as municipal charters, which often banned demolition if hasty and detrimental to urbanization.[46] The proconsular legate of the emperor was authorized to act as his agent in the provinces. Ulpian says that the provincial governor should see to it that public buildings were maintained, control spending on new construction, and appoint technical and administrative personnel if necessary.[47] The emperor could also promote the training of effective construction professionals, in the military and civilian spheres.[48] As commander in chief of the Roman legions, all military construction was technically under his auspices.

Augustus set the standard for Imperial construction beyond Italy, a standard by which other emperors measured themselves, with varying degrees of success.[49] The ancient sources acknowledge Hadrian as the most active Imperial builder in the provinces, as "in almost every city he both built something and arranged for games."[50] Some of this was due, no doubt, to his personal interest in architecture. His decision not to compete with his predecessor in terms of military achievement may, however, have been the basis for his architectural activity, as public building was the most imperial form of peacetime public service. It is admittedly difficult to link Hadrian directly to specific amphitheatrical projects, perhaps due to the ostentatious reticence that one source attributes to him, in that "although he built numberless works everywhere, he never had his name inscribed on them, except for the temple of the Deified Trajan."[51]

Hadrian was himself a provincial, and the most extensive provincial building program in which Hadrian was involved was no doubt at his home town of Italica, where he built one of the largest amphitheaters in the empire.[52] He also traveled widely, which gave him the opportunity to involve himself personally with local projects as he saw fit. Accompanying him on his travels was an architectural work force, organized by Hadrian into efficient military cohorts.[53] In A.D. 121 he visited the northwestern frontier zone, parts of Gaul, and Britain, heading for Spain in the following year.[54] Frontier amphitheaters at Dyrrhachium, Scarbantia, Enge, Isorbrigantium, Camulodunum, Carnuntum, Virunum, Micia, and Flavia Solva date to approximately this period, as do the structure at Tours and renovations at Lugdunum and Isca Silurum. It is tempting to see the direct involvement of the emperor in these projects but impossible to prove.

Indeed, epigraphical evidence for the personal participation of Hadrian in constructing amphitheaters is very slim, with Capua providing a rare example:

> [*colonia Iu*]*lia Felix Aug*[*usta Capua*] *fecit* [*Divus Hadr*]*ianus Aug*[*ustus restituit e*]*t columnas ad*[*iecit Imp. Caes. T. Ael*]*ius Hadrianu*[*s Antoninus Aug.*] *Pius dedicavi*[*t*] [55]

As we saw earlier, Capua first built an amphitheater in the Republican period, which was replaced by the "Campanian Amphitheater," a truly monumental version, in the late first/early second century, later to be restored by Hadrian, as commemorated in this inscription.[56] The first accreditation on the inscription, however, goes to the town of Capua itself, as Roman building could be sponsored by corporate municipalities.

The *Ordo*

The *ordo decurionum*, or municipal council,[57] was granted control of local administration, the municipal charters given them by the central government providing some standardization as to the rights and obligations of local government.[58] This body was traditionally responsible for public works, for providing regular entertainment at public expense, and for maintaining public religion, as is apparent in surviving fragments of municipal charters. Any honors voted individuals had to be ratified first by the *ordo*.

A town whose outward appearance was Romanized gave a good impression to the powers that be, demonstrating its cultural assimilation and concomitant political compliance. Greater recognition of this compliance

by the center, in the form of the bestowal of the *ius Latinum* or the granting of the status of *municipium*, could provide a spur to public building.
Such was the case, for example, at Contributa Ipsca in Baetica and at
Conimbriga in Lusitania.[59] There was also local partisanship, or competition between communities, which found expression in ever more acquisition and embellishment of public amenities. Tacitus provides many examples of such rivalry, two of which center on local amphitheaters. The
arena riot at Pompeii in A.D. 59, for example, has been seen as something
more than fans getting out of control at a sporting event, in that the spectators came to the games already armed (see Fig. 30). The response by
Rome has also been taken as indicative of a less-than-spontaneous conflict between Pompeii and Nuceria. Tacitus tells us that illegal associations had been formed by Pompeiians, possibly at the instigation of one
Livineius, who was exiled for his role in the matter. The motivation towards violence is characterized by Tacitus as *oppidana lascivia*: boosterism
gone bad.[60]

During the turmoil of A.D. 69, one amphitheater was itself the catalyst
for intensification of violent intertown rivalry. Caecina laid siege to the
town of Placentia, with dreadful consequences for the arena:

> In this confrontation the glorious amphitheater, located outside the
> walls, burned. . . . The crowd of townspeople, inclined to be suspi-
> cious, believed the fuel for the fire had been surreptitiously brought
> in by certain of their neighbors, driven by envy and competitive-
> ness, because no other building in Italy was so spacious.[61]

Apparently the inclination toward violent expression of this sort of rivalry was exacerbated by local involvement in larger conflicts, as Capua
and Puteoli "combined municipal competition with civil war," during
the struggle between Vitellius and Vespasian for the Imperial power in
A.D. 69. Nor were they alone in so doing: Tripoli and Lebda likewise used
the context of empire-wide uproar as an excuse for local hostilities.[62]

Sometimes *duoviri*, or priests of the public cult, took responsibility for
the supervision of public works in connection with their office, that is, *ob
honorem*. To what extent these duties were entirely voluntary is questionable, as the *ordo* could play a very active role in directing public service,
sometimes mandating a specific activity to be performed by officials.[63]

FIGURE 30. Depiction of riot at Pompeii in A.D. 59, fresco from Pompeii, courtesy Museo Archeològico di Napoli.

Some building activity took place under duress, as a *munus*, or public duty, imposed by the municipal council.[64] Liability for *munera* was shared by the entire citizen body, from at least the second century after Christ. The form this duty would take was determined on the basis of age, sex, and social status. Women were ineligible for all *munera* involving personal service, since their bodies were considered unsuited to such activity; women were obliged to serve the city with their financial resources instead.[65] Male citizens, however, were liable to personal involvement with city service on many levels, which would have included, at times, the supervision of public construction.[66]

There is little epigraphical attestation for the funding of amphitheaters by the *ordo* as a group.[67] Individual magistrates, acting as magistrates, did apparently undertake this kind of building project, and in providing the source for funding straddle the line between public and private benefaction. The best example of magisterial participation in amphitheater construction comes early on, from Pompeii, where *C. Quinctius C.f. Valgus M. Porcius M.f. duovir. quinq. coloniai honoris caussa spectacula de sua peq. fac. coer. et coloneis locum in perpetuom deder.*[68] The participation here of quinquennial magistrates, the extra-Roman equivalent of the censors, is notable, as is the fact that these two were also responsible for the construction of the odeum in Pompeii.[69] The inscription also makes explicit the fact that they underwrote this project *honoris caussa*, thereby publicizing the link to public office.[70]

The Euergete

Inspired by love of public acclaim and a sense of duty toward one's city and fellow citizens, many individuals sponsored building projects in a "private" capacity, that is, when they were not actively holding magistracies. Like the *viri triumphales* before them, these people provided private impetus and funding, which defines their private character as sponsors, despite the possibility that their funds may have been earned in the service of Rome and despite the otherwise intimately public nature of their lives. Pierre and Monique Clavel-Lévêque are, in fact, convinced that private euergetes were responsible for the majority of provincial buildings.[71] Monuments constituted large public memorials to the donor and his family. Local councils could respond to such philanthropy by rewarding the benefactor with a statue or honorific title.[72] The essential motivation was the enhancement of the power and prestige of the individual, a status that would linger permanently, like the buildings, in the hearts and minds of the community, achieving even a form of immortality.

The action of individuals in the construction of amphitheaters is rarely apparent but discernible. At Lucus Feroniae, M. Silius Epaphroditus was given the title *patronus* because he had paid for the construction and dedication of the colony's amphitheater.[73] Patronage of communities is a widely attested institution in the Roman world.[74] The official procedure by which *patrocinium* could be granted an individual by a community was under official regulation from the time of the later Republic and involved a formal resolution by the local town council, a *decretum decurionum*. In such a decree, the material service of the individual patron was typically not specifically acknowledged. It was apparently inappropriate to suggest a link between a benefaction and the honor conferred; this would seem too much as if the *patrocinium* had been purchased, a commodity haggled over in the public forum. It may also prove disadvantageous to the community to link patron status to a specific time and place; surely patronage of a community was a continuing relationship, with advantages accruing to both sides for years to come. The inscription at Lucus Feroniae is thus distinctive in providing a connection between a particular benefaction, the amphitheater, and the grant of *patrocinium*.

Municipal patronage is likewise connected to the construction of an amphitheater at Tibur. During the reign of Hadrian, M. Tullius Rufus contributed *ad amphitheatri dedicationem HS* ((|)) ((|)) *p.* [*e.*] *et operas n. CC.*[75] Here twenty thousand sesterces, in addition to two hundred man days, are promised toward the completion of an amphitheater. Rufus was acting to fulfill a promise made by his father, M. Tullius Blaesus, who was a prominent citizen of Tibur, priest and curator of the Temple of Hercules Victor, and a municipal patron honored by decree of the Senate.[76] Tibur's arena is small and makes use of a hillside for partial support of the superstructure; nevertheless, the wording of the inscription suggests that the contribution made by the Tullius family would not be sufficient to fulfill the entire construction plan. This sort of contributory or shared beneficence is echoed at other amphitheaters and may be due to the high cost of arena construction. At Sinuessa, Sex. Caecilius Birronianus, who was a *quinquevir*, among other honors, *podium amphitheatri a solo fecit.*[77]

C. Iunius Priscus built the podium, arches, and some silver statues of Neptune for the amphitheater at Arles while a candidate.[78] The same sort of activity was also performed by benefactors of a lower social status, such as the Praenestan freedman *M. Warenus Clari l.* [*T*]*yrann*[*us*] . . . *amphitheatri partem dimid*[*i*]*am in sol*[*o publico dimidiam in privato*]. . . .[79] Here, the restored reading of "half on public land, half on private" makes explicit the overlapping between public and private in the amphitheatrical complex.

Women, as *municipes* without suffrage, were nevertheless also euergetes.[80] A wealthy priestess from Cartima in Baetica sponsored many projects, gifting her town with land for baths, colonnades, statues, and necessary repairs on existing structures.[81] A woman built the aqueduct at Ilugo in Tarraconensis in memory of her spouse and son.[82] The involvement of women in public construction seems typical of the general pattern of public activity by women in the Roman world. Women largely acted as family representatives, to maintain and promote the honor and fame of their families. The family connection also may explain the involvement of Ummidia C.f. Quadratilla, who, using her own funds, financed the building of an amphitheater for the citizens of Casinum.[83]

Ummidia Quadratilla, whose obituary appears in Pliny's *Letters*, seems to have been the daughter of C. Ummidius Quadratus, praetor in A.D. 18, who himself was a native of Casinum.[84] She must have been born between 27 and 30, to make her an octogenarian in around 107, when Pliny announced her death. To whom she was married is not known, but she was survived by a granddaughter and by a grandson, C. Ummidius Quadratus.[85] Pliny knew her as a woman of vigor and discernment, whose gender condemned her to frivolous pastimes; she used to sponsor pantomimes but would never allow her grandson to watch them perform, lest their crudities offend his delicate youth. Her activity in the construction of amphitheater and temple puts the lie to her professed feminine levity and *illum otium sexus*. In keeping with the careful upbringing of her grandson, she followed in the footsteps of her father in building to enhance the family reputation as patrons of the Roman people.[86]

MANAGEMENT

The Romans maintained a minimalist approach toward governmental administration, with as much as possible kept in private hands. The central

authority itself had no mechanism to provide construction and maintenance services, let alone to collect the money needed to pay for those services. Instead, the state contracted these tasks out to the worthiest bid-
der.[87] In essence, then, private interests were directly responsible for most
Roman public building. These contractors did not necessarily themselves
possess the technical knowledge required for the particular project but
rather provided capital and management to run the skilled support structure.[88] And as Plutarch put it, construction by contract is "both better
and faster."[89] The terms of the building contract followed a basic pattern.[90] The *locator*, who was the presiding magistrate in the case of public
works, provided the specifications of the work to be done, which were
more or less detailed depending on the magistrate's willingness to continue his involvement beyond this stage. These specifications included a
discussion of materials.[91]

For state projects, state quarries and brick factories may have provided
the necessary materials.[92] A schedule of deadlines was set to determine
when the work was to be completed (*dies operis*) and when final payment
would be made (*dies pecuniae*).[93] Provision was made for *probatio* and *iudicatio*, or inspection and quality control. Vitruvius' discussion of the legal
aspects of contracting admits that the current system allows for much
waste of funds in its laxity over completion according to the contract.[94] In
fact, he claims that if the contractor finished according to the terms, he
was given public honors by official decree.[95] This suggests that fulfilling
the contract was actually rather extraordinary. The problem is magnified
when one considers that different contractors undertook different parts
of the project, with one corporation handling materials, another labor,
another supervising the actual construction.[96]

Did this practice continue in the Imperial period? We have seen that
Augustus set up curatorial boards to handle maintenance on public works
of various sorts. These boards did have permanent staffs, including technicians and laborers, but these bodies were occupied with maintenance,
not new construction or big repairs, which were still contracted out. The
scale, intensity, and sophistication of building during the Empire mandated that the emperor, although nominally the building sponsor, delegate even the standard obligations of a *locator*, such as the responsibilities
of *probatio*, *iudicatio*, and haggling over contractual particulars.[97]

Some point to an intensified role by the building sponsor or Imperial agent, who may have taken over some of the duties previously filled by the contractor. It is possible, however, to overestimate participation by the central administration in building projects throughout the empire.[98]

Ratio Operis

To set the project in motion, the sponsor needed to draft a *ratio operis* fairly early in the planning stage.[99] This plan of action would include a detailed estimate of necessary materials and labor as well as an outline of projected financial resources. A site had to be chosen and surveyed, and then came the actual architectural planning, crucial in Roman architecture.[100]

The sponsor would probably have to delegate much of the responsibility for the technical aspects of the *ratio operis*, although Vitruvius suggests that the patron be his own architect.[101] The architectural drawings would have been drafted by someone closer to the labor force: the contractor, if qualified, or the contractor's architect/engineer. The sponsor would be more concerned about funding.[102]

As we have seen, the source of the funding varied according to the source of the patronage. The emperor could supply capital from the fisc or use indirect methods, such as allowing the levying of a new tax or redirecting the area's taxes toward the specific project. The financial responsibility could also be divided among several sources; for example, Herodes Atticus shared the cost of the aqueduct in the Troad with the emperor.[103]

If the project were sponsored by the community, how could financial arrangements be made? Funds available for local interests were limited at any given time. The town owned property, and rent was owed for public land being used by private persons. This would include not only agricultural land but also urban lots, rented by businesses for retail purposes.[104] Some of this property may have passed to the community in testaments.[105] Another source of public funds was local tax levied on trade and money changing. Taxes could not, however, be subject to ad hoc manipulation, as new taxes had to be approved by the central government, which was not very likely to happen. Rome did not want communities to drain themselves too much in this way. After all, locals must be sufficiently solvent not only to meet their strictly financial obligations to Rome but to shoulder their nonmonetary Imperial burdens, such as the maintenance of roads, aqueducts, and the Imperial post.[106] Sometimes the expenditures on public building were shared by public and private purses, which appears epigraphically as an acknowledgement of the euergete's specific contribution. This is the context in which we find the participation of Blaesus and an unknown magistrate at Luca, who gave *hic HS C in opus amphithe[atri . . .] in annos decem*.[107]

The combination of public and private is the essence of the *summa honoraria*, an official financial obligation placed on the magistrate entering office.[108] This can be traced back to the notion of property qualifications for public office.[109] The ancient rationale was that property owners had a lot invested in local interests and thus should have more of a say in the local politics. With this privilege came responsibility, as someone who had benefited from his community, socially as well as financially, owed something to it in return. This obligation was recognized materially as the *summa honoraria*.

Summa honoraria were not standardized on an empire-wide basis but varied locally. Quinquennial magistrates at Carthage, for example, paid 38,000 sesterces, while *sufetes* at Themetra only contributed 800 sesterces. Antoninus Pius, when requested to fix the amount of the *summa* paid by decurions in a town in Macedonia, settled on 2,000 sesterces, apparently arbitrarily.[110] This was recognized as a lucrative source for public funds and was manipulated by various towns, as Pliny suggests in his account of a town increasing the number of public offices to increase revenue.[111] *Summa*, originally cash payments for games to be celebrated during the magisterial year, could be converted to payments for monuments intended for public use and benefit. Sometimes a magistrate would add to the *summa*, either in cash or by funding a building project, an expense still described as *ob honorem*. Sometimes a simple offer to fund a project was itself commemorated epigraphically, as *pollicitas ob honorem*, analogous to games promised by candidates for office in the Roman Republic.[112] It has been suggested that the existence of the *summa* system indicates that voluntary munificence was not enough in and of itself to meet the financial needs of towns.[113] While this may be true, more significant is the Roman system of provincial taxation, which traditionally funneled tribute payments away from the periphery. The taxes themselves were originally meant to support the imperialist goals of the city of Rome, to the detriment of the provinces. Later, when the provinces might have need of such financial resources, special arrangements had to be made to supplement a system that had not been structured to answer this need.

Actual prices for buildings are relatively rare epigraphically and difficult to use to formulate a general system of costs. An attempt was made by R. Duncan-Jones, who concentrated on North Africa and Italy, areas that offered the most information.[114] The highest attested building cost in North Africa was 600,000 sesterces, for a temple in Lambaesis, while in Italy the more deluxe constructions were in the range of two million sesterces.

No prices for amphitheaters are attested epigraphically from North Africa, a situation that Duncan-Jones explains by suggesting that these, as the largest freestanding structures, were the most costly of all monuments and thus were probably never built from private resources.[115] We have seen that individuals did, in fact, finance amphitheaters, but in terms of absolute prices, we should, by Duncan-Jones' reasoning, assume a cost for amphitheaters higher than the 600,000 sesterces in North Africa, indeed, higher than the 2,000,000 sesterces paid for lavish buildings in Italy generally. This can be compared with the figure of 10,000,000 sesterces for an unfinished theater in Bithynia that Pliny had to deal with during his stint as Imperial legate.[116] Another theater was built in Spain at a cost of 400,000 sesterces, which may indicate a huge range in theater costs.[117] The two costs we have for amphitheaters both come from Italy, from Tibur and Luca, and give us the figures of 20,000 and 1,000,000 sesterces respectively, again a very wide range.[118] We should note, however, that the wording of the two inscriptions suggests that these funds were not meant to cover the entire cost of the amphitheater but were simply contributions toward the completion of the structure, albeit sizable ones.[119] Extrapolating from so few figures, with provenances ranging widely in time and space, is surely very risky. Is there another way to analyze the construction costs for amphitheaters?

M. K. and R. L. Thornton used areal measurements to formulate a system for comparing building costs for the area within 60 kilometers of Rome itself.[120] They arbitrarily selected one building, the Augustan "Maison Carrée" in Nîmes, as a base and expressed all other buildings in terms of a comparison between the relative amount of labor involved to construct them and that needed for the base. Each building was thus assigned a number of work units. The work-unit allocation has no real meaning, in terms of cash cost or man hours, but is taken as expressing all necessary labor, material, and time.[121] The "Maison Carrée," chosen for its remarkable state of preservation more than for anything else, was arbitrarily assigned 60 work units, which breaks down to eight square meters of temple per work unit.[122] This cost index was further modified according to the extent of the work involved (i.e., to "build" a building was more costly than to "enlarge," which, in turn, was more expensive than to "restore") and to the elaboration of the construction (a colonnade being more austere, presumably, than a temple, although covering a larger area).[123] They altered the system according to building type as well, deciding that aqueducts, theaters, and the Imperial Domus were sufficiently distinct to warrant so doing.[124]

Work units as determined by floor space is a happy relationship, to some extent. After all, we have evidence that ancient contractors based their estimates on areal measurements, as indeed is done today.[125] There are, however, problems in this approach. One such concerns the breaking down of three-dimensional structures into only two dimensions. Consideration of materials and architectural concepts is only taken into account by the Thorntons in a gross fashion, although it is obvious that a building made of cut marble was a great deal more expensive than one of the same size that used earthworks. Further difficulties are apparent when one examines the Thorntons' index of Julio-Claudian building projects and the work units assigned to amphitheatrical structures.

One might reasonably assume that the estimate of cost for an amphitheater would have some relationship to that of the theater, as it can be regarded as the equivalent of two theaters back to back. According to the Thornton methodology, the theater's work units are calculated by dividing the metric area of the theater by eight and multiplying that number by the number of storeys in the individual theater.[126] The Theater of Marcellus, with two storeys and an area of 8,831 square meters, was therefore given 2,208 work units. The amphitheater of Statilius Taurus, however, was assigned a mere 120 work units, Caligula's incomplete amphitheater, 100 work units, and the wooden amphitheater of Nero a paltry 72 work units, despite the lack of specific evidence in the ancient sources for size or nature of construction of these buildings. If, however, one were to apply the Thornton method of theater calculation to the Colosseum, an amphitheater of known dimensions, it would be worth 11,468 work units, more than any building project that they considered. The wide discrepancy between methodology and results, at least in their estimate of amphitheatrical building effort, casts suspicion on the analysis as a whole.

The only way in which the Thornton methodology might be useful is in estimating the costs of amphitheaters relative to each other but only within the different conceptual building types. The utility of this is limited, however, as it seems obvious that a larger amphitheater would be more expensive than a smaller amphitheater of the same type. As we will see, the wide variety of building technique found in the construction of amphitheaters makes cost comparison across the board a difficult thing to achieve in any absolute form.

LABOR

The sponsors of public works did not generally acknowledge "the little people" in dedicatory inscriptions. As we have already seen, only those who paid for the construction and the emperor himself could legitimately be the recipients of honorific epigraphy; references to the laborers employed on public architecture are few and incidental in the corpus of Roman inscriptions.[127] We have already seen a singular reference to labor in amphitheatrical construction, that being the contribution of two hundred *operae*, or man-days, toward Tibur's arena by M. Tullius Rufus.[128] What sort of men actually worked those *operae*? Even to approach this question, one must stretch widely the limited evidence available for public construction in the Roman world. Architectural laborers likely fell into one of four groups: slaves, corvées, convicts, or free workers, hired for pay.

Slaves

It has been postulated that huge gangs of slaves, owned by private individuals who contracted out their services, were regularly employed on the public works.[129] Evidence for the existence of such groups appears in connection with Crassus and with the aqueducts in Rome.

Plutarch explains how Crassus amassed his fortune in urban real estate, by taking advantage of desperate people and desperate times.[130] He bought slaves skilled in architecture and in construction, and when he had more than five hundred of them, he used them on rebuilding properties purchased cheaply from the victims of man-made and natural disaster.[131] He would then lease out his new property, his bits of urban renewal.[132] Plutarch goes on to say that Crassus did not use his builders to construct dwellings for his own use. From this it has been extrapolated that Crassus hired out his gangs for the building projects of others, an assumption that finds no support in Plutarch's account. In fact, quite the opposite is implied. The passage describes Crassus' profiteering through architecture, how the slaves were employed by Crassus to build structures he could rent out to others, not luxury housing for his own use. The description may indicate the transitory nature of their employment by Crassus; his projects were, after all, dependent on disaster. It should also be noted that the biographer is telling of an extraordinary individual, whose unusual habits cannot be taken as evidence of a regular practice in Rome.

The first "Imperial" slave gang was organized by Agrippa as curator of the aqueducts.[133] These slaves were Agrippa's own private property, inherited by Augustus who gave them to the state to perform the routine maintenance of the aqueducts. It may be that other public works, such as the road system, were administered along similar lines, with slave gangs on hand for the regular tasks of maintenance.[134]

It is unlikely, however, for economic reasons, that large groups of slaves were regularly employed on building projects.[135] Romans may have owned small groups of slaves trained as building technicians, which they could contract out for projects requiring their specialized skills.[136] Roman architecture, however, with its preference for concrete, favored the unskilled worker. Why waste the talents of these artisans on heaving and dumping concrete? Furthermore, the slave required year-round total maintenance, which would be extremely costly for a private owner, who would, in turn, pass that cost on to the contractor. Surely a thrifty contractor would prefer to hire free menials at a great savings to himself and to the sponsor.

Such would have been the situation in the city of Rome. The evidence for slaves in provincial trades is even more minimal, but the localized nature of the provincial market would argue against the employment certainly of large numbers of slaves outside Italy.[137]

Corvée

The conscription of private citizens may have been a source of labor for public works in the Roman world.[138] The significance of this practice in the Imperial period should not, however, be overemphasized in the face of little evidence.

The *lex Ursonensis* made allowance for physical labor as a *munus*, with adult men to donate no more than five days a year and their wagons to be made available for public works three days annually.[139] This is the only instance in the corpus of Roman law where such admittedly minimal provision is made; the *munus* of public labor does not appear with the other *munera* in the *Digest*.[140] Its appearance in the *lex Ursonensis* may have been understood as a temporary measure, until the colony acquired its own public slaves, to be invoked only in dire necessity.[141] Its use in Urso for *munitio* may reflect the early usage of corvées in times of military crisis.[142]

Damnati ad Opus Publicum

The Roman Empire had no prison system as such.[143] Instead of this custodial form of incarceration, lower-class criminals convicted of minor offenses were condemned to various forms of hard labor, including the public works.[144] Although the *opus publicum* is often referred to in Roman legal sources as a form of punishment, the impact of convict labor overall in the construction and maintenance of Imperial works in the capital is not clear.[145]

The situation outside Rome is even murkier, with only fleeting, albeit suggestive, evidence. Josephus tells us that Vespasian sent Nero 6,000 prisoners of war from Judaea to provide labor for the canal at the Isthmus of Corinth.[146] Nero's great need for menials on this project and on others is reiterated by Suetonius, who tells us that a call went out for all those in custody throughout the empire to be requisitioned for public building.[147] This instance seems to have been unique, and the systematic exploitation of convicts for major building projects was not otherwise seen at Rome.

The lengthiest piece of literary evidence for the pragmatics of the condemnation *ad opus publicum* comes from Pliny.[148] In his account, the convicts had begun to act as public slaves and were getting paid for their services. Trajan decreed that they should return to their usual duties, such as work at the bath house, on drains, and on the roads. Here the convicts serve sentences of limited duration within the city that condemned them, which presumably provided for their maintenance during their term.[149] Although the tasks seem to have been water and communication maintenance, that is, the public utilities, the sentence was considered humiliating and was accompanied by public flogging and the shaving of half of the convict's scalp. Because of the humiliation and loss of social status, decurions, veterans, and their sons, the whole class of the *honestiores*, were exempted from this kind of punishment.[150] This degradation of the individual is key to understanding the conviction to the *opus publicum*. The *damnatio*, or penal, aspect of the sentence was the chief concern, and the potential economic resource of convict labor was not fully realized, despite the increased need for it in the later empire.

Free Labor

Roman building technique, with its emphasis on concrete, relied heavily on extensive planning prior to construction. It was in this planning process and in the finishing details that technical skill was in demand. The bulk of Roman construction could be done by unskilled labor, "grunts," who were more likely to be free.[151] In addition, the employment of the free poor as *operarii* was a welcome supplement to the *annona*, the dole that provided only bleak bare necessities to the single male citizen.[152] Public works were therefore promoted by the demagogic politician not only to enhance his own prestige by providing a civic ornament for posterity but also to curry favor with the masses by providing them with income.

Roman demagogues were engaged in public works. C. Gracchus was surrounded continually by numbers of contractors and artisans, who were under obligation to him.[153] Appian emphasizes the Gracchan interest in public works and the political benefit to be gained from such an interest. Gracchus' sponsorship of extensive road-building activity had won him the support of a great number of contractors and artisans as clients.[154] Cicero discusses spending on public works as a form of liberality.[155] Public projects, such as docks, temples, and colonnades, were better for posterity than immediate handouts, in Cicero's argument.

The sponsorship of public works as support for the free poor was continued by the emperors. The wish to provide popular relief, *plebiculam pascere*, is also behind Vespasian's rejection of a labor-saving device for the renovation of the Capitolium.[156] Nero's massive reconstruction of Rome after the fire in A.D. 64 and his fixation with luxurious and innovative private building (and the jobs these provided) may be one explanation for his popularity with the Roman masses. Aside from their natural appreciation of his musical talents, the populace of Neronian Rome kissed the hand that fed them.

MILITARY AMPHITHEATERS

The connection between the Roman army and civilian construction was especially important in the provinces. The troops were instrumental to the Romanization process, providing a model for emulation with their enlightened urbanized lifestyle and in practical terms, as they were a rich resource for technical and organizational expertise and a handy labor pool. This became especially important in the later Empire, when the breakdown of the centralized structure and the deterioration of civilian services meant that the army was the only concentration of technicians and labor.[157]

The emperor was the living symbol of the bond between military and civilian, being both commander in chief and First Citizen. Ultimately, the initiative for all works of the legions came from him, taking direct action himself or acting through his legates, who in turn would delegate the Imperial procurator or the local commander to supervise the actual construction process.[158] The civil-military link was acknowledged conceptually by the Emperor Hadrian, who reorganized the work force employed on Imperial projects in Rome according to the legionary hierarchy.[159]

At a lower administrational level, the Imperial architects most familiar from the literary sources have a background in military affairs that goes beyond those skills strictly applicable to public construction. Vitruvius, for example, was in charge of construction and repair of *ballistae* and other engines of war under Augustus.[160] Apollodorus joined Trajan on the northeastern frontier during the Dacian Wars and later distilled that experience into a monograph on the besieging of cities, dedicating the work to the Emperor Hadrian.[161] The creators and the administrators of public works were men of this ilk. Frontinus' major works included a work on strategy as well as the more familiar one on aqueducts. Some of this may be due to the militarism inherent in Roman society and the traditional role of the army as the venue for initiation into the *cursus honorum*, or public service.

On a lower level, technicians would be trained in specializations of the building trade during their first years in the legions. Once their training was complete, they could be moved around the empire independent of their original unit. Their destination would apparently be determined by the provincial governor, who was obliged to lend *ministeria quoque militaria* to the *curatores* of public works, when needed for repair or construction of public buildings.[162] They could also be sent for special problems, as technical troubleshooters, to government officials in need.

The military often controlled the operations at state-owned material resources.[163] The largest brickyards outside the city of Rome were located at legionary headquarters, such as the one at Xanten on the Rhine, which produced bricks used throughout the frontier region. At mines, the legions acted as security forces, guarding the unfortunates condemned *ad metallum*, an effective way of converting a death sentence to useful public service.[164] Besides working as wardens, troops provided organizational and technical expertise at the Roman mines and quarries.[165]

The troops were at times directly involved in the extraction process, as is indicated by the duty roster of *Legio III Cyrenaica*. The men were here assigned various tasks in the quarries: they were to cut lime, burn it for mortar, and gather sand to be used in making concrete. This material would supply military projects, of course, but it apparently could also be used by civilians. The stones for the Forum of Colonia Ulpia Traiana were provided by military work gangs, as was the timber for public buildings in Verulamium.[166]

The military was itself a resource, most notably as a source of manpower and the largest labor force in the empire. The legions filled work gangs particularly on large-scale Imperial projects, such as the aqueduct and road systems. More localized constructions known to have been built by the military were also on a grand scale, with a definite tendency toward the use of such gangs on fortifications and amphitheaters, seldom on temples or arches.[167]

Scale, however, seems to be related only indirectly to this use of the military. It may be that the emperor, ultimate director of this labor force, was more likely to involve the troops in projects of some strategic importance, such as aqueducts, roads, and fortifications. It may be true also that the training received by military technicians pointed them toward more utilitarian projects rather than lavish civilian monuments. One should always be wary of generalizations based on inscriptional evidence; epigraphical acknowledgements are more likely to be given for major works, a tendency that may bias our perception of military building.

Some of these projects, however, were clearly related to specifically civilian interests. Trajan, for example, had a bridge built by soldiers to accommodate the marble trade at Hippo Regius.[168] Probus in Egypt ordered the Roman legions, "who were never allowed to take it easy," to construct bridges, temples, porticos, basilicas, and irrigation works.[169] Troops assigned to the German frontier in A.D. 9 were clearing away trees to build towns for the natives, civilizing the rural landscape by building roads and bridges.[170] It is in activity like this that we can see the use of the military as a tool for Romanization, the imposition of a Mediterranean lifestyle on those subject to Roman rule. This is perhaps even clearer in the development of the agricultural economy of the frontier area. Soldiers under Probus were actively involved in the conversion of land for agriculture, while officers were responsible for assigning land resources to communities, the fields, pastures, and springs commemorated in inscriptions.[171]

The rationale behind developing all this technical expertise in construction was in the tradition requiring the Roman army to build extensive camps on a regular basis to be used for a single night or as permanent legionary headquarters. This ability, basic to Roman military concepts and a major strategic advantage in the field, was a source of amazement to Josephus, as cities seemed to come into being in a matter of minutes.[172] Vegetius Rufus claimed that the Roman army carried a walled town wherever it went, providing a source of strength through security and a real advantage in the field.[173] By Frontinus' time, this truism was condensed into a pithy epigram attributed to Domitius Corbulo: the pick was the weapon with which to beat the enemy.[174] Here is the practical link between martial valor and construction.

The development of these traditional skills was an important part of training the recruits. Once learned, however, soldiers had to keep these skills honed, and thus we find troops on the frontier busily erecting practice or training camps, which show up in the archaeological record as camps located near permanent military bases but without evidence for occupation.[175] Britannia has the largest number of these with more than fifty, mostly in Wales. Nine were constructed in the general vicinity of Tomen-y-Mur, camps that range from around 10 to 44 square meters in size. Using sods of turf cut to a standard size, cohorts would compete against each other in timed construction competitions.[176] Quality was emphasized, and any below-standard work was grounds for punishment.[177] Some of the Welsh practice camps have deliberately been sited on unsuitable terrain, apparently to give troops experience building in difficult situations. It would presumably be a way of maintaining discipline and building physical strength too, to erect practice camps in unpleasant weather in nasty, wet ground.[178]

The link between the military and the amphitheater goes beyond the general association with the public works to touch on the function of the amphitheater as an arena for combats and as such predates the formalization of the amphitheater as a building type.[179] In 105 B.C., the consul, P. Rutilius Rufus, called on *doctores* of the gladiatorial *ludi* in Capua to teach the Roman legionaries a better sword drill, one which would be more versatile and efficient.[180] Thus the training of Roman soldiers was linked to that of gladiators, who were martial models not only of efficiency and versatility but also of bravery and fidelity, even unto death, as is clear from their appearance as rhetorical *topoi* in literature of the Roman world. The link became exceptionally close during crisis situations, when gladiators were occasionally recruited into the Roman army, as happened in the struggle against the Marcomanni under Marcus Aurelius.[181] It is not, therefore, surprising to see the central government adopting arenas as standard operating equipment of the Roman military from the early years of the Principate, the time when we first see clear Imperial manipulation of the amphitheatrical institution. The oldest military amphitheaters are at Segusium and Cemenelum and date to the Augustan installation of cohorts in the area.[182]

Military amphitheaters are characterized by their relatively modest size and practical means of construction. The most common building method made use of earthworks. Once a suitable location, outside the camp proper but adjacent to the walls, was determined, the central arena was dug out, and the dirt was piled and packed around its ellipse. Retaining walls were needed and incorporated available material, whether it be sod, wood, or stone, either quarried locally or gathered from the rubble of arena excavation. Seating was then constructed on top of the earthworks, with varying degrees of luxury displayed. Sometimes stepped ridges were flattened into the earthwork itself; sometimes wooden bleachers were built by the corps of carpenters.

Inscriptions offer direct testimony to the involvement of the military in the construction of amphitheaters. The individuals attested sometimes expanded their military service to include civil duties. At Périgueux, for example, A. Pompeius Dumnomotus, a former military tribune, built the amphitheater as prefect of public works in this technically nonmilitarized area.[183] Sextus Pedius Lusianus Hirrutus, whose distinguished military career may have led to his selection as a quinquennial magistrate, built the amphitheater at Interpromii.[184] At Carnuntum, *C. Domitius Zmaragdus domo Antiochia dec. municipi Ael. Carnunt. [a]mphitheatrum impens. [sua] solo publico fec.*[185] It is assumed that Zmaragdus' Antiochan origin indicates his original presence on the frontier as military personnel, although this is not mentioned in the inscription.

Other inscriptions, particularly a set from Britannia, provide direct evidence for the actual building process. The group from Tomen-y-Mur, with specific, and varying, area measurements incorporated into the inscription, may attest competition among cohorts in speedy amphitheater construction.[186]

The formalization of the military amphitheater seems to some degree dependent on the permanence of the military installation. Legionary headquarters were more likely to build less ephemeral amphitheaters of stone, and, in many places, originally wood and earth constructs were rebuilt in cut stone as the years went by and the camp became a city. This phenomenon belies the argument that the military amphitheaters were not amphitheaters per se but rather should be understood as *ludi*, their elliptical shape and surrounding seating reliant on training concepts instilled by the gladiatorial *doctores* assigned to the legions.[187] Such arguments stress the priority of weapons training and tactical practice in these structures, going so far as to question whether the military amphitheaters were ever used for spectacle, the civil function. An inscription from Carnuntum indicates that one of the loges for dignitaries was reserved for military officials, one for municipal, which would suggest that Carnuntum's military amphitheater was indeed used both for training and to house spectacles.[188] The presence of gladiators on the frontier indicates that the amphitheaters displayed spectacles at least occasionally. The typical lack of provision for special effects in military amphitheaters is more likely due to budgetary considerations than to their exclusive function as training grounds. This is not to deny that these arenas did have a military function: they were built at the same time as the camp, and they can be found in strictly military locations. The amphitheater, as we have seen, was a multipurpose building, and the fact that it filled a fundamental military need does not mean that the soldiers were not also subjected to spectacle.

TECHNOLOGY

Once the sponsor had declared himself or had been selected, the plans were made, and the construction contracts were signed, at last came the actual building of the amphitheater. As with all other aspects of amphitheatrical building projects, the actual construction required choosing, from a variety of options, the method and means best suited to the financial, material and manpower resources of the situation, that is, an amphitheater type that would fit into the terrain and fulfill the needs of the sponsoring municipality.

Golvin analyzes amphitheaters by structural concept, segregating extant buildings into two major categories: the so-called *structure pleine* and *structure creuse*, by which he means amphitheaters that rely on earthworks or modified earthworks for major support and those that utilize freestanding constructs around voids (i.e., vaulting) for weight-bearing elements.[189] The distinction is somewhat arbitrary, and construction of amphitheaters can be better analyzed as falling somewhere along a continuum, ranging from buildings dug entirely from the bedrock to earthworks supported by retaining walls of various degrees of technical sophistication, to entirely freestanding structures making full use of the best in Roman public architecture, combining utility and practicality with classical grace of form. Along this continuum are also ranged amphitheaters that combine structural concepts. Tarraco's amphitheater, for example, is dug out of the bedrock on the northwest but is supported by masonry and concrete vaulting on the southeast.

Earthwork amphitheaters were relatively simpler than those constructed with freestanding voids, and thus tend to be slightly earlier, at least in terms of the monumental examples of this species. The location of the amphitheater in the terrain was important, as it was easier and cheaper to take advantage of natural slopes or hollows, limiting the need for artificial support structures. The arena was usually dug out of the earth, which was then used as the basis of support for at least part of the seating.[190] The remaining seats could be cut out of the hillside. This was the basic form taken by the earthwork structural concept, but architectural embellishments of various sophistication could modify the standard. Retaining walls, for example, could incorporate interior galleries for more efficient movement in the structure.

The heavy, compact character of the earthwork type was the source of its limitations. The fundamental technical problem was in retaining the earthen embankments against the weight of the monument and the inherent tendency of earthworks to settle and spread, exerting a lateral force on retaining walls, which thus had to be quite strong. The problem increased with the size of the structure. It was also difficult to maintain a steep slope on *caveae* that used only embankments for support. The width of the *cavea* could be decreased, but this placed limitations on the size of the amphitheater. Without building a complex infrastructure to retain the soil, like that seen at Verulamium, the earthwork type of amphitheater has an upward limit on size (see Fig. 31).

Efforts were made to solve these problems within the conceptual bounds of the structural type. The most obvious solution was to reinforce the earthworks with more sophisticated means for retention, such as the compartmentalized embankments. Greater familiarity with sophisticated building techniques led to the propagation of the *structure creuse*. *Structure creuse* amphitheaters might also be called "freestanding"; that is, they do not rely on the terrain nor on massive earthworks; radiating walls and vaults are the major weight-bearing structures. They are more complex and require a greater degree of technical sophistication but can be built anywhere a flat area can be created and can be extremely large and elaborate. This actually facilitated the planning process, as the amphitheater could be conceived as a whole from the outset, there being no need to incorporate sloping terrain in an aesthetically meaningful way.

The choice of construction type had a great impact on the financial side of the *ratio operis*. Building an amphitheater supported by earthworks was relatively inexpensive, as the materials could mostly be obtained on the site. Labor was the major expense. Amphitheaters partially or entirely

FIGURE 31. Aerial photograph of mixed edifice at Verulamium, showing earthwork substructure retained by rubble walls, photo by Aerofilms, published in M. I. Finley, *Atlas of Classical Archaeology* (New York: McGraw-Hill, 1977), p. 26.

dug out of bedrock, as was done at Tarraco, were similarly cheap for the same reasons (see Fig. 32). Once masonry came to be a major factor in the building concept, even if only used for veneer and in conjunction with concrete, costs could skyrocket, depending on the local availability of stone. Labor costs also increased, as stonecutting was a skill that required years of training. Higher quality stone was more difficult to work with and thus required even greater skill. A building plan incorporating Graeco-Roman architectural orders, worked in marble, with decorative sculptural elements and the like, was a very expensive building indeed.

Once a conceptual type was chosen, a site well suited to take advantage of natural resources had to be selected. It was easiest to build outside city walls, to avoid demolition of existing structures and to allow space for crowds and amphitheatrical extranea when the structure was in use. The selection process is exemplified by the choice of location for the Colosseum, which combined practical with political considerations. As the property had been considered an Imperial possession, there was no need for Vespasian to purchase additional land or dispossess inhabitants. There was also no need for demolition of existing structures, as the lake bed merely had to be drained of its water to be made usable.[191] Public land that had been usurped for private use was thus graciously returned to the Roman people.

The next step involved the preparation of the area for construction. Depending on the amphitheater type chosen, the labor force could simply clear and level a sufficiently broad expanse or provide additional support for the building. The Flavian Amphitheater, for example, was built on top of a large pad, extending beyond the foundations of the building proper, which provided a unified and cohesive support for the amphitheater. After a space had been cleared, the planners traced the ellipse.

There are several easy ways to form an ellipse, such as stretching a line between two points or a drawing a series of lines perpendicular to the designated long axis. The Roman method of tracing the amphitheatrical ellipse, however, seems to have relied on four centers, from which lines were stretched to determine the outline of the structure and the placement of the radiating walls in the freestanding buildings. The two centers located on the short axis were positioned roughly midway on the bisected axis. The centers on the long axis were located approximately at one-third

FIGURE 32. Amphitheater at Tarraco, showing bedrock that underlay original seating, photograph by author.

intervals. The shape of the ellipse achieved using this method is some-what more elongated than a true ellipse.[192]

The specifics of amphitheater construction from this point can best be understood by example. The most spectacular example, as well as the one that has received the most intensive scrutiny, is the Colosseum. Acclaimed by Martial as one of the world's wonders from its birth, the Flavian Amphitheater was designed to be the most prestigious locale for blood games of power and politics.[193]

Begun in around A.D. 75, the Colosseum, although incomplete, could host games in A.D. 80 for its dedication, with final touches added through-out Domitian's reign. Hordes of laborers, skilled and unskilled, worked on the project, which incorporated 100,000 cubic meters of travertine in the façade alone.[194] Some 400,000 cubic meters were used in the whole building, which would have mandated that two hundred cartloads of stone be brought in each day during construction.[195] The travertine was quarried below Tivoli and taken by barge down the Anio and Tiber rivers and then hauled to the building site.[196] Deep ruts in the paving of the up-per Via Sacra may have been the result of this constant traffic for the Colosseum. Such was the intensity of the pace set by Vespasian, who wanted the positive feedback resulting from rapid completion of an ad-mittedly huge building project.

Slight differences in the construction suggest that the work was di-vided into four quadrants, each let to a different contractor (or under a different supervisor), with varying construction values.[197] This distribu-tion of the burden would allow for constant progress, as would the use of different materials. When winter's onset disallowed the pouring of con-crete, the focus of the work could shift to an area using less concrete.[198] Handling of the different fabrics also suggests a high level of technical so-phistication, as heavy tufa and travertine appear at lower levels, while the relatively less dense peperino, brick, and cement were used on the upper storeys.[199]

The building sequence of the Flavian Amphitheater has been recon-structed by G. Cozzo, whose outline is widely accepted.[200] Once the foundations had been laid, the outer façade of the structure was built to the top of the second storey, decorated with engaged Ionic columns (see Fig. 33). Behind the façade, two concentric walls were next erected. The work crew then put in a series of travertine piers, the main weight-bear-ing elements, to the point at which they made contact with the seating,

FIGURE 33. Colosseum, outer façade, photograph by author.

incorporating concealed springings within the fabric of the piers to support vaults that would be built later in the construction process. When
the piers attained their full height, the annular barrel vaults, destined to
link the concentric walls into a cohesive structural unit, were built, starting with the topmost vault (see Fig. 34). By putting in the topmost vault

FIGURE 34. Colosseum, annular vaulting connecting outer and inner façade, photograph by author.

first, the builders were able to proceed on two fronts: this vault provided support for construction above the second storey[201] and shelter during inclement weather for work below the second storey.[202] The basic structure of the peripheral galleries was now in place. Next the workers fabricated brick arches to link the individual piers, one with the next, in a

FIGURE 35. Colosseum, brick radial vaulting underlying seating, photograph by author.

direction perpendicular to that of the annular, concentric vaults. The brick arches would eventually provide major support for the sloping radial barrel vaults underlying the seating (see Fig. 35). With the construction of the brick arches, all the basic structural elements were in place, forming the skeleton of the Colosseum. It is believed that work had advanced this

FIGURE 36. Colosseum, view of interior, photograph by author.

far by the death of Vespasian in A.D. 79, forming the basic minimum structure within which to hold the dedicatory games in 80.[203]

Under Titus the third tier of the façade was added, which is the extent of the building as it appears in the reliefs from the contemporary Tomb of the Haterii.[204] Domitian built the fourth-storey façade, decorated with

Corinthian pilasters. Piers and vaulting were added to that already *in situ* to allow for a third level of seating. A fourth-storey interior colonnade was then put in, using the Roman Composite order.[205] The Flavian Amphitheater complex was completed by the addition of three levels of arena substructures, including a subterranean link to the contemporary *Ludus Magnus* (see Fig. 36).[206]

TICKETS AND SEATING

Fronto attributes great importance to the Games in the maintenance of the sociopolitical order: "Government is proven no less by its shows than by serious matters . . . the entire populace is united by spectacles."[207] But far from flinging the portals open wide to all comers, Roman law and custom restricted attendance at the spectacles to selected representatives of the *universus populus*. The regulation of seating at the amphitheater must be considered along with other economic aspects of the institution; the whole notion of selective access to the *spectacula* suggests that these structures were built with a particular audience in mind. As with so many aspects of the amphitheater, the basic conceptual formulation of seating was developed during the Early Principate.[208]

The *lex Julia theatralis* was part of Augustus' sweeping program of social reform, intended to represent the restoration of traditional Roman values and customs.[209] In this case, restricted seating in the theater and at other spectacles can be seen as the public replication of the Roman hierarchy in an idealized form. What had been *spectandi confusissimus ac solutissimus mos* was now given order and expanded to cover the seating at gladiatorial shows as well as ludic games.[210]

The lengthiest account of Augustus' specifications is in Suetonius and is more clearly understood with reference to the technical names applied to seating in Roman spectacle buildings.[211] The largest division of seating in the Roman amphitheater, for example, is the *maenianum*. The three *maeniana* in the Colosseum divide the seating area into horizontal sections, which in turn are subdivided into *cunei*, or wedges, *ordines*, or rows, and *loca*, the individual seats. In Augustus' regulations, the *primus subselliorum ordo* was the area reserved for senators. *Ordo* in this context refers to a horizontal row of seats, also called a *gradus*, and in this case was the row closest to the performance area, directly above the podium wall. Vestals were to sit in this section, but *separatim et contra praetoris tribunal*, that is, in their own separate grouping across from the tribunal. The specific word choice for the Vestals' seats in this row is most interesting, as it makes sense in terms of amphitheatrical seating, where tribunals were situated at either end of the arena's short axis, but not in theaters per se, where the tribunal was centrally located in the *cavea* with only the stage placed opposite. Foreign ambassadors, who used to sit with high-ranking Romans, were now to be excluded from this area. Soldiers were separated from civilians, married citizens had their own *ordines*, and boys and their tutors were assigned to their own *cuneus* or wedge. Boys may therefore be understood as having their own sections within the *maeniana* assigned to their particular social group. Women were relegated to watching *ex superiore loco*, usually interpreted as the topmost rows of seating, and no *pullati* were allowed in the *media cavea*.[212]

Other brief references to the *lex Julia theatralis* fill out the picture somewhat. Pliny describes it as clarifying and making more strict the equestrian right of sitting in the first fourteen rows, that is, the first section of seating, which would translate in the amphitheater to the first *maenianum*.[213] Pliny also tells us that citizens who had earned the *corona civica* were privileged to sit between the senators and the equites, which would be the first row of the first *maenianum*.[214]

What was the "extremely lax and confused" system the Augustan regulation was meant to reform? As we have seen, Republican *munera* were held in the Forum Romanum, where the space available for spectators was limited to the area not already taken up by public monuments and the like. Some Roman notables were able to avoid tussling over space limitations by acquiring reserved seating one way or another, but these seem to have been the very few, and the majority of the attendees had to struggle for access to space that could probably not even accommodate the ruling class in its entirety, let alone the enthusiastic population.[215]

Cicero's *Pro Murena*, in its discussion of whether Murena's habits of seat distribution at spectacles constituted electoral bribery or not, has implications for access to seating. The *ambitus* legislation of 63 B.C. was being tested on L. Licinius Murena, currently running for consul. Cicero had played a key role in this legislation, in an effort to tighten up the limitations on candidates' activities. Traditionally, the ruling class, acting as individuals, controlled access to the games sponsored by others of their number by handing out passes to their clientele inside Rome and outside. This had been the "system" for generations, as Cicero explains, that "either out of political ambition or generosity," the well-off Romans see to "the rewards and advantages poorer men acquire . . . according to long-standing tradition."[216] These generous or ambitious members of the upper class had, in turn, apparently received blocks of seating from Roman officials and magistrates, including the consuls and Vestal Virgins, who gave them to friends, family, and connections, the *propinqui et necessarii*.[217]

Part of the new limitations on candidacy for public office concerned *munera* and "whether places at gladiatorial games were to be given to the crowd . . . seemingly in opposition to the *lex Calpurnia*."[218] What particular aspect of giving seats *vulgo tributim* was the problem? The *tributim* is usually interpreted as the key word here, and the distribution of seats according to voting tribe as the crime involved. It does not seem likely that tribal distribution would have been regarded as a questionable practice; the audience may have sat in tribes regularly, as Mommsen contended was the case in the Roman theater.[219] The same may have been true for the gladiatorial spectacles, if we are to understand the *curiae* inscribed on seats in the amphitheaters at Lambaesis and Lepcis Magna as synonymous with *tribus*. Instead, the focus should be shifted to the word *vulgo*. Cicero clarifies later on that the Senate thought it a crime to give seating at spectacles to the crowd, with no discretion.[220] Apparently Murena had given tickets to all and sundry instead of his *amici, propinqui, necessarii*, and *tribuli*, as was the more standard practice. The fact of his candidacy may also have annoyed his rivals. It is likely that Murena, by making a show of providing a plenitude of tickets, wanted to capitalize on the political value of *munera* without actually breaking the law by being an *editor* himself.[221] Cicero argues against the extension of the limitations on editorship to include ticket distribution. He claims that such practices are founded in tradition, that "all these are the obligations of friends and relations, the just returns of poor men, and the official duties of candidates."[222]

The humbler Romans, or those who lacked important tribal or social connections, may have gained access to the *munera* only by paying a steep price for the privilege, a practice suggested by the arena incident from the career of Gaius Gracchus.[223] For *munera* held in the Forum, the magistrates of 123 B.C. built seats all around and rented them out. Gaius saw this as discrimination against the poor, who could not afford to pay for the seats and who could not otherwise even see the show, as their view would be obstructed by the seating structure.[224]

This then was the system used during the Republic: the producers of the individual shows gave blocks of seat passes to political associates and supporters, who did likewise. Any remaining seats could be sold at the discretion of the *editor*. There was considerable reform in the Principate, as was true for so many of Rome's political customs. Augustus enacted legislation to extend the social distinctions enforced previously at the theater to cover the audience at the *munera* as well. He then further elaborated on these regulations, specifying who, exactly, could sit where and with whom, with the result that the traditional aristocratic privilege in seat distribution was limited, because the best seats were barred to all but the aristocrats themselves.[225]

Stratification at spectacles was also enforced outside Rome proper, as part of the municipal charter imposed by the central government. The *lex Ursonensis* provides some information on the strata, where the proximity to the performance was determined by the level of sociopolitical importance.[226] In the lowest seats, next to the arena, were the decurions, with whom sat the augurs, pontiffs, and any Roman senators who might be present. Above this *ordo* were the equites, although whether these were equites by reason of their property or in terms of political function is not clear.[227] Above the equites were *coloni coloniae*, then *incolae*, those who lived in the surrounding area. Those who were not *municipes* were the most distant from the arena, with *hospites*, or resident foreigners, sitting in front of the *adventores*, visitors who were in town perhaps specifically for the *spectacula*.[228]

Is this a replication of the Roman model? The *lex Ursonensis* seems to place more emphasis on the distinction between local and extralocal spectators. This may simply be a realistic acknowledgement of the circumstances for spectacle outside Rome. Rome was inhabited by perhaps a million people, only fifty thousand of whom could be stuffed into the Colosseum.[229] The size of other western amphitheaters was much greater relative to the size of the city and could therefore hope to accommodate more than just the local inhabitants. There was, therefore, need of legislation to regulate this.

It is more important, however, to focus on the apparent emphasis placed on being a *municeps* in the Urso restrictions. This was a two-way relationship between an individual and his home town. He was obliged to perform duties for the *municipium* but was entitled to privileges in return, such as preferred seating at local spectacles. The Roman seating can also be interpreted along these lines, as Augustus did not intend simply to enforce and solidify his idealized image of social stratification but to make a distinction based on level of political involvement and responsibility. Thus foreigners and women, both denied suffrage, were shunted off to the farthest seats to squint down at the distant action. The emphasis placed on traditional Roman dress at public spectacles further stresses this distinction.[230]

Additional evidence from the provinces heightens the complexity of the seating scenario, as it deals with collegial activity in the public sphere. Inscriptions have been gathered from several amphitheaters, which allot seating to what may have been *collegia*, in this case groups of people sharing a profession.[231] At Nîmes, the merchant marines had their own designated section, at Arles, seats were set aside for *pastophori* and *scholasticii*.[232] Golvin tries to fit this practice into the Augustan scheme based on social hierarchy, although he admits that this provincial means of establishing social ranking seems rather different from that in the capitol. It is possible, however, that these *collegia* were allocated seats by the *ordo* due to their corporate sponsorship of part of the building project. Such seating grants were made at Pompeii, when an association of the *magistri* of a suburban district contributed to the renovation of the spectacle seating.[233] Something of this nature may also have happened in Rome in the Late Empire, when the name of a known restorer of the seats in the Colosseum appears in a number of places, possibly indicating his permanent control over those particular *loca*.[234]

The possibility for seat rental may have continued into the Imperial period, as the sources seem to offer some evidence for places at spectacles available for purchase. Dio Cassius tells of a two-day *venatio* given by Caligula in the Circus Maximus to celebrate the birthday of his sister Drusilla; Dio specifically notes that these seats were offered *proika*, "for free," which suggests that the spectacle would not otherwise have been free of charge.[235] This is especially surprising, given the venue. The Circus Maximus held some 200,000 spectators and had few practical means of controlling access. Suetonius describes a situation that took place during Caligula's reign, when some places in the circus were *gratuita loca*, that is, free, and members of the public camped out from the middle of the night to get seats, more than twenty Roman equites among them.[236] This may suggest not only that paying seats existed, but that they were probably expensive, since members of the relatively wealthy equestrian class were driven to camping out for free ones. Alternatively, one could apparently acquire tickets through a *locarius*, or ticket scalper.[237] The situation outside Rome may have been comparable, as one inscription from Cirta speaks of revenue *ex reditibus locorum amphitheatr. diei muneris*, that is, from payment for amphitheater seats on the day of the event. The *lex Ursonensis*, however, makes no reference to payment for seating at spectacles.[238]

Who would be inclined to seek financial profit from amphitheatrical *munera*? Not the euergete acting as an *editor*. The emphasis placed by the ancients on the generosity of such a benefactor excludes the possibility of his somehow recouping his losses. Those motivated by politics and competition for status would find their reward in increased public prestige rather than in a newly swollen wallet.[239]

Ville suggests that the individual city, or the *princeps* at Rome, could collect an entry tax at the *spectacula* (except on seats reserved for the privileged class) to pay for expenses that the *editor* had not taken into account or simply as a source of revenue, as at Cirta. Alternatively, such a tax could support the maintenance of the amphitheater and arena, a task that must be performed whether games were going on or not.[240] The evidence, scanty and incidental as it is, points to no obvious explanation.

Because of the role of the amphitheater as a tool for public manipulation and control, its construction was subject to central control. All amphitheaters, therefore, were built under the auspices of the emperor, who in some cases provided the actual funding and technical means of construction, for both civil and military amphitheaters. Most civil amphitheaters, however, were the creations of local inspiration; they resulted from a corporate impetus, that is, the municipal *ordo*, or from the drive of an ambitious individual euergete, who could use the construction of an amphitheater, a grand gesture of public-minded generosity, to enhance his reputation, maximize his political success, and guarantee some measure of immortality, albeit on a local level.

The means and motivations for amphitheater construction fit snugly into the larger context of Graeco-Roman euergetism, as interpreted by Augustus, the first *princeps*. Under his auspices the administrative system of public construction was revised to bring maintenance under governmental control while allowing the glory from new construction to accrue to private individuals and ultimately to the emperor, as patron of all. Under Augustus the first amphitheater was built in Rome. Under Augustus the amphitheater was incorporated into the Imperial Cult, as part of the venue for public demonstrations of loyalty to the regime. Augustus also designed the audience to be impacted by the amphitheater, by legislating seating restrictions that were ultimately based on the individual's relationship to the regime. These restrictions were in effect throughout the empire, as spectators were granted good seating according to their status as *municipes*. Augustus' demonstrable interest in construction and in the institution of the amphitheater as part of his new Imperial vision make it highly likely that he was the one who mandated that all amphitheater construction be subject to the approval of the *princeps*. Augustus, then, was the means and instrument of the amphitheater, the node for the system of construction.

V. THE MAGIC RING
Human Sacrifice in the Arena

Then out spake brave Horatius,
The Captain of the Gate:
"To every man upon this earth
Death cometh soon or late.
And how can man die better
Than facing fearful odds,
For the ashes of his fathers
And the temples of his gods?"

THOMAS BABINGTON MACAULAY,
Lays of Ancient Rome

HOW ARE WE TO RECONCILE the bloodiness of the arena and the events it sheltered with the arena's centrality in Roman society? The issue is an uncomfortable one. The standard assessment suggests that as the *munera* became purely a spectacle, they became more murderous because the public wanted to see blood.[1] That the people of Rome were able to indulge this degenerate desire was merely due to the degraded status of the professional gladiator. The determination of the trend in scholarship thus to secularize, even to trivialize, the arena does not sufficiently address the fascination it held for Rome and the avid support it enjoyed from the Roman State.[2] We must look elsewhere for elucidation.

One method that may provide some enlightenment is that of ethnographic analogy, in which we look for similar practices outside the Roman context in an effort to construct a general pattern for the purpose of comparison.[3] What function did the ritualized slaughter of human beings play in other societies? Can we see the same forces at work in the Roman example? The sacrificial patterns of the Aztecs, Incas, and Carthaginians and the practitioners of funerary sacrifice in Sumeria, China, and Dahomey offer some insights into the motivation for human immolation and its association with the maintenance of an authoritarian power structure. The practice of human sacrifice in the Roman context also points to a cultural disposition toward this sort of activity, which may have influenced the form taken by the amphitheatrical complex during the Roman Empire. The *munera* must be interpreted as ritual based in the sacrificial structure and imbued with its essence.

The suspicion that gladiatorial combat is a form of human sacrifice affects our assumptions about the social institution symbolized by the amphitheater. I propose that the amphitheater was a politicized temple that housed the mythic reenactment of the cult of Roman statehood. The struggle of the gladiator embodied an idealized and distilled version of the military ethic of *Romanitas*. His death served as a foundation sacrifice that answered the crisis of empire, validating the Roman struggle for power and offering a model for understanding the basis of Roman power.

PATTERNS OF HUMAN SACRIFICE

Human sacrifice may be defined as killing with spiritual or religious motivation, usually accompanied by ritual and performed in a sacred place. In the absence of a temple, a magic ring drawn on the ground would serve.[4] Human sacrifice is a social act, one found usually among human societies at a relatively high level of sophistication. Indeed, the manipulation of broad-based power seems to be intimately connected to the practice of human sacrifice. It is not simply the powerful using the lives of the weak as fodder for the savage hungers of a cruel god. Human sacrifice is a collective activity, undertaken by the representatives of the community on its behalf. It can therefore be taken as evidence not only for high civilization but also for the individual's strong identification with the needs of the unified system and willingness to give them priority above his own.

Human beings have been sacrificed for a variety of purposes: in ceremonies accompanying foundations, at funerals, and as special victims in state cults.[5] René Girard depicts the ritualized killing of human beings not as a mere gift to the deity nor as an act of communion with the entity; instead he draws a close connection between violence in human society and human sacrifice. He connects human immolation with what he calls the "sacrificial crisis" of the state, a response by a primitive society in which the absence of a true judicial system inhibits the prevention of the escalation of violence through secular means. The violence threatens to cause irreparable damage to the social fabric. This crisis must be addressed by the spilling of human blood in an effort to bring back social and cosmic order.[6] Girard places too much emphasis on "primitivity" and the perceived lack of a judicial system; the result is that many known practicers of human sacrifice would be excluded from his pattern. This difficulty is resolved by Hyam Maccaby.

The societal importance of human sacrifice is likewise emphasized by Maccaby, who interprets this kind of immolation as historically connected with some great event or critical situation, especially the foundation of a city, a nation, a tribe, or a religion.[7] When great danger threatens a political or religious body, desperate measures to avert this danger are necessary. The community must be refounded, reborn, with this renewal validated and protected by the offering of a human life.[8] Maccaby sees human sacrifice as "foundation sacrifice," with "foundation" understood not merely as a referral to the physical construction of a city or building but as the construction of a community identity based on political or religious ideology.

The patterns of human sacrifice described by Girard and Maccaby are played out historically over a wide time span, the participants including such disparate groups as early humans in France, ancient Sumerians and Carthaginians, and modern inhabitants of the Andes. Human sacrifice takes place as part of state cult, not in a private context. The ritualized death of human beings is carried out specifically on behalf of the community as a whole, whether that community is understood as a patriarchal tribal unity, as incarnate in the person of the ruler, or as a relatively sophisticated Imperial administration. A closer examination of the human sacrificial pattern in different societies may clarify the function and meaning of this practice.

Aztec and Inca

In the early fifteenth century the Aztecs and Incas transformed their social complexes into the most effective mechanisms for conquest seen in the New World, dominating the largest states ever formed by Native American peoples. They did so through the revision of traditional religious concepts into a militaristic ideology focused on and fed by human sacrifice.[9] The immolation of human beings had long been a part of ancient American cult practice, institutionalized with the earliest rise of complex social systems.[10] The Aztec and Inca Empires centralized the traditional cult and directed it toward purposes of political expansion;

they also greatly increased the demand for victims, whose blood literally fed the state.

The Mexica, or Aztecs, began their rise to power as highly stratified warrior bands, rewarded for their mercenary activity with land and the tribute it produced. As their skill in warfare increased, so did their area of domination and their reliance on tribute in the economic system.[11] The leaders shifted the focus of religious practice to the cult of the sun, dominated by the militant deity Huitzilopochtli, who represented the powers of good in the constant universal struggle against darkness and death. Huitzilopochtli demanded continual expansion of the Aztec Empire because of his ever-growing need for the nourishment provided by human sacrifice, the majority of victims being prisoners of war.[12] Should this nourishment not be provided, then the Mexica, indeed, the entire universe, was threatened with annihilation.[13]

Human sacrifice fueled social mobility as well. The warrior class and the Pochteca, or merchant class, were organized hierarchically, with progress through the ranks joined closely to performance in the Imperial Cult. Acquiring victims for sacrifice, either through capture in battle or by purchase, allowed one to rise in his own social group or even to jump barriers between classes.[14]

For the rulers of the Mexica, Huitzilopochtli's power was a divine parallel to their temporal authority, the hearts of the victims analogous to the tribute demanded by the empire.[15] In addition to the autocratic political rhetoric of the ideology, Aztec rulers manipulated the rituals themselves for political purposes, using the spectacle and blood as a means of impressing, and implicitly threatening, rivals with the power of Huitzilopochtli and the state identified with this deity. For example, Moctezuma II invited enemy leaders to his inaugural celebrations in which the best of their warriors were slaughtered by the thousands, surely a powerful object lesson for those concerned.[16]

The ideological complex surrounding ritual slaughter provided the incentive for social change and military success within Aztec society, but in the long run this momentum could not be maintained. The Aztec imperialist style did not encourage assimilation or integration of conquered territories: the acquisition of tribute was their main concern, and that acquisition was eventually hampered by the ritual decimation of potential food producers. When the growth necessary to the state ideology could no longer be supported, the social dynamism dependent on sacrifice also was stymied. The top-heavy Aztec social structure began to feel the strain from internal conflict. The empire of the Mexicas was crumbling from within by the time Cortés arrived.[17]

The Aztec experience offers several general parallels to the amphitheater. Masses of enemy soldiers were ritually killed in front of large crowds. This event was supposed to inspire militarism. It was seen as something characteristic of the special leadership qualities of the Aztec, as a representation and as an explanation of the process of acquiring an empire; its practice was encouraged as part of the transmission of empire. It had social and political implications for the sponsors of the activity, both the emperor and those lower down on the ladder of power. This general pattern for human sacrifice can also be found south of Tenochtitlan, the details diverging but the overall message remaining consistent.

Although it was once thought that the Inca ruled a peaceful state centered on an innocuous solar cult, scholars have increasingly recognized that human sacrifice was a tool used by the Incas to maintain social, political, and economic control over their expansive empire. Indeed, the extension of imperial control was accomplished by a combination of military conquest and reciprocity, in which the best gift of all was a human sacrificial victim. Once new territory was incorporated, victims continued to be a medium of exchange, as administrative positions were acquired and public works were pushed through by deals made in human blood. Forming both vertical and horizontal ties, victim/gifts bound Inca society together.[18]

The Incas sacrificed numbers of select children, chosen from noble families for the perfection of their health and personal attractiveness. Twice a year, at the solstices, carefully prepared representatives of the best each administrative district had to offer came to the capital of Cuzco. Crops, domesticated animals, and children were paraded in the most lavish finery, accompanied by gorgeous works of art. There the victims were lectured concerning their new role. They were told of the great good their deaths would bring the Incas and of the new status awaiting them as ambassadors to the gods and as localized minor divinities themselves. Solemn processions would then begin at the Temples of the Sun and the

Moon and wend their way out again to the periphery of the empire, making sacrifices at strategic and cultic locations throughout Inca lands.

The child victims were called *capacochas* or *capac hucha*, which can be translated as "royal sin." The explanation of this term centers on the notion that the Inca ruler incorporated the Empire within himself; his illness or misbehavior could have a dreadful effect on the well-being of the state. The victims embodied the ruler's impurities; with their deaths they drew the evil away from the living.[19] The young were also sacrificed to alleviate drought, illness, earthquakes, hunger, and inclement weather, to celebrate a military victory, to ward off military defeat, to encourage the fertility of the earth, to hail an emperor's assumption of power, to commemorate the death of an emperor, to welcome omens of prosperity, and to ameliorate omens of disaster.

Sacrifice was performed in high places, such as the plain of Nazca, where decapitation and the cult of the head played a role in Andean water and fertility cults, or on mountains far above the altitude at which regular human habitation can be sustained.[20] Inca peak sanctuaries were located off the Royal Inca Highway, the major road system that provided communication for the empire. Mountain locations were chosen for a variety of reasons. Mountains have often been seen as sacred areas, as a result of their dominance of the landscape and their inaccessibility. Andean peoples associated mountains with the fertility of the earth, because of the crucial importance of the water supplied by melting snow. The most powerful Andean gods were gods of the mountains.[21] When the Incas conquered the Andean area, they incorporated the pre-Inca sacredness of the mountains into Imperial ideology. Mountains became political boundaries, as the control of water resources was a major concern to Inca administration. The mountains had to be controlled on a spiritual level as well, which the Incas did by removing the cult images of the local mountain gods to the capital city and by building new shrines on the peaks to supplant the local worship with a specifically Inca cult, focused on the Inca ruler. The state cult thus redirected and absorbed the respect, awe, and even terror felt for the mountains.[22]

Like *munera* given in amphitheaters in the Roman sphere, Inca sacrifice can be interpreted as a means of exchange operating on a social rather than an economic level. The provider of the victim would be incorporated into the power structure of the overlords, while the victim was a symbol of the giver's good will and active labor on behalf of the state. The sacrificer was an euergete, and the human token of his status was ritually absorbed by the state at monumental "magic rings" that defined the boundaries, physical and ideological, of the Inca realm.

Carthage

The name "Tophet" in the Bible refers to a place in the Valley of Ben Himmon, south of Jerusalem, where the ancient inhabitants of Israel performed *molech*, the sacrifice of children by fire.[23] The modern attribution of this practice to Phoenician customs, in combination with archaeological evidence, has led some scholars to suggest that the children's cemeteries at Carthage and other Phoenician sites should share the name of "Tophet" equally with the one near Jerusalem.[24]

The Tophet at Carthage was densely populated, with the remains of well over twenty thousand children providing evidence for more or less continuous sacrifice for nearly six centuries, beginning around 750 B.C., roughly contemporary with the founding of the colony.[25] Here young children were offered to the deities Tanit and Ba'al Hammon in a ritual described by Greeks and Romans, a ritual that seems designed to capture the essential purpose of the sacrificial act in as graphic a way as possible. The young victim was placed in the arms of the bronze image of Ba'al Hammon, arms that sloped downward toward a pit or large brazier filled with burning embers.[26] Once the child had been cremated, the ashes were removed and placed in an urn, which in turn was placed in a pit, sometimes lined with cobbles, and then covered over. A burial marker, a *cippus* or stela, was then often placed above the urn. Sometimes several cremations shared an urn; sometimes several urns shared a pit.

The evidence from Carthage, like that from the other examples, belies the traditional, evolutionary perspective of human sacrifice, that is, as human society "progressed" and became increasingly "enlightened" and "civilized," animal sacrifice was preferred to human, only to be eclipsed itself by inanimate symbols of religious communion. At Carthage, however, expansion of the political hegemony, cultural sophistication, and child sacrifice simultaneously peaked, in the fourth and third centuries B.C., due no doubt to the observed effectiveness of child sacrifice in promoting the success and prosperity of Carthage and its elites. The expansion of *molech* was due no less to the increased perception of vulnerability sudden success may awaken.[27]

The epigraphical evidence indicates that child sacrifice was performed, largely by members of the upper class, in fulfillment of unspecified vows. Some have wanted to associate the *molech* with the law of the first born, which in its biblical form demanded that on the eighth day of life, the first born of both men and domesticated animals be handed over to god. The excavators at Carthage question this assumption, given the presence of multiple victims, presumably from the same family, and given the relatively advanced age of some victims, which ranges from neonate to four years.[28]

The ancient writers indicate that civic crises brought on bouts of child sacrifice, which was resorted to as a means of propitiating the gods and averting disaster. Diodorus Siculus describes such a spate of immolation in 308 B.C., inspired by the invasion of Syracusan forces and by a governmental coup. Panicky and anxious to atone for any possible cultic neglect, the nobles of Carthage sacrificed some two hundred of their children.[29] The excavators of Carthage, however, aver that such mass sacrifices were rare, as they have found no evidence for this activity in the archaeological remains.[30] In fact, there is a trend in modern scholarship to secularize child sacrifice at Carthage, with Stager and Wolff suggesting that the motivation for the *molech* was the regulation of population growth, seen as economically desirable for a moneyed class interested in consolidating the wealth of the family. In the latest phase of the Tophet, Carthaginians of poorer classes would have joined their betters in child sacrifice, as a hedge against poverty. The ritual nature of the undertaking thus becomes a matter of "formalization" and "institutionalization," fully supported by Carthage's leaders.

The interpretation of *molech* as population control is weak on several levels. From a purely practical point of view, if one wishes to reduce the population, one should reduce the number of breeding females and therefore practice female infanticide, a preference hinted at by the excavators in their description of infanticide as allowing for sex selection.[31] Females in antiquity endured a lower social status in general, perceived as less desirable in the abstract and in the concrete as a drain on family resources from one who would leave the family unit on marriage anyway.

One would expect, therefore, to find a predominance of female sacrifice victims at Carthage. The admittedly meager evidence does not, in fact, support this. The bones of the Tophet belonged to individuals too young to allow sexing, but the animal victims commingled with them tended to be male and may provide an analogue for the human *molech*. More persuasive evidence can be gained from the biblical references to the practice of *molech*, in which the preferred victims are the *sons* of the participants, not the daughters.[32]

The biblical descriptions refer to the sacrifice of princes; would royalty feel severe economic constraints? Indeed, why would the central government support population control among its elites? In comparison, the Roman State at its peak of prosperity was very much concerned with promoting the fecundity of its ruling classes, not with sponsoring minimal population growth. Given the expansionism of Carthage, surely the limitation of potential leaders and bureaucrats would be seen as disadvantageous to its long-term interests.[33]

The most compelling argument against the interpretation of child sacrifice as birth control is based on the domination of the religious element. To assume a double motivation, religious and economic, in the Punic worshippers of Tanit and Ba'al Hammon is to assume a conscious devaluation of the human victim. The child was due to be discarded anyway; the hungry gods of the Tophet would hardly be satisfied with the rejects of the faithful.[34]

The evidence from the sources suggests that the custom of child sacrifice was linked to the role of the nobility in governance of the state. Child sacrifice at Carthage may have functioned much as did the Incan *capac hucha* system, with the blood of victims cementing the vertical and horizontal power relationships within the social structure. Ultimately, however, we return to *molech* as described by Diodorus Siculus. He clearly identifies Carthaginian human sacrifice as a response to a perceived threat to the state. In Carthage, Girard's "sacrificial crisis" provoked the outpouring of the blood of children, historically in 308 B.C., and archaeologically, over the passage of centuries.[35]

Ur, China, and Dahomey

Sacrifice performed at the royal funeral, in a broad spectrum of cultures, was meant to honor the king and to provide for him hereafter. The ceremony served to increase the social gap between royal and nonroyal: the ability to command such powerful ritual demonstrated the elevated status of the late dynast and strengthened the position of the living ruler. This validation of the social hierarchy therefore resonates with the use of human sacrifice in the New World and in Carthage. And as we have seen elsewhere, this form of sacrifice was undertaken in response to serious social crisis. The occasion served as a means of providing stability during a transitional period. The communal expression of formalized grief acted to channel the range of emotions generated by the political change and to focus those passions on the funeral ceremony itself, a ceremony filled with blood and splendor but a ceremony which had specific limitations in time and space. On a practical level, therefore, the disruption of the social group could thus be managed, controlled by the governing body. The replication of death through the sacrifice of retainers had deeper implications. By incorporating death into the ritual performance, it too becomes subject to control. Death is mastered by the new master.[36]

This practice has a very long history; the unnatural deaths of their retainers at the funerals of the great may be a custom dating as far back as twenty thousand years before Christ, as suggested by burials in the Charente region of France.[37] With increasing cultural sophistication, funeral sacrifices acquired elaborate archaeological documentation.

In 1927 Sir Leonard Woolley began to excavate the royal cemeteries of Ur. There he found the richly decorated tombs of Sumerian royalty of the Early Dynastic period (roughly 2600–2450 B.C.), in which the lordly deceased were fully outfitted for the needs of the next life, which required the presence of their trusty steeds, their musicians, their guards, and their attendants, who had willingly followed their masters into death. In the sixteen tombs excavated by Woolley, dating to around 2800 B.C., the chief corpses, isolated in their own privileged chambers, were accompanied by between six and eighty of their retinue, sacrificed as part of the elaborate ritual surrounding the royal funeral. There was no violence involved: the victims had either drugged themselves into a stupor or had taken a fatal dose of some narcotic prior to burial.[38]

The surviving cuneiform texts from Sumer make no reference to this ritual in connection with the death of kings. For this reason, the burials at Ur have, at times, been interpreted as evidence for fertility celebrations, in which the Corn King or a functional cognate ensures the seasonal growth of the crops with his own ritualized death. Subsequent discoveries of similar, and definitely royal, tombs, albeit from a later period, seem to verify Woolley's reconstruction of Sumerian regal funerals as an expression of political authority rather than the promotion of agricultural fecundity.[39]

Strikingly similar to the royal burials at Ur were the graves at Anyang, of the kings of China's Shang Dynasty, despite the chronological and geographic differences.[40] The central pit housed the king's burial chamber, a wooden room elaborately decorated with paint, inlay, and stucco, much as his quarters in the palace would have been. Once the royal body was interred, the sacrificial ceremony began, with a long period of time allotted for the deposition of grave goods and human victims within the tomb.[41] The king's chamber was surrounded by four sloped passageways, oriented to the points of the compass, which held the beheaded bodies of his retainers, buried in groups of ten; more were buried beneath the floor level of the royal chamber. The king himself was buried in grand isolation.[42]

The key point is that the sacrifice of thousands of retainers at the royal funeral arises alongside developed urbanization, the formation of differentiated social groups, the organization of sophisticated governmental systems, and the spread of sophisticated bronze technology and writing systems. In other words, the use of mass sacrifice of humans is a product of the process of "civilization" and the generation of a state society.[43]

The sacrifices at royal funerals continued throughout much of China's early history. Further archaeological evidence comes from the time of the Wei State, in the fourth and third centuries B.C., when one prince was accompanied by 99 female attendants.[44] Unlike the Sumerian examples, the Chinese custom is documented by contemporary literature. Ssuma Chien records the deaths of the sovereigns of Ts'in in the seventh century B.C., such as Wu, who took 66 people with him into the grave, and Muh, who was followed by 177 of his court, including prominent ministers who apparently freely decided to accompany the ruler. Following the unification of China under the Han Dynasty in the later third century B.C., literary attestation of this custom dies out, although there is archaeological evidence for its continuation into the fourteenth century after Christ.[45]

Evidence of human sacrifice in the West African kingdom of Dahomey comes from several centuries of occasional contacts made by European travelers, beginning with the Portuguese in the fifteenth century.[46] The presence of Europeans on the coast acted as a stimulant to the slave trade, which became a factor in the local economy and a spur to conquest.

There was some tension between the desire for material gain available through slave trafficking and the need for captives to be used as sacrificial victims. Any captives sold as slaves deprived the royal ancestors of victims and vice versa. Nevertheless, the expansionist agenda needed for the acquisition of large numbers of victims also worked for the acquisition of slaves.[47]

A British sea captain named Snelgrove witnessed sacrifice in Dahomey in 1727. Most of the sacrifices were meant to keep the dead king supplied with servants and news from the world of the living. The sociopolitical purpose behind the sacrifices was that common to royal funerals: to ease the transition between rulers and to enhance the status of the new ruler by placing him in a position of authority. This was accomplished at two major festivals: the Grand Custom, or *akhosutanun*, which was the funeral on the death of the ruler, and the Annual Custom, or *khwetanun*, in which his royal heir yearly commemorated his death.[48] Like the Roman funeral *munera*, the Grand Custom was often delayed, here by several years, to acquire enough victims.

A French visitor, M. Lartigue, witnessed the Grand Custom of 1860, which involved the death of perhaps 1,000 victims over several months. These victims included the regular retinue of the deceased king, his wives, his Amazon retinue, and captives from raiding expeditions.[49] A *dokpwegan*, or representative of each class, village, and occupation, was also sacrificed. Thus the whole of Dahomeyan society, symbolically, joined the dead king in his new existence. The remaining residents went into deep mourning, neglecting the necessities of daily life in a demonstration of the impact of the crisis generated by royal death.

The most detailed description of the Annual Custom comes from Richard Francis Burton, who witnessed the events of 1863.[50] The ceremony took place at "victim sheds" or "palace sheds," partially covered platforms erected outside the town. The victims, distinctively clothed in shirts, shorts, and pointed caps, were tied to stools inside the sheds, where they were fed well and attended by slaves for days. The victims were at last placed in baskets, lifted high overhead and tossed from the platforms. After they hit the ground, they were beheaded and mutilated and left as carrion.

The sacrifices of Dahomey were largely part of the royal ancestor cult.[51] In addition to the Grand and Annual Customs, the king was obliged to keep in regular contact with his dead father, reporting on all current events, no matter how trivial, by sending a message via sacrificial victim. Only the king had the prerogative of human sacrifice. The Customs also benefited the whole of Dahomey, as the royal ancestors ensured military victory. Martial success, in turn, guaranteed a continuing supply of victims for the customs, creating a feedback loop not unlike that of the Aztecs.[52] But the ceremonies also provided an occasion for the revalidation of Dahomeyan hierarchy, displayed in lavish, spectacular form before the whole of society present at the Customs. The king was seen to distribute the benefits of the Customs, reinforcing his connections with other elements of the community through exchange of gifts and sacrifices, often using the same backdrop and ritual as the human sacrifices. Gifts were thrown from the platform, just as were the sacrifices. As he handed out the gifts, the king would say, "Eat of life," articulating the true nature of the royal bounty.[53] He also forged other links with other displays of royal prerogatives, dispensing justice, redistributing tribute, making political decisions, and participating in other religious rituals to enhance the impact of the Customary spectacle of authority.

In terms of superficial details, the funeral sacrifices of Ur and China do not provide a direct analog for the early gladiatorial combats, although both involve death in honor of the powerful deceased. The status of the victims is different: the household of the king died in Ur and China, while the *munera* set prisoners of war against each other. The nature of the death also differs, in that the Roman context is much more violent than the Sumerian and Chinese. The West African royal funerals are slightly closer to the early Roman *munera*, in that spectacle played an important role and prisoners of war became a valuable commodity in the course of providing for the Grand Custom and the Annual Custom. Human immolation at Ur, China, and Dahomey is nevertheless analogous to Roman practice, in terms of its administration as a state-run institution and of the close ties to the cult of the sovereign and its clarification of the essential difference between the elevated, almost godlike, status of the ruler and those he ruled. The societal vulnerability caused by the death of the ruler necessitated the response of human sacrifice as a means of offsetting the crisis of the state and marking the transferral of power and the renewal of the social identification of the community. As we have seen, this motivational pattern, of crisis and potential instability answered by human immolation, shapes the sacrificial complex in a variety of societies. It is fully a part of the Roman dynamic of human sacrifice, both in the *munera* and elsewhere.

The Graeco-Roman World

The ancient Mediterranean presents evidence for a different type of funerary sacrifice with human victims: the immolation of prisoners at the tomb of a dead warrior, especially a warrior killed in battle. The classic example of this practice is the activity at the funeral of Patroclus as described by Homer in *Iliad* 23. Achilles makes careful arrangements for this sacrifice, breaking off his murderous rampage, as

> . . . when he wore out his strength in killing, he took twelve captive youths from the river, to be blood satisfaction for dead Patroclus, son of Menoitios.[54]

In contrast to the heedless, bloody-minded excess of Achilles' seeking vengeance on Hector, the sacrifice of twelve Trojan youths was orderly, with exacting specifications apparently planned well in advance. Homer implies that this arrangement was a long-standing one between Achilles and Patroclus, made as part of the cementing of their bond, as Achilles indicates in evoking his dead friend: "For I am now doing for you all that I promised previously. . . . I have sacrificed before the fire twelve splendid children of Troy."[55]

The death of the twelve Trojan youths was accomplished as part of the lighting of the funeral pyre, clearly part of the reverent disposal of the corpse rather than the more secular part of the funeral festivities. After the flames died down, the bones of Patroclus were carefully gathered and placed in a golden jar. The Trojan bones remained among the dead ashes, mingled with what was left of the hero's horses, the other victims sacrificed to Patroclus.[56]

Closer to home, Etruscan Italy may have performed analogous sacrifices in honor of their war dead, to judge from the evidence of the literary sources. Herodotus describes the massacre of Greek prisoners by the Caeretans after Alalia.

> After the ships were destroyed, the Carthaginians and the Etruscans drew lots for the captives; of the Etruscans, the Caeretans got most of them, led them away, and stoned them to death.[57]

Livy describes another immolation of Roman prisoners, this time en acted by the Tarquinians in 358 B.C.: "Nor was the destruction in the line of battle so hard to accept as the fact that the Tarquinians sacrificed 307 Roman captives."[58] The Romans were to take vengeance on Etruscan captives, ritually slaughtering the defeated foe as a means of getting even with Tarquinia.[59] Iconographical evidence from the Etruscan sphere, specifically the frequency of the theme of Trojan sacrifice at Patroclus' funeral on Etruscan pottery, may also point to the customary use of ritual killing as Etruscan public demonstration.[60]

In 72 B.C. another such incident took place, which is most provocative, considering that the actors were, themselves, gladiators. After the defeat of Crixus by a consular army, Spartacus sacrificed 300 Roman prisoners to the spirit of his deceased colleague.[61] Here a distinction in treatment is clearly being drawn between the 300 Romans whom he sacrificed and the totality of the remaining prisoner group, whom he simply destroyed. For Spartacus, this action resonates with multiple meanings. The funeral sacrifice to Crixus is conflated with a foundation sacrifice, as Spartacus immediately sets off for Rome, a new and potentially cataclysmic campaign that would surely warrant the highest sacrifice. The irony of the ritual being performed by a gladiator would not have been lost on the Romans, nor, it is likely, on Spartacus.

Blood sacrifices at funerals can be understood as grossly analogous to regularized animal sacrifice, in its provision of some sort of nutrition to the wispy surviving spirit of the dead, blood being in some sense the distillation of the life force. Human blood, being the most vivid reminder of his former existence, would surely be the most effective nutrient.[62] The sacrifice of a captive had further significance, in that the *anima* of the deceased could thus have its ethical or emotional needs met as well. The death of a prisoner would be morally satisfying to the dead man, as a sort of vengeance exacted upon those responsible for his death.[63] It is in this spirit that Mark Antony killed Hortensius at his brother's tomb.[64]

This interpretation of human funeral sacrifice, however, only scratches the surface of the meaning of immolation. Humans provided victims at the funeral feasts only of great men, never the lowly, and the position of these men as leaders of society is crucial to the understanding of the sacrificial act. The choice of human victims sets the deceased apart from his fellows and emphasizes his importance not merely as a "great man" but also as someone imbued with a more-than-human essence to warrant such honors. The sacrifice acts, therefore, as posthumous exaltation of the community's leader, a validation of the vertical hierarchy. But the performance of human sacrifice is also undertaken in compensation for the loss of such a personage to the community, with the immolation acting as a means of offsetting the debilitation caused by his absence and the social disruption of the resulting rift in the social structure.[65]

The overdetermination or many-layered motivation for human funereal sacrifice can be applied to the obsequies of Patroclus. Achilles, by definition, was driven by rage. No doubt he derived personal satisfaction from killing some of the people responsible for the death of his friend. The satisfaction was meant to be shared by Patroclus, toward whom Achilles directed the sacrifice.[66] The death of the Trojan prisoners took place, however, in a public context, carefully arranged as a performance before a designated audience of military personnel. The heightened ceremony surrounding this sacrifice was intended to revitalize the Achaean sense of community and cohesiveness, strengthened by the blood of a dozen youths of doomed Ilium.[67]

HUMAN SACRIFICE IN ROME
Commuted Sacrifice

The evidence for human sacrifice ever having been a regularized part of Roman cult is elusive and scattered widely but can be analyzed as documentation for several different types of sacrifice.[68] The first type of evidence is in the area of "commuted" human sacrifice, in which, it is suggested, manufactured humanoid figures or some such substitute came to be offered to the deity in place of actual living beings. All instances of "commuted" sacrifice are associated with the religious calendar; all connections with human sacrifice were made by ancient commentators.[69]

The *Compitalia* was celebrated in early January, in honor of the Lares *compitales*. Sacrifice and public games commemorated the holiday, with special sacrifices performed at the crossroads. Macrobius claimed that Tarquinius Superbus had restored an ancient rite belonging to this festival, by sacrificing boys to Mania, or Larunda, mother of the Lares.[70] After the expulsion of the bloodthirsty Tarquins, heads of garlic and poppies took the place of human heads.[71] The link between Tarquinius Superbus and supposed human sacrifice is highly suggestive. The last of the Tarquins came to assume a role in Roman folklore as the stereotypical bloodthirsty and cruel tyrant; on the other hand, the Romans often portrayed the Etruscans as the purveyors of time-honored customs, particularly religious ones. Here, the two motifs are combined as Macrobius fleshes out an explanation for archaic ritual in Roman festal celebrations. The overall result may say more about the role played by Tarquinius Superbus in Roman tradition than about the historical development of cultic practices in the *Compitalia*.

At *Saturnalia* offerings of *sigillaria* were made, small pieces of terracotta or hard-baked dough in human shape, which Macrobius saw as remnants of the human sacrifice offered regularly on that holiday in archaic times.[72] This blood sacrifice was abolished by Hercules upon his return from Spain, and the *sigillaria* substitutes were offered ever after.

Hercules appears again in the gentle role of ameliorator of blood sacrifice, specifically, the immolation connected with the *Argei* celebration of mid-May, then as now a topic of confusion and controversy.[73] The venerability of the festival is acknowledged by Livy, who credits Numa with the establishment of a number of rituals and locations for this festival.[74] Varro offers more specifics, noting that there were twenty-seven shrines of the *Argei* distributed throughout the Subura, Esquiline, Colline, and Palatine districts, named *Argei* after the Greek chieftains who came to Rome with Hercules and eventually settled in Italy.[75] Overcome by nostalgia for their homeland, they flung themselves into the Tiber or gave orders that their remains be given the chance to seek the shores of the Argolid by way of the Tiber. Varro explains that the despair of the Greek settlers is commemorated every year by the pontiffs, who fling twenty-seven small human images made out of wicker into the Tiber, presumably to seek their spiritual home in the Argolid.[76]

By far the lengthiest discussion of the *Argei* appears in Ovid's *Fasti*, wherein he cites no fewer than three traditions concerning the origins of the festivities.[77] The central act, the throwing of effigies woven of rushes from the Pons Sublicius, is briefly described, giving primacy to the Vestals as sacrificial agents. Ovid then assures his audience of the falsity of the senicide or euthanasia *aition* of the *Argei*, in which feeble oldsters were hurled into the river to empower the votes of younger citizens. Ovid also discards the hoary tale that Jove demanded two human lives to be sacrificed to the sickle-bearing Old One in the river, sacrifices commuted by Hercules to *corpora falsa*, an alteration that found favor among the Quirites.

The Tiber himself rises from his bed to explain the true source of the *Argei* to Ovid and his audience. Hercules came to Italy,

> but his followers refused to go any further. A large part of them had come from Argos, now deserted. . . . Often, however, they were touched by bittersweet longing for their homeland, and one, when dying, gave this brief command: "Throw me into the Tiber, so that carried on Tiberine waves my useless dust may reach the Inachian shores." The specifications for burial disturbed his heir: the dead foreigner was buried in Ausonian soil; an image woven of wicker was thrown into the Tiber instead of the master, to find once more its Greek home across the distant seas.[78]

The crucial elements of the myth are present: the Greek companions of Hercules, the longing to reunite with the Greek *patria* at last and the possibility or threat of consigning honored senescents to the waters.[79] In this last version all traces of human sacrifice have been removed, and the heirs of the Argei show proper filial piety in their reluctance to dishonor their parents' corpses by refusing them burial in this way. Their decision to use woven effigies reduces greatly Hercules' particular role as civilizing influence.[80]

The antiquarian interest in the *Argei* shown by Ovid and others was shared by venerable modern aitiologists. One reconstruction relies on a perceived opposition between the *Argei* and the non-Argive populace of Rome.[81] It may be that the *Argei* effigies were supposed to represent Rome's enemies, drawing on the alleged connection between the origin of Rome and ancient Troy, the legendary foe of Argives everywhere. The annual sacrifice of proto-Rome's primal enemy may have been designed to promote military success. This explanation stretches the evidence too much, however, given the lack of bellicose paraphernalia or referents beyond the name *Argei*.

Mannhardt proposed that the effigies symbolized the dying of the "vegetation spirit" in the spring, to be thrown into the water and return anew the next year.[82] He supported this contention by using nineteenth-century European peasant customs as comparanda: the peasants did indeed interact in this way with the image of the vegetation spirit. The date, however, of the Roman rite, in mid-May, is not a very convenient time for the death of the vegetation spirit, being between sowing and harvest time. Mannhardt rationalizes this by suggesting that the ceremony was originally in midsummer but shifted when the calendar was reformed, a solution that is surely far too ingenious.

Frazer saw nothing very vegetal about the ceremony, particularly as the effigies were specifically woven from rushes, not corn, and rushes played no prominent role as a food staple in European agricultural communities.[83] The Vestal Virgins and pontiffs were also not overtly concerned with the ritualization of the agricultural cycle.

Frazer then, like Ovid, brings up a "straw man" explanation for the rites of the *Argei*. He points to Plutarch's reference to the purificatory nature of the *Argei* and its temporal conjunction with the *Lemuria* festival on May 13, suggesting that mid-May may have been a good time to exorcise the demons and evil spirits that had accumulated through the year.[84] He draws a comparison to the biannual practices of Guinea, where the community loudly frightens wicked ghosts and demons into the containment of wickerwork figures, along with ashes from the hearth and other household refuse. The figures are then thrown into the river, whereby they are swept out to sea.[85]

Despite the charm of the Guinea account, little of the atmosphere of exorcism lingers in the Roman *Argei*. Although in some sense the effigies were felt to represent the spirits of the deceased, in myth they were hardly malignant entities but honored forebears and part of Rome's heroic origins, seeking the romantic melancholy of a posthumous return to their homeland.

Frazer no doubt draws on this link with Rome's origins in his interpretation of the *Argei* as a commuted foundation sacrifice. The construction of bridges was a risky undertaking, one that required the ritual appeasement of various divinities and an entire college of priests to do so. The arrogance of humans seeking to overcome natural obstacles might offend the godhead in general; the river god might feel anger and frustration on being robbed of his natural prey by a bridge, which no doubt decreased the number of drowning victims substantially. By throwing in substitute victims made of rushes, the Romans may have been able to pacify the Tiber, lest he rise in anger and snatch his due from Rome's streets in flood. The sacrifice took place on the Pons Sublicius because of its primacy as the first bridge built in Rome, commemorated in the venerable song of the Salii.[86] The annual commuted sacrifice of the *Argei* therefore fits into the proposed pattern of human immolation as a foundation sacrifice of such importance to the archaic Romans as to find its way into the religious calendar, to be commemorated annually, even after its original meaning has been largely dissipated by time.

Not Commuted

There are a number of rituals performed by the Romans in historical times that lack tiny human images but nevertheless smack of human immolation.

The *Ver Sacrum* was a rite common to several of the Italian peoples, in which there still lingered a hint of human blood. The ritual was undertaken in response to crisis in the community, famine, plague, or other imminent danger. All living things born during the spring were designated as sacred to the gods and liable to sacrifice, should the gods act to remove the threatening disaster.[87] The immolation of youthful humans and beasts was later commuted to exile upon maturity, a development that Varro linked to overpopulation.[88]

This sort of emigration formed the basis for the origin myths of several Italian tribes, including the Samnites, the Hirpini, the Picentini, and the Mamertini.[89] The *Ver Sacrum* appears in the Roman context not as this sort of ritualized colonization but as a typical wartime vow; young humans were not among the designated victims. The first instance recorded was in 217 B.C., after Lake Trasimene, when Hannibal's rapacious presence to the north was taken as a sign of divine displeasure, due to Flaminius' neglect of proper ritual ceremony.[90] The Romans turned to the Sibylline Books and vowed games, temples, supplication, and a *Ver Sacrum* in return for the granting of victory, plans officially ratified by the vote of the People.[91] Livy's citation of the official decree contains the basics of the *Ver Sacrum* offering:

> Let the Roman People, the Quirites, offer up in indefeasible sacrifice to Jupiter what the spring shall have produced of swine, sheep, goats, and cattle that shall not have been consecrated to some other deity, beginning with the day which the Senate and People of Rome shall have designated.

Did the *Ver Sacrum* ever involve the death of Italian youths? The historicity of such a sacrifice eludes us, but what is important is its symbolic value to the ancients. They understood the *Ver Sacrum* as commemorative of human immolation, and its association with the foundation of various Italian tribes makes its adherence to the proposed pattern for human sacrifice clear. The shift to the military sphere that took place under the Romans is typical, as the association between human sacrifice and military endeavor is one that permeates Roman thought, as will become apparent.

There is fairly late, Christian, and possibly apocryphal evidence for human immolation at the festival of Jupiter Latiaris, where a gladiator of some sort was regularly put to death, a practice Minucius Felix found appropriate for the son of baleful Saturn.[92] The literary context of these citations is problematic, as the *Feriae Latinae* sacrifices appear as part of what seems to be a standardized list of alleged human sacrifices found worthy of polemic. Other items on the list, notably the Forum Boarium sacrifices and Carthaginian infanticide, are better documented and may argue for the validity of the *Latiaris* immolations as well.

Warde Fowler admits the existence of the Jupiter Latiaris sacrifice but denies the Roman-ness of its character. He suggests that this was a late practice inspired by the bloody rites of Oriental cults, in combination with the jaded brutalization of the Roman mindset by the activities of the arena.[93] His attribution of blame to the arena for this aspect of bloody Roman practices adds a curve to the circularity of the argument: was the arena bloody because of Roman nature or was Roman nature bloody because of the arena? The obscurity of the Jupiter Latiaris ritual in the sources fatally impedes full scholarly analysis, but Jupiter as head of the Capitoline Triad and of the state pantheon may have accepted human victims in another context, that being the execution of justice.

It is difficult to draw a clear distinction between capital punishment and sacrifice to the state gods.[94] After all, in a nonsecular society, he who transgressed the law not only challenged worldly authorities, he angered the divinities represented by those authorities. Capital punishment, as the expiatory sacrifice of the criminal, deflected the rage of the gods from the community and restored the *pax deorum*.[95]

The relationship between execution and expiatory sacrifice is tacitly acknowledged by the Roman criminal code, which refers to the *consecratio*, as it were, of the criminal, in which he is made *sacer* and the property of the gods. We see this in Festus, for whom "he is a *homo sacer* whom the People have condemned because of criminal activity."[96] *Sacer esto* as a penal formula acknowledges the ultimate responsibility of the gods for imposing punishment on convicted criminals: the death of the one convicted is the transferral of jurisdiction from terrestrial to celestial authorities. Execution is simply a means of delivering the malefactor to the gods.

Capital punishment was, at times, openly ritualistic. Pliny tells of the special disposal of the harvest thief, whose death was offered to the goddess Ceres.[97] Punishment of the Vestal who broke her vow of chastity is of this order as well. Her pollution could infect the intimate relationship between the gods and the Roman State, so she was buried alive to turn aside the wrath of the gods at a community that allowed such impiety.[98]

The importance of ritualized capital punishment to the understanding of the arena is readily apparent, as the participants in the *munera* were frequently chosen by the judicial system. Criminals were sentenced to the *ludi* and to the arena. Victimizers of the system thus quite literally became its victims.

The sources are willing to consign human sacrifice to the religious calendar of the distant past, a distancing device if ever there was one. There may be a self-congratulatory element in this, as Romans are depicted as having learned the ways of "civilized" Mediterraneans long, long ago. This is an image common to the European West, where only primitive forebears and Other People offer up human sacrifices. In Rome, much of the ritualized shedding of human blood was placed in its acceptable Roman context in which the widespread slaughter of human beings was not unusual but expected and even demanded: warfare.

War

The success of a particular campaign depended upon the good will of the state gods. The official conclusion of the campaign was marked by sacrifice made in thanks for the glory achieved by divine sanction. The sacrifice was the essential act and the defining characteristic of the Triumph.[99]

Everything centered on the state cult. The triumphator took on the aspect of Jupiter, the procession wended its way toward the Capitolium, and the gods received the best of the booty, to be displayed in permanent tribute to their beneficence, munificence, and magnificence. Given the overwhelming religious aura suffusing the Roman triumph, the execution of the enemy commander takes on new significance.[100]

The placement of the principal captives in the order of the procession marks their true nature as offerings made sacred to the gods. First marched the group of magistrates and senators, a distinct element in the *pompa*. Then came a group of *tubicines*, whose fanfare announced the coming of the "victims and offerings" group, who marched in ascending order of their importance as sacrifices. The material spoils and representations of the conquest came first, followed by the filleted oxen and the Camilli, animal victims and their despatchers. The chief adversaries, bound in chains, rounded off the grouping. The commonality of these three components was indicated by their separation from the rest of the triumphal procession, a separation defined by the presence of the heraldic element, before and behind the group. The next element of the *pompa* was the general as Jove epiphanate, announced and marked by the lictors.[101]

The procession halted at the end of the Sacred Way, where the principal captives were beheaded or strangled. This had to be done before the ritual could continue.[102] The *pompa* then climbed the Capitoline Hill to the temple of Iuppiter Optimus Maximus, where the animal victims were killed. The material spoils were then deposited in the temple, set apart from the mundane world as sacred and special. The sacrifices, therefore, took place in decreasing order of magnitude: humans, animals, and objects.[103]

The distance between the designated victim and the Roman people is apparent in the triumph. The enemy is objectified, apart, one of the spoils of war that properly belonged to the gods. This separation between the victim and the community is, however, often blurred in the Roman context. The victim is strongly identified with the community and its needs and can be comprehended as a symbolic representation of the Populus Romanus. The Roman world fostered a strong tradition of self-sacrifice on behalf of the community, a tradition which can best be understood as *devotio*. Although *devotio* is best known from its Republican military context, the activity appears among civilians and in peacetime as well.

The prime example of the devotion of the selfless civilian is that provided by M. Curtius in 362 B.C. When an ominous chasm opened in the Forum, it was known that the gap could only be filled with Rome's most precious treasure. Livy says:

This was in fact what the priests prophesied must be delivered to that place, if they wanted the Roman Republic to live forever. Then M. Curtius, a youth well-known in warfare, scorned those who doubted whether there was anything more precious to Rome than arms and military prowess, and in the following silence he contemplated the temples of the immortal gods that loomed over the Forum and the Capitol and raising his hands, now to the sky, now to the earth, gaping open to the infernal deities.[104]

Curtius proclaimed his devotion to the state and, clad in armor, mounted on his trusty steed, flung himself into the abyss, which promptly closed over this epitome of manly virtue. Crowds of men and women threw offerings and first fruits after him. Martial flavor suffuses Livy's account, despite the civic context.

The primary use of the *devotio* was on the battlefield, when the military leader offered his own life to the gods in exchange for the destruction of the enemy. Livy provides a detailed description of the ritual involved in association with the Great Latin War of 340–338 B.C.[105] There had been some ambiguity in the auspices taken before a battle in Campania in 340, and then the Roman effort had begun to slip. The consul, Decius, spoke to his colleague, "Marcus Valerius, we need the help of the gods; you're a pontiff of the Roman People, so dictate the ritual formula with which I can devote myself on behalf of the legions."[106] Upon Valerius' advice, Decius put on his toga, veiled his head, thrust out one hand from his toga, touched his chin,[107] and spoke the following while standing on a spear:[108]

O Janus, Jupiter, Father Mars, Quirinus, Bellona, Lares, New Gods, National Gods, Gods who have authority over us and over the enemy, Infernal Gods . . . afflict the enemies of the Roman People, the Quirites, with terror, horror and death. . . . I devote myself, with the legions and auxiliaries of the enemy, to the Infernal Deities and to Earth.[109]

It is notable that, although the consul seeks the blessing and assistance of quite a collection of gods, he offers himself (and the enemy) as victim only to the Infernal Gods, the Di Manes, and to Earth, or Tellus, both chthonic deities. Decius then put on the Gabian cincture and charged into battle.[110] Filled with berserker rage, his terrible aspect threw the Latins into disarray. When he fell, he earned the praise of all the Roman people, since "he averted onto himself alone all the menace and danger from gods above and below." The Latins fled the field in august terror.[111]

Livy goes on to add that the consul, dictator, or praetor who devotes the legions of the enemy need not devote himself but could designate a particular legionary. If the man offered up as substitute victim does in fact die, fine; if not, an image of him must be buried some seven feet below ground as a *piaculum caedi*, an offering to atone for depriving the gods of their due.[112] Should the general devote himself and fail to be killed, he was barred henceforth from full participation in cult practice.[113]

Livy explains his digression into the particulars of the *devotio* by asserting that

I have decided to report these things unchanged from the original way in which they were formally expressed and handed down, exact in the words themselves, even if the memory of all traditional practices, divine and human, has been abolished, preferring everything new and foreign to the ancient and native.[114]

By this, Livy may imply that the battlefield use of *devotio* had gone out of use by his own time, but it seems clear that he finds the practice *priscus*, ancient, and *patrius*, traditionally Roman; this contrasts sharply with Dio Cassius' assessment of the Imperial *devotio*.

The ritual of the *devotio* continued in the Imperial period, although with a definite shift in context and focus. An example of this new style of *devotio* took place during one of Augustus' bouts of illness.[115] Sextus Pacuvius offered his life in return for Augustus' recovery, which Dio, interestingly, disconnects from the Republican *devotio*, asserting that in so doing, Pacuvius followed Iberian sacrificial practice.[116] Comparable instances, with grimmer Imperial responses, took place under Caligula.[117]

The victim of the *devotio* is self-determined. His death is meant to divert divine wrath to the appropriate, non-Roman target. The practice of *devotio* is in many ways analogous to a practice seldom specifically connected to ritual, the custom of single combat.[118] During a lull in battlefield activity, a champion from one side would challenge the opposition to meet him in single combat. The two armies would not participate directly in the action but were spectators to the drama and witnesses to the honor earned by monomachists. These duels seem to have prevailed in the Republic, appearing in the literary record sporadically from prehistoric times until at least 45 B.C. When the leader of the Roman forces, acting as champion, killed the leader of the enemy, he earned the *spolia opima*, the highest military accolade.[119] Here the motivation of self-sacrifice is linked with typically aristocratic military achievement, which takes the form of a battlefield spectacle. The glory and honor to be gained as a champion must have influenced the Roman perception of the *munera*, lending the games some of its golden aura.[120]

The triumph and the *devotio* incorporate human sacrifice into the military sphere as a positive element, which served to enhance the critical nature of the situation. The survival of the Roman State was at risk in warfare. Human immolation in its martial context is very much part of the sacrificial pattern, acting as a means of reestablishing group identity and encouraging renewed success at a time of societal crisis. Sacrifice is more than a positive factor in Roman military success; it is presented as an absolute necessity for the continuance of the community. The power of human sacrifice as a symbol of Rome at war is evident when the image appears in political rhetoric as a perversion of Roman military ideals.

Inflammatory Reports

The literature records other instances of human sacrifice in a military context, notable for the personal, directed hostility apparent in the source. These are not so much simple, descriptive narratives as they are invective. Whether and how much we should disregard the evidence is, therefore, an important consideration.

A contemporary rumor held that the Catilinarian conspirators drank human blood mixed with wine, as reported in Sallust's account of the intrigue. "After the oath, they all tasted it, just as is the custom in solemn rituals . . . and because of this they used to say they would better keep faith with one another, each aware of the other's great shame."[121]

Sallust clearly presents the ritual as typically degraded Catilinarian criminal activity but not as entirely unusual, as even, perhaps, to be expected in such a conspiracy. The sacred aspect of such a plot is a topic Cicero plays with as well. He refers to gruesome rituals performed to sanctify the knife to be used in his own assassination and a blasphemous shrine at which Catiline made spiritual preparations for the murder of Roman citizens, clearly vituperative rhetoric on Cicero's part and only indirect evidence for Catiline's bloody ceremony.[122]

The incident may have been fabricated after the fact by supporters of Cicero, in response to the backlash against the consul's actions. Alternatively, it may reflect a genuine Roman feeling that the risk inherent in actions of this magnitude demands that aid be summoned from all quarters, temporal and divine. Catiline's sacrifice may, in fact, be intended as a form of sympathetic magic, the offering of human blood in expectation of the civil trauma to come.

It was alleged that Julius Caesar sacrificed insubordinate soldiers on the Campus Martius.[123] In 46 B.C. Caesar was wallowing in luxurious celebrations, sheltering the audiences at his games with silk awnings and suchlike, which provoked his soldiers to riot. They wanted handouts, not all this display and pleasure seeking. They stopped their activity only with the arrival of Caesar, whose subsequent actions to discourage such misbehavior were interpreted along ritual lines.

> Two others were killed using the method of sacrifice. And the reasoning behind this I cannot say (for the Sibyl did not speak nor was there any other such oracle), but they were sacrificed in the Campus Martius by the pontiffs and the *flamen Martialis* and their heads were mounted near the Regia.[124]

Dio identifies the appropriate incentive for such ritual killings: the recommendation of the Sibyl at a time of crisis. The lack of such an oracle for this incident leaves him baffled about its true cause. The presence of the *flamen* and *pontifices* lends this event the cachet of traditional state cult. Some have compared the sacrifice to the October Horse ceremony, as the head of the horse, like those of the mutinous soldiers, was hung on the walls of the Regia.[125] Other than this detail, however, the two ceremonies are not markedly similar. Other rationalizations of this "sacrifice" are not forthcoming. Dio is the only source for these sacrifices and may have mistaken a purely military execution on the Campus Martius, somewhere near the *ara Martis*, for some sort of ritual immolation.[126] Caesar's status as pontifex maximus and his consequent association with the Regia may have further confused the issue.

Sextus Pompey was rumored to have sacrificed horses and men to Poseidon as a thank offering for his favor in 38 B.C. There had been storms. Octavian's ships had suffered. Sextus' had not, and in gratitude for this certain sign of favor from his divine forebear, Neptune, he offered up these unusual sacrifices.[127] As with the sacrifice of Caesar, Dio is the only source for Sextus' promotion of this activity. Like Caesar, Sextus Pompey had a reputation for a certain unconventional attitude toward the gods and his own relationship with divinity. These delusions of godhood may have been seen as indicative of widespread innovation in ritual conduct, the danger of which was expressed in the human blood spilled on the alleged altars of the dynasts.

Seneca, in his treatise on clemency, cites notorious incidents of Octavian's cruelty, including the proscriptions, the fact that he killed Romans at Actium, his vengefulness in pursuing Sextus Pompey, and the altars of Perusia, the *arae Perusinae*, after which events Octavian came to see the expedience of *clementia*.[128] The altars of Perusia join those of Caesar and the younger Pompey as examples of altars whose bloodstains poured from human victims.[129] The difference in this case is in the relative abundance of material concerning the incident in question: the violent repression of the resistance at Perusia.[130]

The basic story is that Octavian on the Ides of March in 41 B.C. sacrificed hundreds of Perusians at the altar of the deified Caesar to propitiate the *manes* of his adopted father. Different versions include different details. Dio states that the sacrifice took place at the altar of Divus Julius Caesar, while Suetonius locates it at a shrine of the deceased dictator, and he adds the scheduling detail of the Ides of March. Dio and Suetonius both claim that three hundred victims were involved. Suetonius seizes the opportunity to paint a fairly vehement portrayal of Octavian's brutality, as he describes him as implacably addressing all Perusian suppliants with the phrase "*moriendum esse!*" "You must die!"

Other sources are much more generous to Octavian, distancing him from responsibility for the Perusian slaughter, which they portray as executions more or less justified by the wartime context. Appian's Octavian is forced by the soldiers to execute the Perusians, and the deaths are not sacrificial. The deaths in Velleius' account are very much deemphasized, mentioned only in part of a single sentence, as owing more to the rage of the soldiers than to Octavian's will.[131] Reid agrees with Appian and Velleius Paterculus and attributes the altar, if one in fact existed, to the work of the soldiers, who, in his opinion, were also responsible for launching sling bullets inscribed *divom Iulium* into the town.[132] The existence of war materiel so inscribed has a strong flavor of military ritual, perhaps encouraged by the commander in chief, who stood to profit from such a cult in his soldiery.

Caesar's role in this instance as apparent cult focus for human sacrificial ritual is significant. We have already seen some evidence that links the ancestor cult with the shedding of human blood.[133] Vergil also seems to allude to this practice, in Aeneas' treatment of Italian prisoners of war at the funeral of Pallas. "He bound their hands behind their backs and despatched them to the infernal shades, to sprinkle the flames with sacrificial blood."[134] Vergil apparently ascribes great antiquity to this kind of immolation, which may, in fact, be a genuinely archaic Roman ritual. On the opposite extreme, Vergil may be manufacturing a heroic practice based on Achilles' treatment of the Trojan youths and locating it firmly in the Roman context. The evidence from the Perusian sling bullets and other sources suggests that such incidents were to be found in the Italy contemporary with Vergil.

The true nature of most of these "inflammatory reports" as partisan rhetoric is clear from their context. The most well documented, and therefore most difficult to dismiss, is the *arae Perusinae* episode; the multiplicity of citations of the event is independently supported by the *ballistae*. The connection with Julius Caesar points to the historicity of the event as ritual killing. The appearance of Caesar as object of cult suggests the personal involvement of Octavian, given his willingness elsewhere to countenance and even promote the cult of divus Julius. The victims here need not be considered equivalents of oxen or other standard sacrifices; they can be understood rather as analogous to the victims in a triumph or those convicted of a capital offense, with Julius Caesar in the role of Jupiter cognate.

The Forum Boarium

The most unequivocal example of human sacrifice in the Roman context involves the immolation of two couples, male and female, Greek and Gallic, who were buried alive in the Forum Boarium. The literary references to this event point to the context of the late third century, when perceived danger from outside provoked tumultuous religious response in Rome. They therefore closely fit the pattern of human sacrifice as a response to crisis, in an effort to renew communal identity and morale in a climate of blood-soaked communication with the divine. Not everyone is willing to make this identification of the Forum Boarium sacrifice, and the controversy generated by the literary references warrants further examination.[135]

Dio, as paraphrased by Zonaras, places the sacrifice among the events of 228 B.C., in which an oracle was revealed to the Romans, which claimed that Greeks and Gauls would occupy the city. To avert the prophecy, two Gauls and two Greeks, male and female, were buried alive in the Forum. It was hoped that the victims' "possession" of their tomb would fulfill the letter of the oracle and prevent a larger occupation by hostile Greek and Gallic forces.[136]

This may be the same episode described by Plutarch, dated by him to 226 B.C., a time when Roman fear of a Gallic invasion drove them into the arms of Hasdrubal.[137]

> Their preparation made their fear apparent . . . and the innovations concerning sacrifice. For they have no barbaric nor unnatural practice, but as much as it is possible in their customs concerning the gods they resemble the Greeks,[138] but at the beginning of the war they were driven to act on the instructions of the Sibylline Books and buried alive two Greeks, a man and a woman, and likewise two Gauls in the so-called Cattle Market, and even to this day, in the month of November, they do sacred rituals, unspoken and unwitnessed, with Gauls and Greeks.

Most intriguing, for our purposes, is the "even to this day" and following. The use of the dative, in the relative pronoun as well as in the ethnic adjectives that follow, is unusual. Reid discards the obvious interpretation, choosing to interpret this passage as referring to otherwise unattested secret rites that had some sort of liturgical reference to the Greeks and Gauls. Following so closely on Plutarch's description of what is clearly sacrifice, surely the lack of clarity in Plutarch's expression must imply activity similar to that in the immediately preceding clause rather than demand the invention of obscurely innovative rituals. This passage would thus further bolster Pliny's claim about the continuance of such practices into the Early Empire.

Livy's account of sacrifice in the Forum Boarium places it in 216 B.C., in the aftermath of the disaster at Cannae.[139] The historian describes a scene of terror and panic not only because of the failure of the Roman military and the imminent threat of Hannibal's invasion but also because of prodigies and portents. The Vestals Opimia and Floronia had been convicted of impurity; one had been buried alive, *uti mos est*, the other had committed suicide. The misbehavior of the Vestals, in light of the other ominous occurrences, was seen as indicative of such danger impending for Rome that the decemvirs consulted the books and Fabius Pictor was sent to Delphi to find out what would constitute appropriate ritual propitiation

> and what would be the outcome of such serious disasters. Meanwhile, some extraordinary sacrifices were made, among which were the burial alive of a male and female Gaul and a male and female Greek in the Forum Boarium in a place walled with stone, which had already been tainted with human sacrifices, not a Roman rite at all.[140]

These unusual rites were considered sufficient placation for the gods, leaving the Romans to take extraordinary measures for the defense of the City, including the recommissioning of armor from spoils and the arming of slaves.

Several particulars from the Livian account are notable. First is the connection between Vestal corruption and human sacrifice, not only in terms of the death of the Vestal involved but as a catalyst for further action that resulted in still more human immolation, deemed necessary under the circumstances. Then, Livy does not specify which books of oracles recommended this action although he does state that the decemvirs, the traditional guardians of the Sibylline Books, were the priestly group involved. In both he differs from other accounts of the Forum Boarium sacrifice.[141]

Tzetzes describes the burial of a "Greek and Galatian male-and-female pair . . . in the middle of the forum," in reference to the leadership of Fabius Maximus Verrucosus (Cunctator), which seems to relate to the same incident as the Livian account of 216.[142] Here, the sacrifice is in response to an oracle that threatened that Gaul and Greece would overtake Rome. The Greeks and the Gauls thus represent a threat to Roman well-being, and the sacrifice is intended to secure the failure of the foreign menace.

Plutarch brings up the Forum Boarium sacrifice again in a detailed account from the *Roman Questions*, a context which in itself allows no secure date for the incident.[143] The central issue that has captured Plutarch's concern is the reason Romans discourage human sacrifice among their subjects. He introduces the topic by referring to the Bletonesioi, who, being barbarians, wanted to offer up human victims to the gods. The Romans would not allow it, a refusal that Plutarch finds surprising, citing the Forum Boarium incident as evidence for the Roman use of human sacrifice.

There are two parts to the question Plutarch asks, issues which pertain to the whole institution of human sacrifice in the Roman world. The first part is concerned with divine spheres of influence and whether it is wrong to offer human sacrifice to the gods *(theois)* per se, such offerings being appropriate rather to the *daimosin*, here to be interpreted as infernal deities or Di Manes. The second part of the question deals with the legitimacy of the authority that orders such sacrifice and whether such immolation is wrong when commanded by law and custom *(ethei kai nomoi)* but legitimate when ordered by Sibylline Books *(ek ton Sibylleion)*. This presents the controversy as one over the regular performance of human sacrifice versus its occasional use in extraordinary circumstances. The persistence of the Sibylline Books in the Roman story may suggest that the Romans found only the extraordinary context valid.

Plutarch proceeds to tell the tale of Helvia, a Vestal Virgin whose immodest death by lightning was regarded as indicative of corruption among them. Corruption was found, indeed, and the Vestals were punished. The Sibylline Books were then consulted concerning the purification needed; the oracle ordained the sacrifice of two Greeks and two Gauls.

The Helvia story appears elsewhere in reference to events of the year 114 B.C., which is usually accepted as the appropriate date for this third Forum Boarium sacrifice.[144] These other accounts, however, do not link the Helvia episode causally with the Forum Boarium activity. Livy's account says the Sibyllines demanded the erection of the Temple of Venus Verticordia to atone for the Helvian Vestals, not the sacrifice of foreigners. Plutarch is in fact the only source for human sacrifice in the Forum Boarium in 114, which has been interpreted as the confused conflation of three originally distinct events: sacrifices of the Bletonesioi, that of Helvia, and that of the Gauls and Greeks at the Forum Boarium.[145]

The Bletonesioi appear nowhere else. It may be that these are the inhabitants of Bletisa, in Spain.[146] Reid agrees that the barbarians involved are Iberian but thinks either the manuscript or Plutarch may be in error and that the incident took place among the Lusitanians. He reconstructs the situation as a reference to Spanish rebellion in the mid-second century B.C. Reid's Lusitanians performed these sacrifices as part of their war preparation, the bloodiness of the ritual but a pale precursor of the anti-Roman hostility to come. Livy may describe the same episode, when the immolation of a man and a horse by the Lusitanians provoked Servius Galba to launch a preemptive strike against them, although a peace treaty was still in effect.[147] The argument is strained and problematic, as Reid's identification of the Bletonesioi as rebellious Lusitanians, doomed to be brutally quelled by Roman might, jars with the rest of Plutarch's account, in which a rational exchange of cultural viewpoints leads to no bloodshed on either side.

The corruption of the Vestal Virgins is associated with the Forum Boarium sacrifice in Livy and in Plutarch. Why was an additional sacrifice needed, beyond the death of the Vestals? The imminent threat posed by the state being at war is not sufficient provocation, in Reid's view. After all, the Roman State was so frequently at war.[148] He postulates that Livy and the others derived the story from later annalists, who creatively used the peculiar means of punishing a Vestal in conjunction with the existence of walled underground chambers in the Forum Boarium, very similar to those near the Colline Gate for the Vestal penalty, to weave a tale of human sacrifice connected to the Vestal scandals in 216 and 114. Reid here provides another ingenious rationalization to deny a form of immolation he finds disturbing. Granted, Vestals were walled in, granted, sources say this took place at the Colline Gate. There may have once been a walled chamber in the Forum Boarium. But what possible reason could annalists have for creating the fiction of Gallo-Greek sacrifices out of whole cloth? Livy's account seems to preserve the evidence of Fabius Pictor, an eyewitness to these events. Surely it is easier to accept such testimony at its face value than rely on Reid's hitherto-unknown secret Gallo-Greek rites in the Forum Boarium, whose mystery fostered rumors of human sacrifice.

Others have likewise emphasized the Vestal connection but in a somewhat different manner.[149] Cichorius denied the influence of perceived danger from outside, attributing all human sacrifice to the dreadful sacrilege of Vestal misbehavior. In his analysis, the pollution of the Vestals presented a sufficiently grave threat to the city to warrant extreme ritual actions to remove the pollution. While Vestal misconduct was indeed a serious offense, this reconstruction is also problematic, in that it requires excessive manipulation of the sources. The Forum Boarium events are in all accounts distanced causally, if not chronologically, from Vestal misbehavior; indeed, the sacrifices of 228 are not connected with a Vestal scandal at all.[150]

Eckstein's explanation of these sacrifices emphasizes the consultation of the Sibylline Books as the immediate catalyst for action. The Sibylline Books were usually consulted after a series of portents generated great concern in Roman hearts, as prodigies were seen as indicative of divine displeasure and evil times ahead for Rome, unless decisive actions were taken.[151] In Eckstein's view, the Vestal misbehavior was one in a series of omens that motivated the Sibylline consultation. Human sacrifice was the drastic ritual action recommended by the Books to avert the danger threatening. Thus the Forum Boarium sacrifices fit the pattern of human sacrifices followed so far, as an extraordinary response to a crisis situation.[152]

The promise of Plutarch's "and even now" (*eti kai nun*) seems to bear fruit in later references to the Forum Boarium sacrifices. Pliny, in discussing the miraculous powers attributed to Roman ritual, relates that

> even our own time has seen a male and female Greek, or members of the race with whom the issue then happened to be, buried in the Forum Boarium. The leader of the priestly college of quindecimvirs used to preside over prayer at this rite.[153]

Pliny's "with whom the issue then happened to be" (*cum quibus tum res esset*) suggests the viability of this sort of ritual as a traditional yet flexible Roman response to crisis. Furthermore, the polymath clearly states that this practice continued at least until *nostra aetas*, that is, the mid-first century after Christ.

Reid cannot accept the textual reading of *etiam nostra aetas vidit*, pointing to its incompatibility with Pliny's comments elsewhere.[154] He therefore construes the manuscript as corrupt, the corrected reading to be *nostra civitas*, which would be more consistent with the implication that Romans no longer tolerated human sacrifice as a cultic act. The text as it is does not, however, contradict itself. Pliny's point is clear: not only in the days of Decius' *devotio* and Tuccia's miracle but in *etiam nostra aetate* the *precationes* of Roman priests were highly effective. The temporal aspect of the phrase is vital to the sense of the passage.

The Emperor Aurelian, in A.D. 271 when the Goths and Marcomanni howled at the borders of the empire, called for the renewal of the Forum Boarium rites and ordered that war captives be held for sacrifice if necessary.[155] Here, as during the Republic, the *Libri*, possibly the Sibylline Books, were to suggest the appropriate ritual. Public necessity, *necessitate publica*, is described as the cause or occasion of the ritual activity. Also notable is the matter-of-fact inclusion of captives along with sacrificial animals and luxury items as potential offerings to the gods, as *quemlibet sumptum, cuiuslibet gentis captos, quaelibet animalia* are the designated objects of official action.[156] Victory is requested at public need, with captives submitted at the outset of war.[157] The type of sacrifice enacted in the Forum Boarium during the Republic is again presented as a possibility, the gravity of the situation perceived as indicative of a real threat to Roman well-being. Such danger had been met in the past with the help of human sacrifice. Its extreme nature had been proven effective in calming the disorder of the gods and in focusing the morale of the Romans to meet the difficulties ahead.

THE IDEOLOGY OF HUMAN SACRIFICE

There were authors in the Roman tradition who claimed human sacrifice at Rome came from outside.[158] As we saw earlier, Livy described the Forum Boarium sacrifices as a ritual hardly Roman.[159] Cicero echoes this attitude and refers to human immolation, when performed by foreigners, as something abnormal and disgusting:

> Can anything seem sanctified or religious to those who, even if when, led by some fear, they decided the gods must be placated, desecrate with human sacrifices their altars and temples, so that they are not even capable of practicing their religion without first defiling religion itself with wickedness? Indeed, who does not know that they [the Gauls], to this day, practice that savage and barbarous habit of human sacrifice? Because of this, what kind of trustworthiness, what kind of piety do you think there is for those who even think that the immortal gods can be most easily pleased by the blood and murder of humans? Do you consider your own religious scruples to be in line with those of these witnesses? Do you think you can get any sanctified or moderate testimony from them?[160]

As has been noted, and rightly so, the opinions of intellectuals of the first century B.C. can hardly count as evidence for archaic Roman practices.[161] The fact that "foreign" human sacrifice, surely an extreme ritual if ever there was one, caught on at Rome, suggests that there was already something in the Roman mind-set to incline them toward this sort of activity. The active presence of human sacrifice in the later Republic was strong enough to warrant official response, in the form of the *senatus consultum* formally banning the practice in 97 B.C. Pliny informs us that

> in the 657th year of the city, when Gnaeus Cornelius Lentulus and Publius Licinius Crassus were consuls, a senatorial decree was passed that no human shall be sacrificed, at that time unnatural rites were celebrated openly . . . nor could anyone ever be able to estimate how much is owed to those Romans who lifted these performances, in which to kill a man was considered extremely religious, and even to eat him was considered very wholesome.[162]

The context for this notice is Pliny's discussion of magic. Here apparently the polymath credits the Romans for doing away with human sacrifice in a magical or superstitious context and ritual cannibalism. Reid thinks it unlikely that Pliny could make such a statement about practices he calls *monstra* if the Romans in his time were regularly offering up Greeks in the Forum Boarium.[163] The context is important, however, and relates to Plutarch's suggestion in the *Roman Questions* and to the context we have seen all along for human sacrifice. The appropriate sphere for human immolation was in the atmosphere of imminent threat to the state; frivolous usages of the practice were barbaric and to be avoided by Romans.

Wünsch surmises that there is some indication of the presence of human sacrifice in archaic Roman religion, which was in earliest times abolished from official regular practice, then later revived under foreign influence.[164] The foreign influence Wünsch assumes did not come from the worshippers of bloody Cybele and her ilk but from Greece.

The role Hellenism played in human immolation at Rome is ambiguous. On the one hand, Greece, as personified by Hercules, was portrayed as responsible for dissuading the archaic Romans from the barbarism of human sacrifice. On the other hand, the Sibylline Books persistently appear in conjunction with the immolation of human beings, a connection that Dio, for one, has come to expect in such a context. How are we to reconcile this tension? It must be understood that the presence of Hercules and the Sibylline Books need not indicate the genuine, historical involvement of Greeks. It rather demonstrates a Roman perception about the nature of archaic religion and its organization. Like the Etruscans, the Greeks may have been perceived as a people with sophisticated religious practices that stretched far back into the dim reaches of time. The prestige of old Roman rituals may thus have been enhanced by the overlay of a Greek or Etruscan patina.

Toutain asserts that the claim that human sacrifice was foreign to Roman religion was a pretense, as was the claim that the procedure was found in the Sibylline Books.[165] Whatever the Romans pretended to believe, it is clear that human sacrifice can be found in the oldest strata of Roman religious practices, used, as elsewhere, as a means of propitiating angered deities. The immolation of humans was an ad hoc response to extraordinary crisis situations, intended to propitiate the community of the gods and to draw together the human community in observation of unusually solemn rituals.

The *Munera* as Sacrifice

There are at least two ways of categorizing gladiatorial combat. The current trend in scholarship identifies the *munera* as agonistic, not sacrificial, and is argued most forcefully by Georges Ville and Paul Veyne.[166] To the contrary, the similarities between the *munera* and other forms of human sacrifice, in addition to the evidence for human immolation elsewhere in the Roman system, suggest that an argument can be made for the sacrificial interpretation. The ancient texts, where they address the issue at all, seem to verify this identification, at least in terms of the origin of the *munera*.

Tertullian outlines the development of gladiatorial combat as an amelioration of earlier and more outright employment of blood offerings.

> For at one time, since it was believed that the spirits of the dead were propitiated by human blood, they used to sacrifice captives or purchased slaves of bad quality at funerals. Afterward it was decided to cover up the impiety with pleasure. So then on the appointed day they put those whom they trained (such training! they learn to die!) to use before the tombs of the dead.[167]

The same process is reconstructed by Servius, who claims that the change from simple slaughter to combat to the death was due to the changing perception of human immolation. He claims:

> The custom was to kill captives at the tombs of great men. Because this, after a time, seemed cruel, it was decided that gladiators should fight before the tombs.[168]

Tertullian labeled the transformation a change from impiety, a word choice one might perhaps have expected from a Christian apologist. Servius lacks that particular partisan agenda and calls the new perspective an awareness of *crudelitas*, which can be seen as the need to attain some distance between the act of human sacrifice and the perpetrators thereof.

We have already discussed human funerary sacrifice, whether it be of the retinue of the deceased or of his enemy. The latter practice is dismissed by Ville as irrelevant to human sacrifice, as the simple taking of one death for another is far too banal and too much like vengeance to be ritually significant.

Ville's argument was left here at the time of his death and was taken up again by Paul Veyne, his editor posthumously. Veyne claims that the concept or theme of human sacrifice remained in the Roman imagination after the reality was long gone, a situation he compares to the significance of the Isaac myth for the Jewish mind-set and that of Iphigenia among the Greeks. It was this motif that the Romans attached to the *aition* of the gladiatorial games, when in the Hellenistic frenzy for aetiology some sort of origin for the games had to be concocted.

While Veyne is correct to emphasize the concept of sacrifice in the Roman mentality, his assumption that human immolation is but a dim memory in the historical period must be questioned because of the multiplicity of sacrifice references that appear in the martial context if nowhere else. This "fiction" of sacrificial origins for the *munera* must also be questioned; this is hardly the only explanation for the issue. The derivation of mythic origins is a process of selection, based on cultural linkages perceived by the aetiologists. The shedding of human blood must be purposive, and the strong historical identification with the needs of the state and with *pietas* fosters the identity between *munera* and sacrifice, enough to overcome a more recent distaste for "human sacrifice for its own sake."[169] Locating such rituals in the past allowed contemporary Romans the comfort of distance; it need not reflect the real state of affairs.

Veyne points to the regularity of the phrase *ludi funebres et munus gladiatorium* in the annalistic tradition that Livy follows, seeing in this usage an agonistic collectivity and thus an indication of the true nature of the *munera*. This phrase can conversely be interpreted as demonstrating the distinctiveness of the *munus gladiatorium* from the regular *ludi funebres*. The grouping of *munus* with *visceratio*, which is much more prevalent in the Late Republican and Early Imperial literary accounts, could instead be seen as the idiomatic expression, one that emphasizes still more the separation of the *munera* from the agonistic sphere and the relationship with blood sacrifice.

Veyne, following Malten, compares the agonism of the original gladiatorial combats not to the epic death of the Trojan youths but to the combat between Ajax and Diomedes at the funeral of Patroclus, where the two combatants fought to first blood, not to the death.[170] Veyne claims that this essential dissimilarity to the *munera* is based on the special circumstances of the event. The audience would not have stopped the combat at first blood if Ajax and Diomedes had not been great leaders, if the spectators had not been their comrades-in-arms, if Ajax and Diomedes had been social undesirables or slaves who battled for the promise of freedom, that is, if the context had been that of the Roman practice. The multiplicity of the conditionals, however, surely belies the true parallelism of the practice. The repute of heroic duels, like that of Ajax and Diomedes, enhanced the meaning of the *munera* but did not define it.

The impetus for and explanation of the *munera* comes from the essence of *Romanitas*, its nature stretching far back into Rome's mythohistorical past to the struggle between Romulus and Remus over the foundation of the City. The death of Remus can be interpreted as a foundation sacrifice, vital and necessary to the protection of the city and its future well-being.

The definition of a death as a human sacrifice depends on the religious use to which it is put, not on historical proof that the worshippers actually participated in an openly acknowledged rite in which a human being was put to death for the benefit of the social group. Indeed, only rarely is such acknowledgement seen, as the group involved commonly distances itself from the death, shifting responsibility for the act to accident, to the victim or to malevolence beyond the control of humans. The benefit accrued for the group from the victim's death is the true indicator of human sacrifice.[171]

The immolation of human beings as an integral part of the ceremonial foundation of cities was a practice common to many cultures all over the world. The death of the victim was intended to placate the gods at a critical moment of vulnerability, a moment when they might be expected to display divine indignation at human arrogance in undertaking such a venture. The people involved inflicted pain on themselves by sacrificing one of their own, in hopes of preempting divine retribution, and sent the victim to the other world as their representative and patron.[172]

The myths surrounding human sacrifice often use distancing devices to absolve society of its responsibility for the death as well as to soften the appearance of excessive bloodthirstiness on the part of the gods. The choice of distancing device is suggestive and indicates something about the character of the society involved.

The death of Remus takes place in an admittedly contrived combat, where the victim has become a willing participant in the ritual action. The murder of Remus is justified beforehand as a reasonable response to provocation and after the fact as protection of the sacred boundary of the city. How can one then suggest that ritual was involved? The key indicator is the societal benefit resulting from the death: a great city was established. The inherent goal of the foundation sacrifice was thus met. Another clue lies in Romulus' fate: far from being punished for fratricide, the surviving twin is the eponymous city founder and idealized first king.[173]

Ritual combat cloaks another foundation sacrifice in Rome's mythical history, in the triple duel of the Horatii and Curiatii during the synoecism of Alba Longa and Rome. The question of whether the civic merging of Rome and Alba Longa is at all historical is not really important here. The story of the duel was embedded in early Roman history, essential to the concept of the foundation of a new sociopolitical entity. Such an event needed to be commemorated by a foundation sacrifice. The society involved shielded itself doubly from ritual misfortune by using the distancing device of the ceremonial combat.

The *munera* are a variant on the ritual combat/sacrifice theme, where the victim becomes property of the gods who granted his victory.[174] The analog was hinted at by Rose in the 1920s, who saw the *munera* and other ritual combats as expiatory in some way. The clear association between crises of state and the holding of *munera* can be seen from the attested inception of the practice in the third century. From the outset, *munera* are presented in association with more traditional cultic practice to offset the disaster threatening the community. In 264 and in 216 B.C. the fate of Rome hung in the balance.[175] The violence of the menace called for a drastic response. The appropriateness of the ritualized combat form of sacrifice was enhanced by its roots in Roman mythology and its martial character.

The ritual combat at the heart of the Roman State, acting in conjunction with the tendency toward self-sacrifice, supported the Roman military tradition of dueling champions. The challenge of the champion, fulfilled in combat before the two assembled armies, was redolent of honor and achievement to the Roman viewpoint.[176] It is this heritage that lends some conviction to Veyne's reconstruction of the development of the *munera*.[177] Gladiatorial combat was far more than the simple entertainment Ville and Veyne describe; the pattern of the Roman *munera* can be identified with the mythic foundations of the Roman State and with the fundamental institutions of the Roman Empire.

Augustus as the New Founder of Rome was also faced with a crisis of state. His institutionalization of the Imperial form of the *munera*, sheltered in their official domain of the amphitheater, was in response to this crisis and meant as a preventive measure against further disturbance. The regular refounding of the state through gladiatorial sacrifice would be a source of renewal for the empire. From here on, the *munera* were under the exclusive control of the emperor and sponsored through the West in association with the two key instruments of Empire as established by Augustus: the Imperial Cult and the army. The message of the arena reached a vast audience; the impact of its rhetoric was heightened by its pervasiveness.

The arena was the embodiment of the empire. From the center in Rome came the permission to build the amphitheater, quintessentially Roman in style and mass. The builders acted as the emperor's local agents, in conjunction with other technical arms of the state: the army, its back, and the resources, its blood. The seating arrangements replicated an idealization of the Roman polity. The arena itself was a stage for political performance and the demonstration of power within the existing power structure: the immediate favor of the *editor* set off and depended upon the ultimate authority of the emperor. The message of the central combat was subtler but no less clear. The struggle of the gladiators was strongly reminiscent, if not an actual reenactment, of Rome's foundation sacrifice, the death of Remus at the hands of his brother. Gladiatorial combat was the Imperial process in microcosm, embodying the militarism at the core of Rome's justification of Empire. The Pax Romana had been bought with blood and depended on military victory for its survival.

The gladiator himself was the focus of all this attention, yet he was essentially irrelevant to the overall message: he was not part of the target audience. He was, like the amphitheater itself, simply a means to an end, a channel through which ritual is accomplished. He is thus an analog to Maccaby's Sacred Executioner in the dualistic nature of his role in the ideology of the arena. The Sacred Executioner is the agent of god's will in the performance of the sacrifice. He is thus more than human, assimilated, even though briefly, to the god. The Sacred Executioner is also reviled because of the very nature of his task; he is tainted by the miasma of human blood. He, like the victim, is victimized by his sacred function. He is both deific and vile. The gladiator performed the ritual reenactment of Empire; he was vital and necessary and admirable in so doing. But his identification with that ritual put him outside the rest of society. The *infamis* nature of his task forever separated him from the benefits of his accomplishments and excluded him permanently from the magic ring.

CONCLUSION

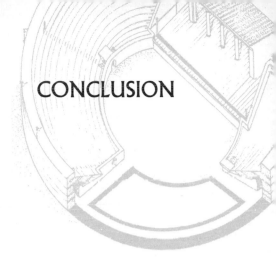

THE MEANING OF THE AMPHITHEATER thus becomes apparent in several spheres of social interaction. A certain structural framework has gradually taken shape, upon which the institution of the amphitheater was raised.

The presence of the first emperor has been a recurrent theme throughout this inquiry. He provided the inspiration for the first monumental amphitheater in Rome, built by his crony Statilius Taurus in 29 B.C. The structure picked up momentum in its spread through the empire, with Augustus providing official support by connecting the amphitheater with the Imperial Cult and with the army. Legislation controlling the construction of amphitheaters in general was likely passed at this time, defining the structure once and for all as an archetypically public building, subject to direct regulation by the central authority. Even more specific regulation governed the use of the amphitheater. The *lex Julia theatralis* was interpreted on the local level in an effort to make the relationship of the individual to the authorities perfectly apparent, even at the Games. The amphitheater was the site of a direct expression of symbolic power. The symbolic interchange between ruler and ruled was codified and monumentalized in the cults of the amphitheater. Again, Augustus was the prime mover in the establishment of the Imperial Cult, in which the symbolically charged cult implements of altar and amphitheater became, for the provincials, the means of expressing loyalty, and, for Augustus, a means of inserting the emperor into the life of the individual as well as that of the province. The identification of the individual with the Roman authority was thereby strengthened on a personal basis.

The most striking role Augustus played in the amphitheatrical complex stems from his image as the New Founder of Rome. The *munera* had, in the last century of the Republic, become a tool for canny politicians to use in building a power base. The expressions of popular favor generated by the presentation of *munera* enhanced one's reputation as a public benefactor. Augustus seems to have taken into consideration the root of the enthusiasm for *munera* and its origin in the human sacrificial complex. The battle between brothers resulting in the death of one twin can be seen as emblematic of Rome's military past and determination to survive. Romans of the Early Empire had also survived a battle between brothers, and the blood spilt by so much civil war could now be interpreted as purgative, as a new foundation sacrifice, which drew together the Roman people in a new identity for a new beginning.

The *munera* formed the basis of a complex of political ritual, meant not so much as a sugar-coated disguise of coercive force as it was the rhetoric of Roman authority enacted. The ritual made use of the traditional symbols of power, laden with the prestige of time but rearranged to give new meaning and significance to the performance and to differentiate the new complex from the old.[1] Nevertheless, these integrated emblems from Roman tradition gave the impression of cultural continuity, an impression vital to the overall meaning of the ritual of the amphitheater, which resonated with the power of Rome.[2] The ritual performance in the arena was a means of Imperial control through directed attitudinal change, the creation and manipulation of mass emotional response, renewed regularly at the behest of the ruling hierarchy. This was a polyvalent ritual, wrapped in layers of meanings to resonate with a diverse viewing public throughout the empire.

In the amphitheater was the reconstitution of the Roman hierarchy through its representatives in the *maeniana*. Here too was the economic power of the empire, capable of commanding and consuming vast resources, a colorful segment of which was now being recirculated into the amphitheatrical circles of power, now being remade into didactic spectacle. This was not gratuitous display, however, not simply exotica; the spectacles served the public good as well as the interests of the Roman center. Here was public pleasure as well as law and order, here was the conquest of the Roman world as well as its integration in the creation of a new balance, a working sociopolitical order. The amphitheater *was* Roman power, Roman agency, the ability to define and construct the space in which significant actions, resonant in a Roman and provincial interpretation, were made real, given active form, drawing on the spirit of the Roman people and the basic impulses of a mythic past to create and to celebrate a new world order.

APPENDIX I. AMPHITHEATERS AND CENTRAL PLACE THEORY

CENTRAL PLACE THEORY (CPT) is a model of urbanization developed in the 1930s by Walter Christaller as a means of understanding the urban pattern of southern Germany.[1] According to this system, inhabited landscape can be broken down into centers and their hinterlands. Centers perform specific services for those dwelling in the surrounding area, including administrative, judicial, commercial, and political functions. The "range" of a given function depends on how far the average person is willing to come to avail himself of it, always keeping in mind the law of minimum effort (for maximum results). While a farmer might not wish to spend more than a few hours each week traveling to and from the marketplace, he might be willing to take more time journeying to important, albeit more distant, religious festivals several times a year.[2] The distance he will travel once yearly to pay taxes, or participate in governmental functions, could be greater still and represents an extreme of the functional range of a major center.

Higher-order centers, those with a larger hinterland, can be distinguished from lower-order centers in that they would perform the same basic functions as any clustered settlement but would have, in addition, specialized services, which might be utilized on a less frequent basis but by a larger segment of the area's population. Higher-order centers thus have lower-order centers as part of their hinterland, and lower-order centers have, in turn, still lower order centers as satellites.

The term "satellite" is particularly appropriate to CPT. Given a featureless landscape, centers of the same order would be spaced at regular intervals equal to approximately twice the range of the highest function, with some slight overlap. Each center would be surrounded by centers of a next-lower order, also spaced at regular intervals, and so forth.

This general model of a hierarchy of centers has been used to analyze urban systems in such far-flung locations as preindustrial China and ancient Mesoamerica.[3] When applied to classical antiquity, I find it particularly appropriate in an ideological sense.[4] Consider how the classical definition of the *polis* always included its hinterland, an element vital to the subsistence of the city if nothing else. Awareness of a functional hierarchy of towns can be found in the ancient literary sources, as in Aristotle's description of the origin of *poleis* in the process of synoecism, surely analogous to the CPT satellite clustering.[5] A more economic approach can be seen in Xenophon's account of the hierarchy of the shoemaking industry as dependent on the urban market.[6] Pausanias ranks towns by their public architecture, as when he wrote disparagingly of Panopeus in Phocis, questioning its right to call itself a *polis* at all, since it had "no government offices, no gymnasium, no theatre, no marketplace, no water descending to a fountain."[7] Pausanias clearly defines cities by their public buildings and hence by the institutions inherent in those buildings.

When CPT is applied to the analysis of the Roman Empire, the results can be used to gauge the impact of Roman civilization in terms of its ability to impose an urban network on the countryside. Such an attempt was published in 1989 by Tønnes Bekker-Nielsen, who took special interest in Roman Gaul.[8]

Bekker-Nielsen combined the city-lists in Pliny, Strabo, and Ptolemy with the *Notitia Galliarum*, as well as with the Antonine Itinerary and the Peutinger Table, and was able to plot this urban scatter in space. By assuming that all these centers were of the same high order, he could discern four basic densities of urban scatter (Types A–D, with A representing the densest dispersion), which he related to social and historical contexts and causes. Like a modern-day Pausanias, he has a checklist of urban functions appropriate to regional centers, including the town council, capitolium, permanent market, and, most importantly for the present study, the amphitheater.[9]

Is such an approach legitimate? Can one actually use amphitheaters as "markers" for the centrality or higher function of urban areas and thus for the degree of Romanization?

The easiest way to compare the amphitheater scatter with the urban scatter as a whole is to make lists. Given the city-list of Gaul culled from Pliny, Strabo, Ptolemy, and the *Notitia Galliarum*, how many of these major centers had an amphitheater? Bekker-Nielsen cites 117 cities, as compared to my list of 77 amphitheaters for the same geographical area, a difference that seems not unreasonable.[10] One might expect the depredations of time to rob us of some structures. Of these 77 amphitheaters, however, 25 were found at sites not on the city-list. Either these 25 were rural amphitheaters or the city-list is incomplete. This discrepancy can, perhaps, be clarified by testing the viability of CPT.

As Bekker-Nielsen did with cities, I first plotted the amphitheaters of the western empire onto a map, then calculated the average intercenter distance (ICD) between a given structure and its two closest neighbors.[11] To estimate the range of the amphitheatrical central function, I multiplied the ICD by 0.625 (instead of only 0.5) to allow for a slight overlap in hinterlands with the closest neighbor. The specific measurements are given in Tables I–VII, with all distances in kilometers.

I. HISPANIAE AND LUSITANIA
Table I.

TOWN NAME	NEIGHBOR A	NEIGHBOR B	AVERAGE ICD
Acinippo	31 (Urso)	69 (Carmo)	50
Aquae Flaviae	88 (Bracara)	197 (Conimbriga)	143
Astigi	56 (Corduba)	31 (Urso)	44
Balsa	135 (Italica)	144 (Hasta Regia)	140
Barcino	81 (Tarraco)	109 (Emporiae)	95
Bracara Augusta	175 (Conimbriga)	88 (Aquae Flaviae)	132
Carmo	13 (Italica)	63 (Astigi)	38
Carthago Nova	69 (Illici)	300 (Ucubis)	185
Conimbriga	175 (Bracara)	197 (Aquae Flaviae)	186
Corduba	31 (Ucubis)	56 (Astigi)	44
Emerita	169 (Italica)	172 (Corduba)	171
Emporiae	188 (Tarraco)	109 (Barcino)	149
Gades	34 (Hasta Regia)	100 (Acinippo)	67

Table I. (*continued*)

TOWN NAME	NEIGHBOR A	NEIGHBOR B	AVERAGE ICD
Hasta Regia	34 (Gades)	69 (Carmo)	52
Illici	69 (Carthago Nova)	338 (Ucubis)	204
Italica	13 (Carmo)	72 (Astigi)	43
Numantia	238 (Toletum)	220 (Segobriga)	229
Segobriga	113 (Toletum)	220 (Numantia)	167
Tarraco	81 (Barcino)	188 (Emporiae)	135
Toletum	219 (Emerita)	113 (Segobriga)	166
Ucubis	31 (Corduba)	69 (Astigi)	50
Urso	31 (Astigi)	31 (Acinippo)	31

N = 22

AVERAGE ICD = 115

RANGE = 72

II. BRITANNIA
Table II.

TOWN NAME	NEIGHBOR A	NEIGHBOR B	AVERAGE ICD
Baginton	82 (Venta S.)	102 (Verulamium)	92
Calleva Atrebatum	70 (Londinium)	56 (Noviomagus)	63
Camulodunum	70 (Durovernum)	70 (Rutupiae)	70
Charterhouse	40 (Isca S.)	42 (Venta S.)	41
Corinium Dob.	56 (Venta S.)	72 (Isca S.)	64
Deva Victrix	72 (Tomen-y-Mur)	142 (Isorbrigantium)	107
Durnovaria	36 (Woodcuts)	64 (Charterhouse)	50
Durovernum C.	18 (Rutupiae)	70 (Camulodunum)	44
Frilford	35 (Calleva)	46 (Corinium Dob.)	40
Isca Silurum	16 (Venta S.)	40 (Charterhouse)	28
Isorbrigantium	142 (Deva)	206 (Baginton)	174
Londinium	40 (Verulamium)	70 (Calleva A.)	55
Moridunum	96 (Isca S.)	108 (Venta S.)	102
Noviomagus	56 (Calleva A.)	84 (Londinium)	70
Rutupiae	18 (Dorovernum)	70 (Camulodunum)	44
Tomen-y-Mur	72 (Deva)	120 (Moridunum)	96
Venta Silurum	16 (Isca S.)	42 (Charterhouse)	29
Verulamium	40 (Londinium)	80 (Calleva A.)	60
Woodcuts	36 (Durnovaria)	62 (Charterhouse)	49

N = 19

AVERAGE ICD = 67

RANGE = 42

III. GALLIAE

A. Narbonensis
Table III.

TOWN NAME	NEIGHBOR A	NEIGHBOR B	AVERAGE ICD
Antipolis	15 (Cemenelum)	35 (Forum Julii)	25
Aquae Sextiae	71 (Arelate)	92 (Arausio)	82
Arausio	21 (Vasio)	50 (Nemausus)	36
Arelate	25 (Nemausus)	50 (Arausio)	38
Baeterrae	25 (Narbo)	100 (Nemausus)	63
Cemenelum	15 (Antipolis)	45 (Forum Julii)	30
Dea Vocontiorum	54 (Valentia)	71 (Vasio)	63
Forum Julii	35 (Antipolis)	45 (Cemenelum)	40
Narbo	25 (Baeterrae)	125 (Nemausus)	75
Nemausus	25 (Arelate)	50 (Arausio)	38
Segusium	167 (Cemenelum)	175 (Antipolis)	171
Tolosa	142 (Narbo)	167 (Baeterrae)	155
Valentia	67 (Vienna)	54 (Dea Vocontiorum)	61
Vasio	21 (Arausio)	71 (Dea Vocontiorum)	46
Vienna	67 (Valentia)	100 (Dea Vocontiorum)	84

N = 15
AVERAGE ICD = 67
RANGE = 42

B. Aquitania
Table IV.

TOWN NAME	NEIGHBOR A	NEIGHBOR B	AVERAGE ICD
Aginnum	71 (Divona)	108 (Vesunna)	90
Alléans	25 (Avaricum)	25 (Derventum)	25
Aquae Neri	92 (Derventum)	117 (Tintignac)	105
Argentomagus	75 (Derventum)	83 (Lim. Pictonum)	79
Aug. Lemovicum	42 (Cassinomagus)	71 (Tintignac)	57
Avaricum	37 (Derventum)	25 (Alléans)	31
Burdigala	112 (Vesunna)	112 (Med. Santonum)	112
Cassinomagus	83 (Vesunna)	42 (Aug. Lemovicum)	63
Catiriacum	37 (Segodunum)	125 (Divona)	81
Derventum	37 (Avaricum)	25 (Alléans)	31
Divona	71 (Aginnum)	83 (Vesunna)	77
Lim. Pictonum	87 (Argentomagus)	37 (Sanxay)	62
Lugd. Convenarum	142 (Aginnum)	192 (Divona)	167
Med. Santonum	100 (Sanxay)	108 (Cassinomagus)	104
Sanxay	37 (Lim. Pictonum)	100 (Med. Santonum)	69

Table IV. (*continued*)

TOWN NAME	NEIGHBOR A	NEIGHBOR B	AVERAGE ICD
Segodunum	37 (Catiriacum)	96 (Divona)	67
Tintignac	84 (Vesunna)	71 (Aug. Lemovicum)	78
Vesunna Pet.	83 (Cassinomagus)	83 (Tintignac)	83

N = 18
AVERAGE ICD = 77
RANGE = 48

C. Lugdunensis
Table V.

TOWN NAME	NEIGHBOR A	NEIGHBOR B	AVERAGE ICD
Ag. Senonum	33 (Triguières)	54 (Autessiodurum)	44
Alauna	117 (Aregenua)	142 (Nov. Lexoviorum)	130
Aquae Segetae	37 (Lugdunum)	137 (Cabillonum)	87
Aregenua	67 (Nov. Lexoviorum)	58 (Noviodunum)	63
Areines	75 (Suindinum)	54 (Cenabum)	65
Augustodunum	88 (Interanum)	62 (Cabillonum)	75
Autessiodurum	33 (Bouzy-la-Forêt)	49 (Interanum)	41
Autricum	67 (Cenabum)	62 (Med. Aulercorum)	65
Bouzy-la-Forêt	29 (Triguières)	33 (Autessiodurum)	31
Cabillonum	62 (Augustodunum)	112 (Lugdunum)	87
Caes. Turonum	71 (Suindinum)	62 (Areines)	67
Canetonum	42 (Gisacum)	37 (Rotomagus)	40
Cenabum	54 (Areines)	62 (Chennevières)	58
Chennevières	33 (Triguières)	42 (Bouzy-la-Forêt)	38
Gennes	21 (Juliomagus)	75 (Suindinum)	48
Gisacum	17 (Med. Aulercorum)	42 (Canetonum)	30
Interanum	49 (Autessiodurum)	33 (Bouzy-la-Forêt)	41
Juliobona	58 (Nov. Lexoviorum)	67 (Rotomagus)	63
Juliomagus	21 (Gennes)	75 (Suindinum)	48
Locmariaquer	67 (Silva Martis)	83 (Mauves)	75
Lugdunum	112 (Cabillonum)	37 (Aquae Segetae)	75
Lutetia Parisiorum	83 (Autricum)	87 (Gisacum)	85
Mauves	17 (Silva Martis)	83 (Locmariaquer)	50
Med. Aulercorum	17 (Gisacum)	42 (Canetonum)	30
Noviodunum	58 (Aregenua)	75 (Suindinum)	67
Nov. Lexoviorum	58 (Juliobona)	46 (Canetonum)	52
Rotomagus	37 (Canetonum)	42 (Gisacum)	40
Silva Martis	17 (Mauves)	67 (Locmariaquer)	42
Suindinum	75 (Juliomagus)	75 (Areines)	75
Triguières	33 (Chennevières)	29 (Bouzy-la-Forêt)	31

N = 30
AVERAGE ICD = 58
RANGE = 36

D. Belgica
Table VI.

TOWN NAME	NEIGHBOR A	NEIGHBOR B	AVERAGE ICD
Aquae Granni	154 (Durocortorum)	70 (Divodurum Med.)	112
Augusta Treverorum	75 (Divodurum Med.)	160 (Aquae Granni)	118
Augustomagus	83 (Samarobriva)	33 (Champlieu)	58
Champlieu	33 (Augustomagus)	87 (Durocortorum)	60
Divodurum Med.	70 (Aquae Granni)	75 (Aug. Treverorum)	73
Durocortorum	112 (Augustomagus)	87 (Champlieu)	100
Gesoriacum	112 (Ribemont)	117 (Samarobriva)	115
Ribemont-sur-Ancre	25 (Samarobriva)	96 (Augustomagus)	61
Samarobriva	83 (Augustomagus)	25 (Ribemont)	54

N = 9
AVERAGE ICD = 83
RANGE = 52

E. Tota Gallia (without administrative boundaries)

The following changes were necessary in order to calculate ICDs without considering the political boundaries between the Gauls:

Table VII.

TOWN NAME	NEIGHBOR A	NEIGHBOR B	AVERAGE ICD
Aginnum	71 (Divona)	100 (Tolosa)	86
Aquae Segetae	42 (Vienna)	37 (Lugdunum)	40
Augustomagus	46 (Lutetia)	33 (Champlieu)	40
Baeterrae	25 (Narbo)	96 (Catiriacum)	61
Catiriacum	108 (Tolosa)	37 (Segodunum)	73
Champlieu	33 (Augustomagus)	58 (Lutetia)	46
Lugd. Convenarum	142 (Aginnum)	104 (Tolosa)	123
Lutetia	46 (Augustomagus)	58 (Champlieu)	52
Lugdunum	37 (Aquae Segetae)	33 (Vienna)	35
Narbo	25 (Baeterrae)	96 (Catiriacum)	61
Octodurus	108 (Segusium)	170 (Lugdunum)	139
Segusium	167 (Cemenelum)	108 (Octodurus)	138
Tolosa	104 (Lugd. Conv.)	100 (Aginnum)	102
Vesontio	142 (Grand)	104 (Cabillonum)	123
Vienna	67 (Valentia)	33 (Lugdunum)	50

N = 74
AVERAGE ICD = 65
RANGE = 41

APPENDIX II. PLINY IN BITHYNIA
Construction in the Provinces
during the High Empire

PLINY THE YOUNGER WAS SENT to Pontus and Bithynia, on the shores of the Black Sea, as a special *legatus Augusti*, around A.D. 109.[1] Pliny's loosely defined duties as a sort of Imperial troubleshooter extraordinaire can be postulated from the nature of his correspondence with the emperor. He was to act as provincial governor in maintaining law and order and, in addition, to act upon Trajan's special agenda.[2]

Pontus and Bithynia, as is clear in the *Letters*, fostered a hotbed of intense competition among the various cities and their leaders, a competition manifested in extravagant euergetism. They were spending a great deal of money on public buildings, each person trying to magnify his own status by enhancing the appearance of his city. Although this goal was in agreement with the overall aims of Roman imperialism, the waste involved in this headlong architectural enthusiasm is all too apparent in Pliny's investigations. The problem was not one of impending fiscal doom in the area but rather an excess of cash and no checks in the system to discourage abuse of local prosperity.[3] It seems that wasteful spending was a particular bugaboo of the frugal Trajan, who tried to cut down on such irresponsible behavior in Italy through the creation of the *curatores civitatium*, with a mandate to control excessive municipal expenditure. Trajan's solution was not, therefore, to modify the system so it could monitor its own spending but to send out special agents, like Pliny and the *curatores*, to do occasional housecleaning.

As far as public architecture was concerned, it seems clear that Pliny was instructed to allow no new projects to commence without specific permission from the central government, which in his case took the form of a personal assent from Trajan. As for projects already underway, Pliny was to investigate the status of the work and the actions and accounts of its sponsors and to make recommendations in accordance with his findings.

As for public building in the Roman world, Pliny's account offers clarification on several major points. The first of these was a major factor in Trajan's decision to send Pliny to Asia Minor in the first place, that being the use of public building by local politicos in the game of civic competition. This had been much the case in Rome during the Republic and was now to be seen in the provinces. This should not, however, be seen solely as indicative of burgeoning Romanization but as the continuation of the Graeco-Roman system of maintaining complex interrelationships between individuals and classes within the city and between the city and the world outside.

One situation detailed in the *Letters* involved the transfer to the city of Prusa of work undertaken by Dio Chrysostom, one of its leading citizens.[4] A certain Eumolpus opposed this, casting aspersions on Dio's honesty by demanding an accounting and exaggerating the seriousness of his charges by manufacturing a hint of *maiestas*.[5] Here the Imperial legate is dragged in unnecessarily, perhaps as part of the competition for renown spreading beyond the city walls of Prusa. Pliny, concerned about the suggestion of *maiestas*, sends the testaments of the principals to Trajan, who dismisses the treason charge and sends the paperwork back to Pliny to verify the accounting.

Dio Chrysostom dominates the scene in Bithynia as a major player in regional politics, although this impression may be a modern bias due to the survival of his *Orationes*, which compounds his apparent influence during Pliny's term. Nevertheless, Dio Chrysostom did have something of an international status and could count himself an acquaintance of the emperor. The attempt to cast aspersions on Dio's reputation and the implied charge of *maiestas*, however, cannot be understood as specifically anti-Roman sentiment, as a desire to drag down the Roman toady, but simply as part of the local rivalry.[6]

Despite the interest of the passage for civic competition on the provincial level, Pliny's description raises many questions about the institution of public building. The basic issue is the practice of transferring a project to the city, from private hands to public. Was the work finished at the time the issue was raised? If not, does this mean that Dio Chrysostom wanted to abdicate the responsibility for *probatio*? Or was he turning over a completed structure for the use of the city as it saw fit? No mention is made of the duty of future maintenance for the work, which would, presumably, be at the discretion of Prusa's local government.

The propensity for involving Imperial officials in local squabbles can be further seen as Pliny was approached by locals about new projects.[7] The caution Pliny shows about initiating new projects has generally been acknowledged as part of his *mandata*, but there is some indication that the proconsul, as chief Roman official in the province, had usually been consulted about major projects before Pliny's arrival as well.[8] Trajan amplified central interference in local projects by making Pliny, as proconsul, responsible for enforcing promises for public building.[9]

Financing was of prime concern, to be considered even before permission for the project was given, let alone a specific estimate made.[10] Pliny never involves the Imperial fisc, favoring instead a combination of local funding sources, presumably in order not to put too much of a burden on any one resource. For the baths at Prusa, Pliny planned to use a combination of the funds he would *revocare et exigere* from private individuals and the money that usually was spent on oil distribution.[11] The first funding source, the money recovered and exacted by Pliny, may be a reference to the penalties stemming from the embezzlement Pliny had earlier described in Prusa.[12] The bath at Claudiopolis was likewise to be funded using money extracted by Pliny, in combination with the *summa honoraria*, the magisterial dues that had been introduced to Asia Minor around this time.[13] Trajan is mainly concerned that no new taxes be levied and no essential funds diverted.[14]

The supply of labor seems to have been considered part of the preconstruction planning process, akin to financing in its manipulation of resources. Manpower is a topic during the discussion of the canal project, designed to link Lake Sophon, near Nicomedia, to the sea, to remove the need for costly land transport of goods locally.[15] Pliny admits that this work will require a large labor force, but he reasons that there is an abundance of available manpower in the city and in the surrounding rural area and that all *libentissime adgressuros* for a project of such public utility. Clearly here labor is a resource, like the *marmora, fructus,* and *ligna* (marble, produce, and wood) mentioned earlier in the passage. The question revolves around the interpretation of *libentissime adgressuros.* What sort of manpower does Pliny believe "will most freely take up" the task? Sherwin-White sees in this an example of municipal corvée, the use of which was legitimized in Urso's municipal charter.[16] This depends on a somewhat too literal translation of *libentissime,* as "for free," that is, without pay. The corvée is usually believed to have been an archaic practice, rarely resorted to, one that would surely have been inappropriate in an urbanized area not lacking the wherewithal to hire free labor.

Pliny's letters from Bithynia preserve some actual building costs: 3,518,000 sesterces for an aqueduct at Nicomedia and 10,000,000 sesterces for the theater at Nicaea.[17] Do these reflect average expenditures in any way? The money spent on the theater is called *sumptuosae* and possibly *frustra,* while the Nicomedians *tantam pecuniam male perdiderunt,* but the verbiage may be inspired more by the current state of the projects: neither is finished and fulfilling its proper function. Thus the expenditures may not represent per se truly excessive amounts of money for building projects. Pliny's contempt is rather inspired by the fact that more money still must be spent to make the facilities usable.[18]

Pliny used a specific formula of key words to persuade Trajan to permit building projects in Bithynia.[19] Measuring strength by repetition, it was most important to appeal to Trajan's dignity (*dignitas, dignissimam, digna, opus dignum*). His reign was an age (*tui saeculi, tuo saeculo, aeternitate tua*), presumably golden and presumably reminiscent of Augustus and his legendary forebears. Projects were described in pragmatic terms (*tuo utilitatem, convenientissimum*) tempered somewhat by appeals to Trajan's aesthetic sense (*quantum pulchritudinis tantum utilitatis, salubritate et amoenitati*). Trajan, like a fond parent, was to indulge (*indulsisti, indulseris*) his humble subjects.

Pliny repeatedly had problems with the technical advisors on projects. The problem was not a lack of architectural sophistication per se, as Asia Minor had long been urbanized. The relative novelty of specifically Roman techniques may have been the source of the difficulty, a lack of familiarity suggested by Nicomedian unwillingness to use Roman-style

bricks for their aqueduct, which Pliny attributed to luxury-loving prodigality, a characteristic Romans often claimed to find among Easterners.[20]
Pliny's request for an architect in this instance would be to fill a training
void rather than to find trustworthy construction staff. Further naïveté
concerning bricks was at issue in Nicaea, where one architect believed
that the brick facing of a concrete wall was the main source of its strength
and that a wall that lacked such a facing would fall apart, despite its unusual massiveness.[21] Pliny does, however, complain about poor surveying
and sketchy preconstruction planning, faults perhaps more indicative of
fraud than simple ignorance of Roman engineering. In 10.17, for example, Pliny is convinced of fraud; he is seeking to recover considerable
sums of money that had, no doubt, been paid *minime legitimis*. In general
Trajan seems willing to overlook Pliny's real personnel problems, reiter-
ating the ready availability of quantities of architects and engineers to be
found in every province.[22] The only grudging assistance Pliny gets in this
matter is a reminder of the existence of military technicians available to
the provincial governor, a resource less convenient for the lag time in
transportation involved.[23]

Trajan seems much more interested in fraud at a higher level, that is,
profiteers among the ruling class. He urges Pliny to find out who was to
blame for wasteful spending.[24] Trajan's solution to uncontrolled spending
was to make sure new works would not strain municipal resources,[25] that
they suit the real needs of the town,[26] and that proper planning take place
ahead of time, including survey, cost estimate, and financial provisions.[27]

NOTES

INTRODUCTION

1. The extended description of the situation is given by Dio Cassius 47.40.

2. A child was born with ten fingers on each hand. A mule gave birth to a weird hybrid offspring.

3. A. Alföldi (*Early Rome and the Latins* [Ann Arbor: University of Michigan Press, 1971], pp. 29–34) discusses the nature of the Latin festival, or the *Latiar*, in terms of its relationship to the growth of Roman expansion and leadership outside the confines of Rome proper. The Roman State saw the maintenance of Jupiter Latiaris as key to its own continued well-being, alongside the Capitoline cult and that of Jupiter Indiges of Lavinium. The high priority given these ritual obligations is emphasized by the fact that consuls were not to leave for their military zones until they had fulfilled them and that the tribune of the plebs, normally forbidden to leave the city, was granted special permission to attend the celebration on the Alban Mount. The signal importance of this festival for the continued prosperity of Rome made any prodigies that occurred during the *Feriae Latinae* especially sinister. Likewise, neglect of this duty brought serious consequences. Flaminius' underhanded avoidance of the festival was punished by the disaster at Lake Trasimene, as we are informed by Livy 21.63. The inescapability of Philippi is suggested by Hirtius and Pansa's neglect of the festival. As Dio (46.33.4–5) puts it, "In no instance where this has happened have the Roman People fared well." See Chapter 5 for allegations of human sacrifice at Jupiter Latiaris.

4. For the relationship between candidacy for political office and *munera*, see Chapter 1. See also G. Ville, *La Gladiature en Occident des origines à la mort de Domitien* (Rome: École française de Rome, 1981), pp. 57–99, who has here collected all the literary references to *munera* and *venationes* in the later Republic. In some instances, games may have been presented by someone currently holding office, but the textual evidence gives no indication that the *munera* were held as part of the "ordinary" games, thus joining the regular annual calendar of festivities presented by the Roman state.

5. Dio Cassius 47.39 = ἀλλ' αὐτός τε ἑαυτοῦ κρείττων τε ἅμα καὶ ἥττων γενόμενος καὶ ἔσφηλεν ἑαυτὸν καὶ ἐσφάλη.

6. J.-Cl. Golvin, *L'Amphithéâtre romain* (Paris: E. de Boccard, 1988), pp. 275–277, estimates that as many as 252 amphitheaters were to be found in the Roman West, compared to 20 in the East. My concentration is on the arenas in Europe, still the greatest concentration, to the neglect of the 38 amphitheaters in Roman North Africa. The games of the East are the focus of L. Robert, *Les Gladiateurs dans l'Orient grec* (Paris: Bibliothèque de l'École des Hautes Études, 1940), while the performance structures in Africa are discussed by J.-Cl. Lachaux, *Théâtres et amphithéâtres d'Afrique proconsulaire* (Aix-en-Provence: Edisud, 1979).

7. The concept of liminality, of "in-betweenness" and sacred commemoration of transitional phases between one status and another, was initially developed by A. van Gennep (*Rites of Passage* [Chicago: University of Chicago Press, 1960]) but significantly developed by V. Turner (*The Ritual Process* [Chicago: Aldine Publishing Company, 1969]), who extended its meaning beyond mere "transitional phase" to incorporate the autonomous, enduring category of people who inhabit and cross the edges of social boundaries and codes, including religious personnel. Turner also recognized liminality in social movements and social principles. M. Douglas continued in this mode (*Purity and Danger* [London: Routledge and Kegan Paul, 1966]), pointing to the taboo quality of liminal people and things, who represent a threat to orderly expectations but also are mysterious, powerful sources of renewal, innovation, and creativity. For a convenient summary of the concept, see B. G. Myerhoff, L. A. Camino, and E. Turner, "Rites of Passage: An Overview," in M. Eliade, ed., *The Encyclopedia of Religion* (New York: MacMillan, 1987), vol. 12, pp. 380–386.

I. BEGINNINGS

1. For an instance where such an architectural manipulation allegedly actually occurred, see the construction attributed to C. Scribonius Curio in 52 B.C., described below.

2. An assessment of how this may have worked is in A. Scobie, "Spectator Security and Comfort at Gladiatorial Games," *Nikephoros*, 1 (1988): 191–243, especially pp. 209–215.

3. For which see T. Wiedemann, *Emperors and Gladiators* (London: Routledge, 1992), pp. 62–67.

4. Among them such exotic suggestions as a Celtic source for gladiators (see M. Planck, *Über den Ursprung der römischen Gladiatorenspiele* [Ulmer Gymn. Programm, 1866], p. 11), which no one else seems to accept. (See, however, the discussion of gladiatorial games in Celtic ritual and society in chapter three.) V. Müller, "Studien zur kretisch-mykenischen Künst II," *JDAI*, 42 (1927): 1–29, suggested an ultimate Hittite origin, thence to Etruria, then Rome, a contention that would drag us dangerously near the morass of the question of Etruscan origins. A bland summary is offered by M. Grant, *Gladiators* (New York: Delacorte Press, 1967), pp. 9–13.

5. Originally put forward by F. Weege, "Oskische Grabmalerei," *JDAI*, 24 (1909): 99–162. See G. Ville, *La Gladiature en Occident des origines à la mort de Domitien* (Rome: Ecole française de Rome, 1981), whose first chapter is devoted to this issue, pp. 1–56. See also J.-P. Thuillier, *Les Jeux athlétiques dans la civilisation étrusque* (Rome: Ecole française de Rome, 1985).

6. Livy 9.40.17: *Campani ab superbia et odio Samnitium gladiatores, quod spectaculum inter epulas erat, eo ornatu armarunt Samnitiumque nomine compellarunt.* Strabo 5.4.13: ἐπὶ τοσοῦτον γὰρ ἐξετρύφησαν ὥστ' ἐπὶ δεῖπνον ἐκάλουν πρὸς ζεύγη μονομάχων. ὁρίζοντες ἀριθμὸν κατὰ τὴν τῶν δείπνων ἀξίαν. Silius Italicus, *Pun.* 11.51–54: *Quin etiam exhilarare viris convivia caede mos olim, et miscere epulis spectacula dira certantum ferro, saepe et super ipsa cadentum pocula respersis non parco sanguine mensis.* Silius' reliance on Livy as source for the *Punica* surely limits his value as independent evidence for Campanian customs.

7. As Ville admits, *Gladiature*, pp. 24–25.

8. Although Livy's 9.40 is part of his description of the campaigns of 309–308, this particular section is an aetiological reference to customs of the Romans and Campanians and not clearly datable.

9. For tomb paintings, see Weege, "Oskische"; P. C. Sestieri, "Tombe dipinti di Paestum," *RIA*, 5–6 (1956–1957): 65–110; C. Nicolet, "Les Equites campani et leurs représentations figurées," *MEFRA*, 74 (1962): 463–517; and A. Pontrandolfo and A. Rouveret, *Le tombe dipinte di Paestum* (Modena: Franco Cosimo Panini, 1992), with the scenes in question, here categorized as "duello," discussed pp. 55–58. See also Ville, *Gladiature*, p. 20.

10. Alternatively, these could be viewed as scenes from the glorious life of the now-dead hero whose tomb this was, meant simply as commemoration of his exploits as a warrior, which is the view espoused by Nicolet, "Equites," and M. Frederiksen, *Campania* (Oxford: Oxford University Press, 1984), pp. 144–145. Nudity would thus be heroization of the deceased, presumably.

11. See Ville, *Gladiature*, pp. 20–23. Of the four vases most probably gladiatorial, a Cumaean hydria in Naples (Inventory number 12796, published by E. Gabrici, "Cuma," *Monumenti antichi*, 22 [1913], col. 693, fig. 238) depicts someone sitting, waiting, on a stool. Another vase, drawn by Tischbein in the last century, has armed men on the sidelines and also displays of acrobats, which points to the representation of spectacle rather than warfare. The funereal context of these performances is indicated by what may be some sort of funeral monument off to the side of the main action. Tischbein vase I.60 in Weege, "Oskische" and S. Reinach, *Répertoire des vases peints grecs et étrusques* (Paris: E. Leroux, 1922–1924), p. 293. See also a Vatican oenochoe published by A. D. Trendall, *Vasi antichi dipinti del Vaticano: Vasi italioti ed etruschi a figure rosse I* (Rome: Citta del Vaticano, 1953–1955), p. 46, pl. xiii, fig. 30 b, c, no. U 42.

12. Frederiksen, *Campania*, pp. 117–129 discusses the Etruscans in Campania. See, more recently, T. J. Cornell, *The Beginnings of Rome* (London: Routledge, 1995), pp. 151–156.

13. Or that all Italy was once under Etruscan sway. See Polybius 2.17.1 and Strabo 5.4.3 and 8.

14. Frederiksen, *Campania*, pp. 125–126. See also D. Ridgway, "The Etruscans," in J. Boardman, N. G. L. Hammond, D. M. Lewis, and M. Ostwald, eds., *Cambridge Ancient History* (Cambridge: Cambridge University Press, 1988), vol. 4, pp. 634–675.

15. Frederiksen, *Campania*, pp. 127–128 and 134–157, who sees the attack on Cumae by "Etruscans" as more a pirate raid than out-and-out nationalistic warfare. See I. Sgobbo, "Gli ultimi Etruschi della Campania," *RAAN*, n.s. 52 (1977): 1–57 for Oscanization of Campania, as well as E. T. Salmon, *Samnium and the Samnites* (Cambridge: Cambridge University Press, 1967).

16. Funeral rituals tend to be conservative.

17. Frederiksen, *Campania*, pp. 134–137 and Salmon, *Samnium*, pp. 50–53. Livy (9.13.6–7) and Strabo (5.4.11) refer to their rustic ways. It is apparent from the archaeological record that when the Samnites took over the more sophisticated area of Campania, it was they and their institutions who were influenced, not the other way around.

18. This question is neglected by the advocates of the Campanian origins of gladiatorial combat. This touches on basic questions about the process of cultural evolution and the rationale by which one society adopts traits of another. I obviously make the assumption here that, generally speaking, a less sophisticated culture tends to be influenced by a more sophisticated one and not the other way around. This is an extension or simplification of the Law of Cultural Dominance, which basically states that a cultural system that more efficiently exploits the resources of a given environment will tend to spread at the expense of less efficient cultural systems, i.e., to dominate them, hence, the Etruscan interest in trade goods of the Eastern Mediterranean. See D. Kaplan, "The Law of Cultural Dominance," in M. Sahlins and E. Service, eds., *Evolution and Culture* (Ann Arbor: University of Michigan Press, 1960), pp. 69–92. For Etruscan orientalizing, see A. Rathje, "Oriental Imports in Etruria in the 8th and 7th centuries B.C.: Their Origins and Implications," in D. and F. Ridgway, eds., *Italy before the Romans* (New York: Academic Press, 1979), pp. 145–183.

19. J. Henzen first proposed an Etruscan origin for the games in *Explicatio Musivi in villa Burghesiana asservati* (Rome, 1845), pp. 74–75, reiterated by, among others, E. Richardson, *The Etruscans* (Chicago: University of Chicago Press, 1964), pp. 229–230 and L. Malten, "Leichenspiel und Totenkult," *MDAI(R)*, 38 (1923–1924): 300–341. Nicolaus, *Ath.* 4.153–154: Τὰς τῶν μονομάχων θέας οὐ μόνον ἐν πανηγύρεσι καὶ θεάτροις ἐποιοῦντο Ῥωμαῖοι. παρὰ Τυρρηνῶν παραλαβόντες τὸ ἔθος.

20. See two references by Tertullian to "the brother of Jove" who, with his hammer, carts away gladiators killed in the arena (*Ad Nat.* 1.10.47: *gladiatorum exsequias cum malleo deducit* and *Apol.* 15.5: *gladiatorum cadavera cum malleo deducentem*). These have been taken as descriptions of arena personnel dressed as the

Etruscan demon Charun; Ville suggests Charun was incorporated into the games under Augustus. See Ville, *Gladiature*, p. 2; Henzen, *Explicatio*, p. 75; and F. DeRuyt, *Charun: Démon étrusque de la mort* (Rome: Institut historique belge, 1934), pp. 191–192. As far as I can tell, this assertion of Ville's is made without concrete evidence. See also G. Ville, "Les Jeux de gladiateurs dans l'empire chrétien," *MEFRA*, 72 (1960): 273–335, especially p. 283.

21. Isidorus, *Etym*. 10.159: *lanista, gladiator, id est carnifex, Tusca lingua appellatus, a laniando scilicet corpora*. Linguistic analysis of *lanista* points to the Etruscan language, on the basis of the -a suffix and the existence of "Lani" as a proper name in Etruscan. See A. Ernout and A. Meillet, *Dictionnaire étymologique de la langue latine* (Paris: C. Klincksieck, 1959), under "lanista."

22. Ville, *Gladiature*, p. 3.

23. Spartacus' *ludus*, for example, was located in Capua. See Plutarch, *Crass*. 8. K. Welch, "The Roman Arena in Late-Republican Italy: A New Interpretation," *JRA*, 7 (1994): 59–80, rightly emphasizes the evidence for Roman, not Capuan, ownership of the Capuan gladiatorial schools (p. 69).

24. *Tarquinius Priscus prior Romanis duo paria gladiatorum edidit quae comparavit per annos XXVI*. The context of this fragment is not entirely clear. It may have come from Suetonius' *de Regibus*, as part of a presumably longer listing of the first Tarquin's significant accomplishments. Alternatively, it may have been located in his books on Roman games and spectacles, as part of a fuller explanation of the nature and origins of the *munera*, a commentary sadly no longer extant. Suetonius fragment in A. Reifferscheid, *C. Suetonii Tranquilli praeter Caesarum libros reliquiae* (Leipzig: B. G. Teubner, 1860), p. 320, quoted and scoffed at by Ville, *Gladiature*, p. 8, n. 32. See below for further comments on the early *munera* in Rome.

25. See below for further comments on the early *munera* in Rome.

26. The oldest artifacts identified as pertaining to gladiatorial combat are Etruscan seventh-century bronze statuettes, nude males holding a sword upright in either hand. These figures may represent *dimachaerii*, gladiators who specialized in the simultaneous use of two swords. Independently proposed by K. A. Neugebauer, "Der älteste Gladiatorentypus," *JDAI(AA)*, 55 (1940): 608–611 and F. Matz, in a review of Hanfmann's *Altetruskische Plastik*, *Gnomon*, 16 (1940): 197–205. There is, of course, a long gap between the production of these statuettes and the appearance of this gladiator type in the Principate.

27. The Tomb of the Augurs, the Tomb of the Olympiades, and the Tomb of Pulcinella, all dating to the latter half of the sixth century. Ville, *Gladiature*, pp. 4–6. See M. Pallottino, *Etruscologia* (Milan: U. Hoepli, 1963), p. 285; A. Baldi, "Perseus e Phersu," *Aevum*, 35 (1961): 131–133; G. Becatti and F. Magi, *Monumenti della pittura antica scoperti in Italia, fasc III.4: Pitture delle tombe degli Auguri e del Pulcinella* (Rome: Istituto Poligrafico dello Stato, 1955).

28. Diagnostic canine or feline ears are no longer extant. It is usually identified as a dog, but the curl and uniform width of the tail, in addition to the grip of the forepaws on the leg of its opponent, seem more reminiscent of a cat. If it is some

kind of wildcat, this might suggest that some sort of trade in wild animals was going on at quite an early date, which may be significant for *venationes*.

29. Among them are Tarquinia's Tomb of the Bigae, Tomb of the Funeral Couch, Tomb of the Pyrrhichistes, and at Chiusi, the Tomb of the Monkey, Tomb of the Colle, and the Tomb of Poggio al Moro.

30. Another ancient exhibition of martial skill that did not involve bloodshed was the *Lusus Troiae*, an equestrian event, at which Roman boys faced off against each other in executing cavalry maneuvers. Its antiquity is unknown, although the name lays claim to the patina of the venerable Trojan past; the Troy Game first appears in the literary sources in connection with Sulla (Plutarch, *Cat. Mai.* 3), although Vergil attributes its introduction to Aeneas upon arrival in Italy (*Aen.* 5.553–603). Although possibly found in Etruria from a very early date (if one considers the late seventh-century Tragliatella oenochoe evidence for the Troy Game), the equestrian nature of this event argues against its depiction in the tomb paintings at issue here. For the Troy Game as a connection between Etruria and early Rome, see K. W. Weeber, "Troiae lusus," *Ancient Society*, 5 (1974): 171–196 and A. Alföldi, *Early Rome and the Latins* (Ann Arbor: University of Michigan Press, 1971), pp. 280–283.

31. Also found in a Hellenic context, both as spectacle in the Panathenaic games and as athletic training. See Lysias, *Accept. Mum. Def.* 1.

32. See, for example, Nicolaus, *Ath.* 14.631; *Digest* 48.19.8.11; and Pliny, *HN* 8.5.

33. The context of the contests shown in Etruscan tombs is also clearly funerary, which would be an unusual milieu for *Pyrrhica*.

34. Some suggestion of this is in J.-Cl. Golvin, *L'Amphithéâtre romain* (Paris: E. de Boccard, 1988), pp. 17–21.

35. See citation in Reifferscheid, *C. Suetonii* and note 24 above.

36. For the Etruscan influence in Rome, see L. Bonfante, "Roman Triumphs and Etruscan Kings: The Changing Face of the Triumph," *JRS*, 60 (1970): 49–66, and *Out of Etruria* (Oxford: BAR International Series, 1981), pp. 93–110 and Rathje, "Oriental Imports." A different model for this cultural interaction, one which questions Etruscan primacy, is presented by Cornell, *Beginnings*, pp. 156–172.

37. For connection between conquest and the official organization of the ordinary games, see Th. Mommsen, *"Ludi Romani," Römische Forschungen* (Berlin: Weidmann, 1864–1879) and G. Jennison, *Animals for Show and Pleasure in Ancient Rome* (Manchester: Manchester University Press, 1937), pp. 42–43.

38. This was the same Maenius who set up the Rostra from the battle of Antium. For the precise location of the column, see F. Coarelli, *Il foro romano* (Rome: Quasar, 1983–1985), vol. 2, pp. 39–53.

39. Festus p. 135M = p. 107 Th: *Maeniana appellata sunt a Maenio censore, qui primus in foro ultra columnas tigna proiecit, quo ampliarentur superiora spectacula.*

40. The term itself would not originate in Samnite practice; it would not make sense for the Samnites themselves to have a gladiator type named "Samnite." This

suggests a perspective external to the Samnites. See P. Meier, "De Gladiatura Romana: Quaestiones Selectae" (Dissertation, Universität Bonn, 1881), pp. 14–20.

41. The discrepancy between the dates for the Samnite wars and the usual third-century introduction of *munera* could be answered by claiming the "Samnite" armature is a relic of the Campanian or Etruscan system, later adopted by the Romans.

42. Livy, *Epit.* 16: *D. Iunius Brutus munus gladiatorium in honorem defuncti patris primus edidit.* See Colvin, *L'Amphithéâtre,* pp. 17–18.

43. Valerius Maximus 2.4.7: *Nam gladiatorium munus primum Romae datum foro Boario Ap. Claudio, M. Fulvio consulibus: dederunt Marcus et Decimus filii Bruti Perae, funebri memoria patris cineris honorando.* Some manuscripts eliminate the "Perae." Valerius Maximus wrote his "Memorable Deeds and Sayings" in the reign of Tiberius, relying on Livy and the annals as sources of information. His close match with Livy's report is likely due to their mutual annalistic source.

44. Ausonius, *Griphus* 36–37: *tris primas Thraecum pugnas tribus ordine bellis Iuniadae patrio inferias misere sepulcro.*

45. Servius, *Ad Aen.* 3.67: *Apud veteres etiam homines interficiebantur, sed mortuo Iunio Bruto cum multae gentes ad eius funus captivos misissent, nepos illius eos qui missi erant inter se composuit, et sic pugnaverunt; et quod muneri missi erant, inde munus appellatum.* On the question of human sacrifice, see Chapter 5.

46. W. Smith, ed., *A Dictionary of Greek and Roman Biography and Mythology* (London: J. Murray, 1876), vol. 2, p. 658 and vol. 1, pp. 507–513 and F. Münzer, "Iunius Brutus," *RE,* 10:1, col. 1023.

47. B. Niebuhr, *The Roman History* (London: C. and J. Rivington, 1827), vol. 1, pp. 522–530.

48. A third son, a child at the deaths of his brothers, is suggested by Posidonius, quoted in Plutarch, *Brut.* 1.

49. Other *cognomina* include Bubulcus, Gracchanus, Norbanus, Paciaecus, Pennus, Pullus, and Silanus.

50. Münzer, *RE,* 10:1, col. 1026 accepts the double *cognomen.*

51. Livy 10.43, 47.

52. T. R. S. Broughton, *The Magistrates of the Roman Republic* (Cleveland: Press of Case Western University, 1968), vol. 1, pp. 201–202 and Münzer, *RE,* 10:1, no. 124. Interestingly, the son of the consul of 266 became dictator in 216, after Cannae, and in the same year as the Aemilian *munera.*

53. Extramural regulation for burials demanded by the Twelve Tables, Table X (Sacred Law). See collection of Twelve Tables in E. H. Warmington, ed., *Remains of Old Latin* (Cambridge, Mass.: Harvard University Press, 1935), vol. 3, pp. 424–513.

54. Henzen, *Explicatio,* pp. 112–113.

55. Meier, "De Gladiatura," pp. 33, cites Plutarch, *Crass.* 8 describing the games of Lentulus.

56. He is, after all, writing some seven centuries after the event, at a time when gladiatorial combat was long established and standardized.

57. Livy 23.30: *Et M. Aemilio Lepido, qui bis consul augurque fuerat, filii tres, Lucius, Marcus, Quintus, ludos funebres per triduum et gladiatorum paria duo et viginti in foro dederunt.*

58. For further comments on the Forum location, see below.

59. Smith, *Biography*, vol. 2, pp. 762–770.

60. Livy 23.30; Polybius 2.21; and Zonaras 8, p. 401.

61. Livy 21.49, 51; 22.9, 33, 35; and 23.30.

62. Further discussion of the link between the dates of the first *munera* and the inception of the institution appears in Chapter 5.

63. M. Valerius Laevinus in Livy 31.50.4. The year 183 B.C. saw the funeral of P. Licinius Crassus, detailed in Livy 39.46. T. Quinctius Flamininus was honored in 174; see Livy 41.28.11. Ville, *Gladiature*, pp. 42–51 lists all instances of *munera* given in the second and third centuries.

64. Servius, *Ad Aen.* 2.1440: *unde ludi Taurei dicti, qui ex Libris Fatalibus a rege Tarquinio Superbo instituti sunt propterea quod omnis partus mulierum male cedebat. alii ludos Taureos a Sabinis propter pestilentiam institutos dicunt, ut lues publica in has hostias verteretur.*

65. Festus p. 351 M = p. 528 Th. Restoration of *in circo Flamonio* to text made by J. Scaliger. See Müller's comment. See also Ville, *Gladiature*, p. 54; F. Altheim, "Taurii, Ludi," in *RE*, 4A:2, cols. 2542–2544; and H. H. Scullard, *Festivals and Ceremonies of the Roman Republic* (Ithaca: Cornell University Press, 1981), p. 156.

66. Ovid, *Fast.* 4.681–682: *missae vinctis ardentia taedis terga ferant volpes.*

67. W. Mannhardt, *Mythologische Forschungen aus dem Nachlasse* (Strassburg: K. J. Trubner, 1884), pp. 108–110 specifies peasants in contemporary France and Germany. See also Scullard, *Festivals*, pp. 101–103.

68. J. G. Frazer, ed., *Publii Ovidii Nasonis: Fastorum Libri Sex* (London: MacMillan and Co. Ltd., 1929), vol. 3, pp. 331–335. Other explanations cite the fox as a safeguard against mildew, or the burning of the fox and the wheat as preventing excessive heat in the summertime.

69. Ovid, *Fast.* 5.371–374: *cur tibi pro Libycis clauduntur rete leaenis imbelles capreae sollicitusque lepus? non sibi, respondit (Flora), silvas cessisse, sed hortos arvaque pugnaci non adeunda ferae.* See also Martial 8.67.4.

70. Pliny, *HN* 18.286.

71. The voting of the annual festival for Flora is described as taking place during the consulship of Laenas and Postumius; *Fasti* 5.327–330. The rabbits' running from their starting boxes had apparently become an axiomatic expression by the late third century. This is suggested by Plautus, whose characters take flight even more quickly than the rabbits in question (*citius extemplo a foro fugiunt quam ex porta ludis cum emissus lepus*), *Persa* 435–436. The uninhibited tone of the *Floralia* is clear from later descriptions, when the prostitutes of Rome claimed the *Floralia*, with its midnight mimes performed in the nude, as their special festival. See Valerius Maximus 2.10.8; Martial 3.86; and Juvenal 6.249–250.

72. Or teaching them amazing tricks: see Pliny's elephants, *HN* 8.2.

73. As recorded by Seneca (*De Brev. Vit.* 13.3) *primus Curius Dentatus in*

triumpho duxit elephantos and Eutropius (2.14.3) *(Curius) Primus Romam elephantos quattuor duxit.* Although Pliny *(HN* 8.6) contests this, saying that this was the first time elephants were in Italy but that Metellus was the first to bring them to Rome. Clearly the experience in Lucania had an impact, as elephants were afterward occasionally called Lucanian cows, as is explained by Varro *(Ling.* 7.389) and Lucretius (5.1302, 1339).

74. Pliny, *HN* 8.6.16–17: *Roma autem in triumpho V annis* (275 B.C.) *ad superiorem numerum additis, eadem plurimos anno DII* (252 B.C.) *victoria L. Metelli pontificis in Sicilia de Poenis captos. CXLII fuere aut, ut quidam, CXL travecti ratibus quas doliorum consertis ordinibus inposuerat. Verrius eos pugnasse in circo interfectosque iaculis tradit, paenuria consilii, quoniam neque ali placuisset neque donari regibus; L. Piso inductos dumtaxat in circum atque, ut contemptus eorum incresceret, ab operariis hastas praepilatas habentibus per circum totum actos. Nec quid deinde iis factum sit auctores explicant qui non putant interfectos.*

75. Livy 39.22.2: *et venatio data leonum et pantherarum, et prope huius saeculi copia ac varietate ludicrum celebratum est.*

76. Livy 44.18.8: *et iam magnificentia crescente . . . ludi, sexaginta tres Africanas et quadraginta ursos et elephantos lusisse.* Were there forty bears and forty elephants, or forty bears-and-elephants? The *Africanae* were apparently some sort of large feline, which the *OLD* (*Africanus* 1c) identifies as possibly panthers.

77. Ville, *Gladiature,* pp. 53–54.

78. *OLD ludere* 6a.

79. Pliny, *HN* 8.24: *Senatus consultum fuit vetus ne liceret Africanas in Italiam advehere. Contra hoc tulit ad populum Cn. Aufidius tribunus plebis, permisitque circensium gratia inportare.* Alternatively, there was a tribune named Gnaeus Aufidius in 114 B.C., whom H. Rackham accepts in the Loeb edition of Pliny as the activist in question. This is that Aufidius whom Cicero knew as a jurist and historian, who was also blind. See mentions in *Tusc.* 5.38, *Dom.* 13, *Fin.* 5.19.

80. And the motivation would depend on the date of the *senatus consultum.* The quote from Pliny merely refers to a *"vetus"* senatus consultum, but *"vetus"* to whom? Pliny? Or Aufidius? If the date is 170, obviously Carthage would be more of a threat, since by 114 Carthage was no longer a political rival. The "tear of Carthage" may be analogous to the suggested motivation for the timing of the Iunian and Aemilian *munera.* The antidemagoguery explanation would probably make more sense at the later date, as this was when individual politicians were coming to the fore more and more. The Aufidius of 170 was the one who accused C. Lucretius Gallus of ill treatment of the Chalcidians (Livy 43.10).

81. Valerius Maximus 2.7.14: *Et L. Paulus, Perse rege superato, eiusdem generis et culpae homines elephantis proterendos substravit; utilissimo quidem exemplo, si tamen acta excellentissimorum virorum humiliter aestimare sine insolentiae reprehensione permittitur. Aspero enim et absciso castigationis genere militaris disciplina indiget, quia vires armis constant; quae, ubi a recto tenore desciverint, oppressura sunt, nisi opprimantur.*

82. Ville, *Gladiature,* pp. 53–54.

83. Valerius Maximus 2.7.13: *everso Punico imperio, exterarum gentium transfugas, in edendis populo spectaculis, feris bestiis obiecit.*

84. See Chapter 5 for discussion of further ties between human sacrifice and the triumph.

85. The losing survivors of the Servile War met a similar fate in 100 B.C. Pliny, *HN* 8.20 and Seneca, *De Brev. Vit.* 13.6.

86. Livy, *Per.* 51 and Appian, *Bel. Afr.* 118.

87. Such as the Thessalian rodeo put on by Claudius; see Suetonius, *Claud.* 21.3.

88. See C. Nicolet, *The World of the Citizen in Republican Rome* (Berkeley: University of California Press, 1980), pp. 345–373 and P. J. J. Vanderbroek, *Popular Leadership and Collective Behavior in the Late Roman Republic* (Amsterdam: J. C. Gieben, 1987), pp. 77–81 and 218–267.

89. Polybius 6.52–54.

90. Appian, *B. Civ.* 1.105–106.

91. In some cases, years lapsed between the funeral proper and the *munera* part of the obsequies. Julius Caesar provides a good example of this: during his aedileship in 65 he sponsored highly elaborate gladiatorial games in honor of his father's decease some twenty years earlier. See Pliny, *HN* 33.53 and Dio Cassius 37.8. Caesar also planned gladiatorial games for his daughter, which suggests an expanded definition (in Caesar's mind at least) of what constituted a public figure deserving of such an honor. See Suetonius, *Caesar* 26.

92. For which see P. Plass, *The Game of Death in Ancient Rome* (Madison: University of Wisconsin Press, 1995), pp. 46–55 and 200–206.

93. Indeed, many of the thugs were themselves professional gladiators.

94. Plutarch, *C. Gracch.* 12.3–4.

95. Access to seating at spectacles held in the Forum was restricted to those who had sufficient "pull" with the sponsors of the spectacle and the current magistrates, who apparently were able to get blocks of seats for redistribution. See Chapter 4 for more detailed discussion of ticketing.

96. See especially Cicero, *Sest.* 106–127 and Vanderbroek, *Popular Leadership*, pp. 77–81. Due to the patterns of seat distribution, this would, of course, be a *selected* cross-section of the public.

97. The regularization of the *munera* in the spectacle calendar is alleged by some to have begun in 105 B.C. under the auspices of the aediles, as was suggested by P. Bucheler, "Die staatliche Anerkennung des Gladiatorenspiels," *RhMus*, 38 (1883): 476–479. This reconstruction is based on Ennodius, *Pan. dict. regi Theod.* 19, in which he says that Rutilius and Manlius (consuls in 105) sponsored gladiatorial combat so that the plebs might be familiar with warfare. Ennodius does *not* say that this was an official, i.e., state-sponsored, activity; in fact, the reference may originate from a tradition related by Valerius Maximus (2.3.2) that these consuls brought in *doctores* from the gladiatorial schools to coach legionaries in sword technique during the military crisis generated by the disastrous defeat at Arausio.

It is more likely that official sponsorship of *munera* as part of magisterial duties began in 42 B.C. See Dio Cassius 47.40.6. See, however, Welch, "Arena," pp. 61–62, who argues for the presentation of *munera* as part of the official games in Republican colonies and possibly in Rome as well during the Late Republic.

98. Cicero, *Mur.* 67. See also below, Chapter 4, section on seating.

99. Suetonius, *Caesar* 10.2.

100. See Cicero, *Sest.* 66.134 and *In Vat.* 15.37.

101. Pliny, *HN* 33.53 and Plutarch, *Caesar* 5. Caesar may represent an extreme, but even Polybius (31.28) attests the scale of growth of *munera*, when he asserts that an heir was more or less expected to spend thirty talents, a fortune equivalent to 750,000 sesterces, to provide such spectacle for his predecessor.

102. The outbursts of street violence could be highly organized as well. See especially Vandenbroek's assessment of Clodius' activities in 57 during the *Ludi Romani*, *Popular Leadership*, pp. 249–251.

103. Most apparent in the presence of the *columna lemniscata* on the Caivano hydria and the monument on the Tischbein vase, cited by Ville as evidence for Campanian gladiatorial combat. See O. Elia, "Caivano. Necropoli pre-romana," *NSA* (1931), pp. 577–614, who calls it armed combat, not gladiatorial but martial. Tischbein vase I.60 in S. Reinach, *Répertoire des vases peints grecs et étrusques* (Paris: E. Leroux, 1922–1924), p. 293.

104. Tertullian, *De Spect.* 12.3: *quos paraverant, armis quibus tunc et qualiter poterant eruditos, tantum ut occidi discerent, mox edicto die inferiarum apud tumulos erogabant.*

105. Servius, *Ad Aen.* 10.519: *sane mos erat in sepulchris virorum fortium captivos necari: quod postquam crudele visum est, placuit gladiatores ante sepulchra dimicare, qui a bustis bustuarii appellati sunt.* The use of contrived combats as a distancing device for communally sanctioned human sacrifice is discussed further in Chapter 5.

106. Except perhaps Servius by implication, as his comment is associated with Italic Turnus' rampage. This could be taken as evidence for Italic as opposed to Etruscan practice.

107. Urn published in U. Tarchi, *L'arte nell'Umbria e nella Sabina* (Milan: Fratelli Treves, 1936–1940), vol. 1, pl. lxx. See also Golvin, *L'Amphithéâtre*, pp. 16–17.

108. Which had very public elements, such as the *elogia* and *pompa funebris* in addition to the *ludi*. The *ludi* probably took place on the eighth day after the interment, the *novendialis*.

109. Discussed by Golvin, *L'Amphithéâtre*, pp. 301–313. See also Welch, "Arena," pp. 69–78.

110. Vitruvius 5.1: *ad spectaculorum rationem utilis dispositio.*

111. See J. Russel, "The Origin and Development of the Republican Forums," *Phoenix*, 22.4 (1968): 304–336.

112. Or does it? Some authorities claim it measures 90 by 35 meters, which is a ratio of 2.57:1. See F. E. Brown, *Cosa: The Making of a Roman Town* (Ann Arbor:

University of Michigan Press, 1980), pp. 30–31, but compare Russel, "Origin," p. 307 and Golvin, *L'Amphithéâtre*, pp. 302–303.

113. P. C. Sestieri, *Paestum* (Rome: Istituto Poligrafico dello Stato, 1967), and F. Castagnoli, *Orthogonal Town Planning in Antiquity* (Cambridge, Mass.: Harvard University Press, 1972), p. 132. Both Paestum and Cosa were founded as Roman colonies in 273 B.C.

114. Luna's forum measures approximately 47 by 82 meters. See S. L. Siena, *Luni: Guida archeologica* (Sarzana, 1985) and T. W. Potter, *Roman Italy* (Berkeley: University of California Press, 1987), pp. 74–75.

115. See Golvin, *L'Amphithéâtre*, pp. 304–306 and A. Maiuri, "Saggi nell'area del foro di Pompei," *NSA*, 3 (1941): 371–404. For Rome, see Golvin, *L'Amphithéâtre*, pp. 18–21 and Coarelli, *Foro*, vol. 2, pp. 125–49. For more details on the Roman Forum, see below.

116. For fuller discussion of functionalism in spectacle settings, see Golvin, *L'Amphithéâtre*, pp. 298–300.

117. F. Canac, *Acoustique des théâtres antiques* (Paris: Editions du Centre National de la Recherche Scientifique, 1967), p. 178, who suggested that the upward capacity limit on theaters was twelve thousand seats.

118. O. Navarre, "Odeum," in Ch. Daremberg, E. Saglio, and E. Pottier, eds., *Dictionnaire des antiquités grecques et romains* (Paris: Hachette et Cie, 1907), vol. 4, pt. 1, pp. 150–152.

119. A. Sorlin-Dorigny, "Stadium," in Ch. Daremberg, E. Saglio, and E. Pottier, *Dictionnaire des antiquités grecques et romains* (Paris: Hachette et Cie, 1911), vol. 4, pt. 2, pp. 1419–1456.

120. A.-C. Bussemaker and E. Saglio, "Circus," in Ch. Daremberg, E. Saglio, and E. Pottier, *Dictionnaire des antiquités grecques et romains* (Paris: Hachette et Cie, 1887), vol. 1, pt. 2, pp. 1187–1201. For all the architectural details of Roman circuses, see J. Humphrey, *Roman Circuses* (Berkeley: University of California Press, 1986).

121. Golvin, *L'Amphithéâtre*, pp. 307–310.

122. In terms of economy, important to the *editores* of *munera* and probably to the builders of Imperial amphitheaters, the more spectators there were, greedily sucking in all the sensation the spectacle offered, the better. There was, no doubt, a careful balance between enhanced visual perception and increased seating capacity, with the Colosseum probably representing the upward limit feasible.

123. See comments above on the seating provided by Maenius et al.

124. Golvin, *L'Amphithéâtre*, pp. 18–21 and Coarelli, *Foro*, vol. 2, pp. 125–149. Some such renovation was necessary, for example, after the fire of 210 B.C.

125. Pseudo-Asconius, *Div. in Caec.* 16–50. For more discussion of seating at *munera*, see Chapter 4 below.

126. Cicero, *Phil.* 9.7.16: *cum talis vir ob rem publicam in legatione mortem obierit, senatui placere Ser. Sulpicio statuam pedestrem aeneam in rostris ex huius ordinis sententia statui, circumque eam statuam locum ludis gladiatoribusque liberos posterosque*

eius quoquo versus pedes quinque habere, quod is ob rem publicam mortem obierit. Note that the privilege is granted to children and descendants without any restrictions, apparently until the end of time. For more on seating, see Chapter 4.

127. As noted earlier, the Basilica Porcia was built during the censorship of M. Porcius Cato in 184. The Basilica Aemilia followed in 179, while M. Aemilius Lepidus and M. Fulvius Nobilior were the very architecturally active censors. The Basilica Sempronia was constructed under the censorship of Ti. Sempronius Gracchus in 170. For the building activity of censors, see Chapter 4 in addition. For seating in colonnades of basilicas, see Vitruvius 5.1. The Basilica Opimia, west of the Temple of Saturn, was added to the Forum in 120; ironically, it commemorated the overthrow of C. Gracchus, son of the builder of the Basilica Sempronia. On the Republican Forum, see F. Coarelli, *Guida archeologica di Roma* (Milano: A. Mondadori, 1974), pp. 53–81 and J. E. Stambaugh, *The Ancient Roman City* (Baltimore: Johns Hopkins University Press, 1988), pp. 106–114.

128. Plutarch's description, in *C. Gracch.* 12.10, may indicate that the tribunals, including the Rostra and the Comitium, were curved. See Welch's reconstructions of Caesar's spectacular accommodations in the Forum, "Arena," pp. 73–75, figs. 6–8.

129. Caesar's renovations of the Forum are described in Golvin, *L'Amphithéâtre*, pp. 45–51 and Coarelli, *Foro*, vol. 2, pp. 233–257.

130. The Basilica Porcia was not rebuilt after the fire.

131. See G. Gatti, "I Saepta Iulia nel Campo Marzio," *L'Urbe*, 2.9 (1937): 8–23 and Nicolet, *World*, pp. 249–250.

132. Coarelli, *Foro*, vol. 2, pp. 244–255.

133. See C. F. Carettoni, "Le gallerie ipogee del foro e i ludi gladiatori forensi," *BCAR*, 76 (1956–1958): 23–44; C. F. Giuliani and P. Verduchi, *L'area centrale del foro romano* (Florence: L. S. Olschki, 1987), pp. 52–66; and Coarelli, *Foro*, vol. 2, pp. 211–213. This is, of course, the forerunner to subterranean arrangements made in later amphitheatrical arenas, the best known being those in the Colosseum.

134. Dio Cassius 43.22.3: καὶ ἀμφιθέατρον ἐκ τοῦ πέριξ πανταχόθεν ἕδρας ἄνευ σκηνῆς ἔχειν προσερρήθη. See also Suetonius, *Caesar* 39.2.

135. Ville, *Gladiature*, p. 70. See Curio's structure of 52, described below, for antecedents.

136. Pozzolana was found particularly in Campania but also elsewhere in central Italy.

137. For concrete details, see H.-O. Lamprecht, *Opus Caementitium: Bautechnik der Römer* (Düsseldorf: Beton-Verlag, 1984), pp. 19–68; J. B. Ward-Perkins, *Roman Architecture* (New York: H. N. Abrams, 1977), pp. 97–99; and W. L. MacDonald, *The Architecture of the Roman Empire I* (New Haven: Yale University Press, 1965), pp. 152–166.

138. Although there were stone theaters defined as Roman, i.e., built under at least nominal Roman auspices, such as those at Pompeii, Cales, and Capua,

which all date to the first half of the second century, these were not entirely free-standing and thus were not Roman in style.

139. The earliest amphitheaters were built in Capua, Cumae, and Liternum at the end of the second century. These early Campanian examples were joined by Puteoli, Telesia, Abella, Teanum, Cales, and Pompeii before the end of the Republic. Paestum, although technically in Lucania, is located close enough to the Campanian amphitheaters to have been influenced by the same factors. The other four Republican amphitheaters include two in Etruria and two in Hispania Baetica, areas that feature more or less prominently in the early history of the *munera*, dovetailing nicely with presumed traditional interests. Varied types of evidence date these buildings: Capua, Cumae, and Liternum are dated to the second century by Johannowsky on the basis of their early type of *opus reticulatum* (W. Johannowsky, "La situazione in Campania," in P. Zanker, ed., *Hellenismus in Mittelitalien* [Göttingen: Vandenhoeck and Ruprecht, 1976], vol. 1, pp. 267–299); Pompeii, by an inscription: *CIL* X.852; Abella, by construction technique (*opus incertum*); Cales, by construction technique; Teanum, by construction technique as well as simplicity of design; Puteoli (small amphitheater), by construction technique, although this is sometimes dated to the Augustan period; Telesia, by construction technique (*opus reticulatum* walls for both amphitheater and for Sullan colony); Paestum, by material used to construct the arena and basis of *cavea*; Sutri *looks* primitive in design as well as execution. The material of Ferentium is comparable to that at Pompeii and Telesia. Carmo's material is like that at Pompeii. Ucubi's context is apparently Caesarean. See Golvin, *L'Amphithéâtre*, pp. 24–25 and 32–44. See also Welch, "Arena," pp. 65–69.

140. See Johannowsky, "Situazione."

141. Some of the wealth was reinvested abroad. Campanian traders established enclaves on Delos and in Asia Minor to protect their interests.

142. Extrapolated from H. Jouffroy, *La Construction publique en Italie et dans l'Afrique romaine* (Strasbourg: AECR, 1986), pp. 1–56.

143. See Appian *B. Civ.* 1.7 and Siculus Flaccus, *De Cond. agr.* p. 135, 20.

144. Sullan colonies themselves met with some resistance, referred to by Cicero, *Ad Fam.* 13.4.

145. See also Welch, "Arena," pp. 60–61, whose findings agree with my own.

146. *CIL* X.852: *C. Quinctius C.f. Valgus M. Porcius M.f. duovir. quinq. coloniai honoris caussa spectacula de sua peq. fac. coer. et coloneis locum in perpetuom deder.*

147. Cicero, in *Pro Sulla* 60–61, describes the colonists as different, by definition, from the locals in terms of political participation, or *suffragium*, and *de ambulatio*, which some have taken as a technical term associated with elections, others, as a reference to their freedom of movement. See P. Castrén, *Ordo Populusque Pompeianus* (Rome: Bardi Editore, 1975), pp. 54–55.

148. For the spread of *munera* and amphitheaters as part of the imposition of a Romanized identity, see Wiedemann, *Emperors*, pp. 1–54.

149. On this issue, see E. S. Gruen, *Culture and National Identity in Republican Rome* (Ithaca: Cornell University Press, 1992), pp. 205–210.

150. There are earlier hints at such constructions, notably for 179 (Livy 40.51) and 174 (Livy 41.27), although the latter structure is described as a *scaena* and not a theater per se. The fact that the censors were apparently responsible for these creations makes it unlikely that they were intended as temporary venues for the year's games. This is the same Nasica who offered wild animals at his aedilician games in 169.

151. This Gruen understands as a ban on seating, period, permanent or temporary.

152. Livy, *Per.* 48: *P. Cornelius Nasica auctore tamquam inutile et nociturum publicis moribus ex senatus consulto destructum est.* Valerius Maximus 2.4.2: *ut scilicet remissioni animorum juncta standi virilitas, propria Romanae gentis nota, esset.* See also L. R. Taylor, *Roman Voting Assemblies* (Ann Arbor: University of Michigan Press, 1966), pp. 30–31 on the desirability of standing for the Roman character.

153. See, for example, M. Bieber, *History of the Greek and Roman Theater* (Princeton: Princeton University Press, 1961), p. 327.

154. See Appian, *B. Civ.* 1.28 and E. Frézouls, "Aspects de l'histoire du théâtre romain," *ANRW* II.12.1 (1983): 353–354.

155. See also Nicolet, *World*, p. 363. Gruen, *Culture*, p. 210 specifies the need for the elite to control artistic expression and its reception, emphasizing the cultural aspect of contemporary political stances rather than the pragmatic needs of spectacular manipulation.

156. Aulus Gellius, *N.A.* 10.1.7. Pompey's theater was allegedly simply the huge and elaborate porch of a relatively tiny temple.

157. Pliny, *HN* 36.24.117 and Plutarch, *Cat. Min.* 45.

158. It sounds very much like a false etymology, and it should be noted that Pliny is writing very much after the fact. We have no evidence for the currency of the word "*amphitheatrum*" until the second century after Christ, "*spectacula*" being used until the Imperial period, then "*amphitheatra*" before the use of the singular came into vogue. See R. Etienne, "La naissance de l'amphithéâtre, le mot et la chose," *REL*, 43 (1966): 213–220. Golvin seems, however, entirely convinced of the historicity of Curio's structure; *L'Amphithéâtre*, pp. 30–32 and pl. 4.

159. In 29 B.C., as attested by Dio Cassius 51.23 and Suetonius, *Aug.* 29.

160. Dio Cassius 59.10. Suetonius, *Caligula* 21 tells us that the project was abandoned by Claudius. *CIL.* VI.1252 refers to the damage to the aqueduct. See Golvin, *L'Amphithéâtre*, p. 54 and also L. Richardson, *A New Topographical Dictionary of Ancient Rome* (Baltimore: Johns Hopkins University Press, 1992), pp. 6–7.

161. Tacitus, *Ann.* 13.31. See Golvin, *L'Amphithéâtre*, pp. 55–56 and Richardson, *Dictionary*, p. 11.

162. Dio Cassius 62.18.

163. Indicated by Suetonius, *Vesp.* 9.1. Between Augustus and Vespasian, amphitheatrical needs were met by Statilius' structure, by a temporary structure built under Caligula, and by Nero's wooden building, as well as by, presumably, traditional means.

164. The spread of amphitheaters outside Italy began in the Republican period, picked up speed under Augustus and peaked around the turn of the century. For more on this, see Chapter 2. For the construction of amphitheaters as politicized public buildings, see Chapter 4.

165. Livy 28.21: *cum dirimi ab tanta rabie nequirent, insigne spectaculum exercitui praebuere documentumque quantum cupiditas imperii malum inter mortales esset.*

166. Dio Cassius 44.6: κἀν ταῖς ὁπλομαχίαις μίαν τινὰ ἀεὶ ἡμέραν καὶ ἐν τῇ Ῥώμῃ καὶ ἐν τῇ ἄλλῃ Ἰταλίᾳ ἀνέθεσαν.

167. "*Legitima*" insofar as they are part of the "ordinary" games, those presented by Rome's magistrates as part of the regular festal calendar.

168. Dio Cassius 47.40. See further interpretation of this passage in the Introduction above.

169. Augustus, *RG* 22.1, echoed by Suetonius, *Aug.* 43. Note the huge increase in scale from the spectacles of the Republic.

170. Dio Cassius 54.2. The wording of Suetonius, *Tibe.* 34 and Dio Cassius 59.14 suggests that gladiators were seen at other public festivals, as subsidiary to the main spectacle. The editorial responsibility was transferred to the quaestors under Claudius, which Tacitus (*Ann.* 11.22) interprets as putting that office up for sale. This would replace their obligation to keep the roads paved, as we are told by Suetonius, *Claud.* 24.2. See K. Hopkins, *Death and Renewal* (Cambridge: Cambridge University Press, 1983), p. 6. For further Augustan control of the spectacles, see below, especially Chapters 4 and 5.

171. Dio Cassius 54.17, which specifies that praetors could spend, from their own resources, three times the amount allocated them from public funds. See also Martial 10.41. Special cases got special accommodations: Trajan gave Hadrian two million sesterces to be used for his praetorian games. See SHA, *Hadr.* 3.8.

172. For the use of ritual in political communication, see, among others, C. Bell, *Ritual Theory, Ritual Practice* (New York: Oxford University Press, 1992), pp. 171–187 and D. I. Kertzer, *Ritual, Politics and Power* (New Haven: Yale University Press, 1988), especially pp. 77–124.

173. Juvenal 10.77–81: *Nam qui dabat olim imperium fasces legiones omnia, nunc se continet atque duas tantum res anxius optat, panem et circenses.* Rephrased by Fronto 2.216.

174. This identification is not unique to the Principate. See Cicero, *Sest.* 106, discussed above. L. Friedländer, *Roman Life and Manners* (London: G. Routledge and Sons, 1908), pp. 5–6 and Hopkins, *Death*, pp. 17–20.

175. Dio Cassius 73.20: καὶ κύριος εἶ καὶ πρῶτος εἶ καὶ πάντων εὐτυχέστατος. νικᾷς. νικήσεις. ἀπ᾽ αἰῶνος. Ἀμαζόνιε. νικᾷς. See also the discourse represented on mosaics, including those at Smirat and in Madrid, discussed by S. Brown, "Death as Decoration: Scenes from the Arena on Roman Domestic Mosaics," in A. Richlin, ed., *Pornography and Representation in Greece and Rome* (New York: Oxford University Press, 1992), pp. 180–211.

176. For spectacles as controlled populism, see Wiedemann, *Emperors*, pp. 165–183.

177. Suetonius, *Claud.* 21. For the importance of spectacles as a venue for communication, see Z. Yavetz, *Plebs and Princeps* (Oxford: Clarendon Press, 1969), pp. 18–24.

178. See Chapter 6, in particular, of Yavetz, *Plebs,* for a discussion of the importance of *levitas popularis,* the "common touch."

179. Gladiators typically came from the ranks of the marginalized in Roman society. They were prisoners of war, criminals, or slaves, with a few free men voluntarily entering the arena. To do so, however, meant an automatic loss of social and civic status, essentially the loss of freedom, while one remained a gladiator. The gladiator was *infamis:* he had no political agency, he was socially untouchable, and he was vulnerable to the sort of physical abuse from which Roman citizens, by law, were protected. The negative aspect of being a gladiator made it an appropriate sentence, in Roman eyes, for those convicted of a capital offense. One was either *damnatus ad ludum,* condemned to the gladiatorial school, which was a life sentence, or *damnatus ad arenam,* condemned to the arena to face a gladiator or wild animal unarmed. This was a death sentence. For a summary of the arena participants, see Ville, *Gladiature,* pp. 227–255; Wiedemann, *Emperors,* pp. 102–127; and J. P. V. D. Balsdon, *Life and Leisure in Ancient Rome* (New York: McGraw-Hill, 1969), pp. 288–330.

180. M. Foucault, *Discipline and Punish* (New York: Pantheon Books, 1977), pp. 47–69.

181. Livy 28.21; see also Silius Italicus, *Pun.* 16.527–548. Interestingly, here Livy distinguishes between these gladiatorial games and funeral games also held: *Huic gladiatorum spectaculo ludi funebres additi pro copia provinciali et castrensi apparatu.*

182. For further exploration of the Iberian approach to combative performance and its relation to local politics, see J. M. Blázquez and S. Montero, "Ritual funerario y status social: los combates gladiatorios prerromanos en la Peninsula Ibérica," *Veleia,* 10 (1993): 71–84.

183. R. May, *Power and Innocence* (New York: Norton, 1972), pp. 243–244.

184. Although the exercise of this sweeping authority may have been relatively infrequent, the institution of the *patria potestas* was fundamental to Roman society. See W. K. Lacey, "*Patria Potestas,*" in B. Rawson, ed., *The Family in Ancient Rome* (Ithaca: Cornell University Press, 1986) and R. Saller, "*Patria potestas* and the Stereotype of the Roman Family," *Continuity and Change* 1 (1986): 7–22.

185. E. Fromm, *The Heart of Man* (New York: Harper and Row, 1964), pp. 32–33. The pathology of the spectators at the Roman games is explored by C. Barton, *The Sorrows of the Ancient Romans: The Gladiator and the Monster* (Princeton: Princeton University Press, 1993).

186. K. Lorenz, *On Aggression* (New York: Bantam Books, 1966). See also G. W. Russell, "Psychological Issues in Sports Aggression," in J. H. Goldstein, ed., *Sports Violence* (New York: Springer-Verlag, 1993), pp. 157–181, who points out that Lorenz has since changed his mind (p. 161).

187. Which has been taken to indicate some premeditation on the part of the rioters, as it was not typical to carry weapons on one's person. For the political context of the riot, see Castrén, *Ordo*, pp. 111–112 and W. O. Moeller, "The Riot of A.D. 59 at Pompeii," *Historia*, 19 (1970): 84–95.

188. Tacitus, *Ann.* 14.17: *levi initio atrox caedes orta inter colonos Nucerinos Pompeianosque gladiatorio spectaculo . . . quippe oppidana lascivia in vicem incessentes probra, dein saxa, postremo ferum sumpsere . . . et rursus re ad patres relata, prohibiti publice in decem annos eius modi coetu Pompeiani.*

189. Suetonius, *Nero* 35.

190. It should, however, be remembered that the notion of "violence" is a cultural construct; one man's violence is another man's legitimate competition. See D. Riches, "The Phenomenon of Violence," in D. Riches, ed., *The Anthropology of Violence* (Oxford: Basil Blackwell Ltd., 1986), pp. 1–27.

191. The paradigm is offered by T. Gould, "The Uses of Violence in Drama," in J. Redmond, ed., *Violence in Drama* (Cambridge: Cambridge University Press, 1991), pp. 1–14.

192. The manipulation of violence in service of the Roman State is discussed on a more individual level in A. W. Lintott, *Violence in Republican Rome* (Oxford: Clarendon Press, 1968). Violence in society has been interpreted as playing a beneficial role, when constructed within parameters of control that support the value system of a given society. See discussion in E. Dunning, "Social Bonding and Violence in Sport: A Theoretical-Empirical Analysis," in Goldstein, *Sports Violence*, pp. 129–146.

193. Hopkins, *Death*, pp. 1–3. Skepticism is expressed by Wiedemann, *Emperors*, pp. 39–40.

194. This is suggested in Tacitus, with reference to decimation, Ann. 14.44: *contra singulos utilitate publica rependitur.*

195. R. Auguet, *Cruauté et civilisation* (Paris: Flammarion, 1970), pp. 239–244 and M. Wistrand, *Entertainment and Violence in Ancient Rome* (Göteborg: Ekblads, 1992), pp. 15–29, who categorizes the assessments; see also Plass, *Game*, pp. 62–77 and 213–224. See, however, ambiguity of reactions acknowledged by Wiedemann, *Emperors*, pp. 128–145.

196. Cicero, *Tusc.* 2.41 calls gladiators *perditi homines aut barbari*, ruined men or barbarians. Tacitus refers to them (*Ann.* 1.76) as *vilis sanguis*, degraded bloodlines, which shamefulness they pass on to their offspring (*Ann.* 11.21). The servile status of many gladiators also made their lives, to some extent, forfeit; they were already "socially dead." See O. Patterson, *Slavery and Social Death: A Comparative Study* (Cambridge, Mass.: Harvard University Press, 1982). Others, as prisoners of war, had already committed the capital offense of resistance to Rome, thus demonstrating their barbarity.

197. Seneca (*Tranq.* 2.4–5) points out, writing about the suicide of a gladiator, that "you must not think that only great men have been gifted with the strength of mind that breaks the bonds of human servitude." Seneca, *Ep.* 77.6 has the classic articulation of the good death.

198. Pliny, *Paneg.* 33: *non enerve nec fluxum, nec quod animos virorum molliret et frangeret, sed quod ad pulchra vulnera contemptumque mortis accenderet, cum in servorum etiam noxiorumque corporibus amor laudis et cupido victoriae cerneretur.*

199. Pliny's exposition is part of his encomium to Trajan, originally delivered as consul in A.D. 95. Trajan may have taken Pliny's view to heart, providing ten thousand edifying examples of such Roman ideals in the games celebrating his Dacian victory. The moral value of *munera* in promoting "contempt for death" is recognized also by Cicero, *Tusc.* 2.41 and claimed by Ammianus Marcellinus 14.6 as one of the bases of Rome's enduring authority.

2. A SCATTER OF CIRCLES

1. See J. Rykwert, *The Idea of a Town* (Princeton: Princeton University Press, 1976) for discussion of the foundation ritual and its meaning for urbanism. For extension of foundation rituals to western provinces, see W. Mierse, "Augustan Building Programs in the Western Provinces," in K. A. Raaflaub and M. Toher, eds., *Between Republic and Empire: Interpretations of Augustus and His Principate* (Berkeley: University of California Press, 1990), pp. 308–333. For exploration of the implications of urbanization in antiquity, see W. L. MacDonald, *The Architecture of the Roman Empire II* (New Haven: Yale University Press, 1986), pp. 248–273 and J. Rich and A. Wallace-Hadrill, eds., *City and Country in the Ancient World* (New York: Routledge, 1991). The extent of urbanization in La Tène society, prior to Roman conquest, is considered in P. S. Wells, *Culture Contact and Culture Change* (Cambridge: Cambridge University Press, 1981) and chapter 2 of B. W. Cunliffe, *Greeks, Romans and Barbarians: Spheres of Interaction* (New York: Methuen, 1988).

2. For recent discussion of the Romanization process as locally interactive, see, among others, C. R. Whittaker, *Frontiers of the Roman Empire* (Baltimore: Johns Hopkins University Press, 1994), pp. 1–9, 98–131; S. K. Drummond and L. H. Nelson, *The Western Frontiers of Imperial Rome* (Armonk, New York: M. E. Sharpe, 1994); D. B. Saddington, "The Parameters of Romanization," in V. A. Maxfield and M. J. Dobson, eds., *Roman Frontier Studies 1989: Proceedings of the XVth International Congress of Roman Frontier Studies* (Exeter: University of Exeter Press, 1991), pp. 413–418. For an overly minimalist view of this interaction, see R. MacMullen, "Notes on Romanization," reprinted in *Changes in the Roman Empire: Essays in the Ordinary* (Princeton: Princeton University Press, 1990), pp. 56–66.

3. For a fuller explanation of the methodology employed, see Appendix 1.

4. See, among others, P. Grimal, *Roman Cities* (Madison: University of Wisconsin Press, 1983), p. 57 and T. Bekker-Nielsen, *The Geography of Power* (Oxford: British Archaeological Reports, 1989), pp. 4–13 and Table 2.1. Similar assertion made by J.-Cl. Golvin, *L'Amphithéâtre romain* (Paris: E. de Boccard, 1988), p. 265, although T. Wiedemann, *Emperors and Gladiators* (New York: Routledge, 1992), pp. 41–46, acknowledges the role of the amphitheater in Romanization, and rightly so.

5. See Appendix 1: with N as twenty-two amphitheaters, the average distance between centers (or intercenter distance [ICD]) was 115 kilometers, with a range for each of some 72 kilometers, which is closest to Bekker-Nielsen's least-dense Type D dispersion, with its average ICD of 105.7 kilometers and a range of 66.1 kilometers. Spanish amphitheaters better fit the 2:1 ratio of successive urbanization types set up by Bekker-Nielsen, being almost twice the Type C figures of 58.5 and 36.6 for ICD and range respectively.

6. Bekker-Nielsen specifically cites the tribe of the Aedui in central Gaul as a case in point of such a phenomenon: *Geography*, p. 31. For a summation of the changing situation in Gaul during the first half of the first century, see Cunliffe, *Greeks*, pp. 80–105.

7. Of course, our knowledge about scarcity or prevalence of amphitheaters depends on the current state of archaeological evidence, as does our knowledge about urbanization spread.

8. They are Bracara Augusta, which was visible in the eighteenth century, Carmo, Carthago Nova, Conimbriga, Emerita, Emporiae, Illici, Italica, Segobriga, Tarraco, Toledo, and Ucubis. Evidence for the others is literary and epigraphical.

9. Livy 28.21 and Valerius Maximus 8.11. For the description of the second-century games in Spain at the death of Viriathus, see Appian, *Hisp.* 6.75. See Golvin, *L'Amphithéâtre*, pp. 21 and 42. For the pre-Roman duels in Spain, see J. M. Blázquez and S. Montero, "Ritual funerario y status social: los combates gladiatorios prerromanos en la Península Ibérica," *Veleia*, 10 (1993): 71–84.

10. Possibly they were motivated by factors analogous to those in Celtic society, for which see Chapter 3.

11. The numerous bull events in the festival calendar of Spain are described by T. Mitchell, *Blood Sport: A Social History of Spanish Bullfighting* (Philadelphia: University of Pennsylvania Press, 1991), pp. 13–24. Mitchell, however, perceives the link between Roman *venationes* and modern Spanish tauromachy as indirect in historical terms (p. 40), suggesting that the *corrida*'s heritage can be traced to medieval *capeas* but no further. He does, however, acknowledge a striking similarity in social meaning, both events endowed with political and psychosexual significance in the expression of both *majismo* and *machismo* (pp. 160–168). For further interpretation of the modern bullfight as an expression of human civilization and control, see G. Marvin, "Honour, Integrity and the Problem of Violence in the Spanish Bullfight," in D. Riches, ed., *The Anthropology of Violence* (Oxford: Basil Blackwell Ltd., 1986), pp. 118–135.

12. J.-M. Blázquez et al., *Historia de España antigua* (Madrid: Ediciones Cátedra, 1978), vol. 2, pp. 685–689.

13. The Augustan amphitheaters are Emerita and Tarraco, while the Julio-Claudian are at Segobriga, Conimbriga, and Emporiae.

14. Vitruvius 5.1.3–4. See discussion in Chapter 1.

15. This is acknowledged by Golvin in the case of Urso, *L'Amphithéâtre*, pp. 252 and 265.

16. See S. Keay, *Roman Spain* (Berkeley: University of California Press, 1988), p. 116, who points to the impetus in public building between the third century B.C. and the Early Empire.

17. Likewise, the earlier military pacification of the peninsula makes Iberia an unlikely spot for the placement of frontier amphitheaters, for which see below.

18. Strabo (3.4.13) assures us that the population of the Iberian peninsula preferred these areas for settlement.

19. J.-M. Blázquez, *Economía de la Hispania romana* (Bilbao: Ediciones Najera, 1978), pp. 392–395. Gaul, however, also has its share of outsized amphitheaters; see below.

20. Surpassed only by Rome's Colosseum, capacity of some fifty thousand and Capua's Hadrianic phase, which seated around thirty-seven thousand. The later phase of Carthage's amphitheater had a capacity roughly that of Italica's. See Golvin, *L'Amphithéâtre*, pp. 283–289, for relative dimensions.

21. Similar conjunctions can be found in Lugdunum, Narbo, Samarobriva Ambianorum (Amiens), Augusta Treverorum (Trier), and Colonia Agrippinensis (Cologne). The link between Imperial Cult and amphitheaters is explored in greater depth in Chapter 3.

22. Given a sample of nineteen known British amphitheatrical structures, the average ICD is 67 kilometers with a range of 42 kilometers. This would match up with the high side of Bekker-Nielsen's Type C pattern, Bekker-Nielsen, *Geography*, p. 31. His Type C has an average ICD of 58.5 kilometers and a range of 36.6 kilometers, to be found in southwest and northern Gaul.

23. For an overall discussion of this matter, see M. Millett, *The Romanization of Britain* (Cambridge: Cambridge University Press, 1990).

24. Hence York is not included in my statistical analysis. Scholars postulate, however, that it was located to the southeast of the legionary fortress. Early maps of York show streets in the vicinity taking an elliptical curve, possibly to respect an elliptical structure, such as an amphitheater. See P. Ottaway, *The Book of Roman York* (London: B. T. Batsford, Ltd., 1993), pp. 33–34. See also J. Wacher, *The Towns of Roman Britain* (London: B. T. Batsford, Ltd., 1995), p. 176.

25. Baginton is a strange case. This was some sort of a circular construction incorporated into the fortress walls. Some view it as a *gyrus*, or arena for cavalry drills and weapons practice, which function is assumed for all military arenas.

26. These include Corinium Dobunnorum, Durnovaria, Moridunum, Isorbrigantium, Rutupiae, and Charterhouse-upon-Mendip, which was a mining site opened up and guarded by the military. Connection to military is especially clear for Durnovaria and Corinium Dobunnorum, where the first, timber phase of the amphitheater dates approximately to the time when the military garrison would still have been in the vicinity. Rutupiae, as the chief port of Britannia, had great strategic significance throughout the Roman period.

27. The first phase of the London amphitheater is contemporary with a notable effort to rebuild Britannia's most important city after the destruction caused during the Boudiccan revolt in A.D. 60. This period also saw the rise of the first

forum, basilica, and public baths in Londinium. The arena, however, is set apart from the civic structures. See note in *Current Archaeology*, 109 (1988): 49–50; D. Perring, *Roman London* (London: B. T. Batsford, Ltd., 1991), pp. 60–63; and G. Milne, *Roman London* (London: B. T. Batsford, Ltd., 1995), pp. 48–60. See also summary in P. Salway, *Oxford Illustrated History of Roman Britain* (Oxford: Oxford University Press, 1993), pp. 111–113.

28. See examples of military labor gangs taking credit for their work on building stones at Tomen-y-Mur (*RIB* 420–428), Isca Silurum (*RIB* 336–355), and Deva Victrix (*RIB* 467–474). Further discussion of legionary amphitheater building is in Chapter 4.

29. An aspect of frontier life emphasized by M. C. Bishop in "On Parade: Status, Display and Morale in the Roman Army," in H. Vetters and M. Kandler, eds., *Akten des 14. Internationalen Limeskongresses 1986 in Carnuntum* (Vienna: Österreichische Akademie der Wissenschaften, 1990), pp. 21–30.

30. See discussion on importance of the horse to British amphitheaters in M. Fulford, *The Silchester Amphitheatre* (London: Society for the Promotion of Roman Studies, 1989), pp. 187–190.

31. For the connection between amphitheaters and the legions, see also Golvin, *L'Amphithéâtre*, pp. 154–156, and J.-Cl. Golvin and C. Landes, *Amphithéâtres et gladiateurs* (Paris: Editions du CNRS, 1990), pp. 203–216. K. Welch ("The Roman Arena in Late-Republican Italy: A New Interpretation," *JRA*, 7 [1994]: 59–80) suggests this connection should be pushed back into the Late Republic.

32. Civilian contexts for amphitheaters included Venta Silurum (Caerwent), Calleva Atrebatum (Silchester), Noviomagus Regnensium (Chichester), Frilford, Canterbury, Verulamium (St. Albans), and Woodcuts, which had a tiny arena measuring only 50 by 70 feet.

33. See discussion below and in Chapter 3 in connection with Celtic cult practice. Frilford's amphitheater has not yet been excavated, but a speculative overview of the site is available in B. C. Burnham and J. Wacher, *The "Small Towns" of Roman Britain* (London: B. T. Batsford, Ltd., 1990), pp. 178–183. Woodcuts is also somewhat peculiar. It dates to the beginning of the fourth century, making it the latest British amphitheater by a century or more. The town itself is a mere village. This rural amphitheater may perhaps be analogous to the mixed edifices, on which see below.

34. See A. Hönle and A. Henze, *Römische Amphitheater und Stadien* (Zurich: Edition Antike Welt, 1981), pp. 137–153 on this big moment in the history of their construction.

35. Possible expansion of Cogidubnus' territories under Vespasian, coincident with significant construction at what may have been his palace at Fishbourne, was argued by B. W. Cunliffe, *Excavations at Fishbourne 1961–1969* (London: Society of Antiquaries, 1971), pp. 13–14. The urbanization process in southern Britannia may have been due to the influence of a pro-Roman client king; see W. S. Hanson, *Agricola and the Conquest of the North* (London: B. T. Batsford Ltd., 1987), pp. 75–77.

36. The "Northeastern Frontier" includes arenas located in the provinces of Upper and Lower Germania (8 and 3 amphitheaters respectively), Upper and Lower Pannonia (5 and 1), Dacia (5), Noricum (3), Lower Moesia (1), and Dalmatia (4). Of the eight amphitheaters in Germania Superior, two (Vesontio and Octodurus) appear on the maps with Gaul. Two sites in Pannonia Superior (Aquincum and Carnuntum) have two amphitheaters, one civilian and one military.

37. For the Roman frontier as a zone of particularly intense interaction and as the nursery for a border society distinct from those of the immediately adjacent regions, see Whittaker, *Frontiers* and Drummond and Nelson, *Western Frontiers*, as well as, among others, M. van der Veen, "Native Communities in the Frontier Zone: Uniformity or Diversity?" in Maxfield and Dobson, *Roman Frontier Studies*, pp. 446–450 and J. H. F. Bloemers, "Relations between Romans and Natives: Concepts of Comparative Studies," in Maxfield and Dobson, *Roman Frontier Studies*, pp. 451–454. For a more comparative approach, see also the seminal work by O. Lattimore, *Inner Asian Frontiers of China* (New York: American Geographical Society, 1940).

38. Today known as Petronell and Budapest. See Golvin, *L'Amphithéâtre*, pp. 135–138.

39. C. Domitius Zmaragdus by name, *CIL* III.14359.

40. Interestingly, the sizes of the amphitheaters are reversed at Carnuntum and Aquincum, the civilian structures housing some 18,000 and 8,000 respectively, while the military ones held 8,000 and 16,000 or so.

41. See "Vetera" on map 3. Unfortunately, little is known of the amphitheater apart from its probable location. See Golvin, *L'Amphithéâtre*, p. 255 and P. La Baume, "Römische Köln," *BJ*, 172 (1972): 271–292. For the Imperial Cult in the amphitheater, see Chapter 3.

42. There are, however, some legionary or major fortifications that seem to lack an arena of their own, including Potaissum, Troesmis, Durostorum, Novae, Singidunum, Viminacium, Poetovio, Vindobona, Lauriacum, Castra Regina, Argentorate, Acumincum, and Novaesium. How did these fill their amphitheatrical needs? Most were located very near to installations that did have amphitheaters. Some (Troesmis, Durostorum, and Novae) were in the far eastern area, fairly close to the Black Sea, and only became legionary headquarters after the annexation of Dacia. It may be that Hadrian's emphasis on civil rather than military affairs distracted him from the provision of the amphitheatrical accommodations in this remote area. Our evidence may also be at fault. Poetovio, home to *legiones VIII Augusta* and *XIII Gemina*, stood on the bank of the river Drau, which has since destroyed the legionary camp and possibly any amphitheatrical remains as well. The *limes Raetiae*, from Mogontiacum to Lauriacum, is the part of the frontier system most bereft of amphitheaters. Military activity in this area began in the late first century B.C., but legions were withdrawn from the area by Tiberius and not permanently stationed here again until the Marcomannic wars in the middle of the second century after Christ, by which time the heyday of amphitheater construction was past. The provinces of Upper and Lower Moesia

in general are quite bereft of amphitheaters, with the Severan construction at Marcianopolis the sole example. The Greek East, with its relative disdain for amphitheaters, may have been influential here. Alternatively, our relative lack of information about the area may have distorted our impressions of Roman Moesia.

43. The amphitheaters at Iader and Salonae were last seen in the seventeenth century.

44. Salonae was colonized by Julius Caesar around 47 B.C. It is thought that Epidaurum was also a colony of Caesar's, in gratitude for the support of the Italian settlers in the Civil Wars. Iader was a colonia of Octavian's, dated to 33 B.C. Aequum is Claudian.

45. See Golvin, *L'Amphithéâtre*, pp. 206–207, who gives a capacity of 19,600 for the amphitheater. Compare the amphitheatrical presence at basically all provincial capital cities, including Carnuntum and Aquincum in the relative vicinity.

46. These include Epomanduodurum, Virinum, Scarbantia, and Ovilava. Flavia Solva may also fall into this category, in that it was located on an ancient roadway later bypassed by the Roman system.

47. See below, and Chapter 3 on Celtic cult in the arena. See also Golvin, *L'Amphithéâtre*, p. 262 n. 146.

48. Given fifteen examples from Narbonensis, the average ICD is 67 kilometers, and the range, 42 kilometers. Aquitania possessed some eighteen amphitheaters, with an average ICD of 77 kilometers and a range of 48 kilometers. Lugdunensis' thirty amphitheaters rendered an average ICD of 58 kilometers and a range of 36 kilometers. There were only nine amphitheaters in Gallia Belgica, which rendered the highest average ICD, 83 kilometers, and the range of 52 kilometers. To eliminate possible bias resulting from conforming too closely to artificially imposed political boundaries, I did a further study without considering the barriers between the Galliae, adding Octodurus and Vesontio, more properly part of Germania Superior, which yielded an average ICD of 65 kilometers and a range of 41 kilometers. These results, especially those achieved for Lugdunensis, were closest to Bekker-Nielsen's Type C, which, as defined by Bekker-Nielsen, has an average ICD of 58.5 kilometers and a range of 36.6 kilometers.

49. See comments in R. Duncan-Jones, *Economy of the Roman Empire* (Cambridge: Cambridge University Press, 1982), pp. 261–262 and R. Haywood, "Roman Africa," in T. Frank, *Economic Survey of Ancient Rome* (Baltimore: Johns Hopkins Press, 1933–1940), vol. 4, pp. 1–119, especially p. 112. See also G. Forni, "L'indàgine demogràfica e gli anfiteatri in Dacia," *Apulum*, 13 (1975): 111–134. Forni seems to take his results much more literally, as an expression of the population of the urban center at time of construction. Note also the earlier discussion of disjunction between amphitheater capacity and size of city in the Iberian peninsula.

50. N. J. G. Pounds ("The Urbanization of the Classical World," *Annals of the Association of American Geographers*, 59 [1969]: 135–157) uses the area of traces of

urban settlement for his calculations. The dearth of other comparanda to be found was striking.

51. See Golvin, *L'Amphithéâtre*, pp. 225–236; A. Grenier, *Manuel d'archéologie gallo-romaine* (Paris: Editions A. et J. Picard, 1958), vol. 3.2, pp. 886–928; and G.-C. Picard, "Les Théâtres ruraux de Gaule," *RA* (1970): 185–192. Golvin lists thirty-three of these constructions, which I have revised to thirty-five, three of which are in Britannia and twenty-one in Lugdunensis. I eliminated Lixus because it is in Mauretania and thus outside the area of my concern. I further eliminated Moingt and Bonne because they did not exist in Grenier, the source Golvin cited for his knowledge of them. I added to the list the first phase of the "theater" at Canterbury, which looks, in plan at least, like one half of a typical Romano-British amphitheater, as well as the building at Ribemont-sur-Ancre, which clearly alternated between functioning as a theater and an amphitheater.

52. Due to a complete lack of epigraphical evidence and little architectural variation, the mixed edifices cannot be dated with any more specificity than "pre-Hadrianic" and "Hadrianic and after." See Chapter 3 for further discussion of the function of this "Celtic" type of amphitheater.

53. The stage at Senlis is only 11.5 by 5.5 meters and that at Aregenua is 10 by 4 meters.

54. M. Bieber, *History of the Greek and Roman Theater* (Princeton: Princeton University Press, 1961), especially pp. 408–428.

55. Such is Golvin's opinion.

56. A more extensive discussion of building costs and considerations is in Chapter 4.

57. See Vitruvius 5.3.

58. Greater precision concerning the nature of these spectacles is considered in Chapter 3.

59. The mean capacity was only 6,000.

60. In Roman times known as Burdigala, Mediolanum Santonum, Caesarodunum Turonum, Vesunna, Limonum Pictonum, and Augustoritum Lemovicum.

61. I refer to Nîmes and Arles.

62. One similiarity is the building material, which made use of *opus vittatum* augmented by iron. See Golvin, *L'Amphithéâtre*, p 162, who finds the resemblance to Saintes especially striking. Capacity is 33,250.

63. This is Golvin's contention, *L'Amphithéâtre*, pp. 216–217.

64. *CIL* XIII.4038, restored by L. Maurin and M. Thauré, "Inscriptions révisées ou nouvelles du musée archéologique de Saintes," *Gallia*, 38 (1980): 197–213.

65. This program included laying out the street system and constructing the Germanicus arch. See L. Maurin, N. Laurenceau, and G. Vienne, *Recherches archéologiques à Saintes en 1978* (Saintes: Société d'archéologie et d'histoire de la Charente-Maritime, 1979), pp. 121–129. For the amphitheater in particular, see Golvin, *L'Amphithéâtre*, pp. 124–126 and J. Doreau, J.-Cl. Golvin, and L. Maurin,

L'Amphithéâtre gallo-romain de Saintes (Paris: Centre National de la Recherche Scientifique, 1982).

66. Golvin, *L'Amphithéâtre*, pp. 160-161 and Grenier, *Manuel*, vol. 3.2, pp. 670-674. For population shift explained as a reversion to earlier Gallic settlement patterns, see P.-A. Février, "L'Habitat dans la Gaule méridionale," *CLPA*, 24 (1975): 7-25 and G. Barruol, "La Résistance des substrats préromaine en Gaule méridionale," in D. M. Pippidi, ed., *Assimilation et résistance* (Paris: Les Belles Lettres, 1976), pp. 389-405.

67. *CIL* XIII.932 and 11045 a and b. Note the Celtic *cognomen* of this individual, indicating perhaps some level of collaboration between Imperial administration and locals. See also L. Maurin, *Saintes antique* (Saintes: Société d'archéologie et d'histoire de la Charente-Maritime, 1978), p. 192 n. 62. A relative was also involved, but the *cognomen* of this person has been obliterated.

68. This type of temple has been seen as a survival from pre-Roman wooden prototypes originally built in association with burial precincts and dedicated apparently to chthonic entities. For the Gallo-Roman *fanum*, see Chapter 3. See A. Brisson and J.-J. Hatt, "Les Nécropoles hallstattiennes d'Aulnay-aux-Planches," *Revue Archéologique de l'Est*, 4 (1953): 193-233.

69. See S. L. Dyson, "Native Revolts in the Roman Empire," *Historia*, 20 (1971): 239-274 and "Native Revolt Patterns in the Roman Empire," *ANRW* II.3 (1975): 138-175.

70. The revolts extend even beyond the Flavian period, if one considers the formation of the Gallic Empire under Postumus to be inspired by similar anti-Roman motivations.

71. See Chapter 3 on the Imperial Cult for activity at Lugdunum.

72. See N. Chadwick, *The Druids* (Cardiff: Wales University Press, 1966), pp. 5 and 41-50 for the political threat constituted by the Druids. See also H. Last, "Rome and the Druids: A Note," *JRS*, 39 (1949): 1-5 and Dyson, "Native Revolt Patterns," pp. 157-158, where he notes the possible significance of the name "Sacrovir" as indicative of Druidic ties and the connection to ominously well organized non-Roman institutions.

73. Pliny, *HN* 30.13. See Dyson, "Native Revolt Patterns."

74. Suetonius, *Claud*. 25.

75. See discussion in J.-J. Hatt, *Celts and Gallo-Romans* (London: Barrie and Jenkins, 1970), pp. 243-245. Another amphitheater possibly to be linked to the Sacrovir rebellion is the mixed edifice at Canetonum, site of an unrecovered hoard buried during the turmoil.

76. Golvin, *L'Amphithéâtre*, p. 190; Grenier, *Manuel*, vol. 3, part 1, pp. 250-251; and R. Couraud, "L'Amphithéâtre de Limoges, premiers sondages octobre 1966," *Bull. de la Soc. Arch. et Hist. du Limousin*, 94 (1967): 49-63.

77. A discussion of the revolt's composition and leadership can be found in B. Levick, "L. Verginius Rufus and the Four Emperors," *RhMus*, 128 (1985): 318-346. Gallic support came from the Aedui, Sequani, Arverni, and Allobroges, some of whom had been resistant to Roman interests in Gaul since the second

century B.C. For a survey of this interaction, see C. Ebel, *Transalpine Gaul: The Emergence of a Roman Province* (Leiden: E. J. Brill, 1976). Other support came from the governor of Britannia, M. Trebellius Maximus, the quaestor of Baetica, A. Caecina Alienus, and Iulius Civilis, the future leader of a revolt with clearer separatist leanings. For Vindex' revolt as an example of "true" Romanization, i.e., the absorption of Roman values to the extent that Republican ideals of *libertas* and such were the guiding force behind his actions, see the important article by C. M. Kraay, "The Coinage of Vindex and Galba," *NC*, 9 (1949): 129–149. See also P. A. Brunt, "The Revolt of Vindex and the Fall of Nero," *Latomus*, 18 (1959): 531–559. Of course, separatism may be achieved at the same time as the goals of personal opportunism or Republicanism, a double motivation accepted by A. Momigliano, "Nero," in S. A. Cook, F. E. Adcock, and M. P. Charlesworth, *CAH* (New York: MacMillan Co., 1934), pp. 702–742, especially pp. 739–740.

78. This may have been more nationalistic in motivation than is usually argued, depending of course on how one defines "nationalism." The most "nationalist" sentiment that can be extrapolated from these Gallic revolts is the striving for a political-ethnic coalition independent of the Roman hegemony, one supported perhaps by oracles of Celtic type. See Dyson, "Native Revolt Patterns," pp. 158–160. It has been suggested that Tacitus tried to make Vindex' goals seem more nationalist: L. J. Daly, "Verginius at Vesontio: The Incongruity of the Bellum Neronis," *Historia*, 24 (1975): 75–100. Dyson points out that the first news of the revolt came from the governor of Aquitania. See Suetonius, *Galba* 9.

79. Given the nonspecific dating of the mixed edifices (pre-Hadrianic or post-Hadrianic), one could feasibly add some sixteen more to this list. See Golvin, *L'Amphithéâtre*, pp. 225–236.

80. On the revolt of Vindex, see V. Rudich, *Political Dissidence under Nero: The Price of Dissimulation* (London: Routledge, 1993), pp. 210–212 and J. Sancery, *Galba ou l'armée face au pouvoir* (Paris: Les Belles Lettres, 1983), pp. 37–46.

3. ORDER AND STRUGGLE: CULT IN THE AMPHITHEATER

1. A. F. C. Wallace, *Religion: An Anthropological View* (New York: Random House, 1966), pp. 25–29 summarized views of Durkheim, Weber, and others in this regard. This is, of course, only one way of many in which to study religion. See also V. Turner, *The Anthropology of Performance* (New York: PAJ Publications, 1986) and D. I. Kertzer, "The Role of Ritual in Political Change," in M. J. Aronoff, ed., *Culture and Political Change* (New Brunswick: Transaction Books, 1983), pp. 53–73. For the use of myth and ritual to integrate social tensions and oppositions, see, in general, C. Lévi-Strauss, "The Structural Study of Myth," in T. Sebeok, ed., *Myth: A Symposium* (Bloomington: Indiana University Press, 1955), pp. 81–106 and C. Bell, *Ritual Theory, Ritual Practice* (New York: Oxford University Press, 1992), pp. 30–37.

2. Cicero, *Har. Resp.* 19: *pietate ac religione omnes gentes superavimus*. See similar sentiments expressed in *Nat. D.* 2.3. Public business was conducted in accompaniment with religious ritual, such as sacrifice and procession; even the locations

for the enactment of public business were religious. Senate meetings were held at various temples, the Senate building had an altar inside, indeed, the establishment of the *pomerium* through inauguration made the city of Rome into a *templum*. See A. Wardman, *Religion and Statecraft among the Romans* (London: Granada, 1982), pp. 6–7.

3. An etymological link can be drawn between *religio* and the verb *ligare*, "to bind," emphasizing the inherent connective nature of Roman cult. See *OLD*. Participation in public cult was a means of establishing public status, a fact acknowledged by Augustus in his revival and expansion of religious offices to enhance cohesion in his New Rome.

4. See, e.g., Valerius Maximus 4.1.10. Discussed by W. V. Harris (*War and Imperialism in Republican Rome, 327–70 B.C.* [Oxford: Clarendon Press, 1985], pp. 118–125 and 265–266), who points to the traditional prayer of the censors following each purification of Rome and to the prayer at the *Ludi Saeculares*, like the *lustratio* a cleansing and inaugural ritual for Rome.

5. Livy describes declaration of war by fetial priests in 1.32. See the *evocatio* of Juno, patron goddess of Veii, expressed in mythohistoric form in Livy 5.21–23. Arnobius explains that "the Romans used to distribute the cults of conquered cities among private families or award them state recognition" (*Adv. Nat.* 3.38).

6. See Polybius 6.56, where he articulates his admiration for Rome's ability to marshall the power of religion to the domination of its empire. Of course, the inverse is also true: decadence and the self-destructive tendencies of the Roman state are attributed to lack of religiosity, articulated especially during the Late Republic; see, among others, Horace, *Carm.* 3.6.

7. D. Fishwick, *The Imperial Cult in the Latin West* (Leiden: E. J. Brill, 1987), vol. 1.1, pp. 126–130 and L. R. Taylor, *The Divinity of the Roman Emperor* (Middletown, Conn.: American Philological Association, 1931), pp. 146–148. See also S. R. F. Price, *Rituals and Power: The Roman Imperial Cult in Asia Minor* (Cambridge: Cambridge University Press, 1984) pp. 239–248 on the "function" of the Imperial Cult.

8. Suetonius, *Aug.* 52 and Dio Cassius 51.20.

9. Roma seems to have been equivalent to the Hellenistic city goddess Tyche, as a deified personification of a political force. As such, she had been associated with cultic acknowledgement of various Republican *imperatores*, including, for one, Flamininus. This established tradition in the East no doubt played some role in Octavian's decision.

10. Dio Cassius in 51.20 acknowledges this decision as a crucial precedent in the history of Imperial interaction. See also Suetonius, *Aug.* 52 and Tacitus, *Ann.* 4.37.

11. This is discussed at length by Fishwick, *Imperial Cult*, vol. 1.1, pp. 97–149. See also Taylor, *Divinity*, pp. 208–209 and R. Turcan, "L'autel de Rome et d'Auguste 'ad confluentem'," *ANRW* II.12.1 (1982): 607–644.

12. Livy, *Per.* 139: *ara divi Caesaris ad confluentem Araris et Rhodani dedicata sacerdote creato C. Iulio Vercondaridubno Aeduo.*

13. Suetonius (*Claud.* 2) narrows the chronology to a specific day, as *Claudius natus est Iullo Antonio Fabio Africano conss Kal Aug Luguduni eo ipso die quo primum ara ibi Augusto dedicata est.* Some have taken this to mean that the altar was dedicated on August 1, 10 B.C., the day and year of the emperor Claudius' birth, hence Suetonius' emphatic *eo ipso die.* See A. Degrassi, *I fasti consolari dell'Impero romano* (Rome: Edizioni di Storia e Letteratura, 1952), p. 5 and H. Mattingly, *Coins of the Roman Empire in the British Museum* (London: Trustees of the British Museum, 1923–1962), vol. 1, p. cxiii. The Latin can, however, be taken as specific to the day and not necessarily the year, the phrase, therefore, being interpreted as Suetonius' use of the anniversary of a recent major event as a chronological marker. In this reading, *primum* would translate as something like "originally," as in *OLD*, *primum* 5. The connection to the altar was acknowledged by Claudius himself, who issued fifty-year coins depicting the altar in A.D. 41.

14. Dio Cassius 54.32: τοὺς πρώτους αὐτοῦ, προφάσει τῆς ἑορτῆς ἣν καὶ νῦν περὶ τὸν τοῦ Αὐγούστου βωμὸν ἐν Λουγδούνῳ τελοῦσι, μεταπεμψάμενος.

15. A role in quelling rebellion has been postulated for the Concilium, in that their refusal to participate in such affairs may have provided an example for others or in that councilmembers themselves may have been Imperial informers. See J. A. O. Larsen, *Representative Government in Greek and Roman History* (Berkeley: University of California Press, 1955), pp. 130–142 and A. J. Christopherson, "The Provincial Assembly of the Three Gauls in the Julio-Claudian Period," *Historia*, 17 (1968): 351–366. See also J. Deininger, *Die Provinziallandtage der römischen Kaiserzeit von Augustus bis zum Ende des dritten Jahrhunderts n. Chr.* (Munich: Beck, 1965).

16. Caesar, *B.G.* 1.31, 2.5, 3.16–17, 4.11, 5.54, 7.32, 8.21–22. Bibracte council: 7.63. See also his reference to the assemblies of the Druids, 4.14.

17. See M. MacNeill, *The Festival of Lughnasa* (Oxford: Oxford University Press, 1962), pp. 418–430 for summary of the significance of the feast of Lug, particularly in Ireland.

18. Lug may be identified with the Welsh deity Lleu Llau Gyffes found in the Third Branch of the *Mabinogion*, who, like Lug, is known for his many talents; indeed, the Welsh name translates as the Bright One of the Skillful Hand. See G. A. Wait, *Ritual and Religion in Iron Age Britain* (Oxford: British Archaeological Reports, 1986), vol. 1, pp. 217–218 and 221.

19. Caesar, *B.G.* 6.17. See also P. MacCana, *Celtic Mythology* (London: Hamlyn, 1970), pp. 27–29 and M. Dillon and N. K. Chadwick, *The Celtic Realms* (London: Weidenfeld and Nicolson, 1967), pp. 143–149. In fact, Mercury is the god most commonly referred to in Romano-Celtic inscriptions, with a multitude of different epithets.

20. Audin reconstructs such a cult center as including a pair of pillars, an architectural choice mirrored in the later Imperial cult. Audin has, alas, little archaeological evidence on which to base his reconstruction. A. Audin, "L'Omphalos de Lugdunum," in M. Renard, ed., *Hommages à Albert Grenier* (Brussels: Collection Latomus, 1962), vol. 1, pp. 152–164.

21. Suetonius (*Gaius* 20) tells of oratorical contests in which the loser was thrown into the river. Christian martyrs, after their bodies were exposed and burned, had their remains dumped in the river (Eusebius, *Hist. Eccl.* 5.1.62). This practice is found at Rome, as the appropriate punishment for parricides was the *poena cullei*, in which the criminal was sewn into a sack with an assortment of animals and thrown into the river, or the sea, if convenient. See description in Cicero, *Inv. Rhet.* 2.148, among others. Discussion in M. Radin, "The Lex Pompeia and the Poena Cullei," *JRS*, 10 (1920): 119–130. Here the river acts primarily as a convenient means of disposal for the body. Its symbolic value should also be considered: the water is, itself, a realm separate from that of everyday human interaction. It may thus act as a means of transferring the corpse from the world of the living to that of the dead, a metaphorical Styx, as it were. For the Celtic water cult, see below.

22. Fishwick, *Imperial Cult*, vol 1.1, pp. 112–120.

23. See L. Gagé, "La Théologie de la Victoire impériale," *Revue Historique*, 171 (1933): 1–43 and J. R. Fears, "The Theology of Victory at Rome: Approaches and Problems," *ANRW* II.17.1 (1981): 736–826.

24. Notable examples include Scipio Africanus, Marius, Sulla Felix, and Pompey; see Fears, "Theology of Victory," pp. 773–802.

25. Described by Dio Cassius 43.14. Like other ancient sources, Dio includes this "cult image" among the excessive honors granted Caesar, which may eventually have provoked his assassination.

26. For the Augustan program of material persuasion in general, see P. Zanker, *The Power of Images in the Age of Augustus* (Ann Arbor: University of Michigan Press, 1988). See also specific comments on Imperial Cult, ibid., pp. 302–323.

27. Dio Cassius 15.20.

28. Contemporary with the Ara Augusti at Lugdunum.

29. The crown of laurel was granted to victorious Roman generals; the crown of oak was presented to a soldier who had saved the life of a comrade. The altar was depicted in all its glory on commemorative coins minted at Lugdunum periodically throughout the Julio-Claudian years, as seen in Figure 17 (*BMC* 565). See also Mattingly, *BMC*, vol. 1, pp. 92–97, nos. 548–560, 565–588.

30. The inscription recording this is *ILTG* 217. See A. Grenier, *Manuel d'archéologie gallo-romaine* (Paris: Editions A. et J. Picard, 1958), vol. 3.2, pp. 685–688; A. Grenier, *Manuel d'archéologie gallo-romaine* (Paris: Editions A. et J. Picard, 1960), vol. 4.2, pp. 505–516; and J. Guey and A. Audin, "La Dédicace de l'amphithéâtre des Trois Gaules," *Bulletin des Monuments et Musées Lyonnaises*, 2 (1958): 59–67. This is based on a restoration of a lacuna to read *amphitheatri* [*arenam cum p*]*odio*.

31. *CIL* XIII.1036. C. Julius Rufus was exceptionally Romanized, even for his family. His grandfather, C. Julius Gedomo, had been granted Roman citizenship after Caesar's conquest but had retained a Celtic name as *cognomen*, as did his son. Rufus eschewed even this vestige of his Celtic roots. Indeed, it has been suggested

that this may indicate his language of choice was Latin. See A. King, *Roman Gaul and Germany* (Berkeley: University of California Press, 1990), p. 66.

32. Fishwick, *Imperial Cult*, vol. 1.1, pp. 133–135 and A. Audin and M. Le Glay, "L'Amphithéâtre des Trois-Gaules à Lyon," *Gallia*, 28 (1970): 67–89, and *Gallia*, 37 (1979): 85–98.

33. Fishwick, *Imperial Cult*, vol. 1.1, pp. 120–125 arguing against, among others, Turcan's interpretation in "L'autel."

34. *CIL* XII.6038 and M. Gayraud, *Narbonne antique des origines à la fin de IIIe siècle* (Paris: E. de Boccard, 1981), pp. 384–409.

35. Fishwick, *Imperial Cult*, vol. 1.1, pp. 137–139.

36. Tacitus, *Ann.* 1.39.1: *interea legati ab senatu regressum iam apud aram Ubiorum Germanicum adeunt.*

37. Tacitus, *Ann.* 1.57: *sacerdos apud aram Ubiorum creatus.*

38. J.-Cl. Golvin, *L'Amphithéâtre romain* (Paris: E. de Boccard, 1988), p. 255. There was also an inscription to Nemesis; see below.

39. Fishwick, *Imperial Cult*, vol. 1.1, pp. 141–144.

40. Pomponius Mela 3.13; Pliny, *HN* 4.111; and Ptolemy, *Geog.* 2.6.3.

41. See F. Diego Santos, "Die Integration Nord- und Nordwestspaniens als römische Provinz in der Reichspolitik des Augustus," *ANRW* II.3 (1975): 523–571 for argumentation.

42. See discussion for Flavian period in R. Etienne, *Le Culte impérial dans la péninsule ibérique d'Auguste à Dioclétien* (Paris: Boccard, 1958), pp. 447–459.

43. J. Alarcão in *PECS*, p. 162, who mentions in passing epigraphical evidence for a temple of the Imperial Cult at Bracara Augusta. It is also the findspot of at least two inscriptions (*CIL* II.2416 and 2426) that mention a *sacerd(os) Rom(ae) et Aug(usti) conventus Bracaraug(ustani).*

44. Fishwick, *Imperial Cult*, vol. 1.1, pp. 148–149, building on a foundation laid by, among others, M. Krasheninnikoff, "Über die Einführung des provinzialen Kaisercultus im römischen Westen," *Philologus*, 53 (1894): 147–189.

45. This tighter link between assembly and cult was emphasized by Th. Mommsen, *Römisches Staatsrecht* (Leipzig: S. Hirzel, 1876–1888), vol. 3, pp. 743–744.

46. Quintilian, *Inst.* 6.3.77. See Tiberian coins described in A. Burnett, M. Amandry, and P. P. Ripollès, *Roman Provincial Coinage* (London: British Museum Press, 1992), especially nos. 218, 221, 225, and 231.

47. *CIL* II.6097, tentatively dated to the Augustan period by letterforms.

48. Golvin, *L'Amphithéâtre*, pp. 164–165.

49. Fishwick, *Imperial Cult*, vol. 1.1, pp. 171–179. Admittedly, the use of the term *flamen* here is somewhat troubling. The specific date of the establishment of the provincial assembly at Tarraco is not clear. The general belief is that it coincides with the organization of the provincial cult in the early first century. See S. J. Keay, *Roman Spain* (Berkeley: University of California Press, 1988), pp. 60–61 and 157–158 and F. Albertini, *Les Divisions administratives de l'Espagne romaine* (Paris: Boccard, 1923), pp. 83–104. There is very slight evidence for some sort of

altar celebrating Augustus at Emerita, but it is, alas, highly questionable. See Fishwick, *Imperial Cult*, vol. 1.1, pp. 180–183 and C. H. Sutherland, "Aspects of Imperialism in Roman Spain," *JRS*, 24 (1934): 31–42. This is most disappointing, because the amphitheater at Emerita dates to 8 B.C., when Augustus himself was in the area; see Golvin, *L'Amphithéâtre*, pp. 109–110.

50. Fishwick, *Imperial Cult*, vol. 1.1, pp. 165–167. Fishwick concentrates too much on the "Tarraco model" for the worship of *divus* Augustus, given that there is evidence for both types of worship at Tarraco in a relatively short interval of time, which makes the reconstruction of a specific, distinct model somewhat risky.

51. D. Fishwick, *The Imperial Cult in the Latin West* (Leiden: E. J. Brill, 1987), vol. 1.2, pp. 295–300.

52. Roma suffers from lack of specific interest at this time.

53. Fishwick, *Imperial Cult*, vol. 1.2, pp. 240–256; Golvin, *L'Amphithéâtre*, pp. 192–193; Gayraud, *Narbonne*, pp. 384–409; and A. Grenier, *Manuel d'archéologie gallo-romaine* (Paris: Editions A. et J. Picard, 1958), vol. 3.1, pp. 128–142.

54. Details such as honors due the *flamen* and his wife and expenditure for certain ritual items. See *CIL* XII.6038.

55. See L. Rossi, *Trajan's Column and the Dacian Wars* (Ithaca: Cornell University Press, 1971), especially pp. 146–148 and 185–186 and F. Lepper and S. Frere, *Trajan's Column* (Gloucester: Alan Sutton, 1988), pp. 81 and 152, pls. xxv and lxxiii.

56. Fishwick, *Imperial Cult*, vol. 1.2, pp. 301–307.

57. Deininger, *Provinziallandtage*, pp. 118–119.

58. Golvin, *L'Amphithéâtre*, p. 129.

59. Deininger, *Provinziallandtage*, pp. 116–117.

60. Golvin, *L'Amphithéâtre*, pp. 262–263.

61. *CIL* III.773 and 7506.

62. J. J. Wilkes, *Dalmatia* (London: Routledge and K. Paul, 1969), p. 200. Scardona's sanctuary is identified as Trajanic on the basis of its accommodations, i.e. the *ara*, and the known Trajanic interest.

63. J. Fitz, "The Excavations in Gorsium," *A Arch Hung*, 24 (1972): 1–52.

64. It is possible, however, that Oescus, not Troesmis, was the provincial center. The first amphitheater on Trajan's Column has been tentatively identified with Oescus, which would be a nice match with the proposed scenario.

65. Fourteen of the thirty Rhine-Danube amphitheaters date to the second century, 7 to the first, and 1 to the third. Eight are undated.

66. Such is the impression given by the current state of information. This may all change as we learn more about the militarized zone.

67. See Fishwick, *Imperial Cult*, vol 2.1, pp. 574–584. For the ability of ritual to foster political hierarchies, see Kertzer, "Role," pp. 59 and 65–67.

68. See Chapters 1 and 5 for more detailed discussion of the sociopolitical meaning of the *munera*.

69. There is little discussion of these edifices in the scholarly literature, particularly in terms of function, which is the most intriguing part of the whole problem. See brief references to the topic in G. Coulon, *Les Gallo-Romains: Au carrefour de deux civilisations* (Paris: A. Colin, 1985), pp. 65–67 and G.-C. Picard, "Les théâtres ruraux de Gaule," *RA* (1970): 185–192. For water sanctuaries, see Grenier, *Manuel*, vol 4.2.

70. It may be that these "hard primitivists" all rely on Posidonius, whose early first-century B.C. travels took him to southern Gaul and thus allowed him firsthand access to information concerning the Celts. These "Posidonians" include Strabo, Diodorus Siculus, and Athenaeus, who all acknowledge the man directly, and Lucan, Pomponius Mela, Tacitus, and Julius Caesar, whose reliance on Posidonius is less straightforward. How much did he rely on literary sources of information about the Gauls? After all, he was actually in Gaul, talking to real live Celts, and should not have to depend on someone else's study. The obvious reason is to save time: Caesar had to make immediate decisions as to projected actions of his Gallic foe. It is possible that he could not afford to wait and conduct his own study but fell back on learned publications of a fairly recent date. For Caesar as utter copyist, see J. J. Tierney, "The Celtic Ethnography of Posidonius," *Proceedings of the Royal Irish Academy*, 60 (1960): 189–275, especially pp. 211–218 and 223–224. For Caesar as independent, see D. Nash, "Reconstructing Poseidonios' Celtic Ethnography," *Britannia*, 12 (1976): 111–126. See also N. Chadwick, *The Druids* (Cardiff: Wales University Press, 1966), p. 11; J. Malitz, *Die Historien des Poseidonios* (Munich: Beck, 1983); and S. Piggott, *The Druids* (London: Thames and Hudson, 1968), pp. 92–98. See also Wait, *Ritual*, p. 191.

71. They are called the Alexandrian group because of their common connection to Hellenistic scholarship as it was fostered in that city. This stance seems to stem from Timaeus, writing circa 300 B.C., and Timagenes and Alexander Cornelius Polyhistor, rough contemporaries of Posidonius. Polybius and Livy may fall into this group, both acknowledging Timaeus' work in preparing their presentations on the North Italian Celts. See Chadwick, *Druids*, p. 11 and Piggott, *Druids*, pp. 98–99.

72. The tendency of ancient historians to rely on earlier textual sources, instead of conducting primary research themselves, may skew the evidence. The last centuries before the turn of the millennium were a period of massive cultural change for the Celtic peoples. Contact with the Mediterranean led to conflict and adaptation, the forms thereof varying both locally and temporally. The Celts contemporary with Timaeus likely led different lives from those encountered by Posidonius or Caesar. For the transformation of Iron Age western Europe and the extent of urbanization in La Tène society, prior to Roman conquest, see, among others, P. S. Wells, *Culture Contact and Culture Change* (Cambridge: Cambridge University Press, 1981); J. Collis, *The European Iron Age* (London: B. T. Batsford Ltd., 1984); and D. Nash, "Celtic Territorial Expansion and the Mediterranean World," in T. Champion and J. Megaw, eds., *Settlement and Society: As-*

pects of West European Prehistory in the First Millennium B.C. (Leicester: Leicester University Press, 1985), pp. 45–67.

73. Posidonius was a historian and geographer. His ethnographic passages were supplemental color. The limited interest in Celts apparent in what was a primary source for our primary sources should be a warning. Another trend to be aware of is the increasing tendency to paraphrase and condense commentary still further in the later writers. See Tierney, "Celtic Ethnography," p. 222.

74. For "the Other" in antiquity, see F. Hartog, *The Mirror of Herodotus: The Representation of the Other in the Writing of History* (Berkeley: University of California Press, 1988); E. Hall, *Inventing the Barbarian* (Oxford: Oxford University Press, 1989); Y. A. Dauge, *Le Barbare: Recherches sur la conception romaine de la barbarie et de la civilisation* (Brussels: Collection Latomus, 1981); and M. Clavel-Lévêque, *Puzzle gaulois: Les Gaules en mémoire* (Paris: Les Belles Lettres, 1989), pp. 307–336.

75. K. H. Jackson, *The Oldest Irish Tradition: A Window on the Iron Age* (Cambridge: Cambridge University Press, 1964) and C. O'Rahilly, ed., *Táin Bó Cúailnge from the Book of Leinster* (Dublin: Dublin Institute for Advanced Studies, 1967), pp. xiii-xiv.

76. Being mentioned, by title at least, in the Cín Dromma Snechta, or the Book of Druimm Snechtai, now no longer extant. The earliest surviving manuscripts are the so-called Lebor na hUidre, or the Book of the Dun Cow, and the Book of Leinster, both from the twelfth century. See J. Gantz, *Early Irish Myths and Sagas* (New York: Penguin, 1981), pp. 20–21 and R. Thurneysen, *Die irische Helden- und Königsage bis zum siebzehnten Jahrhundert* (Halle: M. Niemeyer, 1921).

77. The flip side to this is that the Irish vernacular may, admittedly, be an isolated insular perversion.

78. Although, interestingly, the Druids do not seem as much a distinct and institutionalized part of the sociopolitical power structure in the vernacular as in the ancient Graeco-Roman sources. The extent to which evidence from the tales matches with what is known of Iron Age material culture is considered by J. P. Mallory, "The World of Cú Chulainn: The Archaeology of the Táin Bó Cúailnge," in J. P. Mallory, ed., *Aspects of the Táin* (Belfast: December Publications, 1992), pp. 103–159. J. Carney suggested that the tales largely originated in medieval Ireland, the creation of Christian literati who consciously archaized to construct their pre-Christian "fairyland." See J. Carney, *Studies in Irish Literature and History* (Dublin: Dublin Institute for Advanced Studies, 1955) and H. L. C. Tristram, "La Razzia des vaches de Cuailnge et les archéologues," *Études Celtiques*, 29 (1991): 403–414. Extreme skepticism concerning the existence of the Celts as a unified historical ethnic group is expressed by M. Chapman, *The Celts: The Construction of a Myth* (New York: St. Martin's Press, 1992).

79. The appearance of a Christian overlay, however, points to another potential problem: the monkish redactor. To please his contemporary, Christian audience, and to salve his own conscience as well, the transcriber of the tales may have

altered the original, transforming gods into men, for example, or he may have omitted some parts entirely. The notable lack of a unifying conceptual organization in Celtic religion as it appears in the Irish vernacular may be due to such deliberate neglect on the part of the redactor. This may also help explain why the Druids do not seem as much a distinct and institutionalized part of the sociopolitical power structure in the vernacular as in the ancient sources. To grant them such a sophisticated organization would make them too much like Christian monks and thus grant them seeming legitimacy. See Chadwick, *Druids*, pp. 56–58 and MacCana, *Celtic Mythology*, pp. 132–135, who minimizes the censorship of the monks, given the often anti-Christian bent of what has survived. Discussed at length in K. McCone, *Pagan Past and Christian Present in Early Irish Literature* (Kildare: An Sagart, 1990). See also K. H. Jackson, *A Celtic Miscellany: Translations from the Celtic Literatures* (Harmondsworth: Penguin, 1971).

80. Fragments of the Four Branches (the tales of Pwyll, Branwen, Manawydan, and Math) are in Peniarth 6, a manuscript from the early thirteenth century. The earliest extant manuscript to preserve tales, the Llyfr Gwyn Rhydderch, or White Book of Rhydderch, dates to the first half of the fourteenth century. The title *Mabinogion* was supplied by Lady Charlotte Guest, who in 1849 first published an English translation of the tales. The name was generated by the fact that the first four major tales end with "so ends this branch of the *mabinogi*," or words to that effect. Guest assumed that *mabinogi* was a tale for children, as *mab* can be translated as "boy." What it actually means is not clear: it may refer to the story of someone's heroic youth, but no specific hero cycle has been preserved. It perhaps may stem from the interpretation of *mab* as "descendant" and thus be the tales of Wales' divine dynasties. See J. Gantz, *The Mabinogion* (Harmondsworth: Penguin, 1976), pp. 29–32.

81. Celtic and Roman tradition meet in the epigraphic record from postconquest Gaul and Britain, but this, like the literary sources, is of limited value to our understanding of the nature of Celtic cult. The reason for this has to do with the whole idea of syncretism and the process of *interpretatio Romana*. The postconquest Gauls began to commemorate their dedications to local divinities with Latin inscriptions. Most cited the name of the indigenous deity and that of his Roman cognate. The problem lies in the identification of cognate divinities. Hundreds of Celtic divine names appear in the inscriptions, most of them only in a single instance, yet they are identified with only a handful of Roman gods. How are we to explain this? It seems clear that the nature of godhood in the Celtic world does not correspond exactly to that of Rome. Indeed, unlike the Roman pantheon, the Celtic divinities, for the most part, do not seem to be defined by function but rather are closely connected to the land and its protection and fertility. The deities represented only once epigraphically, according to this interpretation, would be sacred only to that particular area. Can we then still discuss "Celtic religion" as a unit, given the geographic particularism apparent in the inscriptions? The similarity of ritual, religious artifacts and iconography found throughout the Celtic world suggests that although the names of deities changed with the

landscape, Celts shared a common functional relationship with deity. Support for this comes from the wide distribution of images of certain types of deity, notably the wheel/sky god, the hammer/cauldron god, the antler-headed god, the hooded trio and the Matres, who are identified often as, respectively, Jupiter/Taranis, Sucellus (patron of protection and abundance), Cernunnos (the fertility god), and the *genii cucullati*, which may in fact be a warmly dressed version of the Matres, who represented fertility, agricultural and human. The identification of these images with deities in the vernacular is more problematic, as the specifically divine attributes have disappeared in the tales. The antler-headed god, however, has been linked functionally to Conall Cernach, Finn and Cú Rói, the hammer/cauldron god is the Dagda, and the Matres are the various tutelary goddesses. See E. Thevenot, *Divinités et sanctuaires de la Gaule* (Paris: Fayard, 1968) and "L'Interprétation gauloise des divinités romaines," in M. Renard, ed., *Hommages à Albert Grenier* (Brussels: Collection Latomus, 1962), vol. 1, pp. 1476–1490. See also P. F. Bober, "Cernunnos: Origin and Transformation of a Celtic Divinity," *AJA*, 55 (1951): 13–51 and P. Lambrechts, *Contributions a l'étude des divinités celtiques* (Bruges: "De Tempel," 1942).

82. Caesar, *B.G.* 6.17. See also P.-M. Duval, *Les Dieux de la Gaule* (Paris: Presses universitaires de France, 1957), p. 94 for a handy table of potential functional parallels.

83. Caesar, *B.G.* 6.18. Strabo, like Caesar, is something of a syncretist, but he gives less information about the specific nature of Celtic divinities. He refers to cult practice on islands, which seems to have been chthonic in character. The women of the Samnitae, dwelling on an island off the mouth of the Loire river, were possessed by "Dionysus" and performed ecstatic initiations and roofing ceremonies. In this most intriguing story, Strabo relates that these women once yearly removed the roof from their temple and were ritually obliged to replace it before sunset of the same day. Apparently one woman was designated a victim and was made to drop her roofing materials, at which point she was torn to pieces by the other priestesses, who raced around the temple shouting "*Euoi!*" (the typical Greek Dionysiac shriek) until the madness passed (or perhaps until the roofing was finished). Strabo also informs us that a sanctuary to "Demeter and Kore" was located on an island off the coast of Britain; see 4.4.6. Lucan, unlike Strabo and Caesar, does not translate the names of Celtic gods into their Graeco-Roman equivalents. The *Pharsalia* preserves apparently Celtic divine names, those being Teutates, Esus, and Taranis. See Lucan 1.444–446, to which a scholiast in Berne has added explanations of the various types of human sacrifice appropriate to each deity: Teutates received drowned victims, Esus' victims were hanged from trees, and fire dispatched the human offerings to Taranis.

84. Wait, *Ritual*, pp. 203–204.

85. The Welsh vernacular does not suggest a Celtic pantheon so much as whisper of one. Its major characters appear vestigially divine only when set next to their Irish counterparts, an identification not at all obvious when considering the Welsh material in isolation. The *Mabinogion* tells of three dynasties of

humanized gods, of which the family of Dôn has most retained its divinity, being roughly cognate to the Tuatha dé Danaan, the children of Irish Danu. The main difference between the Irish and Welsh tradition is the complete absence of Welsh tutelary goddesses: the female divinities, such as Rhiannon, Arianrhod, and Branwen, are more associated with birds and sorcery than with the land.

86. Wait, *Ritual*, pp. 220–224.

87. Wait, *Ritual*, pp. 228–232 and J.-L. Brunaux, *The Celtic Gauls: Gods, Rites and Sanctuaries* (London: Seaby, 1988), pp. 5–9.

88. See *Pwyll Pendeuic Dyuet* or "Pwyll, Lord of Dyved," in Gantz, *Mabinogion*, pp. 45–65. Pwyll is offered the reward of the wife of Arawn for his victory; his refusal of this prize Gantz interprets as a gloss on the original Celtic version and as evidence of the influence of contemporary Christian/chivalric values.

89. *Maccgnimrada Con Culaind*, or *The Boyhood Deeds of Cú Chulainn*, is found in the Book of the Dun Cow. Translation in Gantz, *Early Irish Myths*, pp. 134–146. See also *Táin Bó Cúailnge* 608–824.

90. Indeed, much of the *Táin Bó Cúailnge*, Cú Chulainn's epic defense of the Ulstermen, focuses on his duels at river fords. See, for example, the Aided Fraích episode (*Táin Bó Cúailnge* 833–857), the Aided Lethain (946–972), the Aided na Rígamus (1685–1693), the Aided Lóich meic Mo Femis (1874–2037), and Comrac Maind (2523–2566). The *gáe bolga* was used to kill Lóch and Fer Diad; in the latter case, the weapon was hurled by Cú Chulainn in his epic rage and pierced a sensitive part of Fer Diad's body. Whether the weapon was originally intended for this use, or whether this is another example of the extremity of Cú Chulainn's warp or battle distortion, is another question. Literally, *gáe bolga* means "gapped spear," which may point to its identification with a Celtic javelin described by Diodorus Siculus (5.30) as having a broken or barbed spiral point, which parallels the *gáe bolga* in *Táin Bó Cúailnge* 3344–3359. See A. Ross, *The Pagan Celts* (London: B. T. Batsford, Ltd., 1986), p. 10.

91. *Táin Bó Cúailnge* 2955–2962.

92. The *Fled Bricrend*, or *Bricriu's Feast*, is also in the Lebor na hUidre. Translation of the tale can be found in Gantz, *Early Irish Myths*, pp. 221–256.

93. See also the almost anthropomorphized rising of rivers in the *Táin*, e.g., the Colptha and the Sechaire in the Aided Úaland, *Táin Bó Cúailnge* 1002–1029.

94. J. Toutain, *Les Cultes païens dans l'Empire romain*, III, (Paris: Leroux, 1920), p. 408.

95. Grenier, *Manuel*, vol. 4.2, pp. 725–786.

96. The pre-Roman type, also known as the "Belgic type" of sanctuary, enclosed the central cult focus with a ditch and palisade. The central focus was sometimes a building, sometimes a covered pit or a cluster of posts. See Brunaux, *Celtic Gauls*, pp. 10–24 and J. Webster, "Sanctuaries and Sacred Places," in M. Green, ed., *The Celtic World* (London: Routledge, 1995), pp. 445–464.

97. Grenier, *Manuel*, vol. 4.2, pp. 553–567 and Coulon, *Gallo-Romains*, pp. 67–68.

98. Grenier, *Manuel*, vol. 4.2, pp. 572–577.

99. Ibid., pp. 583–586.

100. This is rather interesting, as Tintignac is in the heart of Aquitania while Vieil-Evreux is northwest of Paris; Gisacus seems more mobile than most Celtic divinities.

101. Grenier, *Manuel*, vol. 3.2, pp. 950–955. See also M. Baudot, "Le Problème des ruines de Vieil-Evreux," *Gallia*, 2 (1943): 191–206. Gisacus is mentioned here in *CIL* XIII.3197 and 3204, which seems to be a bilingual inscription.

102. Grenier, *Manuel*, vol. 4.2, pp. 730–733 and vol. 3.2, pp. 921–924.

103. The menhir is known today as la Roche du Vieux Garçon, which surely it is. See Grenier, *Manuel*, vol. 4.2, pp. 733–737.

104. The implications of this are intriguing, as this may represent a functional connection between the amphitheatrical games and Celtic use of human sacrifice. For the sacrificial complex, see Chapter 5.

105. Grenier, *Manuel*, vol. 3.2, pp. 904–909.

106. Mentioned in a panegyric delivered in A.D. 311 at Trier. See J.-J. Hatt, "La Vision de Constantin au sanctuaire de Grand et l'origine celtique du labarum," *Latomus*, 9 (1950): 427–436.

107. Picard's understanding of the rural sanctuaries emphasizes the Romanized architecture as Imperial propaganda, meant to remind the provincials of the creature comforts now accessible to them through Romanism. He does not really address the issue of whether the distinctively Gallic architectural style was carried over into the function of the complex. See Picard, "Théâtres ruraux." As should be apparent, I find the combination of Roman and local taste as representative of a dynamic interaction pervasive in the sanctuaries at all levels.

108. A. Grenier, "Hercule et les théâtres gallo-romains," *REA*, 42 (1940): 636–644.

109. Other deities are shown in atypical fashion on Gallo-Roman pottery, notably Mercury, in scenes that seem to emphasize the comedic trickster aspect of his nature.

110. Found in *Culhwch ac Olwen*, or *How Culhwch Won Olwen*, which may have been the first of the Welsh tales to assume its current form. Translation in Gantz, *Mabinogion*, pp. 134–176.

111. Beltane, also known as Cétshamain, was a celebration of the vernal equinox and the coming of the growing season. See G. Webster, *The British Celts and Their Gods under Rome* (London: B. T. Batsford, Ltd., 1986), pp. 30–35 on the major seasonal festivals.

112. See MacNeill, *Lughnasa*, with a summary pp. 418–430. She found the vestiges of such festivals at 195 sites in Ireland.

113. Faction fighting also occurred in Rome at the festival of the October Horse, in which men from the Subura annually faced off against their counterparts from the Via Sacra. See W. Warde Fowler, *The Roman Festivals of the Period of the Republic: An Introduction to the Study of the Religion of the Romans* (London: MacMillan, 1899), p. 242.

114. H. D. Inglis, *Ireland in 1834* (London: Whittaker, 1835), vol. 2, pp. 46ff.

115. *Mar is duine a bhí ionnam-sa nach dtiocfadh 'un láithreach/ Thar éis nár coir náireach bhí ariamh mo dhiaidh;/ Ach buille bhata a bhualadh Domhnach a' Mháma/ Mar isé bhí gnásúil ariamh sa tír,/ 'S gan cuimhne bheith agam-sa air lá'r na bháireach/ Ach iad a bheith ag baint sásta amach an bhliain dár geionn.* Quoted in MacNeill, *Lughnasa*, p. 425.

116. See MacNeill, *Lughnasa*, p. 429. M. Green notes the presence of warrior gods at healing sanctuaries, capable of combating illness; see M. Green, *Symbol and Image in Celtic Religious Art* (London. Routledge, 1989), pp. 64–69.

117. Polybius 2.17. Strabo agrees, adding that only now, under Roman rule, have they been compelled to lay aside their arms and take up farming (4.1.2; see also 4.1.5).

118. Polybius 2.20.

119. Strabo 4.4.2.

120. E.g., Strabo 4.1.5, 4.1.12, 4.4.3.

121. See Diodorus Siculus 5.28, where the comparison is made to Ajax.

122. Polybius 2.35 and Caesar, *B.G.* 2.29. Note, however, the unusual noisiness of that courage, i.e., the Celtic Tumult, the miraculously panic-causing capabilities of which are described in, e.g., Livy 5.38–39 and Polybius 2.29. The Tumult is given epic form in the *Táin Bo Cúailnge*, when Cú Chulainn goes into a dreadful sort of battle trance: "His first distortion came upon Cú Chulainn so that he became horrible, many-shaped, strange and unrecognisable. . . . His face became a red hollow. He sucked one of his eyes into his head. . . . The other eye sprang out on to his cheek. His mouth was twisted back fearsomely. . . . The torches of the war-goddess, the virulent rain-clouds, the sparks of blazing fire were seen in the clouds and in the air above his head with the seething of fierce rage that rose above him. His hair curled about his head like branches of red hawthorn. . . . The hero's light rose from his forehead. . . . As high, as thick, as strong, as powerful and as long as the mast of a great ship was the straight stream of dark blood which rose up from the very top of his head and became a dark magical mist . . . and he came forth in this manner to attack his enemies." (O'Rahilly, *Táin Bó Cúailnge*, pp. 201–202).

123. See Polybius 2.31 and 3.62 for Celtic suicide.

124. The best known are the "Large" and the "Small" Gallic groups, both sponsored by the kings of Pergamum. The "Large" group, which once included the Ludovisi Suicidal Gaul and the Capitoline Dying Gaul, was set up originally in Pergamum itself, while the "Small" group, so called because of its less-than-lifesize porportions, was located on the Acropolis in Athens.

125. See J. J. Pollitt, *Art in the Hellenistic Age* (Cambridge: Cambridge University Press, 1986), pp. 83–97 and R. R. R. Smith, *Hellenistic Sculpture* (New York: Thames and Hudson, 1991), pp. 99–104.

126. See, among others, Ross, *Pagan Celts*, pp. 40–45.

127. See M. Millett, *The Romanization of Britain* (Cambridge: Cambridge University Press, 1990), pp. 9–39 and B. Cunliffe, *Iron Age Communities in Britain* (London: Routledge, 1978), pp. 334–343.

128. Fullest treatment of this is in Caesar, *B.G.* 6.13–15, who does admit that the Aedui, for one, had an elected magistrate called a *vergobret* (*B.G.* 1.16). The warriors may have constituted a sodality transcending tribal boundaries, as suggested by the Gaesatae described by Polybius and paralleled by the Fenian bands in historical Ireland. See Ross, *Pagan Celts*, p. 50. For sodalities among the Celts, see B. Arnold, "Rank and Status in Early Iron Age Europe," in B. Arnold and D. B. Gibson, eds., *Celtic Chiefdom, Celtic State* (Cambridge: Cambridge University Press, 1995), pp. 43–52.

129. Caesar, *B.G.* 6.11–12.

130. The Irish legal tracts go back, in written form, to the seventh century but seem to be based on tradition dating back much earlier than this, possibly transmitted through the centuries in verse form, not unlike the vernacular epics. The major collections are the Crith Gablach and the Lebor na Cert; see D. A. Binchy, ed., *Corpus Iuris Hibernici* (Dublin: Dublin Institute for Advanced Study, 1978) and F. Kelly, *A Guide to Early Irish Law* (Dublin: Institute for Advanced Study, 1988).

131. One extreme example of this is described by Strabo 4.2.3 and Athenaeus 4.37 p. 152, in which Loverius, king of the Arverni in the mid-second century B.C., demonstrated the wealth of his tribe and his own capacity for generous leadership by hosting a massive feast, which lasted for days on end in a 2¼ square mile compound built especially for the occasion. Loverius also distributed gold to the residents of the surrounding countryside and even tossed a bag of gold to a passing bard, who had arrived too late for the meal. For the feast in general, see S. James, *The World of the Celts* (London: Thames and Hudson, 1993), pp. 70–71; M. Dietler, "Driven by Drink: The Role of Drinking in the Political Economy and the Case of Early Iron Age France," *Journal of Anthropological Archaeology*, 9 (1990): 352–406; and A. Appadurai, *The Social Life of Things: Commodities in Cultural Perspective* (Cambridge: Cambridge University Press, 1986).

132. See M. Dietler, "Early 'Celtic' Socio-political Relations: Ideological Representation and Social Competition in Dynamic Comparative Perspective," in B. Arnold and D. B. Gibson, *Celtic Chiefdom, Celtic State*, pp. 64–71, who, however, believes that feasting displays or "commensal politics" supplanted martial ones as a means of political competition.

133. J. Filip, *Celtic Civilization and Its Heritage* (Wellingborough, England: Collet's, 1977), p. 93.

134. Athenaeus 4.36, p. 152: ἐν κύκλῳ. μέσος δ' ὁ κράτιστος. ὡς ἂν κορυφαῖος χοροῦ. διαφέρων τῶν ἄλλων ἢ κατὰ τὴν πολεμικὴν εὐχέρειαν. ἢ κατὰ τὸ γένος. ἢ κατὰ πλοῦτον . . . ἐφεξῆς δ' ἑκατέρωθε κατ' ἀξίαν ἧς ἔχουσιν ὑπεροχῆς.

135. See A. Ross, *Everyday Life of the Pagan Celts* (London: B. T. Batsford, Ltd., 1970), pp. 63–71 and *Pagan Celts*, pp. 45–50.

136. See Polybius 2.19, which describes how, in 299 B.C., the Celtic effort is undermined by their "undisciplined habits." At the victory celebrations, they drunkenly quarrel over the booty, which leads to fighting and soon the death of the majority of the army and the destruction of the booty to boot.

137. *Bricriu's Feast* presents a female analog to this ranking by combat, with the Word Battle of the Women of Ulster, which, like the duelling, breaks out at a communal feast. See Ross, *Pagan Celts*, pp. 84–85.

138. The principle is evident in the breach in an episode of the *Táin Bó Cúailnge* when Cú Chulainn has to battle Ferchú Loingsech and his twelve followers at one time. *Táin Bó Cúailnge* 2510–2531.

139. Athenaeus 4.40, p. 154.

140. Diodorus Siculus 5.28. ἐκ τῶν τυχόντων πρὸς τὴν διὰ τῶν λόγων ἅμιλλαν καταστάντες, ἐκ προκλήσεως μονομαχεῖν πρὸς ἀλλήλους. The use of reviling as a "warm-up" before coming to blows is a recurrent motif in the *Táin*, one purpose of which is articulated by Cú Chulainn to his charioteer, Láeg, whom he asks to taunt him to greater efforts, should Cú Chulainn seem to be flagging. See *Táin Bó Cúailnge* 3267–3275.

141. Athenaeus 4.40, p. 154: "Ἄλλοι δ' ἐν θεάτρῳ, λαβόντες ἀργύριον ἢ χρύσιον, οἳ δὲ οἴνου κεραμείων ἀριθμόν τινα, καὶ πιστωσάμενοι τὴν δόσιν, καὶ τοῖς ἀναγκαίοις ἢ φίλοις διαδωρησάμενοι.

142. See Millett, *Romanization*, p. 36.

143. Discussed by Ross, *Pagan Celts*, pp. 89–93, who sees the establishment of this harmony moving from the top down, with the *fírinne flátha*, the justice of the king, mediating between the divine and human plane.

144. Vitruvius 1.7.1. In fact, it seems that only the mixed edifice at Senlis housed a Hercules sanctuary; see Golvin, *L'Amphithéâtre*, p. 337.

145. See Martial, *De Spec.* 22.3 and Statius, *Silv.* 1.6.62.

146. See, in this line, M. B. Hornum, *Nemesis, the Roman State, and the Games* (Leiden: E. J. Brill, 1993).

147. See examples in Homer, *Il.* 3.156, 5.335, 13.122, 14.80, *Od.* 1.350, 2.136, 20.330, et al. and Hesiod, *Theog.* 223 and *Op.* 197–200.

148. Athenaeus 8.334c and Apollodorus, *Bibl.* 3.127. In the form of a goose, she is finally ravished at Rhamnous and later gives birth to Helen. Thus we see a connection drawn between Nemesis and Rhamnous, her most famous cult center, at a very early date. This points to a shrine of some antiquity in that vicinity, even though extant remains date back only to the fifth century. Scholarship has been distracted by Pausanias' description (1.33) of the sanctuary at Rhamnous, which he connects to Athenian victory at Marathon, often interpreted as meaning that the cult of Nemesis there only dates back to the fifth century. The evidence of the *Cypria* militates against this, surely, as does the great paucity of Marathon or Persian references in the decorative scheme of the temple as described by Pausanias, i.e., if Marathon were the sole inspiration for this cult to a newly personified deity, then one *would* see Marathon references and would *not* see the obscure iconography that Pausanias did. For further details, see M. Miles, "A Reconstruction of the Temple of Nemesis at Rhamnous," *Hesperia*, 58 (1989): 131–249 and C. W. J. Eliot in *PECS*, p. 753

149. Further early evidence for Nemesis comes from Athens, where the *Nemesia* annually celebrated and/or propitiated the dead, in fear of Nemesis as the

agent of vengeance for the deceased. Nemesis' cult at Smyrna was also of great antiquity, although her character here seems more like Aphrodite than Artemis, with the Graces dancing holy attendance upon her. Pausanias 9.35.6 refers to statues of the Charites by Boupalos. See L. R. Farnell, *The Cults of the Greek States* (Oxford: Oxford University Press, 1896), vol. 2, pp. 487–500 for Aphrodite-Nemesis connection. Another peculiarity of the Smyrna cult is Nemesis' double nature, mentioned in the description of Alexander's dream of Smyrna and verified by the material record; see Pausanias 7.5.3. The reasoning behind the duality of Nemesis at Smyrna is a much-debated issue, summed up by B. C. Dietrich, *Death, Fate and the Gods* (London: Athlone Press, 1965), pp. 170–172. These and other oddities of cult suggest that Nemesis here, as in Attica, was the ancient chthonic deity of the place, whose original, more polyvalent, character faded over time to become specific to what was suggested by the epithet. H. Herter, "Nemesis," *RE*, 16:2, col. 2353, suggests that the cult of Smyrna had been transported there by Ionic settlers from Attica. Others credit the Smyrna cult with the establishment at Rhamnous. The question is not crucial to our interests. Later coins of Smyrna show the Nemeseis wearing the mural crown, an attribute also of Tyche, a.k.a. Fortuna, for the importance of which to Nemesis, see below.

150. Solinus 7.26, apparently a confusion with the well-known statue of Nemesis, which Pausanias says was a work of Pheidias; the artist was actually Agoracritus. Dietrich, *Death*, pp. 157–176.

151. Modern assumptions about what constitutes a "real" god may differ from ancient; there is a tendency among scholars to interpret divinities who represent abstract qualities as artificial and, by implication, as superficial. Because these deities are judged as lacking the depth of personality and dynamism of gods with more substantive mythological backgrounds, it is assumed that any cult they attracted was likewise lacking in some basic religious feeling. Others, rightly, argue that such a distinction was not made in antiquity. See J. R. Fears, "The Cult of Virtues and Roman Imperial Ideology," *ANRW* II.17.2 (1981): 827–948, and, with reference to Nemesis, Hornum, *Nemesis*, p. 8.

152. Vanth is often associated with Charun, as seen in the frescoes from the François tomb, among others. Dietrich, *Death*, pp. 145–152. This may be significant for the history of Nemesis' association with the *spectacula*, given the allegedly Etruscan background of the *munera* and Charun's role as one of the stock characters of the arena (see Chapter 1). It may be that the Imperial Nemesis has incorporated some essence of Vanth over the centuries of transition between Hesiod and the Roman amphitheaters. This is, admittedly, speculative.

153. Herter, *RE*, 16:2, cols. 2338–2352 and H. Volkmann, "Studien zum Nemesiskult," *Archiv für Religionswissenschaft*, 26 (1928): 295–321 gives a similar argument. Herter's understanding of the meaning of the cult of Nemesis is based very much on evidence from these cult centers, which in turn has a Hellenic/philosophical bias, filled with the ethical resonance of Nemesis as the divine retributive force of outraged divinity.

154. Evidence from Herter can be organized as shown in Tables VIII and IX.

Table VIII. Nemesis in the Greek East

EAST	GREECE & THE AEGEAN	ASIA MINOR	SYRIA	MACEDON & THRACE	TOTAL
Cities	17	71	17	14	119
Coins	6	61	8	11	86
Epigraphy	11	11	4	3	29 (19)
Sculpture	8	3	5	7	23 (15)
Altars	5	2	1	1	9 (7)
Shrine*	4	3	4	1	12 (6)
Misc	1	4	–	–	5
City (coin only)	5	54	7	9	75
City (no coin)	12	17	10	5	44 (31)

*"Shrine" was defined as a range of architectural entities, from niche to temple, all being locations set aside specifically for the worship of Nemesis.
Numbers in parentheses represent purely Greek totals; all pieces known to be of Roman context were removed from consideration.

Table IX. Nemesis in the West

WEST	LIMES	GERMANY & GAUL	BRITAIN	SPAIN	ITALY	TOTAL
Cities	28 (29)	4 (7)	4 (7)	5 (8)	12	53 (61)
City (coin)	5	–	–	–	–	48 (56)
Coins	5	–	–	–	–	5
Epigraphy	51	4	3	4 (16)	13	75 (87)
Sculpture	10	1	3	–	5	19
Altars	5 (7)	–	–	1 (2)	4	10 (13)
Shrines	7 (8)	(4)	(3)	1 (4)	3	11 (22)
Misc	–	–	–	1	–	–

Numbers in parentheses represent the maximum modification of the catalog in RE on the basis of reinterpretation of the amphitheatrical evidence.

For the best statistical picture of the Nemesis cult, I first eliminated coins from the database as inadequate evidence for actual worship. By so doing, I was able to excise from the list many cities in the East and five in the West, which only appeared in the catalog as findspots for coins. I then eliminated material from the Greek sphere known to have Roman context, to get a more purely Greek picture of Nemesis. The results are striking. Thirty-one cities of the East offered evidence for the cult of Nemesis. Of the 52 pieces of material evidence involved, the weightiest category was epigraphy, with 19 examples (37%), followed by sculpture

(29%), altars (14%), and shrines (12%), of which there were only 6. Compare this to the West, where fifty-six cities had some indication of Nemesis worship, involving a total of 142 material examples. Again, inscriptions were most plentiful, with 61% of the evidence, followed by shrines (16%, which translates into 22 *nemesea*), sculpture (13%), and altars (9%). To give these numbers some meaning in terms of context, all the Nemesis shrines of the West, and indeed most of the other types of evidence, are linked with amphitheaters. For a considerably more detailed collection and analysis of the literary and epigraphic evidence for Nemesis, see Hornum, *Nemesis*, particularly Chapter 3 and his catalogs in appendices 1 and 2. His general conclusions agree with my own.

155. Asia Minor still leads, in terms of amount of evidence, suggesting that Smyrna may indeed have been an influential sanctuary.

156. See A. von Premerstein, "Nemesis und ihre Bedeutung für die Agone," *Philologus*, 53 (1894): 400–415 and A. García y Bellido, *Les religions orientales dans l'Espagne romaine* (Leiden: E. J. Brill, 1967), pp. 82–89. See also L. Foucher, "Némésis, le griffon et les jeux d'amphithéâtre," *Mélanges d'histoire ancienne offerts à William Seston* (Paris: E. de Boccard, 1974), pp. 187–195.

157. The gladiator, strictly speaking, fought against other human beings in ordered combat; the beast-fighter was designated a *venator* or a *bestiarius*. See Chapter 1 for a summary of *munus legitimum*.

158. Argued by Volkmann, "Studien," reiterated by Herter in *RE*, 16:2, cols. 2336–2337.

159. Nemesis is also connected with the theater but only in the Eastern Empire. See Hornum, *Nemesis*, p. 50.

160. SHA, *Max. et Balb.* 8.6, the only literary source that addresses Nemesis as the goddess of the amphitheatrical events.

161. *CIL* II.1125 and 10430, for example.

162. This interpretation of Nemesis is not alien to the Greek cultic context but rather the literary one. She is fairly reminiscent of Farnell's Nemesis, the Artemis-like chthonic deity, whose relationship with her worshipper is meant to alleviate the uncertainty of the fate of the individual. She combines the morally ambivalent qualities of the original Erinyes and the Etruscan Vanth, and like Vanth, she is a chthonic huntress and conveyor of the soul of the dead.

163. Such is the contention of Alicia Canto, based on her work on Nemesis inscriptions at Italica. See A. M. Canto, "Les Plaques votives avec plantae pedum d'Italica," *ZPE*, 54 (1984): 183–194. Nemesis here has the epithet *Caelestis*, which Canto wants to see as indicative of a syncretized polyvalent Carthaginian/Hellenistic goddess redolent of Iberian cosmopolitanism. The Hellenic influence in southern Spain is somewhat questionable, but the whole issue is merely touched on by Canto and is not central to her argument concerning the inscriptions. Obviously I find the Fortuna connection more persuasive.

164. Indeed, Hornum notes that of the ninety inscriptions to Nemesis of the games, only ten can be reasonably connected to participants. See Hornum, *Nemesis*, pp. 70–73 and appendix 2.

165. See Canto, "Plaques." The *sacerdos* from Italica is *AE* 1952 n. 121. The inscription for Corduba is *CIL* II.2195. Canto's "best foot forward" interpretation meets with skepticism from K. M. D. Dunbabin, "Ipsa deae vestigia . . . Footprints Divine and Human on Graeco-Roman Monuments," *JRA*, 3 (1990): 85–109.

166. See Hornum, *Nemesis*, pp. 73–74.

167. According to the evidence in *RE*, where *Augusta* had 28 examples, *Ultrix*, 11 (mostly literary, as one would expect, given the cult interpretation espoused above), *Regina*, 10, and *Sancta*, 8. Hornum's analysis of the epigraphic epithets of Nemesis quantifies this further: out of a total of 166, 51 used *Augusta* or *Sebaste* or some derivative of these. See Hornum, *Nemesis*, pp. 36–40 and table 3.

168. Herter, *RE*, 16 : 2, col. 2373. See also Hornum, *Nemesis*, pp. 15–18.

169. H. Mattingly and E. Sydenham, *The Roman Imperial Coinage* (London: Spink and Son, 1923–1981), vol. 1, p. 126 (Claudius), vol. 2, pp. 9 and 31–33, 50 (Vespasian), 311 (Trajan), 327 and 401–402, 439, 444 (Hadrian).

170. See ibid., vol. 2, pp. 9 and 31–33. In 68/9 there was a Nemesis issue in Spain, which also used the *Pax Augusta* legend (grasping at rhetorical straws, surely, in so doing), and another with the legend *Salus Generis Humani*. Trajan and Hadrian have restored Nemesis coins during their reigns, possibly dating back to the Republican period for the original type. Hadrian's Nemesis has the wheel, bridle, and branch as attributes, all of which are to be found with Fortuna as well (ibid., vol. 2, pp. 311, 401–402).

171. See Hornum, *Nemesis*, pp. 56–70 and Golvin, *L'Amphithéâtre*, pp. 337–340.

172. Golvin, *L'Amphithéâtre*, pp. 109–111, 135–136, and 164–165, and García y Bellido, *Religions orientales*, pp. 89–94. It is believed that Carnuntum's shrine was in this location, although it has not been preserved. The altars were found in that area.

173. The link to Nemesis is not indisputable in these chapels. An inscription to Nemesis was found at the military amphitheater at Aquincum but without provenance. The chapel at Senlis is especially problematic, as a statuette of "Hercules" was found in the location. Other chapels, outside our area, include those at Stobi (which is definitely a *nemeseum*) and at Lambaesis and Theveste in North Africa. Other evidence for worship of Nemesis, disassociated from possible shrines and mostly outside our area of interest, includes the amphitheatrical altars from Savaria and Caesarea and a relief from Gortyna. Some have identified substructures at Salone as chapels, but this is not generally acknowledged as likely.

174. Golvin, *L'Amphithéâtre*, p. 128 and pl. 12.2. See also R. P. Wright, "Roman Britain in 1966: The Inscriptions," *JRS*, 57 (1967): 203–210.

175. Golvin, *L'Amphithéâtre*, p. 136 and pl. 14.6.

176. Corinium Dobunnorum: Golvin, *L'Amphithéâtre*, p. 87, and Wright, "Inscriptions." Aquincum (civil): Golvin, *L'Amphithéâtre*, p. 137 and pl. 14.4.

177. Flavia Solva: Golvin, *L'Amphithéâtre*, p. 91 and pl. 8.4. Ulpia Traiana: Golvin, *L'Amphithéâtre*, p. 129 and pl. 14.7.

178. A similar interpretation of Nemesis' presence at the games is given by Hornum, *Nemesis*, pp. 74–88.

4. THE SYSTEM OF CONSTRUCTION

1. The meaning of the mosaic for the impact of violent images in Roman society is discussed by S. Brown, "Death as Decoration: Scenes from the Arena on Roman Domestic Mosaics," in A. Richlin, ed., *Pornography and Representation in Greece and Rome* (New York: Oxford University Press, 1992), pp. 180–211. See also K. M. D. Dunbabin, *The Mosaics of Roman North Africa: Studies in Iconography and Patronage* (Oxford: Clarendon Press, 1978), pp. 67–70 and M. A. Beschaouch, "La mosaïque de chasse à l'amphithéâtre découverte à Smirat en Tunisie," *Comptes rendus de l'académie des inscriptions et belles-lettres* (Paris: Librarie C. Klincksieck, 1966), pp. 134–158.

2. *Hoc est habere, hoc est posse.*

3. See, among others, P. Veyne, *Bread and Circuses: Historical Sociology and Political Pluralism* (London: Penguin, 1990) and R. MacMullen, *Roman Social Relations* (New Haven: Yale University Press, 1974), pp. 60–61.

4. This is especially true given the public nature of life in ancient cities. The poorer the citizen, the more likely would he be to spend less time in his own squalid apartment and more time in the deluxe public accommodations built for him by a local euergete.

5. Plutarch (*Cat. Mai.* 18.3) expresses this viewpoint: πλούτου γὰρ ἀφαίρεσιν οἱ πολλοὶ νομίζουσι τὴν κώλυσιν αὐτοῦ τῆς ἐπιδείξεως. See also Apuleius, *Met.* 5.10.

6. There are hints at the existence of private amphitheaters. The amphitheater of Statilius Taurus may have been one such, as the Statilii seem to have taken responsibility for its maintenance and may have actually rented it out for games. See J.-Cl. Golvin, *L'Amphithéâtre romain* (Paris: E. de Boccard, 1988), pp. 52–53.

7. The distinction between public and private building tended to blur as it related to the construction funded and/or sponsored by public individuals in the Roman world. On the dichotomy between public and private buildings, see C. Edwards, *The Politics of Immorality in Ancient Rome* (Cambridge: Cambridge University Press, 1993), pp. 137–172.

8. Tacitus, *Ann.* 4.62–63, who makes the contrast between the former motivations and the latter "sordid" one quite clear. See A. Scobie, "Spectator Security and Comfort at Gladiatorial Games," *Nikephoros*, 1 (1988): 191–243, especially pp. 227–228.

9. Tacitus, *Ann.* 4.62–63, says fifty thousand people were killed or maimed, and Suetonius, *Tib.* 40, claims twenty thousand. Both estimates are excessive, given that the seating capacity of the Colosseum, the largest amphitheater ever built, was slightly over fifty thousand and twenty thousand could be considered a good-sized amphitheater.

10. Tacitus, *Ann.* 4.63: *neve amphitheatrum inponeretur nisi solo firmitatis spectatae.*

11. Ibid.: *abundantia pecuniae et municipali ambitione*. Suetonius' brief account of the matter suggests that Tiberius turned the disaster into an opportunity for public relations, making himself accessible to all, a sharp contrast to his previous behavior at Capri and environs.

12. *Digest* 50.10.3: *Macer libro secundo de officio praesidis. Opus novum privato etiam sine principis auctoritate facere licet, praeterquam si ad aemulationem alterius civitatis pertineat vel materiam seditionis praebeat vel circum theatrum vel amphitheatrum sit. Publico vero sumptu opus novum sine principis auctoritate fieri non licere constitutionibus declaratur. Inscribi autem nomen operi publico alterius quam principis aut eius, cuius pecunia id opus factum sit, non licet.* "From book two of Macer's Official Duties: New construction privately funded may be built without authorization from the princeps, except when it leads to rivalry with another of the city or offers the opportunity for sedition or is a circus, theater, or amphitheater. But it is proclaimed by law that new construction built with public funds may not go up without Imperial authorization. Nor may any name be inscribed on any public work, excepting only the emperor and the person who paid for the construction."

13. Although Macer himself lived during the Severan period, in this instance his citation must reflect earlier statutes, such as the *constitutiones* of which he speaks, for the simple reason that the vast majority of Roman amphitheaters predate the third century. Surely the regulation of amphitheater construction depends upon the contemporary, ongoing process of said construction.

14. Alternatively, the restrictions could relate to the increasing involvement of the central government in the rate of Romanization. Although provincials were encouraged to emulate Roman ways, of which Roman civic structures were a highly visible part, they could not be allowed to bankrupt themselves in so doing. After all, an impoverished provincial was resistant to taxation. The problem of overenthusiastic euergetism and its solution, in the form of special Imperial legates or troubleshooters, was considered at some length by Pliny the Younger during his tenure as Imperial legate in Bithynia, for which see Appendix 2.

15. The exception is T. Crispius Reburrus, who *fecit* (possibly) the substructures of the arena at Nîmes, see *CIL* XII.3315 and Golvin, *L'Amphithéâtre*, p. 189 n. 306.

16. In 377 B.C., to be specific. See Livy 6.32. The wall was still being built in 353 (Livy 7.20), using army labor. What does this mean? Did this actually happen? Or was Livy being anachronistic? If so, does that mean that army labor was at work during the Early Principate in the city of Rome? The aediles were credited with a role in city planning after the Gallic sack in 390 B.C. See D. E. Strong, "The Administration of Public Building in Rome during the Late Republic and Early Empire," *BICS*, 15 (1968): 97–109. For specifically censorial activity, see A. Astin, "The Role of Censors in Roman Economic Life," *Latomus*, 49 (1990): 20–36.

17. Ap. Claudius Caecus' building program was funded by support of the populace, as were his expansionist goals for Rome.

18. Polybius (6.13) calls public building the chief civil expense of Rome's treasury in the second century. See below.

19. The sources hint at senatorial opposition to censorial plans, which presumably would not arise if the Senate were responsible for those plans in the first place. Given also the contentiousness of the Senate and the inherent unwieldiness of working in committees, the likelihood of a coherent, far-reaching plan for public construction being realized *in toto* by the Senate seems rather small. If anything, censors-elect would have presented more or less detailed plans for construction to the Senate for ratification and funding allocation. See Strong ("Administration," pp. 97–98), who waffles a bit on the intensity of senatorial involvement at the planning stage.

20. One example of this kind of special funding comes from 179 B.C., when the entire *vectigal*, or tax, was set aside for public building; half that sum was allocated a decade later. *Praesens pecunia* was assessed after the *probatio* had been performed for maintenance contracted out in the previous quinquennium. See Livy 27.10 and 34.6. *Vectigal* of 179 in Livy 40.46 and of 169, Livy 44.16. This period is the best documented. It is thus impossible to say whether special allocations for censorial projects were regularly made.

21. The censors could get a special extension of their term to see the contract through, but this was exceptional. See, for example, Livy 45.15. Other arrangements could be made, as was the case in the third century, when the censors responsible for the construction of the Anio Vetus were appointed *duumviri aquae perducendae*, the special committee in charge of continuing the aqueduct, when their censorship lapsed. See Frontinus, *De Aq.* 1.6.

22. It has been suggested that in the interregnum between censorships, building activity still in progress was handled by the consuls. See F. W. Walbank, *A Historical Commentary on Polybius* (Oxford: Oxford University Press, 1957), vol. 1, pp. 694–697. Or, it may have been that the next censors could be delegated the responsibility for the *probatio*. Cicero, *In Verr.* 2.1.130.

23. Livy, *Epit.* 20 and Festus p. 89 M.

24. Events discussed in Appian, *B. Civ.* 1.28.125 and Velleius Paterculus 1.15. See also Chapter 1.

25. For early ludic constructions, there are the Circus Maximus, from the regal period, and the Circus Flaminius.

26. In 193 B.C., the aediles used the money accumulated from fines to finance a building program that focused on commercial utility. During this and the following year, several porticoes and some sort of market building by the Tiber, perhaps to be identified with the Porticus Aemilia, were built. See Livy 35.10 and 41.

27. See Chapter 1 above.

28. Strong, "Administration," p. 99 and M. K. and R. L. Thornton, *Julio-Claudian Building Programs: A Quantitative Study in Political Management* (Wauconda, Ill.: Bolchazy-Carducci, 1989), p. 32.

29. Curio may or may not have been aedile at the time. Plutarch thought he was, probably because it was customary to give such games, loosely called funerary, as aedile. We know he ran for aedile in 51 but did not win despite his efforts. See Pliny, *HN* 36.15.116–120; Plutarch, *Cat. Min.* 45; Cicero, *Ad Fam.* 8.9, 8.10.

30. One example of the potential impact such aedilician presentations could have may be the *Ludi Romani* in 213 B.C., which constituted the first major public action of L. Cornelius Scipio, later Africanus, prior to his acquisition of an extraordinary command. See Livy 25.2.

31. For the seminal practitioners of this sort of bounty, see L. Pietilä-Castrén, *Magnificentia Publica: The Victory Monuments of the Roman Generals in the Era of the Punic Wars* (Helsinki: Societas Scientiarum Fennica, 1987).

32. For the strong connection between military success and the will of the gods, see P. Brunt, "Laus Imperii," in P. D. A. Garnsey and C. R. Whittaker, eds., *Imperialism in the Ancient World* (Cambridge: Cambridge University Press, 1978), pp. 159–191, especially pp. 163–168.

33. Strong, "Administration," p. 103.

34. See Chapter 1.

35. Dio Cassius 54.8. There was also a curator of public buildings and shrines, about which we unhappily know very little.

36. Dio Cassius 51.23: τοῦ δὲ δὴ Καίσαρος τὸ τέταρτον ἔτι (29 B.C.) ὑπατεύοντος ὁ Ταῦρος ὁ Στατίλιος θέατρόν τι ἐν τῷ Ἀρείῳ πεδίῳ κυνηγετικὸν λίθινον καὶ ἐξεποίησε τοῖς ἑαυτοῦ τέλεσι καὶ καθιέρωσεν ὁπλομαχίᾳ καὶ διὰ τοῦτο στρατηγὸν ἕνα παρὰ τοῦ δήμου κατ' ἔτος αἱρεῖσθαι ἐλάμβανε.

37. The maintenance of the structure seems to have been undertaken by his family, as their household were acknowledged epigraphically as arena personnel. See Golvin, *L'Amphithéâtre*, pp. 52–53.

38. See below for particulars of the Colosseum's construction. For building by the emperor, and the peculiar public/private nature of the emperor's finances, see, among others, Veyne, *Bread*, pp. 292–482.

39. R. MacMullen, "Roman Imperial Building in the Provinces," *HSCP*, 64 (1959): 207–235.

40. This is especially true for the censors of 174 B.C., who directed building projects at *coloniae* and *municipia* outside Rome, using local funding to support them. See Livy 41.27.5.

41. The acknowledgement of Italy and the provinces as integral to the Roman Empire was an ongoing process in the later Republic, no doubt catalyzed by events of the Civil War and the dissolution of the Second Triumvirate, in which the entire Mediterranean was involved to a greater or lesser extent. The universality of Augustus' outlook is apparent in the *Res Gestae*, when he refers to the oath of allegiance made to him by all of Italy, the Gauls, the Spains, Africa, Sicily, and Sardinia (section 25) and when he claims to have attained his supreme authority by universal consent (section 34).

42. Philostratus (*V.S.* 1.25, 1.8, 2.1 and 2.9) describes the efforts of Fronto and Chaeremon, among others, acting as go-betweens and successfully acquiring million-sestertius grants for their provincial clients. Acting as a legate for one's *municipium* could be a *munus* for the citizen; see below.

43. See W. Mierse, "Augustan Building Programs in the Western Provinces," in K. A. Raaflaub and M. Toher, eds., *Between Republic and Empire: Interpretations*

of Augustus and His Principate (Berkeley: University of California Press, 1990), pp. 308–333, who discusses architectural style of buildings in southern Gaul and Spain as indicative of Augustan ideology. See also the discussion of architecture as imperialist text in W. L. MacDonald, *The Architecture of the Roman Empire II* (New Haven: Yale University Press, 1986), pp. 248–273.

44. Public building being considered supplemental support of the free poor: help the poor to help themselves.

45. See *Ep.* 10.70: *indulsisti* and 10.90: *indulseris. Dignissimam*: see *Ep.* 10.37. *Digna, dignum*: see *Ep.* 10.41 and 10.70. See also Appendix 2, for Pliny's experiences in general.

46. See also Suetonius, *Vesp.* 8, in Rome: *vacuas areas occupare et aedificare, si possessores cessarent, cuicumque permisit* and SHA, *Hadr.* 18.2 *constituit inter cetera, ut in nulla civitate domus aliqua transferendae ad aliam urbem ullius materiae causa dirueretur.*

47. *Digest* 1.16.7.1.

48. Alexander Severus subsidized architects, engineers, and their students, trying to address the increasing scarcity of skilled technicians in the empire.

49. MacMullen, "Roman Imperial Building," p. 207.

50. SHA, *Hadr.* 19.2: *in omnibus paene urbibus et aliquid aedificavit et ludo edidit.* Note the pairing of public building and games.

51. SHA, *Hadr.* 19.9: *cum opera ubique infinita fecisset, numquam ipse nisi in Traiani patris templo nomen suum scripsit.* See also SHA, *Hadr.* 7.6. That this was not entirely the case is indicated by a number of inscriptions acknowledging the emperor's support of projects, among them the amphitheater at Capua, for which see below.

52. See A. García y Bellido, *Colonia Aelia Augusta Italica* (Madrid: Instituto español de arqueología, 1960).

53. Aurelius Victor, *Caes.* 14.4–5.

54. Probably. Hadrian's itinerary and travel dates are disputed. See B. W. Henderson, *The Life and Principate of the Emperor Hadrian* (London: Methuen and Co., 1923), Appendix B, pp. 279–294.

55. *CIL* X.3832.

56. Capua's amphitheater was 165 by 135 meters in overall dimensions, seating some thirty thousand spectators, the second largest in capacity after the Flavian Amphitheater. See Golvin, *L'Amphithéâtre*, p. 204 and and J. Beloch, *Campanien: Geschichte und Topographie des antiken Neapel und seinen Umgebung* (Breslau: Morgenstern, 1890), pp. 351–353. The structure at Capua was clearly modeled on the Colosseum, with which it shares several features not found elsewhere, such as the double peripheral gallery.

57. Here the word "municipal" is not meant in its technical sense, i.e., as an anglicized adjectival form of *municipium*, which had a particular meaning in the administrative hierarchy of Roman cities. Rather, "municipal" here indicates the corporate action of the town council, as opposed to that of an individual or the emperor.

58. Such as those partially extant for Heraclea, Urso, Malaga, and Tarentum. See the handy translated collection in E. G. Hardy, *Three Spanish Charters* (Oxford: Oxford University Press, 1912). For administration in the provinces, see N. Mackie, *Local Administration in Roman Spain A.D. 14–212* (Oxford: British Archaeological Reports, 1983), especially pp. 118–132 and 103–104; she is most informative on the particulars of municipal administration. See also A. Lintott, *Imperium Romanum: Politics and Administration* (London: Routledge, 1993), pp. 132–145 on local constitutions in the western provinces.

59. Contributa Ipsca built a temple to Vespasian (*CIL* II.1570). See J. de Alarcão and R. Etienne, *Fouilles de Conimbriga* (Paris: E. de Boccard, 1977), vol. 1, pp. 87–112 for the building program at Conimbriga.

60. Tacitus, *Ann.* 14.17. The passage is quoted in Chapter 1. Analysis of conflict in P. Castrén, *Ordo Populusque Pompeianus* (Rome: Bardi Editore, 1975), pp. 111–112 and W. G. Moeller, "The Riot of A.D. 59 at Pompeii," *Historia*, 17 (1970): 84–95, especially p. 94.

61. Tacitus, *Hist.* 2.21: *In eo certamine pulcherrimum amphitheatri opus, situm extra muros, conflagravit . . . municipale vulgus, pronum ad suspiciones, fraude inlata ignis alimenta credidit a quibusdam ex vicinis coloniis invidia et aemulatione, quod nulla in Italia moles tam capax foret.*

62. Tacitus, *Hist.* 3.57: *municipalem aemulationem bellis civilibus miscebant.* See *Hist.* 4.50 for Tripoli and Lebda. The ongoing competitive situation in Asia Minor is documented in Dio Chrysostom, *Or.* 38–48 and in Pliny the Younger; see also Appendix 2.

63. For example, they instructed two sevirs, appointed officials, to build theater seats at Aurgi in Tarraconensis (*CIL* II.3361). One council demanded that a certain citizen sponsor a building project apparently on the basis of his avoidance of civic duties despite his eligibility for decurial status (*CIL* II.6449).

64. The *Digest* goes into some detail on these obligations of a *municeps* in 50.1–4.

65. *Digest* 50.4.3.3: *corporalia munera feminis ipse sexus denegat.*

66. Decurions, once they left office, were subject to the *munus* of curatorship, which seems to have been an administrative post without the social benefits usually attached to public office: the rank of curator had no honorific insignia, it was not part of the municipal *cursus*, and it offered no advantage in the struggle for social status and ranking. The duties of a curator involved service as ambassador and as public advocate, in addition to the supervision of public construction, repairs, and maintenance. In some cases, the curator may have fulfilled some financial responsibilities, which elsewhere would have been done by a quaestor. For more on curators, see G. P. Burton, "The Curator Rei Publicae: Towards a Reappraisal," *Chiron*, 9 (1979): 465–487 and R. Duncan-Jones, "The Procurator as Civic Benefactor," *JRS*, 64 (1974): 79–85. The establishment of the supervision of public work as a *munus* may have been because magistrates were unwilling or unable to perform this extra function, possibly because of the scope of the duty involved.

67. Capua (see above) is the solitary example.

68. *CIL* X.852.

69. *CIL* X.854. Valgus was the brother-in-law of P. Servilius Rullus, mentioned by Cicero (*Leg. Agr.* 3.2.8, 13; 4.14) as a fraudulent evicter of tenants and a profiteer, who sold land received from Sulla back to the decemvirs. Porcius owned rich vineyards and exported their products to Gaul, where amphoras bearing his stamp have been found in abundance. See R. Etienne, "La naissance de l'amphithéâtre, le mot et la chose," *REL*, 43 (1966): 213–220, especially pp. 214–215.

70. See Chapter 1, above, for the placement of Pompeii's amphitheater in a more general historical context.

71. M. Clavel-Lévêque and P. Lévêque, *Villes et structures urbaines dans l'Occident romain* (Paris: Les Belles Lettres, 1984), p. 122. Whether this holds true for amphitheaters is a matter of some controversy, as Duncan-Jones argues on the basis of finances; see below and R. P. Duncan-Jones, *The Economy of the Roman Empire: Quantitative Studies* (Cambridge: Cambridge University Press, 1982), p. 75.

72. Mackie, *Local Administration*, pp. 119–120.

73. *CIL* XI.3938: *quod amphithe[a]tru[m] col. Iul. Felici Lucofer. s.p.f. dedicavitque.* See F. Coarelli, "Lucus Feroniae," *Studi Classici e Orientali*, 25 (1975): 164–166 for particulars of the amphitheater.

74. On which, see, among others, J. Nicols, "Zur Verleihung öffentlicher Ehrungen in der römischen Welt," *Chiron*, 9 (1979): 243–260; L. Harmand, *Le Patronat sur les collectivités publiques des origines au bas empire* (Paris: Presses universitaires de France, 1957); and T. F. C. Blagg, "Architectural Patronage in the Western Provinces of the Roman Empire," in A. King and M. Henig, eds., *The Roman West in the Third Century* (Oxford: British Archaeological Reports, 1981), pp. 167–188.

75. *CIL* XIV.4259. The amphitheater at Tibur is a modest one, lacking even an annular gallery behind its small but respectable façade. The overall dimensions of the building are a mere 85 by 65 meters, and it seated possibly six thousand. See Golvin, *L'Amphithéâtre*, pp. 198 and 287.

76. *CIL* XIV.4258.

77. *CIL* X.4737.

78. *CIL* XII.697. Candidate for what is unclear, since the inscription is heavily restored. Apparently, however, goal-oriented use of the amphitheater was still considered a persuasive means of swaying the electorate even in the provinces, even in the second century.

79. *CIL* XIV.3010. Note the use of the Claudian letter *W*.

80. For discussion of which, see, among others, R. MacMullen, "Women in Public in the Roman Empire," *Historia*, 29 (1980): 208–218 and J. Nicols, "Patrona Civitatis: Gender and Civic Patronage," in C. Deroux, ed., *Studies in Latin Literature and Roman History*, vol. 5 (Brussels: Collection Latomus, 1989), pp. 117–142. See also women present in the lists of benefactors cited by R. P. Duncan-Jones, *The Roman Economy* (Cambridge: Cambridge University Press, 1976), pp. 227–235.

81. *CIL* II.1956.

82. Mackie, *Local Administration*, p. 119.

83. The same inscription (*CIL* X.5183) notes her responsibility for the construction of a temple.

84. This may have been the C. Ummidius C.f. Quadratus who is credited with the construction of Casinum's Tabularium in *CIL* X.5182. See Pliny, *Ep.* 7.24.

85. Sherwin-White suggests that he was born a Severus, but was adopted into his grandmother's line, hence his name. See A. N. Sherwin-White, *The Letters of Pliny: A Historical and Social Commentary* (Oxford: Oxford University Press, 1966), p. 431.

86. Pliny, *Ep.* 7.24.

87. E. Badian, *Publicans and Sinners* (Oxford: Oxford University Press, 1972), p. 15 and *passim*.

88. Badian, in *Publicans*, p. 37, thinks that publicans specializing in building contracts were more likely to retain specialized staff and support to handle their projects.

89. Plutarch, *An vit. ad infel. suff.* 3: εἶθ᾽ αἱροῦνται τὸν ἀπ᾽ ἐλάττονος δαπάνης ταὐτὸ ποιοῦντα καὶ βέλτιον καὶ τάχιον.

90. Badian, *Publicans*, p. 71. Compare Vitruvius 5.1.6 and 10 praef. 1–2.

91. If the contractor provided everything, this should be considered *emptio* rather than *locatio*, which was regarded as the purchase only of expertise. See *Digest* 18.1.20. Some contracts stipulated the materials to be used and how they would be purchased, although there is some disagreement on this in the *Digest*, whether the *locator* paying for materials by the unit measure should buy them as measured in the final product or as measured at the quarry (or wherever), i.e., the amount needed to get eventually to the final product. See *Digest* 19.2.30 and 19.2.36.

92. See *CIL* VI.1585 and 485.

93. Half the payment agreed on was made to the contractor up front, once he had provided some form of security, preferably property. If the contractor fulfilled his obligations, then he received the other half after *probatio*. If, however, he did not finish by the date agreed upon, he would forfeit a percentage of the final payment.

94. Vitruvius 10 praef. 1–2. There was an upward limit placed on how much waste would affect the treasury. If the contractor went 25% over the estimate, public funds absorbed the loss. If he went more than 25% over, the difference was taken from his security.

95. Vitruvius' "ideal" contractor is conflated with the architect and would be, like Vitruvius, a man of some consequence and thus more liable to public honors anyway.

96. See, for example, the contract for transport of columns in *Digest* 19.2.25.7.

97. This is probably the explanation behind Flavian equestrian appointments, as when Vespasian put L. Vestinus in charge of the rebuilding of the Capitolium, and when Titus, after a fire in the city, designated a board of equestrians

to organize the efforts. See Tacitus, *Hist.* 4.53: *curam restituendi Capitolii* and Sue-tonius, *Titus* 8: *urbis incendio . . . praeposuitque compluris ex equestri ordine.* Titus also directed that the knickknacks or decorative objets d'art of the Imperial residence be used to provide financial support for the construction.

98. Frank may go too far in his reconstruction of the Imperial system based on scattered evidence from Asia Minor. T. Frank, *An Economic Survey of Ancient Rome* (Baltimore: Johns Hopkins University Press, 1938), vol. 4, pp. 837–849.

99. Indeed, Vitruvius 1.1.10 emphasizes the necessity of having the specifi-cations at hand during the contract stage. See R. Ling, "The Mechanics of the Building Trade," in F. Grew and B. Hobley, eds., *Roman Urban Topography in Britain and the Western Empire* (London: Council for British Archaeology, 1985), pp. 14–27, especially pp. 14–17.

100. Roman use of concrete construction allowed for the lion's share of the work to be done by unskilled laborers, who relied on the accuracy and practicality of the plan.

101. Vitruvius 6 praef. 5–6. Vitruvius also has great expectations for the edu-cation of an architect, so his ideal patron-architect may have been as rare as a philosopher-king. In this matter, see Frontinus' uncertainty about his own quali-fications as *curator aquarum, De Aq.* praef 2.

102. Columella (*Rust.* 5.1.3) says that architects scorn to price buildings for themselves, leaving that task to cost surveyors.

103. Philostratus, *V.S.* 2.1.

104. See *Digest* 18.1.32, which specifies that the land was public and only the business was heritable or alienable; see also *CIL* II.2129. Mackie, *Local Adminis-tration*, p. 125, points out that communities could charge for the use of the water supply, as documented by *CIL* II.1643.

105. See *Digest* 50.10 and Pliny, *Ep.* 10.70, 71.

106. *Digest* 49.18.4; 50.4.1.2; 50.4.18.15. For Trajan's negative attitude toward new local taxes, see Pliny, *Ep.* 10 *passim* and Appendix 2.

107. *CIL* XIV.4259 and *CIL* XI.1527. It is not clear as to what was the contri-bution of Luca's "Magistrate X." Was it 100,000 sesterces annually? Or 100,000 total, 10,000 annually for 10 years?

108. R. P. Duncan-Jones, *Structure and Scale in the Roman Economy* (Cam-bridge: Cambridge University Press, 1990), pp. 174–184 and *Economy: Quantita-tive Studies*, pp. 83–86.

109. First mentioned in the Roman sphere in connection with constitutions imposed on Greece in the second century. See Livy 34.51 and Pausanias 7.16.

110. J. H. Oliver, "A New Letter of Antoninus Pius," *AJP*, 79 (1958): 52–60.

111. Pliny, *Ep.* 10.112 and 113.

112. *Pollicitates* for construction were enforceable and heritable, to varying de-grees. See *Digest* 50.12 and *passim.* Trajan made his special agent, Pliny, respon-sible for extracting such promises. The *Digest* puts the provincial governor in charge.

113. Duncan-Jones, *Economy: Quantitative Studies*, p. 88.

114. Ibid., *passim*. See also H. Jouffroy, *La Construction publique en Italie et dans l'Afrique romaine* (Strasbourg: AECR, 1986).

115. Duncan-Jones, *Economy: Quantitative Studies*, p. 75.

116. Pliny, *Ep.* 10.39. The extant remains of the theater in Nicaea measure a maximum of 85 by 55 meters, covering an area of some 4,800 square meters (area of this theater would thus be [pi] x [55][55] divided by 2, or 4,749.3 square meters). Compare this to the Theater of Marcellus, whose area was 8,831 square meters. Of course, this does not take into account the seating on various levels but rather simply the construction in plan.

117. *CIL* VIII.5365.

118. These are the Blaesus and the "Magistrate X" inscriptions mentioned above under *summa*. Apparently, 20,000 sesterces was spent on Tibur's amphitheater, plus 200 *operae*. Luca may have received 1,000,000 sesterces, if we accept the larger figure possible, otherwise 100,000 sesterces. See note above.

119. *Ad amphitheatri dedicationem* and *in opus amphitheatri*.

120. Thornton and Thornton, *Building Programs*, pp. 15–23.

121. The decision made by the Thorntons to abandon absolute estimates of building cost was based on lack of evidence. As noted above, there are very few pieces of evidence for the purchasing power of a sestertius in terms of public building, and these pieces cannot be connected to make any sort of coherent picture, biased as they are by regional factors, inflation, and by their very paucity. Estimating building cost as measured by man-hours involved is also problematic, given the difficulty in reconstructing a realistic picture of preindustrial skills and methods as applied to the sophistication of Roman architecture.

122. The "Maison Carrée" measures 32 by 15 meters, i.e., 480 square meters of ground space.

123. Assigning specific relative value to this set of construction terms seems very shaky indeed, as there is absolutely no guarantee of consistency in word choice among the literary or epigraphic sources.

124. Thornton and Thornton, *Building Programs*, p. 132.

125. Cato, *Agr.* 14.3 and the *lex municipii Tarentini*.

126. Eight being, of course, the square meterage of one work unit.

127. The military is an exceptional case in this regard; see below.

128. *CIL* XIV.4259.

129. For Roman slavery in general, see, among others, K. R. Bradley, *Slaves and Masters in the Roman Empire: A Study in Social Control* (New York: Oxford University Press, 1987); M. I. Finley, *Ancient Slavery and Modern Ideology* (London: Chatto and Windus, 1980); K. Hopkins, *Conquerors and Slaves* (Cambridge: Cambridge University Press, 1978); J. C. Dumont, *Servus: Rome et l'esclavage sous la République* (Rome: École française, 1987); and W. L. Westermann, *The Slave Systems of Greek and Roman Antiquity* (Philadelphia: American Philosophical Society, 1955). Modern scholarship on slavery emphasizes the status and mobility of

the individual slave, touching on slaves in groups primarily as a source of agricultural labor. Relatively little has been done on the use of slaves in public building.

130. Plutarch, *Crass.* 2.

131. Crassus acquired the possessions and estates of men proscribed by Sulla, and he would purchase, at great reduction, property while it was in the process of being destroyed by fire or by some other disaster, a not-uncommon occurrence in ancient Rome.

132. The text does not specify the subsequent rebuilding and lease, but Plutarch does say that Crassus owned most of Rome, so he must, to a large extent, have retained the property he acquired.

133. Frontinus, *De Aq.* 98.

134. By the time of Frontinus' term as curator, two gangs of state-owned slaves, numbering some seven hundred, including skilled workmen, were on hand constantly for maintenance of aqueducts. Some upkeep of aqueducts still had to be contracted, and the terms of contract required a minimum number of slave workmen whose movements were apparently strictly controlled. *Architecti*, *fabri*, and *mensores* appear in the Imperial *columbaria*. See W. L. Westermann, "*Sklaverei*," *RE* Supplement 6, cols. 1035–1036 and R. H. Barrow, *Slavery in the Roman Empire* (New York: Dial Press, 1928), pp. 131–132, who claims that the state, however, possessed no female slaves and thus no way to replace the work force naturally. The perpetual need to restock their slave force by purchase must have been a constant drain on state coffers.

135. This is argued by P. A. Brunt, "Free Labour and Public Works," *JRS*, 70 (1980): 81–100.

136. Such is suggested by Vitruvius 7.1.3. See also T. Frank, *An Economic Survey of Ancient Rome* (Baltimore: Johns Hopkins University Press, 1940), vol. 5, pp. 235–236. Slaves were, in fact, more likely to be skilled craftsmen, whose training was financed by their masters, with an eye to the future earning power of the artisan.

137. See P. Garnsey, "Non-Slave Labour in the Roman World," and C. R. Whittaker, "Rural Labour in Three Roman Provinces," both in P. Garnsey, ed., *Non-Slave Labour in the Greco-Roman World* (Cambridge: Cambridge Philological Society, 1980), pp. 34–47 and 73–99. Both problematize the supposed dualism of the statuses "slave" and "free," acknowledging a number of ambiguous levels of independence between the two in Rome's social economy. Barrow, *Slavery*, pp. 125–129, points to the decline of Italian industry toward the end of the first century and the growth of provincial workshops causing a problem for Italian slave-holding industrialists. At the same time, there were changes in society that made "competition" between free and slave labor more intense: the price of skilled slaves increased as it became more difficult to get them, let alone train them. The result was that there was a preference for free labor.

138. The Capitolium was apparently built in the regal period by a corvée of the *plebs*; Cicero and Livy refer to this fact. Both, however, cite the event in an argumentative context; although the thrust is rather different, both arguments

rely on the archaism of the practice. Cicero (*In Verr.* 2.5.48) uses the event as another nostalgic example of the good old days, when Romans were frugal and performed good, honest labor. Livy (1.56) says that the corvée was conjoined with the use of public funds, which is confusing in itself. What were the funds for? If the labor of free citizens could be compelled, could not the talents of professional architects and the necessary material be requisitioned as well? Livy makes the incident an example of Tarquinian arrogant misuse of Roman citizens, who were also forced to work on the Circus Maximus and the Cloaca Maxima: worthy projects both but filthy labor. The authors locate the practice firmly in the past.

139. See text in Hardy, *Spanish Charters*, p. 44, section 98. See also Lintott, *Imperium Romanum*, pp. 132–145 and Sherwin-White, *Letters*, p. 623. On corvée in Pliny's Bithynia, see Appendix 2.

140. *Digest* 50.1–4.

141. Lintott mentions the use of corvée in connection with military occupation: *Imperium Romanum*, pp. 92–95. See also Barrow, *Slavery*, p. 131.

142. Similar motivation existed for the rebuilding of the Via Domitia; see Cicero, *Font.* 8.18. Three inscriptions from the third century may refer to citizen labor, as they mention work done *per colonos*. *CIL* VIII.8701 and 8828 are from the reign of Severus Alexander, *CIL* VIII.8777 is from that of Gordian. The troubled nature of the period may have led builders to recall an archaic practice. It is also possible that these *coloni* received some compensation for their efforts. Mention of labor on inscriptions is very rare, and the lack of detail on these examples can support no conclusions.

143. For "chain-gangs" as preferred to incarceration, see F. Millar, "Condemnation to Hard Labour in the Roman Empire," *PBSR*, 52 (1984): 124–147.

144. Offenses included diurnal house-breaking (see Paulus, *Digest* 47.18.2) or adhering to Christianity under the Emperor Licinius (Eusebius, *Vit. Const.* 2.20.3). Paulus says their condition was like that of the deportee, i.e., they suffered loss of property, rights of testament, and rights of inheritance.

145. In Rome, for example, the major public facility requiring a fairly constant source of labor was the aqueduct system, which we know was maintained by the Imperial *familiae* or by contractors, who did not apparently have access to the convict labor pool.

146. Josephus, *B.J.* 3.540. This may be the source for the allegation that Judaean prisoners of war provided labor for the Colosseum, for which see below.

147. Suetonius, *Nero* 31.

148. Pliny, *Ep.* 10.31, 32. See commentary in Sherwin-White, *Letters*, pp. 602–606.

149. The maximum mentioned is ten years. This is in contrast to *damnatio ad metallum*, *in ludum* and *ad gladium*, which were life sentences, and, in the case of the mines, virtual death sentences. The *Digest* (48.19.8) says that escapees from the *opus publicum* received a doubled sentence, a life sentence, or a transfer to the mines, which were much worse.

150. Note *social* status, not civic. Removal of suffrage does not apparently occur.

151. See economic reasons given by Brunt, "Labour," p. 93 and above. There is, however, evidence for skilled free (or freed) workmen in the rolls of the *collegia fabrum* in Rome. Varro (*Rust.* 1.17) says that free men, being more expendable than nonfree, should be used for dangerous work.

152. The *operarius* was a day-laborer, who could be hired on a day-to-day basis or for a set period of time but was paid a daily rate. The *operarius* had to be maintained during his stint, i.e., he had to be fed (*Digest* 38.1.50.1). An *operarius* could also be a freedman, who owed his patron a set number of *operae*, which the patron (or his heir) could lease to someone else. In this case, travel time for the freedman was included in the reckoning of *operae* (*Digest* 38.1.9.1). It is likely that the *annona* was always considered a low-income supplement rather than a mainstay. See Brunt, "Labour," p. 94.

153. Plutarch, *C. Gracch.* 6.3: πλῆθος ἐργολάβων, τεχνιτῶν. This motivation was attributed to leaders in classical Greece and appears in Plutarch's portrait of Pericles, where his building program is presented as a way for the poor to share in Athens' fortune through payment for construction labor. Plutarch, *Per.* 12.5.

154. Appian, *B. Civ.* 1.23.

155. Cicero, *Off.* 2.52–60.

156. Suetonius, *Vesp.* 18 and Dio Cassius 66.10.2.

157. An interesting situation developed in fourth-century Britain, however, where individual towns took over maintenance of Hadrian's Wall. Ling, "Mechanics," p. 14, attributes it to the poverty of the central government. It could, however, indicate a relatively low priority of Britain in the Imperial scheme.

158. Ling, "Mechanics," p. 14. See also *RIB* 1092.

159. Aurelius Victor, *Caes.* 14.5.

160. Vitruvius 1 praef. 2.

161. See translation in E. LaCoste, "Les poliorcetiques d'Apollodore de Damas," *REG*, 3 (1890): 230–281.

162. *Digest* 1.16.7.1.

163. R. Davies, *Service in the Roman Army* (Edinburgh: Edinburgh University Press, 1989), pp. 63–65. Evidence exists for military involvement in the extraction of lead, silver, gold, iron, bronze, coal, lime, tufa, trachyte (a volcanic rock with feldspar, mica or hornblende), and other assorted building stone in Britain and Germany.

164. Military as guards: *CIL* III.12067–12069, Josephus, *B.J.* 6.18; pseudo-Origen, *Phil.* 9.12; Eusebius, *De Mar. Pal.* 13.1.

165. Labor and expertise of the troops: *CIL* III.25, 75, 12286. The mine at Charterhouse-on-Mendip is serviced by an amphitheater.

166. *CIL* XIII.8036 for Colonia Ulpia Traiana. S. Frere, *Britannia* (Cambridge, Mass.: Harvard University Press, 1967), p. 204 discusses Verulamium. The army of Germania Inferior seems to have largely monopolized the area's resources, providing tufa, trachyte, and mortar in addition to tiles and bricks for

civil construction. H. von Petrikovits, *Das Römische Rheinland: Archäologische Forschungen seit 1945* (Cologne: Westdeutscher Verlag, 1960), p. 116.

167. MacMullen, "Roman Imperial Building," pp. 216–217.

168. *CIL* VIII.10117.

169. SHA, *Probus* 9: *quos otiosos esse numquam est passus.* Compare Suetonius, *Aug.* 18 and Dio Cassius 51.18.

170. Dio Cassius 56.18.2, 56.20.1–2. See also troops at Abila repairing roads: *CIL* III.199 201.

171. SHA, *Probus* 9 and *CIL* III.2883, 9864a, 9973: *agri et pascua et fontes.*

172. Josephus, *B.J.* 3.76–84.

173. Vegetius Rufus 1.21.

174. Frontinus, *Strat.* 4.7.2.

175. Davies, *Service*, pp. 125–139.

176. Vegetius Rufus 3.8 and *CIL* VIII.18042b. There is what appears to be an illustration of this on Trajan's Column (C. Cichorius, *Die Reliefs der Traianssäule* [Berlin: G. Reimer, 1896–1900], pl. 65).

177. Vegetius Rufus 1.25. Augustus liked making troops stand at attention in front of the *praesidium* holding a sod of turf; see Suetonius, *Aug.* 24.

178. See Tacitus, *Ann.* 13.35, where the rebellious troops add this practice to their list of grievances that catalyzed rebellion in A.D. 14.

179. G. Ville, *La Gladiature en Occident des origines à la mort de Domitien* (Rome: Ecole Française de Rome, 1981), pp. 294–295 and Golvin, *L'Amphithéâtre*, pp. 154–156.

180. Valerius Maximus 2.3.2.

181. See also recruitment in other crises: Caesar, *B.C.* 1.14 (Lentulus plans to outfit gladiators as cavalry); Velleius Paterculus 2.58.2 and Appian, *B. Civ.* 3.49 (assassins of Julius Caesar); Tacitus, *Hist.* 2.11, 23, 34–35, 43, 3.57, 76 (uproar of A.D. 69); Suetonius, *Aug.* 14 (at Perugia); Herodian 7.11 (Maximinus).

182. See Chapter 2 above.

183. *CIL* XIII.11045: *Tu. P. L[. . . petru]cor. A. Pomp. Dumnom. [. . . t]rib. mil. leg. [. . .]ae. praef. fabr. amphit[heatrum cum] ornament[is omnibus] D.S.P.D.A. Pomp. A. Pomp. Ter[tulli f. . . .]s perficien[dum curavit] idemq. dedicavit.*

184. *CIL* IX.3044: [S]ex. Pedio Sex. f. An. Lusium Hirruto prim. pil. leg. XXI pra[ef] Raetis Vindolicis valli[s P]oeninae et levis armatur. IIIIvir. i.d. praef. Germanic[i] Caesaris quinquennalici [i]uris ex s.c. quinquen. iterum. Hic amphitheatrum d.s.p. fecit. M. Dullius M.f. Gallus.

185. *CIL* III.14359.

186. *RIB* 339 Caerleon: *cohortis III c[enturia] Rufini Primi*; *RIB* 343 Caerleon: *coh[ortis] X c[enturia] Fl[avi] Iulin[i]*; *RIB* 344 Caerleon: *c[enturia] Cl[audi] Cup[iti]*; *RIB* 420 Tomen-y-Mur: *c[enturia] And[. . .] p[edes] XXXIX*; and *RIB* 423 Tomen-y-Mur: *c[enturia] Iul[i] Perpetui p[edes] XXI.*

187. See I. Richmond, "Trajan's Army on Trajan's Column," *PBSR*, 13 (1935): 1–40, especially pp. 30–31.

188. See J. Kolendo, "La répartition des places aux spectacles et la stratification sociale dans l'Empire romain, à propos des inscriptions sur les gradins des amphithéâtres et théâtres," *Ktema*, 6 (1981): 301-315.

189. Golvin, *L'Amphithéâtre*, pp. 75-148, 157-223, and 407. Hills count as earthworks in this analysis, as indeed they are, only of a naturally occurring variety.

190. This technique could also be used when the terrain was rocky rather than earthy. Digging an arena and *cavea* out of the bedrock is, however, more difficult and thus costlier, although the rubble thus acquired was a more effective building material.

191. The utility of the lake bed for foundations of the amphitheater is acknowledged by all, but there is some confusion as to the exact reason why this is such an ideal spot on which to build a huge building. Some say the weight of the lake compacted the subsoil, obviating the need for massive foundations and limiting the amount of "settling" under the Colosseum's weight. Others say the softness of the saturated earth would make it very easy to lay the foundations of the structure. One cannot, obviously, have it both ways, and the "compact subsoil" viewpoint seems most advantageous to me.

192. See discussion by J. A. Wright, in an appendix of R. E. M. Wheeler and T. V. Wheeler, "The Roman Amphitheatre at Caerleon, Monmouthshire," *Archaeologia*, 78 (1928): 111-218 and Golvin's discussion, *L'Amphithéâtre*, pp. 403-406. Golvin says this method derives from that used for Roman theaters, thus showing a further link between these monuments to Roman spectacle. Discussion of precise methodology of design, both the layout and the architectural elements, in M. W. Jones, "Designing Amphitheaters," *MDAI(R)*, 100 (1993): 391-442.

193. Martial, *Spect.* 2.

194. It is popularly believed that thousands of Judaean prisoners of war were used as menial laborers on the Flavian Amphitheater. This may be true, to some extent, but the sophistication of the construction techniques would require a large number of skilled workmen as well, who may not have been captured in Judaea.

195. Similar gross amounts of tufa, brick, and concrete were used, along with three hundred tons of iron clamps, removed during the Middle Ages.

196. Frank, *Survey*, vol. 5, p. 221 and Strabo 5.3.10-11.

197. The northwest quadrant in particular is not up to standard and has thus suffered more from modern traffic.

198. Frontinus, *De Aq.* 1.23, points out that concrete sets best between April and November.

199. The uppermost storey, built under Domitian, also used smaller blocks, which would have been both easier to lift to that height and would not put so much stress on the support. This storey also incorporates reused materials, presumably from the Domus Aurea.

200. G. Cozzo, *Ingegneria romana* (Rome: Libreria Editrice Mantegazza di P.

Cremonese, 1928), pp. 203–253. See also summaries in F. Sear, *Roman Architecture* (Ithaca: Cornell University Press, 1982), pp. 135–144; P. MacKendrick, *The Mute Stones Speak* (New York: W. W. Norton and Co., 1983), pp. 291–292; L. Richardson, *A New Topographical Dictionary of Ancient Rome* (Baltimore: Johns Hopkins University Press, 1992), pp. 6–11; and, especially, Golvin, *L'Amphithéâtre*, pp. 173–180. A dissenting voice is that of R. Rea, who believes that too much weight has been placed on the *Chronica Urbis Romae*, the source that attributes the upper level to Domitian. Indeed, Rea sees Titus as the "real" builder of the Flavian Amphitheater. R. Rea, "Le antiche raffigurazioni dell'Anfiteatro," in A. M. Reggiani, ed., *Anfiteatro Flavio: Immagine testimonianze spettacoli* (Rome: Edizioni Quasar, 1988), pp. 23–46, especially 28–35.

201. Support both in terms of scaffolding and for materials to be used in building.

202. The "infilling," or building of stairways and median vaults, could thus proceed during the winter as much as the weather allowed, given the reluctance of concrete to cure properly in cold, wet weather.

203. There were no arena substructures at the time of the dedication, therefore there was nothing present to be flooded out by the *naumachia* presented during the games. This does not, however, mean that the Colosseum housed the *naumachia*, at this or any other time. Dio Cassius (66.25) is the only source to locate them specifically in the Amphitheater, and it is more likely that Titus made use of the already-available Augustan *naumachia* accommodations near the Tiber instead of trying somehow to flood the new arena. There is no trace in the extant remains of any accommodation for naval battles in the Colosseum. Rea suggests that the reference is not to naval battles but to exhibitions in ships, thus falling into the realm of theatrical props and not requiring the presence of water. See Rea, "Antiche raffigurazioni," pp. 36–37.

204. It is possible that this depiction was not meant to be understood as a detailed, realistic representation but as an artistic shorthand. The coins of A.D. 80 show all four storeys of the façade, but coins were notorious for commemorating the completed project years before its actual completion date.

205. The date of construction of the interior colonnade is disputed. P. Colagrossi, *L'Anfiteatro Flavio nei suoi venti secoli di storia* (Firenze. Libreria Editrice Fiorentina, 1913), pp. 32–34 suggests that the different choice of order is key and that Titus finished the façade but not the interior colonnade, which was built under Domitian.

206. A slightly different sequence of construction is given by Richardson, *Dictionary*, who takes the *Chron.* more literally, and suggests that Vespasian was responsible for the first two arcades of the façade and the lower two levels of seating, that Titus added the next level of the exterior and the third and fourth levels of seating in time for the games of A.D. 80. Domitian, he believes, added the top storey of the façade with its decorative bronze shields. See *Chron.* 146.

207. Fronto, *Princ. Hist.* 17: *imperium non minus ludieris quam seriis probari . . . spectaculis universum populum conciliari.* This is contrasted to the grain dole, which only appeases individuals.

208. See discussion of reserved seating in Ville, *Gladiature*, pp. 430–440 and Golvin, *L'Amphithéâtre*, pp. 346–354. A useful assemblage of information was made available in F. W. Ritschl, *Die Tesserae Gladiatore der Romer* (Munich: Straub, 1864).

209. The motivation attested publicly for this set of restrictions is the "scandal" that arose when a senator was not offered a seat in Puteoli's crowded theater.

210. There are indications that, during the Republic, seats in theaters had been reserved for the different social orders. Special senatorial seating was mandated in 194 B.C. (Livy 34.44, 54.3–8), which may reflect customary procedure from even earlier. Equestrian seating in the first fourteen rows probably also dates to the second century but was abolished by Sulla and restored by the *lex Roscia* in 67 B.C. See E. Rawson, "*Discrimina Ordinum*: The *Lex Julia Theatralis*," *PBSR*, 55 (1987): 83–114.

211. Suetonius, *Aug.* 44. See discussion of relationship between façade, *maeniana*, and access passages in the Colosseum in R. Rea, "Recenti osservazioni sulla struttura dell'Anfiteatro Flavio," in Reggiani, *Anfiteatro*, pp. 9–22, especially 11–15.

212. Calpurnius Siculus (7.26–27) verifies that the women were indeed seated with the rabble, as *pulla sordida veste inter femineas spectabat turba cathedras.* The meaning of *pullati* here is not quite clear. It may refer to those wearing dark cloaks in mourning or it may be a reference to dark foreign cloaks, i.e., nontogas. For togas as symbolic of return to Roman tradition under Augustus, see P. Zanker, *The Power of Images in the Age of Augustus* (Ann Arbor: University of Michigan Press, 1988), pp. 162–165.

213. Pliny, *HN* 33.32.

214. See also *CIL* VI.32098, from the Colosseum: *qu]i(bus) in theatr(o) lege pl(ebis) ve[scito sedere l]icet p(edes) XII.* Rawson ("*Discrimina Ordinum*") notes that here theatrical law is applied to the amphitheater and that surely the reference to a law passed by the plebiscite cannot be post-Augustan. The inscription itself implies that the *lex Julia theatralis* was considerably detailed, if it went into allottments in terms of footage.

215. For reserved seating as a civic honor, see examples of Maenius and Servius Sulpicius Rufus noted in Chapter 1. How many could the Forum accommodate? Let us first assume, based on the incised seat dividers still visible in many amphitheaters, that each spectator took up a space approximately 0.4 meters wide on the bench. Assume further that the seating surrounded an arena 48 by 17.8 meters in size (thus accommodating the means of access to Caesar's substructures from the surface). Seated on the first row could be 328 people. Let us further assume, for ease of calculation, that ten rows were set up. In the city of Rome 3,280

seated people is a fairly small proportion of the population and definitely on the small side in relation to amphitheatrical capacity.

216. Cicero, *Mur.* 72: *Quod enim tempus fuit aut nostra aut patrum nostrorum memoria quo haec sive ambitio est sive liberalitas non fuerit ut locus et in circo et in foro daretur amicis et tribulibus? Haec homines tenuiores praemia commodaque a suis tribulibus vetere instituto adsequebantur.*

217. Cicero, *Mur.* 73 and *Ad Att.* 2.1.5.

218. Cicero, *Mur.* 67: *si gladiatoribus vulgo locus tributim [datus] . . . contra legem Calpurniam factum videri.* As will become clear, the literary usage of *locus* is not the equivalent of the more technical use found in the amphitheaters, i.e., *locus* as an individual seat, some 0.4 meters in width. The singular in the sources seems to refer to a block of seating, as it is frequently distributed to plural entities.

219. Th. Mommsen, *Die Römischen Tribus in Administrativer Beziehung* (Altona: J. F. Hammerich, 1844), p. 206.

220. Cicero, *Mur.* 73: *Senatus . . . crimen putat . . . locum ad spectandum dare . . . vulgo, passim.*

221. It being illegal to give *munera* during one's candidacy; see Chapter 1.

222. Cicero, *Mur.* 73: *omnia haec sunt officia necessariorum, commoda tenuiorum, munia candidatorum.*

223. Rawson ("*Discrimina Ordinum,*" p. 97) thinks that if certain tribes had no magistrates in office, then those tribes were simply left out of the ticket distribution. They could, of course, rely on their extratribal social connections.

224. Plutarch, *C. Gracch.* 12.3: θεωρητήρια κύκλῳ κατασκευάσαντες ἐξεμίσθουν. ταῦτα ὁ Γάϊος ἐκέλευεν αὐτοὺς καθαιρεῖν, ὅπως οἱ πένητες ἐκ τῶν τόπων ἐκείνων ἀμισθὶ θεάσασθαι δύνωνται.

225. As for who was responsible for the actual distribution in the Imperial period, the Arval Brethren inscriptions acknowledge the *praefectus annonae* (*CIL* VI.2059). Later activities point up the importance of the urban prefect. The *lex Ursonensis* seems to grant this duty at the municipal level to the presiding magistrate, whose decision was ratified by the *ordo.* See sections 125–127 of the *lex Ursonensis,* in Hardy, *Spanish Charters,* pp. 51–54.

226. *Lex Ursonensis,* section 126.

227. Rawson, ("*Discrimina Ordinum,*" p. 101) favors property class, while Golvin (*L'Amphithéâtre,* pp. 347–348) thinks it a municipal social function, based on his interpretation of an inscription from Lugdunum (*CIL* XIII.1921), which refers to *equites romani a plebe,* sort of leaders of the plebs rather than actual political functionaries.

228. Circumvention of these restrictions was punishable by a harsh fine of 50,000 sesterces; see sections 140–141 of the *lex Julia* on municipalities; *CIL* I.593; and E. G. Hardy, *Roman Laws and Charters* (Oxford: Oxford University Press, 1912), pp. 136–163.

229. Although we do have evidence that foreigners could find places to sit in the Flavian Amphitheater. *CIL* VI.32098 (l and m) reserved seats for people of

Gades. Justin (43.5.10) says that Massiliotes were entitled to sit with the Senate because they had helped Rome pay ransom to the Gauls in 390 B.C.

230. We have no indication that outside Rome women were segregated to the top section. Probably not, as some individual women had seats reserved by inscriptions (such as Gavia Quieta in Gaul, *CIL* XIII.1197). But then, women were liable to *munera*, albeit of a restricted type, outside Rome. In fact, women may have had relatively more local power outside Rome, as there were fewer aristocrats overall who could move beyond the local sphere of prestige, and thus women were not necessarily depriving men of their euergetical glory by getting involved in public affairs. It is outside Rome that we see building activity specifically by women as well, such as Ummidia Quadratilla, the Spanish *flamenica*, and Eumachia at Pompeii.

231. See list provided by J. Kolendo, "Deux amphithéâtres dans une seule ville: le cas d'Aquincum et de Carnuntum," *Archeologia* (Warsaw), 30 (1979): 39–55.

232. *CIL* XII.3316 (Nîmes) and *CIL* XII.714 (Arles). The *pastophori*, like the *scholasticii*, were more of a professional guild, as a group of priests of Isis. See Golvin, *L'Amphithéâtre*, pp. 348–349. Compare the situation of the College of the Arval Brethren in Rome, who had reserved seating guaranteed them by the *praefectus annonae* (*CIL* VI.2059).

233. *CIL* X.853.

234. *CIL* VI.1763; see also *CIL* VI.32172 and 32183. This was Rufius Caecina Felix Lampadius, urban prefect in A.D. 429. See J. R. Martindale, *The Prosopography of the Later Roman Empire* (Cambridge: Cambridge University Press, 1971–1980), vol. 2, p. 655. By the fifth century, gladiatorial combats were no longer held, but intense interest in the Colosseum remained, presumably because of the *venationes* held there until the sixth century, although evidence is quite scanty for this period. Reserved seating was very much the rage especially in Odoacer's reign (A.D. 476–483), with 195 names appearing on the seats. For late activity, see R. S. Bagnall, A. Cameron, S. R. Schwartz, and K. A. Worp, *Consuls of the Later Roman Empire* (Atlanta: Scholars Press, 1987), pp. 8–9 and A. Chastagnol, *Le Sénat romain sous le règne d'Odoacre* (Bonn: Habelt, 1966), p. 44.

235. Dio Cassius 59.13.8.

236. Suetonius, *Gaius* 26.6.

237. Martial, *Spect.* 5.24.9 calls the gladiator Hermes the "darling of the ticket scalpers" or *divitiae locariorum. Locarius* is otherwise unattested.

238. *CIL* VIII.6995.

239. As is implied in Petronius 45.13, where in return for gladiatorial games, an *editor* is given applause as an even exchange. Compare the "improper" motivation in Fidenae for *munera* editorship and amphitheater patronage, and the official efforts made to ensure that henceforth those in control of seats not be liable to such motivations.

240. Alexander Severus allegedly designated that taxes paid by prostitutes and procurers were to go toward restorations on spectacle buildings, specifically, the

Theater of Marcellus, the Circus Maximus, the Stadium of Domitian, and the Amphitheater. See SHA, *Alex. Sev.* 24.

5. THE MAGIC RING: HUMAN SACRIFICE IN THE ARENA

1. P. Veyne's comments on the subject are as an editor to G. Ville's manuscript of *La Gladiature en Occident des origines à la mort de Domitien* (Rome: Ecole française de Rome, 1981), p. 16.

2. The trend being that led by Ville, as elucidated by Veyne and followed by J.-Cl. Golvin, *L'Amphithéâtre romain* (Paris: E. de Boccard, 1988), pp. 15-17. C. Barton, "The Scandal of the Arena," *Representations*, 33 (1991): 1-36 and K. M. Coleman, "Fatal Charades: Roman Executions Staged as Mythological Enactments," *JRS*, 80 (1990): 44-73 do not directly address the issue but discuss gladiatorial combat as a secular event. P. Plass, *The Game of Death in Ancient Rome* (Madison: University of Wisconsin Press, 1995) rightly understands the ritual nature of the *munera*, although his approach differs from my own. The pervasiveness of this denial of human sacrifice is indicated by P. Tierney, *The Highest Altar: The Story of Human Sacrifice* (New York: Viking, 1989), pp. 10-23. Others seem content merely to allude to the possibility of gladiatorial combat's identification as sacrifice, as does D. Fishwick, *The Imperial Cult in the Latin West* (Leiden: E. J. Brill, 1987), vol. 2.1, pp. 574-575 but in terms of origin only and not as essential to the *munera*.

3. The use of ethnographic analogy has a long tradition in anthropology. Comparative history is becoming more widespread as well, as crafting general patterns for understanding human societies can be a helpful tool of analysis. This is not to say that all civilizations are "really" the same but rather that similar responses to similar stimuli can be found, with the details shaped by culture and context. Comparative analysis can also be a means of avoiding particularism and a method of problematizing field-driven paradigms. Further advantages discussed by T. Skocpol and M. Somers, "The Uses of Comparative History in Macrosocial Inquiry," *CSSH*, 22 (1980): 174-197.

4. Paraphrased from N. Davies, *Human Sacrifice in History and Today* (New York: Morrow, 1981), p. 15.

5. A. Green, *The Role of Human Sacrifice in the Ancient Near East* (Missoula, Mont.: Scholars Press, 1975), pp. 3-17.

6. R. Girard, *Violence and the Sacred* (Baltimore: Johns Hopkins University Press, 1977), p. 23. See also Davies, *Human Sacrifice*, pp. 26-27.

7. H. Maccaby, *The Sacred Executioner: Human Sacrifice and the Legacy of Guilt* (New York: Thames and Hudson, 1982), pp. 7-10.

8. Maccaby's primary interest is in human sacrifice as it pertains to Judaism and Christianity and how the institution figures in the relationship between the two cults. He points to the sacrifice of Isaac as a foundation sacrifice central to the Jewish concept of self-identity and to the relationship between Yahweh and his chosen people. The centrality of human immolation was picked up by the

Christians later and transferred to the death of Jesus Christ; his execution as a political criminal was transformed into a sacrifice on behalf of mankind (specifically the Christian segment) and acted as a new foundation for God's new chosen people, emblematic of the redefined relationship with the divinity. Maccaby suggests further that the notion of human sacrifice permeated Christian persecution of the Jews, as anti-Semitic propaganda alleged the ongoing ritual immolation of babies and virgins was a deliberate Jewish perversion of Christian symbols.

9. See G. W. Conrad and A. A. Demarest, *Religion and Empire: The Dynamics of Aztec and Inca Expansionism* (Cambridge: Cambridge University Press, 1984); J. M. Ingham, "Human Sacrifice at Tenochtitlan," *CSSH*, 26 (1984): 379–400; and Davies, *Human Sacrifice*, pp. 198–241.

10. For pre-Aztec human sacrifice at Teotihuacan, see R. Cabrera Castro, "Human Sacrifice at the Temple of the Feathered Serpent," and C. Serrano Sanchez, "Funerary Practices and Human Sacrifice in Teotihuacan Burials," in K. Berrin and E. Pasztory, eds., *Teotihuacan: Art from the City of the Gods* (New York: Thames and Hudson, 1993), pp. 100–107 and 108–115.

11. This tribute took the form of raw materials, manufactured goods, and food, the last of which became more and more important as the population of Tenochtitlan overburdened its environment. E. Calnek ("Settlement Pattern and Chinampa Agriculture at Tenochtitlan," *American Antiquity* 37, no. 1 [1972]: 104–115) estimates that the local horticulture of individual families in the capital city could provide only about 15% of the food needed by the urban population. The burden of supplying food was mainly met by the closer provinces, while more distant areas sent a higher proportion of luxury goods as tribute. See Ingham, "Human Sacrifice," p. 382 and J. Broda, "El tributo en trajes guerreros y la estructura del sistema tributario mexicana," in P. Carrasco and J. Broda, *Economía, política e ideología en el México prehispánico* (Mexico City: Centro de Investigaciones Superiores, 1978), pp. 175–194.

12. Scholars have attempted to measure Huitzilopochtli's growing hunger in terms of numbers of human victims. S. F. Cook, "Human Sacrifice and Warfare as Factors in the Demography of Pre-colonial Mexico," *Human Biology* 18 (1946): 81–102 estimated some fifteen thousand people were immolated annually by the Aztecs; most think this is conservative. The biggest festivals were held to celebrate imperial victories or for major events in the reign of the king. The dedication of the Great Temple at Tenochtitlan in 1487 lasted four days and consumed some ten thousand victims. See Conrad and Demarest, *Religion and Empire*, p. 47.

13. See Fray Bernardino de Sahagun, in C. E. Dibble and A. J. O. Anderson, eds., *Florentine Codex: General History of the Things of New Spain* (Salt Lake City: University of Utah Press, 1950–1969), vol. 6, pp. 114–115; H. de Alvarado Tezozomoc, *Crónica mexicana* (Mexico City: Secretaría de Educación Pública, 1944), pp. 22–23; and Conrad and Demarest, *Religion and Empire*, pp. 38–52. The last suggest that unsuccessful military campaigns heightened the Aztec motivation for conquest, on the understanding that Huitzilopochtli and his cronies were weak

and hungry and that cataclysmic doom was imminent if they did not receive sacrificial sustenance.

14. Conrad and Demarest, *Religion and Empire*, pp. 51–52. See also E. Calnek, "The Internal Structure of Tenochtitlan," in E. Wolf, ed., *The Valley of Mexico: Studies in Pre-Hispanic Ecology and Society* (Albuquerque: University of New Mexico Press, 1976), pp. 287–302.

15. As Ingham puts it, the "images of the gods reified superordination (and subordination)." See Ingham, "Human Sacrifice," p. 379.

16. It may be argued that the prevalence of human sacrifice in Mesoamerica would have dulled the impact of such demonstrations. Few societies in ancient America would have been able, however, to rival the spectacles of the Aztec, in numbers of victims, if nothing else.

17. Ingham, "Human Sacrifice," pp. 394–397 and Conrad and Demarest, *Religion and Empire*, pp. 53–60.

18. J. H. Rowe, "Inca Policies and Institutions relating to Cultural Unification," in G. A. Collier, R. Rosaldo, and J. D. Wirth, eds., *Inca and Aztec States 1400–1800: Anthropology and History* (New York: Academic Press, 1982), pp. 93–118. See also Tierney, *Highest Altar*, p. 29.

19. The dual aspect of the *capac hucha* as both victim and god, perfection and sin, has analogs elsewhere in the ideology of human sacrifice. See below.

20. The Centro de Investigaciones Andinas de Alta Montaña has thus far documented 120 sacrificial cult sanctuaries on mountain tops, 80 of which are located above 17,000 feet. See A. Beorchia, "El enigma de los santuarios indígenas de alta montaña," *Revista CIADAM*, 5 (1987).

21. For the literal incorporation of sacred mountains in *capac hucha* ritual, see R. T. Zuidema, "Bureaucracy and Systematic Knowledge in Andean Civilization," in Collier, Rosaldo, and Wirth, eds., *Inca and Aztec States*, pp. 419–458.

22. Tierney, *Highest Altar*, pp. 57–59 and R. T. Zuidema, "Shafttombs and the Inca Empire," *Journal of the Steward Anthropological Society*, 9 (1978): 133–178.

23. See Jeremiah 7:30–33, 32:35 and 2 Kings 17:16–17. The Tophet was dismantled in the seventh century, according to 2 Kings 23:10. The translation of "*mlk*" as a technical term for this type of sacrifice, and not as "Moloch," the name of an otherwise unattested Phoenician deity, is the focus of P. G. Mosca, "Child Sacrifice in Canaanite and Israelite Religion: A Study in Mulk and Molech" (Dissertation, Harvard University, 1975).

24. See S. Brown, *Late Carthaginian Child Sacrifice* (Sheffield, England: Sheffield Academic Press, 1991); L. E. Stager and S. R. Wolff, "Child Sacrifice at Carthage— Religious Rite or Population Control?" *BAR*, 10 (1984): 31–51; L. E. Stager, "Carthage: A View from the Tophet," in W. Huss, ed., *Karthago* (Darmstadt: Wissenschaftliche Buchgesellschaft, 1992), pp. 353–369; and E. Lipinski, "Sacrifice d'enfants à Carthage et dans le monde sémitique oriental," in E. Lipinski, ed., *Studia Phoenicia VI: Carthage* (Leuven: Uitgevery Peeters, 1988), pp. 151–185. The identification of these as sacrificial cemeteries is not universally accepted,

25. According to legend, Dido founded Carthage around 800 B.C. Servius (*Ad Aen.* 4.459) places it 40 years before Rome's foundation, while Velleius Paterculus (1.6) says it was 65 years prior to that event, and Justin (18.6) says it was 72 years. Other accounts locate it in relation to Troy's fall, such as Eusebius (*Chron.* no. 971), who puts it 133 years afterward. The earliest occupation of the city site can be dated archaeologically to the mid-eighth century; for a discussion of the issues surrounding the foundation date, see S. Lancel, *Carthage: A History* (Oxford: Blackwell, 1995), pp. 20–34.

26. See description in Diodorus Siculus 20.14, echoed by Cleitarchus in a scholia to Plato, *Resp.* 337A, F. Jacoby, *Die Fragmente der griechischen Historiker* (Leiden: E. J. Brill, 1962), vol. 2, pt. B: IIB p745 f9. These classical descriptions are not entirely unproblematic, as they stem from a tradition generally hostile to the Carthaginians. M. Weinfeld downplays their importance as evidence for genuine sacrificial customs, seeing them primarily as anti-Phoenician slander. See M. Weinfeld, "The Worship of Molech and of the Queen of Heaven and Its Background," *Ugarit-Forschungen*, 4 (1972): 133–154.

27. Military success was likely one of the favors to be gained from Tanit and Ba'al Hammon, as suggested by the Diodorus passage and by analogy with Isaiah 30:28–31:9, as well as by Tanit's very nature as goddess of love and war. Compare this to the military context of human immolation in the Roman world; see below.

28. Stager suggests that that these double or paired interments represent the same ritual as the single-victim examples. The scenario he reconstructs has the parents vowing their next child to the deity in exchange for specific divine favor. Should the child be stillborn, the parents would substitute their youngest living child for the less-desirable victim. Obviously, Stager emphasizes a sacrificial impetus different from my own. See Stager, "Carthage," pp. 363 and 369. The epigraphic and literary evidence concerning child sacrifice is recounted by Brown, *Late Carthaginian Child Sacrifice*, pp. 21–33. The archaeological evidence for the presence of Tophets, at Carthage and elsewhere in North Africa, Sicily, and Spain, is collected by Brown as well, pp. 37–76.

29. In addition to three hundred adults who were under suspicion and sacrificed themselves voluntarily: Diodorus Siculus 20.14, with independent verification from Lactantius, *Div. Inst.* 1.21.

30. Although it is not certain that such would in fact be visible in the archaeological record, given the prescribed ritual. The excavators looked for mass burial and mixing of bones and found none. There is, however, no reason to assume that in 308 B.C. all two hundred children were tossed into Ba'al Hammon's arms at once. Surely the usual practices would have been followed, with each family retaining the bones for individual burial, a point rightly raised by W. Röllig in the discussion following Stager's paper, "Carthage," p. 367.

31. Stager and Wolff, "Child Sacrifice," p. 40.

32. Jeremiah 7:31, 2 Chron. 28:3–4 and 2 Kings 21:6.

33. Stager admits puzzlement over the use of child sacrifice in contexts where doing so would have had a definitely negative impact on the community, particularly in the earliest days of the settlement of Carthage. He suggests that the option of animal substitution, or *mulk > immor*, would lessen the "suicidal" effects of child sacrifice on the vulnerable young city. See Stager, "Carthage," pp. 361–362.

34. They would not, apparently, be satisfied with victims of lower social status substituted for the children of the prominent, as is indicated by Diodorus Siculus. See also Brown, *Late Carthinigian Child Sacrifice*, pp. 23 and 172.

35. S. Ribichini interprets the sacrifices at Carthage and elsewhere as exceptional responses to crises, in S. Moscati, *The Phoenicians* (Milan: Bompiani, 1988), p. 120.

36. For the theoretical basis of funerary sacrifice, see D. Hughes, *Human Sacrifice in Ancient Greece* (London: Routledge, 1991), pp. 49–70 and W. Burkert, *Homo Necans: The Anthropology of Ancient Greek Sacrificial Ritual and Myth* (Berkeley: University of California Press, 1983), pp. 48–58.

37. Suggested by Davies, *Human Sacrifice*, p. 32.

38. See L. Woolley, *Excavations at Ur* (London: E. Benn, 1954), pp. 39–90 and Davies, *Human Sacrifice*, pp. 28–31. Royal wives may have been considered a part of this essential entourage and encouraged to commit suicide to accompany their husbands.

39. Some scholars, however, have found hints at the royal mortuary ritual in a fragmentary passage from the *Epic of Gilgamesh*, which describes, apparently, the burial of a royal male, complete with attendants, musicians, concubine, valet, wife, and son; persistence of the rite even after the rise to power of Sargon and the Akkadians is supported archaeologically. It may also be suggested in the "Exultation of Inanna" by Enheduana, the daughter of Sargon. See L. Woolley, with P. R. S. Moorey, ed., *Ur "of the Chaldees"* (London: Herbert Press, 1982), pp. 51–103, especially pp. 91–93 for possible literary references.

40. The Shang Dynasty was roughly 1523 to 1028 B.C. See Davies, *Human Sacrifice*, pp. 37–40.

41. This could have taken as long as three years, a time period customarily given over to mourning in China. See Li Chi, *Anyang* (Seattle: University of Washington Press, 1977), pp. 84–88.

42. K. C. Chang, *The Archaeology of Ancient China* (New Haven: Yale University Press, 1986), pp. 327–328. Description of this practice was known from inscriptions on oracle bones, even prior to the excavations at Anyang; there the practice was called *fa*. See H. G. Creel, *Studies in Early Chinese Culture* (Baltimore: Waverly Press, 1937), pp. 214–218.

43. See K. C. Chang, *Early Chinese Civilization: Anthropological Perspectives* (Cambridge, Mass.: Harvard University Press, 1976), p. 35 and Li Chi, *The Beginnings of Chinese Civilization* (Seattle: University of Washington Press, 1957), pp. 15–16. The reconciliation of this "barbarous custom" with such significant advances has proved a troublesome problem for many scholars of Bronze Age

China. See Creel, *Studies*, p. 204. Li Chi suggests that the practice is, quite literally, "barbarian," transmitted by the barbarous western Sumerians who may have influenced the development of bronze technology as well. See *Anyang*, p. 254.

44. S. N. Kramer, *The Sacred Marriage Rite* (Bloomington: Indiana University Press, 1969), p. 118. For continued use of human sacrifice in China, see H. G. Creel, *The Birth of China* (New York: Frederick Ungar Publishing Co., 1954), pp. 204–214.

45. The textual silence may be due to growing uncertainty as to the appropriateness of the custom, as indicated by Chinese philosophical writings that expressed concern over the social cost of Muh's funeral extravagance. See, for example, song 278 of Shih Ching, in A. Waley's translation, *The Book of Songs* (New York: Grove Press, 1960). Chang uses this song to argue for a continuous reluctance among the common people to participate in the ritual for the previous thousand years or so, surely a problematic assumption: see *Early Chinese Civilization*, pp. 52–53.

46. See Davies, *Human Sacrifice*, pp. 144–153.

47. The needs of the ancestors were given priority over the economic advantages from slave trade. See D. Ronen, *Dahomey: Between Tradition and Modernity* (Ithaca: Cornell University Press, 1975), pp. 21–22.

48. Literally, "the king's head thing" and "the yearly head thing" respectively. See W. J. Argyle, *The Fon of Dahomey: A History and Ethnography of the Old Kingdom* (Oxford: Clarendon Press, 1966), pp. 106–118.

49. The "Amazon retinue" was a corps of female guards who, at the death of the king, went on a destructive rampage, smashing all the personal possessions of the ruler before committing suicide themselves.

50. R. F. Burton, ed. by C. W. Newbury, *A Mission to Gelele, King of Dahome* (New York: Praeger, 1966), vol. 1, pp. 348–386 and vol. 2, pp. 1–62 and 253–269. See also accounts in F. E. Forbes, *Dahomey and the Dahomians* (London: Longman, Brown, Green and Longmans, 1851), vol. 2, pp. 20–174 and A. Le Herissé, *L'Ancien Royaume du Dahomey* (Paris: E. Larose, 1911), pp. 182–194.

51. There were also human sacrifices when the king went to war, built a new palace, or finalized a new treaty.

52. J. A. Skertchly claimed that Dahomeyans were convinced that the discontinuance of the Customs would erode the "glory of the kingdom" and that the dead kings would transfer their loyalty and support to the enemies of Dahomey. See *Dahomey as It Is* (London: Chapman and Hall, 1874), p. 181.

53. Described by Le Herissé, *L'Ancien Royaume*, p. 188. The gifts and sacrifices were made in a specific order: first rum, cloth, cowries, then animal victims, including fowl, sheep and goats, and bulls, then the human victims. The order is not unlike that in the triumphal sacrificial display; see below.

54. Homer, *Il*. 21.26–28: ὁ δ' ἐπεὶ κάμε χεῖρας ἐναίρων, ζωοὺς ἐκ ποταμοῖο δυώδεκα λέξατο κούρους, ποινὴν Πατρόκλοιο Μενοιτιάδαο θανόντος.

55. Homer, *Il.* 23.19–23: χαῖρέ μοι, ὦ Πάτροκλε, καὶ εἰν ᾽Αΐδαο δόμοισι. πάντα γὰρ ἤδη τοι τελέω τὰ πάροιθεν ὑπέστην . . . δώδεκα δὲ προπάροιθε πυρῆς ἀποδειροτομήσειν Τρώων ἀγλαὰ τέκνα, σέθεν κταμένοιο χολωθείς. See also *Il.* 18.336–337 and 23.179–183.

56. Homer, *Il.* 23.235–242.

57. Herodotus 1.167: Τῶν δὲ διαφθαρεισέων νεῶν τοὺς ἄνδρας οἵ τε Καρχηδόνιοι καὶ οἱ Τυρσηνοὶ διέλαχον, τῶν δὲ Τυρσηνῶν οἱ ᾽Αγυλλαῖοι ἔλαχον τε αὐτῶν πολλῷ πλείστους καὶ τούτους ἐξαγαγόντες κατέλευσαν. Their action led to various prodigies, for which the Delphian oracle suggested the institution of regular games and sacrifices. See J.-P. Thuillier, *Les Jeux athlétiques dans la civilisation étrusque* (Rome: École française de Rome, 1985), pp. 53–55.

58. Livy 7.15.

59. Livy 7.19: *pro immolatis in foro Tarquiniensium Romanis*.

60. See G. Camporeale, "Achle," in *LIMC*, vol. 1.1, pp. 200–214 and O. Touchefeu, "Aias," in *LIMC*, vol. 1.1, pp. 312–336. Using artistic motifs and relative prevalence of one scene or another for evidence of social institutions is problematic, for the main reason that we do not know who selected the motifs, whether the ceramic workshops of Greece proper or the Etruscan clientele who purchased the vases. Given, however, the presence of the scene on nonimports, notably the paintings in the François Tomb in Vulci, we can feel more confidence in a genuine Etruscan preference for scenes of Trojan sacrifice at the funeral of Patroclus.

61. Appian, *B. Civ.* 1.117: ὁ δὲ Σπάρτακος τριακοσίους ῾Ρωμαίων αἰχμαλώτους ἐναγίσας Κρίξῳ, δυώδεκα μυριάσι πεζῶν ἐς ῾Ρώμην ἠπείγετο, τὰ ἄχρηστα τῶν σκευῶν κατακαύσας καὶ τοὺς αἰχμαλώτους πάντας ἀνελὼν καὶ ἐπισφάξας τὰ ὑποζύγια, ἵνα κοῦφος εἴη.

62. Homer, *Od.* 11.146–149 refers to the general beneficial quality of blood, which enables the shades in Hades to have rational conversations with Odysseus. This is, of course, not human blood and has no hint of vengeance about its acquisition.

63. Ville, *Gladiature*, pp. 10–11.

64. Plutarch, *Brut.* 28.1.

65. The death of the great man therefore generates a version of the sacrificial crisis described by Girard and Maccaby.

66. See Patroclus as "target" in *Il.* 23.30: σέθεν, and 23.180: ἅμα σοί.

67. See Hughes, *Human Sacrifice*, pp. 49–56. See also A. Henrichs, "Human Sacrifice in Greek Religion: Three Case Studies," in J. Rudhardt and O. Reverdin, eds., *Le Sacrifice dans l'antiquité* (Geneva: Fondation Hardt, 1981), pp. 195–235, who notes a distinction drawn ritually between human and animal sacrifice in the way the victim is handled after death and in the targeting of the ritual.

68. W. Smith, ed., *Dictionary of Greek and Roman Antiquities* (London: J. Murray, 1880), vol. 2, pp. 582–583; J. Toutain, "Sacrificium-Rome," in Ch. Daremberg and E. Saglio, eds., *Dictionnaire des antiquités grecques et romaines* (Paris:

Hachette et Cie, 1877–1919), vol. 4, pt. 2, pp. 976–977 and R. Wünsch, "Roman Human Sacrifice," in J. Hastings, ed., *The Encyclopedia of Religion and Ethics* (New York: Charles Scribner's Sons, 1914), vol. 6, pp. 858–862.

69. A vague example of "commuted" human sacrifice is August's *Volcanalia*. According to Festus p. 238 M, live fish were offered to the god instead of human victims, and the small fish attained some notoriety from their role in the festival. Varro, however, says in *LL* 6.20 that the people drive their animals over a fire during the *Volcanalia*. There is no commuted human sacrifice, and no live fishes, small or otherwise, are at all involved in Varro's description of the festival.

70. Macrobius, *Sat.* 1.11.1 and 1.7.34.

71. *Oscilla* were also offered up, masks or figures meant to be hung in trees or at the door to *periculum expiare*, or avert danger, as part of the rites of expiation and purification performed during this festival. These *oscilla* have been interpreted as analogous in function to the *sigillaria*, for which see below.

72. Macrobius, *Sat.* 1.11.48.

73. Dionysius of Halicarnassus 1.38; Varro, *Ling.* 5.45, 7.44; Ovid, *Fast.* 5.621–660; Aulus Gellius, *N.A.* 10.15; Macrobius, *Sat.* 1.2.47; and Livy 1.21.

74. Livy 1.21: *multa alia sacrificia locaque sacris faciendis, quae Argeos pontifices vocant.*

75. Varro, *Ling.* 5.45 and 7.44.

76. *Argei fiunt e scirpeis simulacra hominum XXVII; ea quotannis de Ponte Sublicio a sacerdotibus publice deici solent in Tiberim.* The fact that Varro does not refer to these *simulacra* explicitly as one-time human sacrifices may be significant, as he refers in 5.50 and 5.52 to primary source material, the *In Sacris Argeorum scripta*, which surely would have provided him with solid evidence for such an assessment.

77. Ovid, *Fast.* 5.621–660.

78. Ibid. 5.650–660: *at comites longius ire negant. magnaque pars horum desertis venerat Argis . . . saepe tamen patriae dulci tanguntur amore, atque aliquis moriens hoc breve mandat opus: "mittite me in Tiberim, Tiberinis vectus ut undis litus ad Inachium pulvis inanis eam" displicet heredi mandati cura sepulcri: mortuus Ausonia conditur hospes humo, scirpea pro domino Tiberi iactatur imago, ut repetat Graias per freta longa domos.*

79. The connection between the term "Argei" and Greece is challenged by L. Clerici, who suggested that the festival was part of the ritual purification of the city following the invasion of the Gauls. Livy 5.50 tells of the formation of a priestly college to deal with this, whose members were *ex iis qui in Capitolio atque arce*. Over time, Clerici proposes that the "Arceii," or dwellers on the Arx, metamorphosed into "Argei," a highly speculative suggestion not supported by the literary evidence. See L. Clerici, "Die Argei," *Hermes*, 77 (1942): 89–100.

80. Thereby allowing the archaic Romans themselves to appear civilized and progressive.

81. Wünsch, "Roman Human Sacrifice," pp. 860–861.

82. W. Mannhardt, *Wald- und Feldkulte* (Berlin: Gebruder Borntraeger, 1875–1877), pp. 265–273.

83. J. G. Frazer, ed., *Fasti* (Cambridge, Mass.: Harvard University Press, 1931), pp. 425–429 and in *Publii Ovidii Nasonis: Fastorum Libri Sex* (London: MacMillan and Co. Ltd., 1929), vol. 4, part 7, pp. 9–110.

84. Plutarch, *Rom.* 86.

85. Frazer is followed more recently by D. P. Harmon, who points to the purificatory role of the Vestals in May and wants, in the Argei, to see the Roman evil dead punished by nonburial in a less risky way. Such demons, when consigned to the Tiber, get swept out to sea and are unable to wreak vengeance on the responsible Romans. See "The Public Festivals of Rome," *ANRW* II.16.2 (1978): 440–1468.

86. The bridge connection is also drawn by J. Hallett, "Over Troubled Waters: The meaning of the Title Pontifex," *TAPA*, 101 (1970): 219–227. Frazer's reconstruction does, however, do away with any explanation of the term Argei, as does Mannhardt's. See further R. E. A. Palmer, *The Archaic Community of the Romans* (Cambridge: Cambridge University Press, 1970), who denies any relationship with human sacrifice.

87. Spring being defined as the time between March 1 and the end of April, i.e., between the Kalends of March and those of May.

88. Varro, *Rust.* 3.16. See also Paulus in Festus p. 379 M. Dionysius of Halicarnassus (1.16) says that propitiation was one motive for a *Ver Sacrum*. Another was the need to give thanks for a victory or for unusual prosperity. Sources are collected and commented upon by W. Eisenhut, "Ver Sacrum," in *RE*, 15A, col. 917 and by J. Heurgon, *Trois études sur le "ver sacrum"* (Brussels: Latomus, 1957).

89. Festus p. 158 M and Pliny, *IIN* 3.110.

90. Livy 22.9–10.

91. *Ibid.: iniussu populi voveri non posse.* It is interesting that although the Sibylline Books blamed disaster on an offended Mars, the deities propitiated by the *Ver Sacrum* et al. were Jupiter, Venus, and Mens.

92. Minucius Felix 30.4; Tatian, *Ad Gr.* 129; and Tertullian, *Apol.* 9. Tatian and Tertullian specify that a *bestiarius* was the victim. Porphyry, *Abst.* 2.56 also alludes to the sacrifice as a contemporary occurrence, but he does not specify the social status of the victim.

93. W. Warde Fowler, *The Religious Experience of the Roman People* (London: MacMillan and Co. Ltd., 1911), p. 112 n. 31.

94. Davies, *Human Sacrifice*, p. 16.

95. Th. Mommsen, for one, proclaims the sacrificial origin of capital punishment: *Römisches Strafrecht* (Leipzig: Verlag von Duncker and Humblot, 1899), pp. 900–904.

96. Festus p. 318 M: *homo sacer is est quem populus iudicavit ob maleficium.* See also Servius, *Ad Aen.* 6.609 for the penal formula.

97. Pliny, *HN* 18.12.

98. See Plutarch, *Rom.* 22 and *Numa* 10. J. S. Reid, "Human Sacrifices at Rome and Other Notes on Roman Religion," *JRS*, 2 (1912): 34–52 says the bloodless nature of the Vestal punishment is due to their status as daughters of the state. There is generally an unwillingness to spill blood in the punishment of family crime, as we see with parricides, who were sewn into a sack and drowned. Reid stubbornly refuses to consider Roman cult practice as including human sacrifice.

99. Smith, *Antiquities*, vol. 2, pp. 894–899. Ville denies the connection: *Gladiature*, p. 17. See M. LeMosse, "Les éléments techniques de l'ancien triomphe romain et le problème de son origine," *ANRW* I.2 (1972): 442–453 and H. Wagenvoort, *Roman Dynamism: Studies in Ancient Roman Thought, Language and Custom* (Oxford: B. Blackwell, 1947). See also E. Kunzl, *Der römische Triumph* (Munich: Beck, 1988).

100. H. S. Versnel, *Triumphus* (Leiden: Brill, 1970), pp. 94–131 points to the common elements in festival, funeral, and triumphal processions.

101. See descriptions of triumphal processions in Dio Cassius 51.21; Plutarch, *Aem.* 33–34; Appian, *Pun.* 66; Livy 26.21.7, 34.52; Tacitus, *Ann.* 2.41; SHA, *Aurel.* 33; and Pliny, *HN* 5.5, to name a few.

102. Josephus, *B.J.* 7.5.

103. Cicero, *In Verr.* 5.30, Livy 26.13. Cicero (*In Verr.* 5.7) rants for some time about the inadvisability of being merciful to the enemy, who should properly be whipped, burned, crucified, etc., the last resort of a desperate country being the pardon of its prisoners of war. R. Heidenreich, "Tod und Triumph in der römischen Kunst," *Gymnasium*, 58 (1951): 326–340 recognized the sacrificial nature of the deaths of prisoners at the triumph, comparing them to the deaths of gladiators at public funerals.

104. Livy 7.6.3–4: *id enim illi loco dicandum vates canebant, si rem publicam Romanam perpetuam esse vellent. Tum M. Curtium, iuvenem bello egregium, castigasse ferunt dubitantes an ullum magis Romanum bonum quam arma virtusque esset, et silentio facto temple deorum immortalium quae foro imminent Capitoliumque intuentem et manus nunc in caelum nunc in patentes terrae hiatus ad deos manes porrigentem.*

105. Livy 8.9–10.

106. Livy 8.9.4: *deorum ope, M. Valeri, opus est; agedum, pontifex publicus populi Romani, praei verba quibus me pro legionibus devoveam.* The phrasing of Decius' request may suggest that the ritual was rare and arcane enough that Decius would not necessarily know how to proceed.

107. This was probably not the same hand both stretching out and touching the chin, as oaths were usually accompanied by holding out one hand, downward or upward depending on whether chthonic or celestial deities were involved in the oath.

108. The spear he stands on cannot fall into enemy hands. If it does, an expiatory sacrifice of a *suovetaurilia* must be made to Mars. Livy 10.14.

109. *Iane Iuppiter Mars pater Quirine Bellona Lares Divi Novensiles Di Indigetes Divi quorum est potestas nostrorum hostiumque Dique Manes . . . hostesque populi Romani Quiritium terrore formidine morteque adficiatis . . . legiones auxiliaque hostium mecum Deis Manibus Tellurique devoveo.*

110. The Gabian cincture, in which some of the toga is wadded into a sort of belt and some is pulled up to cover the head, is associated with usages significant for our purposes, notably with military sacrifices, with the Temple of Janus, the founding of cities, and Decian devotions. See also Livy 5.46 and Vergil, *Aen.* 5.755, 7.611.

111. Livy 8.10.7: *omnes minas periculaque ab deis superis inferisque in se unum vertit.*

112. Compare commuted human sacrifice discussed above.

113. Livy 8.10.14.

114. Livy 8.11.1: *Haec, etsi omnis divini humanique moris memoria abolevit nova peregrinaque omnia priscis ac patriis praeferendo, haud ab re duxi verbis quoque ipsis, ut tradita nuncupataque sunt, referre.*

115. Dio Cassius 53.20 and Valerius Maximus 2.6.11.

116. The Spanish attribution of this practice is interesting, given their apparent predilection for bloody games, noted by Scipio Africanus. Valerius Maximus (2.6.11) also connects it with "Spanish" practice, in that Celtiberian soldiers also practiced a sort of inverse *devotio*: they vowed to protect their leader or die trying. If he should die, so should they. The inhabitants of the Iberian peninsula will be discussed below.

117. Suetonius, *Gaius* 27 and Dio Cassius 59.8. See also Suetonius, *Nero* 36. For the death of Antinous, who may have offered his life for Hadrian so that the emperor could accomplish his goals, see Dio Cassius 69.11: ὅτι ἐθελοντὴς ἐθανατώθη ἑκουσίου γὰρ ψυχῆς πρὸς ἃ ἔπραττεν ἐδεῖτο ἐτίμησεν ὡς καὶ πόλιν ἐν τῷ χωρίῳ ἐν ᾧ τοῦτ' ἔπαθε καὶ συνοικίσαι καὶ ὀνομάσαι ἀπ' αὐτοῦ.

118. See S. P. Oakley, "Single Combat in the Roman Republic," *CQ*, 35 (1985): 392–410, who has a long list of examples from the literature.

119. Which only happened three times: with Romulus, Cossus, and Marcellus, although it was claimed by Crassus.

120. Oakley ("Single Combat," pp. 392–410) wants to link the practice to primitive warfare, in which the outcome of the war overall depended on the result of the duel. She suggests that this particular importance of the monomachy vanished early on in Rome, and it became primarily a means of demonstrating one's military prowess for competitive Roman politicos. She says that traces of its earlier critical role in warfare linger on in myths like that of the Horatii. A different interpretation of the Horatii story appears below.

121. Sallust, *Cat.* 22: *post exsecrationem omnes degustavissent, sicuti in sollemnibus sacris fieri consuevit . . . atque eo dictitare fecisse quo inter se fidi magis forent, alius alii tanti facinoris conscii.* The episode is alluded to in later accounts with more

elaboration. Minucius Felix (30.5) calls it a sacrifice, and Tertullian (*Apol.* 9) specifies the divinity as Bellona.

122. Cicero, *1 Cat.* 6, 9, *2 Cat.* 6.

123. See Reid, "Human Sacrifices," p. 41.

124. Dio Cassius 43.24: ἄλλοι δὲ δύο ἄνδρες ἐν τρόπῳ τινὶ ἱερουργίας ἐσφάγησαν. καὶ τὸ μὲν αἴτιον οὐκ ἔχω εἰπεῖν (οὔτε γὰρ ἡ Σίβυλλα ἔχρησεν οὔτ' ἄλλο τι τοιοῦτο λόγιον ἐγένετο) ἐν δ' οὖν τῷ Ἀρείῳ πεδίῳ πρός τε τῶν ποντιφίκων καὶ πρὸς τοῦ ἱερέως τοῦ Ἄρεως ἐτύθησαν καὶ αἵ γε κεφαλαὶ αὐτῶν πρὸς τὸ βασίλειον ἀνετέθησαν.

125. G. Wissowa, *Religion und Kultus der Römer* (Munich: Beck, 1912), for example, makes the comparison, p. 355 n. 3.

126. See above for the connection between execution and human sacrifice.

127. Dio Cassius 48.48: καὶ ὁ Σέξτος ἔτι καὶ μᾶλλον ἤρθη καὶ τοῦ τε Ποσειδῶνος υἱὸς ὄντως ἐπίστευεν εἶναι καὶ στολὴν κυανοειδῆ ἐνεδύσατο ἵππους τε καὶ ὥς γε τινές φασι. καὶ ἄνδρας ἐς τὸν πορθμὸν ζῶντας ἐνέβαλε.

128. Seneca, *De Clem.* 1.11.

129. Reid, "Human Sacrifices," pp. 42–45.

130. The sources include Dio Cassius 48.14; Appian, *B. Civ.* 5.48; Velleius Paterculus 2.74; and Suetonius, *Aug.* 15.

131. Velleius Paterculus 2.74: *magis ira militum quam voluntate saevitum ducis.*

132. Inscriptions from the bullets thus constitute material evidence for the essential truth of the story. See *Eph. Epigr.* 6.59, no. 64 and *CIL* XI.6721.

133. See sections above on funerary sacrifices and the *devotio.*

134. Vergil, *Aen.* 11.81–82: *vinxerat et post terga manus, quos mitteret umbris inferias, caeso sparsurus sanguine flammas.*

135. A. M. Eckstein ("Human Sacrifice and Fear of Military Disaster in Republican Rome," *AJAH*, 7 [1982]: 69–95) felt equal need to respond to this scholarly flutter. See also Reid, "Human Sacrifices," pp. 34–41; F. Schwenn, *Menschenopfer bei den Griechen und Römern* (Giessen: Verlag von Alfred Topelmann, 1915); Wissowa, *Religion*, pp. 60, 420–421, 542; C. Bemont, "Les Enterrés vivants du Forum Boarium," *MEFRA*, 72 (1960): 133–146; and C. Cichorius, "Staatliche Menschenopfer," *Römische Studien* (Leipzig: Teubner, 1922), pp. 7–21.

136. Zonaras 8.19: Λογίου δέ ποτε τοῖς Ῥωμαίοις ἐλθόντος καὶ Ἕλληνας καὶ Γαλάτας τὸ ἄστυ καταλήψεσθαι Γαλάται δύο καὶ Ἕλληνες ἕτεροι ἔκ τε τοῦ ἄρρενος καὶ τοῦ θήλεος γένους ζῶντες ἐν τῇ ἀγορᾷ κατωρύγησαν ἵν' οὕτως ἐπιτελὲς τὸ πεπρωμένον γενέσθαι δοκῇ καὶ τι κατέχειν τῆς πόλεως κατορωρυγμένοι νομίζωνται.

137. Plutarch, *Marc.* 3: ἐδήλου δὲ καὶ τὸν φόβον αὐτῶν ἥ τε παρασκευὴ . . . καὶ τὰ περὶ τὰς θυσίας καινοτομούμενα. βαρβαρικὸν μὲν γὰρ οὐδὲν οὐδ' ἔκφυλον ἐπιτηδεύοντες. ἀλλ' ὡς ἔνι μάλιστα ταῖς δόξαις Ἑλληνικῶς διακείμενοι καὶ πρᾴως πρὸς τὰ θεῖα. τότε τοῦ πολέμου συμπεσόντος ἠναγκάσθησαν εἶξαι λογίοις τισὶν ἐκ τῶν Σιβυλλείων. καὶ δύο μὲν Ἕλληνας. ἄνδρα καὶ γυναῖκα. δύο δὲ Γαλάτας ὁμοίως ἐν τῇ καλουμένῃ βοῶν ἀγορᾷ κατορύξαι ζῶντας. οἷς ἔτι

καὶ νῦν ἐν τῷ Νοεμβρίῳ μηνὶ δρῶσιν Ἕλλησι καὶ Γαλάταις ἀπορρήτους καὶ ἀθεάτους ἱερουργίας. For invasion fear and subsequent treaty making (the so-called Ebro Treaty), see Polybius 2.13 and 22.

138. Reid, "Human Sacrifices," p. 37 notes the contradictory attitude of Plutarch, who here decries the Romans' abandonment of Hellenic principles, but has no such comment to make about the sacrifice of Persian captives before the battle of Salamis, described in *Them.* 30 and *Aris.* 9.

139. Livy 22.57, probably using Fabius Pictor as his source, given the presence of the latter as ambassador to Delphi.

140. Livy 22.57: *et quaenam futura finis tantis cladibus foret. Interim ex fatalibus libris sacrificia aliquot extraordinaria facta; inter quae Gallus et Galla, Graecus et Graeca in foro bovario sub terram vivi demissi sunt in locum saxo consaeptum, iam ante hostiis humanis, minime Romano sacro, imbutum. Placatis satis, ut rebantur, deis.* The earlier instance Livy alludes to with *iam ante hostiis humanis* may be that which took place in 228 (Zonaras/Dio Cassius) or 226 (Plutarch).

141. Livy's reference to other extraordinary sacrifices made is tantalizing. After the Ver Sacrum of the previous year and now these human sacrifices, one wonders what extremes remain.

142. Tzetzes, *In Lyc. Alex.* 603: Ἑλληνικὸν καὶ Γαλατικὸν ἀνδρόγυνον . . . ἐν μέσῃ τῇ ἀγορᾷ.

143. Plutarch, *Quaest. Rom.* 83.

144. As in Orosius 5.15.20–21; Livy 63; and Obsequens 37.

145. C. Bemont, "Enterrés," pp. 143–146 and Reid, "Human Sacrifices," p. 39.

146. This was suggested by Cichorius, "Staatliche Menschenopfer."

147. Livy, *Epit.* 49. Such is Reid's contention. Other evidence for Spanish human sacrifice can be found in Strabo 3.3.6.

148. Perhaps, but not always against such a foe as Carthage, and surely not with such setbacks as Cannae.

149. Cichorius, "Staatliche Menschenopfer."

150. At least, not without undue strain. A Vestal trial is presented in Livy, *Epit.* 20, which is only approximately this time period, as it better fits with a date of 230 B.C. See Eckstein, "Human Sacrifice and Fear," pp. 75–81.

151. See Varro, *Rust.* 1.1.3 and Pliny, *HN* 11.105 among others, cited by Eckstein, "Human Sacrifice and Fear," p. 72.

152. Eckstein, "Human Sacrifice and Fear," *passim.* So why Greeks and Gauls? Reid ("Human Sacrifices," pp. 38–39) found these ethnicities incomprehensible, in terms of immediate presence as potential foes. Pliny, *HN* 28.12 offers an explanation of the immolation, which seems to have involved the sacrifice of members of the nation against whom Rome was at war, as *pars pro toto* sympathetic magic. If this was indeed the case, then Gauls may make some sense in 226 and 216, but Greeks? H. Diels (*Sibyllinische Blätter* [Berlin: Georg Reimer, 1890], p. 86) believes that the sacrifice of Greeks in 216 was due to the defection of Gelo, Hiero's

son, after the battle of Cannae. Reid thinks this unlikely, as Gelo died soon after the battle, before the death of his father, and Hiero was solidly pro-Roman. Wissowa (*Religion*, pp. 420–421) suggests that Greek sacrifice had become programmatic, which Reid calls "a somewhat arbitrary assumption." The presence of Greeks may have had something to do with the defection of Capua and the South Italian cities to the Carthaginian cause. It is curious, however, that all examples say Greeks and Gauls, and Pliny's specifications in accordance with current international affairs are not seen in the extant sources. Eckstein ("Human Sacrifice and Fear," p. 81) follows G. De Sanctis, *Storia dei Romani* (Florence: Nuova Italia, 1953), vol. 4.2.1, pp. 319–320 in suggesting that Greeks and Gauls may have had symbolic value as archetypal "enemies of Rome." Gauls had actually invaded the city in the distant past, just as Greeks had invaded Troy, the legendary origin of the Roman people, in an even more distant past. Another possibility was offered by Schwenn, *Menschenopfer*, which depended on the Sibylline Books being reflective of Etruscan religious traditions, the Celts and the Greeks being historical threats to Etruria.

153. Pliny, *HN* 28.12: *boario vero in foro Graecum Graecamque defossos aut aliarum gentium cum quibus tum res esset etiam nostra aetas vidit. cuius sacri precationem qua solet praeire XVvirum collegii magister.*

154. Specifically, the reference to the ban on human sacrifice decreed by the Senate in 97 B.C., as cited in Book 30. See discussion below.

155. The author of the *Historia Augusta*, admittedly a problematic source, quotes Aurelian's letter to the Senate (SHA, *Aurel.* 20): *agite igitur et castimonia pontificum cartimoniisque sollemnibus iuvate principem necessitate publica laborantem. inspiciantur Libri; si quae facienda fuerint celebrentur; quemlibet sumptum, cuiuslibet gentis captos, quaelibet animalia regia non abnuo sed libens offero, neque enim indecorum est dis iuvantibus vincere. sic apud maiores nostros multa finita sunt bella, sic coepta.*

156. There is no direct reference to the ethnicity of the victims and the desirability of a match with that of the foe, although it is implied with the phrase *cuiuslibet gentis*. The combination of men, animals, and spoils as wartime sacrifices is also seen in the triumph; see above.

157. Compare the pre-Salamis situation hinted at above, Plutarch, *Them.* 30 and *Aris.* 9.

158. The absence of Roman human sacrifice at Rome is also supported by Wissowa, *Religion*, pp. 420–421.

159. Livy 22.57: *minime Romano sacro.*

160. Cicero, *Font.* 31: *Postremo his quicquam sanctum ac religiosum videri potest qui, etiam si quando aliquo metu adducti deos placandos esse arbitrantur, humanis hostiis eorum aras ac templa funestant, ut ne religionem quidem colere possint, nisi eam ipsam prius scelere violarint? Quis enim ignorat eos usque ad hanc diem retinere illam immanem ac barbaram consuetudinem hominum immolandorum? Quam ob rem quali fide, quali pietate existimatis esse eos qui etiam deos immortalis arbitrentur hominum scelere et sanguine facillime posse placari? Cum his vos testibus vestram religionem coniungetis,*

ab his quicquam sancte aut moderate dictum putabitis? Note that Cicero blasts those who offer human victims to the immortal gods, not to the honored dead. This may be coincidental, but given Plutarch's *Quaest. Rom.* above, it may not.

161. Wünsch, "Roman Human Sacrifice," p. 861.

162. Pliny, *HN* 30.12: *DCLVII demum anno urbis Cn. Cornelio Lentulo P. Licinio Crasso cos senatusconsultum factum est ne homo immolaretur, palamque in tempus illud sacra prodigiosa celebrata . . . nec satis aestimari potest quantum Romanis debeatur, qui sustulere monstra, in quibus hominem occidere religiosissimum erat, mandi vero etiam saluberrimum.*

163. Reid, "Human Sacrifices," p. 35.

164. Wünsch, "Roman Human Sacrifice," p. 862.

165. Toutain, "Sacrificium," pp. 976–977.

166. Ville, *Gladiature*, p. 17.

167. Tertullian, *De Spect.* 12.2–3: *Nam olim, quoniam animas defunctorum humano sanguine propitiari creditum erat, captivos vel mali status servos mercati in exsequiis immolabant. Postea placuit impietatem voluptate adumbrare. Itaque quos paraverant, armis quibus tunc et qualiter poterant eruditos, tantum ut occidi discerent, mox edicto die inferiarum apud tumulos erogabant.*

168. Servius, *Ad Aen.* 10.519: *mos erat in sepulcris virorum fortium captivos necari; quod postquam crudele visum est, placuit gladiatores ante sepulcra dimicare.* See also 3.67, where Varro appears as the possible source for Servius' information, if not for Tertullian's as well. Ville wants to break the link between Varro and Servius/Tertullian by claiming that the Varro attribution refers to the custom of tearing cheeks as bloodletting for the dead, while sacrifice at the tombs is merely popular legend tidied up here by Servius. The break at the *quare* (in 3.67), which Ville postulates, is not so clear to me.

169. See above on the discussion of Pliny's comment on the ban on human sacrifice.

170. L. Malten, "Leichenspiel und Totenkult," *MDAI(R)*, 38 (1923): 300–340.

171. Maccaby, *Executioner*, p. 101.

172. Ibid., p. 11.

173. The connection between foundation sacrifice and the death of Remus is acknowledged by T. P. Wiseman, *Remus: A Roman Myth* (Cambridge: Cambridge University Press, 1995), pp. 117–125. Wiseman, however, sees political meaning in the myth particular to the plebeians' acquisition of political authority in the Early Republic.

174. Maccaby, *Executioner*, p. 12.

175. It may not be coincidental that the threat came from the Carthaginians, whose use of human sacrifice was well known in antiquity; see above.

176. See Oakley, "Single Combat," especially pp. 408–410.

177. See above. This receives some support by Barton, "Scandal," as well, although she differs in her understanding of the gladiatorial attitude, which I find more akin to that of the *samurai* committing *seppuku*. His glory is not the slavish

delight of catering to the audience's whims. It is through achievement *despite* the bloodlust of the audience that the gladiator "wins."

CONCLUSION

1. Indeed, in just this way had Augustus reshaped the material imagery of Rome as a whole, to create a transcendant vision of a renewed, idealized Rome. For Augustan rhetoric in art and architecture, see P. Zanker, *The Power of Images in the Age of Augustus* (Ann Arbor: University of Michigan Press, 1988).

2. For ritual as the exercise of power, see, among others, P. Bourdieu, *Outline of a Theory of Practice* (Cambridge: Cambridge University Press, 1977); C. Geertz, *Negara: The Theatre State in Nineteenth Century Bali* (Princeton: Princeton University Press, 1980); and C. Bell, *Ritual Theory, Ritual Practice* (New York: Oxford University Press, 1992).

APPENDIX I. AMPHITHEATERS AND CENTRAL PLACE THEORY

1. W. Christaller, *Die zentralen Orte in Süddeutschland* (Jena: Gustav Fischer, 1933). See also T. Bekker-Nielsen, *The Geography of Power* (Oxford: British Archaeological Reports, 1989), pp. 4–13, for general discussion relevant to the approach taken here.

2. See Bekker-Nielsen, *Geography*, p. 32, for man-hours consumed in specific distances.

3. See G. W. Skinner, "Marketing and Social Structure in Rural China," *Journal of Asiatic Studies*, 24 (1964–1965): 3–42, 195–228, 363–399 and K. Flannery, ed., *The Early Mesoamerican Village* (New York: Academic Press, 1976).

4. N. J. G. Pounds, "The Urbanization of the Classical World," *Annals of the Association of American Geographers*, 59 (1969): 135–157.

5. Aristotle, *Pol.* 1.1.9.

6. Xenophon, *Cyr.* 8.2.5.

7. Pausanias 10.4.1 (Loeb translation).

8. Bekker-Nielsen, *Geography*.

9. Bekker-Nielsen, *Geography*, table 2.1. The *Notitia Dignitatum* is a fourth-century document concerning the administrative make-up of the empire as it was in late antiquity, listing the officials by location with a brief description of the duties involved. The manuscript of the western half of the empire survives. The Peutinger Table is a map of the Roman world, also dating to the fourth century, intended for use by the traveler, as it concentrates on useful information rather than realistic representation of topography. Likewise, the Antonine Itinerary, a late third-century text, concentrates on travel distances between locations.

10. Ibid., appendices II and III.

11. Which amphitheaters? My basic list came from the *Princeton Encyclopedia of Classical Sites*, but this has been added to and subtracted from during the course of my reading. Especially useful during this study has been J.-Cl. Golvin, *L'Amphithéâtre romain* (Paris: E. de Boccard, 1988).

APPENDIX 2. PLINY IN BITHYNIA: CONSTRUCTION IN THE PROVINCES DURING THE HIGH EMPIRE

1. The date is argued. The only reference to an absolute date is the mention of Calpurnius Macer (10.42, 61) as governor of Moesia Inferior, an office he held A.D. 111–112. Other indirect evidence, such as the incompleteness of Trajan's building program in Rome (*Ep.* 10.18), offers less precise chronology. See A. N. Sherwin-White, *The Letters of Pliny: A Historical and Social Commentary* (Oxford: Oxford University Press, 1966), pp. 80–81.

2. Sherwin-White discusses the particular problems of the area and Pliny's mission there, in the introduction to his commentary on Book 10, *Letters*, pp. 525–555.

3. Dio Chrysostom would later (52.30.3) assert that cities should be discouraged from building, lest they exhaust their financial resources.

4. Pliny, *Ep.* 10.81–82.

5. Because of the possible contamination of Imperial Cult implements by the graves of Dio's wife and son. Alternatively, Eumolpus may be alleging the crime of intramural burial. The lack of clarity may have itself been a ploy by Eumolpus to allow Pliny the choice of a range of perceived criminal activity.

6. Dio Chrysostom had had problems all along; see, for example, *Or.* 38.

7. See, e.g., Pliny, *Ep.* 10.23, 10.37, 10.41, 10.70, 10.90.

8. Dio, at least, did so. *Or.* 40, 45, 47. This would of course have been necessary for an amphitheater anyway, see Chapter 4.

9. Pliny, *Ep.* 10.40. Enforcement of promises for public works, from the individual or from his heirs after his death, is dealt with in *Digest* 50.12.14.

10. Pliny, *Ep.* 10.23, 10.39, 10.90.

11. Pliny, *Ep.* 10.23. Sherwin-White (*Letters*, p. 594) agrees with Hardy's identification of this oil as edible olive oil supplied to the poor as part of the *annona*. See E. G. Hardy, *Pliny's Correspondence with Trajan* (London: MacMillan, 1889).

12. Pliny, *Ep.* 10.17.

13. The *exigentibus* at Claudiopolis may also be a reference to fines for embezzlement, i.e., *publica pecunia . . . male collocetur*. For *summa*, see also Pliny, *Ep.* 10.112–113 and Sherwin-White, *Letters*, pp. 722–727.

14. Pliny, *Ep.* 10.24. Apparently olive oil for the poor is not considered essential.

15. Introduced in *Ep.* 10.41.

16. Sherwin-White, *Letters*, pp. 622–623. See section 98 of the *lex Ursonensis* (Coloniae Genetivae Juliae) and Chapter 4 on corvée.

17. Pliny, *Ep.* 10.37 and 10.39.

18. Compare the sums, for example, to that spent in the Troad by Herodes Atticus (Philostratus, *V.S.* 2.1): seven million drachmas, or approximately twenty-eight million sesterces.

19. Pliny's appeals are as follows: 10.23: *quod alioqui et **dignitas** civitatis et **saeculi tui** nitor postulat*; 10.37: *et **utilitatem operis et pulchritudinem saeculo tuo***

esse dignissimam; 10.41: *intuenti mihi et fortunae tuae et animi magnitudinem* **convenientissimum** *videtur demonstrari opera non minus* **aeternitate tua** *quam gloria* **digna, quantumque pulchritudinis tantum utilitatis** *habitura*; 10.70: *quod* **indulsisti** *fieri . . . cuius beneficio elegans opus* **dignum**que *nomine tuo fiet*; 10.90: *si tu, domine, hoc genus operis et* **salubritati et amoenitati** *valde sitientis coloniae* **indulseris**. Emphasis added.

20. *Ep.* 10.37.

21. *Ep.* 10.39. This wall is a multilayered source of controversy. The text as it stands attributes this twenty-two-foot wall to a gymnasium, which has caused later scholars no end of confusion. What element of a gymnasium, or even of a Roman bath if one wants to push the text that far, would need such a substantial wall? This is either more evidence of Bithynian illiteracy in Roman technology or a problem with the text. It may be that the wall belongs with the theater, where it is still an example of anxious overbuilding, albeit a less extreme one. See Sherwin-White, *Letters*, pp. 618–619.

22. *Ep.* 10.18: *in omni provincia inveniuntur*; see also 10.40.

23. *Ep.* 10.42 and 10.61. As these were nonmilitarized zones, military technicians had to come all the way from Moesia Inferior, which was apparently the closest legionary headquarters.

24. *Ep.* 10.38–39.

25. *Ep.* 10.24, 10.91.

26. *Ep.* 10.40.

27. *Ep.* 10.42, 10.91.

BIBLIOGRAPHY

Albertini, E., *Les Divisions administratives de l'Espagne romaine* (Paris: E. de Boccard, 1923).

Alföldi, A. *Early Rome and the Latins* (Ann Arbor: University of Michigan Press, 1971).

Altheim, F., "Taurii, Ludi," in *RE*, 4A:2, cols. 2542–2544.

Appadurai, A., *The Social Life of Things: Commodities in Cultural Perspective* (Cambridge: Cambridge University Press, 1986).

Argyle, W. J., *The Fon of Dahomey: A History and Ethnography of the Old Kingdom* (Oxford: Clarendon Press, 1966).

Arnold, B., "Rank and Status in Early Iron Age Europe," in B. Arnold and D. B. Gibson, eds., *Celtic Chiefdom, Celtic State* (Cambridge: Cambridge University Press, 1995), pp. 43–52.

Astin, A., "The Role of Censors in Roman Economic Life," *Latomus*, 49 (1990): 20–36.

Audin, A., "L'Omphalos de Lugdunum," in M. Renard, ed., *Hommages à Albert Grenier* (Brussels: Collection Latomus, 1962), vol. 1, pp. 152–164.

Audin, A., and M. Le Glay, "L'Amphithéâtre des Trois-Gaules à Lyon," *Gallia*, 28 (1970): 67–89.

———, "L'Amphithéâtre des Trois-Gaules à Lyon," *Gallia*, 37 (1979): 85–98.

Auguet, R., *Cruauté et civilisation* (Paris: Flammarion, 1970).

Badian, E., *Publicans and Sinners* (Oxford: Oxford University Press, 1972).

Bagnall, R. S., A. Cameron, S. R. Schwartz, and K. A. Worp, *Consuls of the Later Roman Empire* (Atlanta: Scholars Press, 1987).

Baldi, A., "Perseus e Phersu," *Aevum*, 35 (1961): 131–133.

Balsdon, J. P. V. D., *Life and Leisure in Ancient Rome* (New York: McGraw-Hill, 1969).

Barrow, R. H., *Slavery in the Roman Empire* (New York: Dial Press, 1928).

Barruol, G., "La Résistance des substrats préromaine en Gaule méridionale," in D. M. Pippidi, ed., *Assimilation et résistance* (Paris: Les Belles Lettres, 1976), pp. 389–405.

Barton, C., "The Scandal of the Arena," *Representations*, 33 (1991): 1–36.

———, *The Sorrows of the Ancient Romans: The Gladiator and the Monster* (Princeton: Princeton University Press, 1993).

Baudot, M., "Le Problème des ruines de Vieil-Evreux," *Gallia*, 2 (1943): 191–206.

Becatti, G., and F. Magi, *Monumenti della pittura antica scoperti in Italia, fasc. III.4: Pitture delle tombe degli Auguri e del Pulcinella* (Rome: Istituto Poligrafico dello Stato, 1955).

Bekker-Nielsen, T., *The Geography of Power* (Oxford: British Archaeological Reports, 1989).

Bell, C., *Ritual Theory, Ritual Practice* (New York: Oxford University Press, 1992).

Beloch, J., *Campanien: Geschichte und Topographie des antiken Neapel und seinen Umgebung* (Breslau: Morgenstern, 1890).

Bemont, C., "Les Enterrés vivants du Forum Boarium," *MEFRA* 72 (1960): 133–146.

Beorchia, A., "El enigma de los santuarios indígenas de alta montaña," *Revista CIADAM*, 5 (1987).

Beschaouch, M. A., "La Mosaïque de chasse à l'amphithéâtre découverte à Smirat en Tunisie," *Comptes rendus de l'Académie des Inscriptions et Belles-Lettres* (Paris: Librarie C. Klincksieck, 1966), pp. 134–158.

Bieber, M., *History of the Greek and Roman Theater* (Princeton: Princeton University Press, 1961).

Binchy, D. A., ed., *Corpus Iuris Hibernici* (Dublin: Dublin Institute for Advanced Study, 1978).

Bishop, M. C., "On Parade: Status, Display and Morale in the Roman Army," in H. Vetters and M. Kandler, eds., *Akten des 14. Internationalen Limeskongresses 1986 in Carnuntum* (Vienna: Österreichische Akademie der Wissenschaften, 1990), pp. 21–30.

Blagg, T. F. C., "Architectural Patronage in the Western Provinces of the Roman Empire," in A. King and M. Henig, eds., *The Roman West in the Third Century* (Oxford: British Archaeological Reports, 1981), pp. 167–188.

Blázquez, J.-M., *Economía de la Hispania Romana* (Bilbao: Ediciones Najera, 1978).

Blázquez, J.-M., et al., *Historia de España antigua* (Madrid: Ediciones Cátedra, 1978).

Blázquez, J.-M., and S. Montero, "Ritual funerario y status social: los combates gladiatorios prerromanos en la Peninsula Ibérica," *Veleia*, 10 (1993): 71–84.

Bloemers, J. H. F., "Relations between Romans and Natives: Concepts of Comparative Studies," in V. A. Maxfield and M. J. Dobson, eds., *Roman Frontier Studies 1989: Proceedings of the XVth International Congress of Roman Frontier Studies* (Exeter: University of Exeter Press, 1991), pp. 451–454.

Bober, P. F., "Cernunnos: Origin and Transformation of a Celtic Divinity," *AJA*, 55 (1951): 13–51.

Bonfante, L., *Out of Etruria* (Oxford: BAR International Series, 1981).

————, "Roman Triumphs and Etruscan Kings: The Changing Face of the Triumph," *JRS*, 60 (1970): 49–66.

Bourdieu, P., *Outline of a Theory of Practice* (Cambridge: Cambridge University Press, 1977).

Bradley, K. R., *Slaves and Masters in the Roman Empire: A Study in Social Control* (New York: Oxford University Press, 1987).

Brisson, A., and J.-J. Hatt, "Les Nécropoles hallstattiennes d'Aulnay-aux-Planches," *Revue Archéologique de l'Est*, 4 (1953): 193–233.

Broda, J., "El tributo en trajes guerreros y la estructura del sistema tributario mexicana," in P. Carrasco and J. Broda, *Economía, política e ideología en el México prehispánico* (Mexico City: Centro de Investigaciones Superiores, 1978), pp. 175–194.

Broughton, T. R. S., *The Magistrates of the Roman Republic* (Cleveland: Press of Case Western University, 1968).

Brown, F. E., *Cosa: The Making of a Roman Town* (Ann Arbor: University of Michigan Press, 1980).

Brown, S., "Death as Decoration: Scenes from the Arena on Roman Domestic Mosaics," in A. Richlin, ed., *Pornography and Representation in Greece and Rome* (New York: Oxford University Press, 1992), pp. 180–211.

————, *Late Carthaginian Child Sacrifice* (Sheffield, England: Sheffield Academic Press, 1991).

Brunaux, J.-L., *The Celtic Gauls: Gods, Rites and Sanctuaries* (London: Seaby, 1988).

Brunt, P. A., "Free Labour and Public Works," *JRS*, 70 (1980): 81–100.

————, "Laus Imperii," in P. D. A. Garnsey and C. R. Whittaker, eds., *Imperialism in the Ancient World* (Cambridge: Cambridge University Press, 1978), pp. 159–191.

————, "The Revolt of Vindex and the Fall of Nero," *Latomus*, 18 (1959): 531–559.

Bucheler, P., "Die staatliche Anerkennung der Gladiatorenspiels," *RhMus*, 38 (1883): 476–479.

Burkert, W., *Homo Necans: The Anthropology of Ancient Greek Sacrificial Ritual and Myth* (Berkeley: University of California Press, 1983).

Burnett, A., M. Amandry, and P. P. Ripollès, *Roman Provincial Coinage* (London: British Museum Press, 1992).

Burnham, B. C., and J. Wacher, *The "Small Towns" of Roman Britain* (London: B. T. Batsford, Ltd., 1990).

Burton, G. P., "The Curator Rei Publicae: Towards a Reappraisal," *Chiron*, 9 (1979): 465–487.

Burton, R. F., ed. by C. W. Newbury, *A Mission to Gelele, King of Dahome* (New York: Praeger, 1966).

Bussemaker, A.-C., and E. Saglio, "Circus," in Ch. Daremberg, E. Saglio, and E. Pottier, eds., *Dictionnaire des antiquités grecques et romains* (Paris: Hachette et Cie, 1877–1919), vol. 1, pt. 2, pp. 1187–1201.

Cabrera Castro, R., "Human Sacrifice at the Temple of the Feathered Serpent," in K. Berrin and E. Pasztory, eds., *Teotihuacan: Art from the City of the Gods* (New York: Thames and Hudson, 1993), pp. 100–107.

Calnek, E., "The Internal Structure of Tenochtitlan," in E. Wolf, ed., *The Valley of Mexico: Studies in Pre-Hispanic Ecology and Society* (Albuquerque: University of New Mexico Press, 1976), pp. 287–302.

———, "Settlement Pattern and Chinampa Agriculture at Tenochtitlan," *American Antiquity*, 37 (1972): 104–115.

Camporeale, G., "Achle," in *LIMC*, vol. 1.1, pp. 200–214.

Canac, F., *Acoustique des théâtres antiques* (Paris: Editions du Centre National de la Recherche Scientifique, 1967).

Canto, A. M., "Les Plaques votives avec plantae pedum d'Italica," *ZPE*, 54 (1984): 183–194.

Carettoni, C. F., "Le gallerie ipogee del foro e i ludi gladiatori forensi," *BCAR*, 76 (1956–1958): 23–44.

Carney, J., *Studies in Irish Literature and History* (Dublin: Dublin Institute for Advanced Studies, 1955).

Castagnoli, F., *Orthogonal Town Planning in Antiquity* (Cambridge, Mass.: Harvard University Press, 1972).

Castrén, P., *Ordo Populusque Pompeianus* (Rome: Bardi Editore, 1975).

Chadwick, N., *The Druids* (Cardiff: Wales University Press, 1966).

Chang, K. C., *The Archaeology of Ancient China* (New Haven, Conn.: Yale University Press, 1986).

———, *Early Chinese Civilization: Anthropological Perspectives* (Cambridge, Mass.: Harvard University Press, 1976).

Chapman, M., *The Celts: The Construction of a Myth* (New York: St. Martin's Press, 1992).

Chastagnol, A., *Le Sénat romain sous le règne d'Odoacre* (Bonn: Habelt, 1966).

Christopherson, A. J., "The Provincial Assembly of the Three Gauls in the Julio-Claudian Period," *Historia*, 17 (1968): 351–366.

Cichorius, C., *Die Reliefs der Traianssäule* (Berlin: G. Reimer, 1896–1900).

———, "Staatliche Menschenopfer," *Römische Studien* (Leipzig: Teubner, 1922), pp. 7–21.

Clavel-Lévêque, M., *Puzzle gaulois: Les Gaules en mémoire* (Paris: Les Belles Lettres, 1989).

Clavel-Lévêque, M., and P. Lévêque, *Villes et structures urbaines dans l'Occident romain* (Paris: Les Belles Lettres, 1984).

Clerici, L., "Die Argei," *Hermes*, 77 (1942): 89–100.

Coarelli, F., *Il foro romano* (Rome: Quasar, 1983–1985).

———, *Guida archeologica di Roma* (Milano: A. Mondadori, 1974).

———, "Lucus Feroniae," *Studi Classici e Orientali*, 25 (1975): 164–166.

Colagrossi, P., *L'anfiteatro flavio nei suoi venti secoli di storia* (Firenze: Libreria Editrice Fiorentina, 1913).

Coleman, K. M., "Fatal Charades: Roman Executions Staged as Mythological Enactments," *JRS*, 80 (1990): 44–73.

Collis, J., *The European Iron Age* (London: B. T. Batsford Ltd., 1984).

Conrad, G. W., and A. A. Demarest, *Religion and Empire: The Dynamics of Aztec and Inca Expansionism* (Cambridge: Cambridge University Press, 1984).

Cook, S. F., "Human Sacrifice and Warfare as Factors in the Demography of Pre-colonial Mexico," *Human Biology*, 18 (1946): 81–102.

Cornell, T. J., *The Beginnings of Rome* (London: Routledge, 1995).

Coulon, G., *Les Gallo-Romains: Au carrefour de deux civilisations* (Paris: A. Colin, 1985).

Couraud, R., "L'Amphithéâtre de Limoges, premiers sondages octobre 1966," *Bulletin de la Société Archéologique et Historique du Limousin*, 94 (1967): 49–63.

Cozzo, G., *Ingegneria Romana* (Rome: Libreria Editrice Mantegazza di P. Cremonese, 1928).

Creel, H. G., *The Birth of China* (New York: Frederick Ungar Publishing Co., 1954).

———, *Studies in Early Chinese Culture* (Baltimore: Waverly Press, 1937).

Cunliffe, B. W., *Excavations at Fishbourne 1961–1969* (London: Society of Antiquaries, 1971).

———, *Greeks, Romans and Barbarians: Spheres of Interaction* (New York: Methuen, 1988).

———, *Iron Age Communities in Britain* (London: Routledge, 1978).

Daly, L. J., "Verginius at Vesontio: The Incongruity of the Bellum Neronis," *Historia*, 24 (1975): 75–100.

Dauge, Y. A., *Le Barbare: Recherches sur la conception romaine de la barbarie et de la civilisation* (Brussels: Collection Latomus, 1981).

Davies, N., *Human Sacrifice in History and Today* (New York: Morrow, 1981).

Davies, R., *Service in the Roman Army* (Edinburgh: Edinburgh University Press, 1989).

De Sanctis, G., *Storia dei Romani* (Florence: Nuova Italia, 1953).

de Alarcão, J., and R. Etienne, *Fouilles de Conimbriga* (Paris: E. de Boccard, 1977).

de Alvarado Tezozomoc, H., *Crónica mexicana* (Mexico City: Secretaría de Educación Pública, 1944).

de Sahagun, Fray Bernardino, in C. E. Dibble and A. J. O. Anderson, eds., *Florentine Codex: General History of the Things of New Spain* (Salt Lake City: University of Utah Press, 1950–1969).

Degrassi, A., *I fasti consolari dell'Impero romano* (Rome: Edizioni di Storia e Letteratura, 1952).

Deininger, J., *Die Provinziallandtage der römischen Kaiserzeit von Augustus bis zum Ende des dritten Jahrhunderts n. Chr.* (Munich: Beck, 1965).

DeRuyt, F., *Charun: Démon étrusque de la mort* (Rome: Institut historique belge, 1934).

Diego Santos, F., "Die Integration Nord- und Nordwestspaniens als römische Provinz in der Reichspolitik des Augustus," *ANRW* II.3 (1975): 523–571.

Diels, H., *Sibyllinische Blätter* (Berlin: Georg Reimer, 1890).

Dietler, M., "Driven by Drink: The Role of Drinking in the Political Economy and the Case of Early Iron Age France," *Journal of Anthropological Archaeology*, 9 (1990): 352–406.

———, "Early 'Celtic' Socio-Political Relations: Ideological Representation and Social Competition in Dynamic Comparative Perspective," in B. Arnold and D. B. Gibson, eds., *Celtic Chiefdom, Celtic State* (Cambridge: Cambridge University Press, 1995), pp. 64–71.

Dietrich, B. C., *Death, Fate and the Gods* (London: Athlone Press, 1965).

Dillon, M., and N. K. Chadwick, *The Celtic Realms* (London: Weidenfeld and Nicolson, 1967).

Doreau, J., J.-Cl. Golvin, and L. Maurin, *L'Amphithéâtre gallo-romain de Saintes* (Paris: Centre National de la Recherche Scientifique, 1982).

Douglas, M., *Purity and Danger* (London: Routledge and Kegan Paul, 1966).

Drummond, S. K., and L. H. Nelson, *The Western Frontiers of Imperial Rome* (Armonk, New York: M. E. Sharpe, 1994).

Dumont, J. C., *Servus: Rome et l'esclavage sous la République* (Rome: École française, 1987).

Dunbabin, K. M. D., "Ipsa deae vestigia . . . Footprints Divine and Human on Graeco-Roman Monuments," *JRA*, 3 (1990): 85–109.

———, *The Mosaics of Roman North Africa: Studies in Iconography and Patronage* (Oxford: Clarendon Press, 1978).

Duncan-Jones, R. P., *The Economy of the Roman Empire: Quantitative Studies* (Cambridge: Cambridge University Press, 1982).

———, "The Procurator as Civic Benefactor," *JRS*, 64 (1974): 79–85.

———, *Structure and Scale in the Roman Economy* (Cambridge: Cambridge University Press, 1990).

Dunning, E., "Social Bonding and Violence in Sport: A Theoretical-Empirical Analysis," in J. H. Goldstein, ed., *Sports Violence* (New York: Springer-Verlag, 1993), pp. 129–146.

Duval, P.-M., *Les Dieux de la Gaule* (Paris: Presses universitaires de France, 1957).

Dyson, S. L., "Native Revolt Patterns in the Roman Empire," *ANRW* II.3 (1975): 138–175.

———, "Native Revolts in the Roman Empire," *Historia*, 20 (1971): 239–274.

Ebel, C., *Transalpine Gaul: The Emergence of a Roman Province* (Leiden: E. J. Brill, 1976).

Eckstein, A. M., "Human Sacrifice and Fear of Military Disaster in Republican Rome," *AJAH*, 7 (1982): 69–95.

Edwards, C., *The Politics of Immorality in Ancient Rome* (Cambridge: Cambridge University Press, 1993).

Eisenhut, W., "Ver sacrum," in *RE*, 15A, col. 917.

Elia, O., "Caivano: Necropoli pre-romana," *NSA* (1931): 577–614.

Ernout, A., and A. Meillet, *Dictionnaire étymologique de la langue latine* (Paris: C. Klincksieck, 1959).

Etienne, R., *Le Culte impérial dans la péninsule ibérique d'Auguste à Dioclétien* (Paris: Boccard, 1958).

———, "La Naissance de l'amphithéâtre, le mot et la chose," *REL*, 43 (1966): 213–220.

Farnell, L. R., *The Cults of the Greek States* (Oxford: Oxford University Press, 1896).

Fears, J. R., "The Cult of Virtues and Roman Imperial Ideology," *ANRW* II.17.2 (1981): 827–948.

———, "The Theology of Victory at Rome: Approaches and Problems," *ANRW* II.17.1 (1981): 736–826.

Février, P.-A., "L'Habitat dans la Gaule méridionale," *CLPA*, 24 (1975): 7–25.

Filip, J., *Celtic Civilization and Its Heritage* (Wellingborough, England: Collet's, 1977).

Finley, M. I., *Ancient Slavery and Modern Ideology* (London: Chatto and Windus, 1980).

Fishwick, D., *The Imperial Cult in the Latin West* (Leiden: E. J. Brill, 1987–1992).

Fitz, J., "The Excavations in Gorsium," *A Arch Hung*, 24 (1972): 1–52.

Forbes, F. E., *Dahomey and the Dahomians* (London: Longman, Brown, Green and Longmans, 1851).

Forni, G., "L'indàgine demogràfica e gli anfiteatri in Dacia," *Apulum*, 13 (1975): 111–134.

Foucault, M., *Discipline and Punish* (New York: Pantheon Books, 1977).

Foucher, L., "Némésis, le griffon et les jeux d'amphithéâtre," *Mélanges d'histoire ancienne offerts à William Seston* (Paris: E. de Boccard, 1974), pp. 187–195.

Frank, T., *Economic Survey of Ancient Rome* (Baltimore: Johns Hopkins University Press, 1933–1940).

Frazer, J. G., ed., *Fasti* (Cambridge, Mass.: Harvard University Press, 1931).

———, *Publii Ovidii Nasonis: Fastorum Libri Sex* (London: MacMillan and Co. Ltd., 1929).

Frederiksen, M., *Campania* (Oxford: Oxford University Press, 1984).

Frere, S., *Britannia* (Cambridge, Mass.: Harvard University Press, 1967).

Frézouls, E., "Aspects de l'histoire du théâtre romain," *ANRW*, II.12.1 (1983): 353–354.

Friedländer, L., *Roman Life and Manners* (London: G. Routledge and Sons, 1908).

Fromm, E., *The Heart of Man* (New York: Harper and Row, 1964).

Fulford, M., *The Silchester Amphitheatre* (London: Society for the Promotion of Roman Studies, 1989).

Gabrici, E., "Cuma," *Monumenti antichi*, 22 (1913): 9–871.

Gagé, L., "La Théologie de la Victoire impériale," *Revue Historique*, 171 (1933): 1–43.

Gantz, J., *Early Irish Myths and Sagas* (New York: Penguin, 1981).

———, *The Mabinogion* (Harmondsworth: Penguin, 1976).

García y Bellido, A., *Colonia Aelia Augusta Italica* (Madrid: Instituto español de arqueología, 1960).

———, *Les Religions orientales dans l'Espagne romaine* (Leiden: E. J. Brill, 1967).

Garnsey, P., "Non-Slave Labour in the Roman World," in P. Garnsey, ed., *Non-Slave Labour in the Greco-Roman World* (Cambridge: Cambridge Philological Society, 1980), pp. 34–47.

Gatti, G., "I Saepta Iulia nel Campo Marzio," *L'Urbe*, 2.9 (1937): 8–23.

Gayraud, M., *Narbonne antique des origines à la fin de IIIe siècle* (Paris: E. de Boccard, 1981).

Geertz, C., *Negara: The Theatre State in Nineteenth Century Bali* (Princeton: Princeton University Press, 1980).

Girard, R., *Violence and the Sacred* (Baltimore: Johns Hopkins University Press, 1977).

Giuliani, C. F., and P. Verduchi, *L'area centrale del foro romano* (Florence: L. S. Olschki, 1987).

Golvin, J.-Cl., *L'Amphithéâtre romain* (Paris: E. de Boccard, 1988).

Golvin, J.-Cl., and C. Landes, *Amphithéâtres et gladiateurs* (Paris: Editions du CNRS, 1990).

Gould, T., "The Uses of Violence in Drama," in J. Redmond, ed., *Violence in Drama* (Cambridge: Cambridge University Press, 1991).

Grant, M., *Gladiators* (New York: Delacorte Press, 1967).

Green, A., *The Role of Human Sacrifice in the Ancient Near East* (Missoula, Mont.: Scholars Press, 1975).

Green, M., *Symbol and Image in Celtic Religious Art* (London: Routledge, 1989).

Grenier, A., "Hercule et les théâtres gallo-romains," *REA*, 42 (1940): 636–644.

———, *Manuel d'archéologie gallo-romaine* (Paris: Editions A. et J. Picard, 1931–1960).

Grimal, P., *Roman Cities* (Madison: University of Wisconsin Press, 1983).

Gruen, E. S., *Culture and National Identity in Republican Rome* (Ithaca: Cornell University Press, 1992).

Guey, J., and A. Audin, "La Dédicace de l'amphithéâtre des Trois Gaules," *Bulletin des Monuments et Musées Lyonnaises*, 2 (1958): 59–67.

Hall, E., *Inventing the Barbarian* (Oxford: Oxford University Press, 1989).

Hallett, J., "Over Troubled Waters: The Meaning of the Title Pontifex," *TAPA*, 101 (1970): 219–227.

Hanson, W. S., *Agricola and the Conquest of the North* (London: B. T. Batsford Ltd., 1987).

Hardy, E. G., *Roman Laws and Charters* (Oxford: Oxford University Press, 1912).

———, *Three Spanish Charters* (Oxford: Oxford University Press, 1912).

Harmand, L., *Le Patronat sur les collectivités publiques des origines au bas empire* (Paris: Presses Universitaires de France, 1957).

Harmon, D. P., "The Public Festivals of Rome," *ANRW* II.16.2 (1978): 440–1468.

Harris, W. V., *War and Imperialism in Republican Rome, 327–70 B.C.* (Oxford: Clarendon Press, 1985).

Hartog, F., *The Mirror of Herodotus: The Representation of the Other in the Writing of History* (Berkeley: University of California Press, 1988).

Hatt, J.-J., *Celts and Gallo-Romans* (London: Barrie and Jenkins, 1970).

————, "La Vision de Constantin au sanctuaire de Grand et l'origine celtique du labarum," *Latomus*, 9 (1950): 427–436.

Haywood, R., "Roman Africa," in T. Frank, *Economic Survey of Ancient Rome* (Baltimore: Johns Hopkins University Press, 1938), vol. 4, pp. 1–119.

Heidenreich, R., "Tod und Triumph in der römischen Kunst," *Gymnasium*, 58 (1951): 326–340.

Henderson, B. W., *The Life and Principate of the Emperor Hadrian* (London: Methuen and Co., 1923).

Henrichs, A., "Human Sacrifice in Greek Religion: Three Case Studies," in J. Rudhardt and O. Reverdin, eds., *Le sacrifice dans l'antiquité* (Geneva: Fondation Hardt, 1981), pp. 195–235.

Henzen, J., *Explicatio Musivi in villa Burghesiana asservati* (Rome, 1845).

Herter, H., "Nemesis," *RE* 16:2, cols. 2338–2380.

Heurgon, J., *Trois études sur le "ver sacrum"* (Brussels: Latomus, 1957).

Hönle, A. and A. Henze, *Römische Amphitheater und Stadien* (Zurich: Edition Antike Welt, 1981).

Hopkins, K., *Conquerors and Slaves* (Cambridge: Cambridge University Press, 1978).

————, *Death and Renewal* (Cambridge: Cambridge University Press, 1983).

Hornum, M. B., *Nemesis, the Roman State, and the Games* (Leiden: E. J. Brill, 1993).

Hughes, D., *Human Sacrifice in Ancient Greece* (London: Routledge, 1991).

Humphrey, J., *Roman Circuses* (Berkeley: University of California Press, 1986).

Ingham, J. M., "Human Sacrifice at Tenochtitlan," *CSSH*, 26 (1984): 379–400.

Inglis, H. D., *Ireland in 1834* (London: Whittaker, 1835).

Jackson, K. H., *A Celtic Miscellany: Translations from the Celtic Literatures* (Harmondsworth: Penguin, 1971).

————, *The Oldest Irish Tradition: A Window on the Iron Age* (Cambridge: Cambridge University Press, 1964).

James, S., *The World of the Celts* (London: Thames and Hudson, 1993).

Jennison, G., *Animals for Show and Pleasure in Ancient Rome* (Manchester: Manchester University Press, 1937).

Johannowsky, W., "La situazione in Campania," in P. Zanker, ed., *Hellenismus in Mittelitalien* (Göttingen: Vandenhoeck and Ruprecht, 1976), vol. 1, pp. 267–299.

Jones, M. W., "Designing Amphitheaters," *MDAI(R)*, 100 (1993): 391–442.

Jouffroy, H., *La Construction publique en Italie et dans l'Afrique romaine* (Strasbourg: AECR, 1986).

Kaplan, D., "The Law of Cultural Dominance," in M. Sahlins and E. Service, eds., *Evolution and Culture* (Ann Arbor: University of Michigan Press, 1960).

Keay, S. J., *Roman Spain* (Berkeley: University of California Press, 1988).

Kelly, F., *A Guide to Early Irish Law* (Dublin: Institute for Advanced Study, 1988).

Kertzer, D. I., *Ritual, Politics and Power* (New Haven: Yale University Press, 1988).

————, "The Role of Ritual in Political Change," in M. J. Aronoff, ed., *Culture and Political Change* (New Brunswick: Transaction Books, 1983), pp. 53–73.

King, A., *Roman Gaul and Germany* (Berkeley: University of California Press, 1990).

Kolendo, J., "Deux amphithéâtres dans une seule ville: Le cas d'Aquincum et de Carnuntum," *Archeologia* (Warsaw), 30 (1979): 39–55.

————, "La Répartition des places aux spectacles et la stratification sociale dans l'empire romain, à propos des inscriptions sur les gradins des amphithéâtres et théâtres," *Ktema*, 6 (1981): 301–315.

Kraay, C. M., "The Coinage of Vindex and Galba," *NC*, 9 (1949): 129–149.

Kramer, S. N., *The Sacred Marriage Rite* (Bloomington: Indiana University Press, 1969).

Krasheninnikoff, M., "Über die Einführung des provinzialen Kaisercultus im römischen Westen," *Philologus*, 53 (1894): 147–189.

Kunzl, E., *Der römische Triumph* (Munich: Beck, 1988).

La Baume, P., "Römische Köln," *BJ*, 172 (1972): 271–292.

Lacey, W. K., "Patria Potestas," in B. Rawson, ed., *The Family in Ancient Rome* (Ithaca, New York: Cornell University Press, 1986), pp. 121–144.

Lachaux, J.-Cl., *Théâtres et amphithéâtres d'Afrique proconsulaire* (Aix-en-Provence: Edisud, 1979).

LaCoste, E., "Les Poliorcetiques d'Apollodore de Damas," *REG*, 3 (1890): 230–281.

Lambrechts, P., *Contributions a l'étude des divinités celtiques* (Bruges: "De Tempel," 1942).

Lamprecht, H.-O., *Opus Caementitium: Bautechnik der Römer* (Düsseldorf: Beton-Verlag, 1984).

Lancel, S., *Carthage: A History* (Oxford: Blackwell, 1995).

Larsen, J. A. O., *Representative Government in Greek and Roman History* (Berkeley: University of California Press, 1955).

Last, H., "Rome and the Druids: A Note," *JRS*, 39 (1949): 1–5.

Lattimore, O., *Inner Asian Frontiers of China* (New York: American Geographical Society, 1940).

Le Herissé, A., *L'Ancien Royaume du Dahomey* (Paris: E. Larose, 1911).

LeMosse, M., "Les Éléments techniques de l'ancien triomphe romain et le problème de son origine," *ANRW* I.2 (1972): 442–453.

Lepper, F., and S. Frere, *Trajan's Column* (Gloucester, Alan Sutton: 1988).

Levick, B., "L. Verginius Rufus and the Four Emperors," *RhMus*, 128 (1985): 318–346.

Lévi-Strauss, C., "The Structural Study of Myth," in T. Sebeok, ed., *Myth: A Symposium* (Bloomington: Indiana University Press, 1955), pp. 81–106.

Li Chi, *Anyang* (Seattle: University of Washington Press, 1977).

————, *The Beginnings of Chinese Civilization* (Seattle: University of Washington Press, 1957).

Ling, R., "The Mechanics of the Building Trade," in F. Grew and B. Hobley, eds., *Roman Urban Topography in Britain and the Western Empire* (London: Council for British Archaeology, 1985), pp. 14–27.

Lintott, A., *Imperium Romanum: Politics and Administration* (London: Routledge, 1993).

————, *Violence in Republican Rome* (Oxford: Clarendon Press, 1968).

Lipinski, E., "Sacrifice d'enfants à Carthage et dans le monde sémitique oriental," in E. Lipinski, ed., *Studia Phoenicia VI: Carthage* (Leuven: Uitgevery Peeters, 1988), pp. 151–185.

Lorenz, K., *On Aggression* (New York: Bantam Books, 1966).

Maccaby, H., *The Sacred Executioner: Human Sacrifice and the Legacy of Guilt* (New York: Thames and Hudson, 1982).

MacCana, P., *Celtic Mythology* (London: Hamlyn, 1970).

McCone, K., *Pagan Past and Christian Present in Early Irish Literature* (Kildare: An Sagart, 1990).

MacDonald, W. L., *The Architecture of the Roman Empire I* (New Haven: Yale University Press, 1965).

————, *The Architecture of the Roman Empire II* (New Haven: Yale University Press, 1986).

MacKendrick, P., *The Mute Stones Speak* (New York: W. W. Norton and Co., 1983).

Mackie, N., *Local Administration in Roman Spain A.D. 14–212* (Oxford: British Archaeological Reports, 1983).

MacMullen, R., "Notes on Romanization," reprinted in R. MacMullen, ed., *Changes in the Roman Empire: Essays in the Ordinary* (Princeton: Princeton University Press, 1990), pp. 56–66.

————, "Roman Imperial Building in the Provinces," *HSCP*, 64 (1959): 207–235.

————, *Roman Social Relations* (New Haven: Yale University Press, 1974).

————, "Women in Public in the Roman Empire," *Historia*, 29 (1980): 208–218.

MacNeill, M., *The Festival of Lughnasa* (Oxford: Oxford University Press, 1962).

Maiuri, A., "Saggi nell'area del foro di Pompei," *NSA*, 3 (1941): 371–404.

Malitz, J., *Die Historien des Poseidonios* (Munich: Beck, 1983).

Mallory, J. P., "The World of Cú Chulainn: The Archaeology of the Táin Bó Cúailnge," in J. P. Mallory, ed., *Aspects of the Táin* (Belfast: December Publications, 1992), pp. 103–159.

Malten, L., "Leichenspiel und Totenkult," *MDAI(R)*, 38 (1923–1924): 300–341.

Mannhardt, W., *Mythologische Forschungen aus dem Nachlasse* (Strassburg: K. J. Trubner, 1884).

————, *Wald- und Feldkulte* (Berlin: Gebruder Borntraeger, 1875–1877).

Martindale, J. R., *The Prosopography of the Later Roman Empire* (Cambridge: Cambridge University Press, 1971–1980).

Marvin, G., "Honour, Integrity and the Problem of Violence in the Spanish Bullfight," in D. Riches, ed., *The Anthropology of Violence* (Oxford: Basil Blackwell Ltd., 1986), pp. 118–135.

Mattingly, H., *Coins of the Roman Empire in the British Museum* (London: Trustees of the British Museum, 1923–1962).

Mattingly, H., and E. Sydenham, *The Roman Imperial Coinage* (London: Spink and Son, 1923–1981).

Matz, F., review of Hanfmann's *Altetruskische Plastik, Gnomon*, 16 (1940): 197–205.

Maurin, L., *Saintes antique* (Saintes: Société d'archéologie et d'histoire de la Charente-Maritime, 1978).

Maurin, L., N. Laurenceau, and G. Vienne, *Recherches archéologiques à Saintes en 1978* (Saintes: Société d'archéologie et d'histoire de la Charente-Maritime, 1979).

Maurin, L., and M. Thauré, "Inscriptions révisées ou nouvelles du musée archéologique de Saintes," *Gallia*, 38 (1980): 197–213.

May, R., *Power and Innocence* (New York: Norton, 1972).

Meier, P., "De Gladiatura Romana: Quaestiones Selectae" (Dissertation, Universität Bonn, 1881).

Mierse, W., "Augustan Building Programs in the Western Provinces," in K. A. Raaflaub and M. Toher, eds., *Between Republic and Empire: Interpretations of Augustus and His Principate* (Berkeley: University of California Press, 1990), pp. 308–333.

Miles, M., "A Reconstruction of the Temple of Nemesis at Rhamnous," *Hesperia*, 58 (1989): 131–249.

Millar, F., "Condemnation to Hard Labour in the Roman Empire," *PBSR*, 52 (1984): 124–147.

Millett, M., *The Romanization of Britain* (Cambridge: Cambridge University Press, 1990).

Milne, G., *Roman London* (London: B. T. Batsford, Ltd., 1995).

Mitchell, T., *Blood Sport: A Social History of Spanish Bullfighting* (Philadelphia: University of Pennsylvania Press, 1991).

Moeller, W. G., "The Riot of A.D. 59 at Pompeii," *Historia*, 19 (1970): 84–95.

Mommsen, Th., *"Ludi Romani," Römische Forschungen* (Berlin: Weidmann, 1864–1879).

———, *Die römischen Tribus in administrativer Beziehung* (Altona: J. F. Hammerich, 1844).

———, *Römisches Staatsrecht* (Leipzig: S. Hirzel, 1876–1888).

———, *Römisches Strafrecht* (Leipzig: Verlag von Duncker und Humblot, 1899).

Mosca, P. G., "Child Sacrifice in Canaanite and Israelite Religion: A Study in Mulk and Molech" (Dissertation, Harvard University, 1975).

Moscati, S., *The Phoenicians* (Milan: Bompiani, 1988).

Müller, V., "Studien zur kretisch-mykenischen Künst II," *JDAI*, 42 (1927): 1–29.

Münzer, F., "Iunius," *RE*, 10.1, cols. 960–962.

———, "Iunius Brutus," *RE*, 10.1, cols. 1020–1030.

———, "Iunius Brutus Pera, D.," *RE*, 10.1, col. 1026.

———, "Iunius Brutus Scaeva," *RE*, 10.1, cols. 1026–1027.

Myerhoff, B. G., L. A. Camino, and E. Turner, "Rites of Passage: An Overview," in M. Eliade, ed., *The Encyclopedia of Religion* (New York: MacMillan, 1987), vol. 12, pp. 380–386.

Nash, D., "Celtic Territorial Expansion and the Mediterranean World," in T. Champion and J. Megaw, eds., *Settlement and Society: Aspects of West European*

Prehistory in the First Millennium B.C. (Leicester: Leicester University Press, 1985), pp. 45–67.

———, "Reconstructing Poseidonios' Celtic Ethnography," *Britannia*, 12 (1976): 111–126.

Navarre, O., "Odeum," in Ch. Daremberg, E. Saglio, and E. Pottier, eds., *Dictionnaire des antiquités grecques et romains* (Paris: Hachette et Cie, 1877–1919), vol. 4, pt. 1, pp. 150–152.

Neugebauer, K. A., "Der älteste Gladiatorentypus," *JDAI(AA)*, 55 (1940): 608–611.

Nicolet, C., "Les Equites campani et leurs représentations figurées," *MEFRA*, 74 (1962): 463–517.

———, *The World of the Citizen in Republican Rome* (Berkeley: University of California Press, 1980).

Nicols, J., "Patrona Civitatis: Gender and Civic Patronage," in C. Deroux, ed., *Studies in Latin Literature and Roman History* vol. 5 (Brussels: Collection Latomus, 1989), pp. 117–142.

———, "Zur Verleihung öffentlicher Ehrungen in der römischen Welt," *Chiron*, 9 (1979): 243–260.

Niebuhr, B., *The Roman History* (London: C. and J. Rivington, 1827).

O'Rahilly, C., ed., *Táin Bó Cúailnge from the Book of Leinster* (Dublin: Dublin Institute for Advanced Studies, 1967).

Oakley, S. P., "Single Combat in the Roman Republic," *CQ*, 35 (1985): 392–410.

Oliver, J. H., "A New Letter of Antoninus Pius," *AJP*, 79 (1958): 52–60.

Ottaway, P., *The Book of Roman York* (London: B. T. Batsford, Ltd., 1993).

Pallottino, M., *Etruscologia* (Milan: U. Hoepli, 1963).

Palmer, R. E. A., *The Archaic Community of the Romans* (Cambridge: Cambridge University Press, 1970).

Patterson, O., *Slavery and Social Death: A Comparative Study* (Cambridge, Mass: Harvard University Press, 1982).

Perring, D., *Roman London* (London: B. T. Batsford, Ltd., 1991).

Picard, G.-C., "Les Théâtres ruraux de Gaule," *RA* (1970): 185–192.

Pietilä Castrén, L., *Magnificentia Publica: The Victory Monuments of the Roman Generals in the Era of the Punic Wars* (Helsinki: Societas Scientiarum Fennica, 1987).

Piggott, S., *The Druids* (London: Thames and Hudson, 1968).

Planck, M., *Über den Ursprung der römischen Gladiatorenspiele* (Ulm: Ulmer Gymn. Programm, 1866).

Plass, P., *The Game of Death in Ancient Rome* (Madison: University of Wisconsin Press, 1995).

Pollitt, J. J., *Art in the Hellenistic Age* (Cambridge: Cambridge University Press, 1986).

Pontrandolfo, A., and A. Rouveret, *Le tombe dipinte di Paestum* (Modena: Franco Cosimo Panini, 1992).

Potter, T. W., *Roman Italy* (Berkeley: University of California Press, 1987).

Pounds, N. J. G., "The Urbanization of the Classical World," *Annals of the Association of American Geographers*, 59 (1969): 135–157.

Price, S. R. F., *Rituals and Power: The Roman Imperial Cult in Asia Minor* (Cambridge: Cambridge University Press, 1984).

Radin, M., "The Lex Pompeia and the Poena Cullei," *JRS*, 10 (1920): 119–130.

Rathje, A., "Oriental Imports in Etruria in the 8th and 7th Centuries B.C.: Their Origins and Implications," in D. and F. Ridgway, eds., *Italy before the Romans* (New York: Academic Press, 1979), pp. 145–183.

Rawson, E., "*Discrimina Ordinum*: The *Lex Julia Theatralis*," *PBSR*, 55 (1987): 83–114.

Rea, R., "Le antiche raffigurazioni dell'anfiteatro," in A. M. Reggiani, ed., *Anfiteatro flavio: immagine testimonianze spettacoli* (Rome: Edizioni Quasar, 1988), pp. 23–46.

———, "Recenti osservazioni sulla struttura dell'anfiteatro flavio," in A. M. Reggiani, ed., *Anfiteatro flavio: immagine testimonianze spettacoli* (Rome: Edizioni Quasar, 1988), pp. 9–22.

Reid, J. S., "Human Sacrifices at Rome and Other Notes on Roman Religion," *JRS*, 2 (1912): 34–52.

Reifferscheid, A., *C. Suetonii Tranquilli praeter Caesarum libros reliquiae* (Leipzig: B. G. Teubner, 1860).

Reinach, S., *Répertoire des vases peints grecs et étrusques* (Paris: E. Leroux, 1922–1924).

Rich, J., and A. Wallace-Hadrill, eds., *City and Country in the Ancient World* (New York: Routledge, 1991).

Richardson, E., *The Etruscans* (Chicago: University of Chicago Press, 1964).

Richardson, L., *A New Topographical Dictionary of Ancient Rome* (Baltimore: Johns Hopkins University Press, 1992).

Riches, D., "The Phenomenon of Violence," in D. Riches, ed., *The Anthropology of Violence* (Oxford: Basil Blackwell Ltd., 1986), pp. 1–27.

Ridgway, D., "The Etruscans," in J. Boardman, N. G. L. Hammond, D. M. Lewis, and M. Ostwald, eds., *Cambridge Ancient History* (Cambridge: Cambridge University Press, 1988), vol. 4, pp. 634–675.

Ritschl, F. W., *Die Tesserae gladiatore der Romer* (Munich: Straub, 1864).

Robert, L., *Les Gladiateurs dans l'Orient grec* (Paris: Bibliothèque de l'École des Hautes Études, 1940).

Ronen, D., *Dahomey: Between Tradition and Modernity* (Ithaca: Cornell University Press, 1975).

Ross, A., *Everyday Life of the Pagan Celts* (London: B. T. Batsford Ltd., 1970).

———, *The Pagan Celts* (London: B. T. Batsford, Ltd., 1986).

Rossi, L., *Trajan's Column and the Dacian Wars* (Ithaca: Cornell University Press, 1971).

Rowe, J. H., "Inca Policies and Institutions relating to Cultural Unification," in G. A. Collier, R. Rosaldo, and J. D. Wirth, eds., *Inca and Aztec States 1400–1800: Anthropology and History* (New York: Academic Press, 1982), pp. 93–118.

Rudich, V., *Political Dissidence under Nero: The Price of Dissimulation* (London: Routledge, 1993).

Russel, J., "The Origin and Development of the Republican Forums," *Phoenix*, 22.4 (1968): 304–336.

Russell, G. W., "Psychological Issues in Sports Aggression," in J. H. Goldstein, ed., *Sports Violence* (New York: Springer-Verlag, 1993), pp. 157–181.

Rykwert, J., *The Idea of a Town* (Princeton: Princeton University Press, 1976).

Saddington, D. B., "The Parameters of Romanization," in V. A. Maxfield and M. J. Dobson, eds., *Roman Frontier Studies 1989: Proceedings of the XVth International Congress of Roman Frontier Studies* (Exeter: University of Exeter Press, 1991), pp. 413–418.

Saller, R., "Patria Potestas and the Stereotype of the Roman Family," *Continuity and Change*, 1 (1986): 7–22.

Salmon, E. T., *Samnium and the Samnites* (Cambridge: Cambridge University Press, 1967).

Salway, P., *Oxford Illustrated History of Roman Britain* (Oxford: Oxford University Press, 1993).

Sancery, J., *Galba ou l'armée face au pouvoir* (Paris: Les Belles Lettres, 1983).

Schwenn, F., *Menschenopfer bei den Griechen und Römern* (Giessen: Verlag von Alfred Topelmann, 1915).

Scobie, A., "Spectator Security and Comfort at Gladiatorial Games," *Nikephoros*, 1 (1988): 191–243.

Scullard, H. H., *Festivals and Ceremonies of the Roman Republic* (Ithaca: Cornell University Press, 1981).

Sear, F., *Roman Architecture* (Ithaca: Cornell University Press, 1982).

Serrano Sanchez, C., "Funerary Practices and Human Sacrifice in Teotihuacan Burials," in K. Berrin and E. Pasztory, eds., *Teotihuacan: Art from the City of the Gods* (New York: Thames and Hudson, 1993), pp. 108–115.

Sestieri, P. C., *Paestum* (Rome: Istituto Poligrafico dello Stato, 1967).

———, "Tombe dipinti di Paestum," *RIA*, 5–6 (1956–1957): 65–110.

Sgobbo, I., "Gli ultimi Etruschi della Campania," *RAAN*, n.s. 52 (1977): 1–57.

Sherwin-White, A. N., *The Letters of Pliny: A Historical and Social Commentary* (Oxford: Oxford University Press, 1966).

Siena, S. L., *Luni: Guida archeologica* (Sarzana, 1985).

Skertchly, J. A., *Dahomey as It Is* (London: Chapman and Hall, 1874).

Skocpol, T., and M. Somers, "The Uses of Comparative History in Macrosocial Inquiry," *CSSH*, 22 (1980): 174–197.

Smith, R. R. R., *Hellenistic Sculpture* (New York: Thames and Hudson, 1991).

Smith, W., ed., *A Dictionary of Greek and Roman Biography and Mythology* (London: J. Murray, 1876).

Smith, W., ed., *Dictionary of Greek and Roman Antiquities* (London: J. Murray, 1880).

Sorlin-Dorigny, A., "Stadium," in Ch. Daremberg, E. Saglio, and E. Pottier, eds., *Dictionnaire des Antiquités Grecques et Romains* (Paris: Hachette et Cie, 1877–1919), vol. 4, pt. 2, pp. 1419–1456.

Stager, L. E., "Carthage: A View from the Tophet," in W. Huss, ed., *Karthago* (Darmstadt: Wissenschaftliche Buchgesellschaft, 1992), pp. 353–369.

Stager, L. E., and S. R. Wolff, "Child Sacrifice at Carthage—Religious Rite or Population Control?" *BAR*, 10 (1984): 31–51.

Stambaugh, J. E., *The Ancient Roman City* (Baltimore: Johns Hopkins University Press, 1988).

Strong, D. E., "The Administration of Public Building in Rome during the Late Republic and Early Empire," *BICS*, 15 (1968): 97–109.

Sutherland, C. H., "Aspects of Imperialism in Roman Spain," *JRS*, 24 (1934): 31–42.

Tarchi, U., *L'arte nell'Umbria e nella Sabina* (Milan: Fratelli Treves, 1936–1940).

Taylor, L. R., *The Divinity of the Roman Emperor* (Middletown, Conn.: American Philological Association, 1931).

———, *Roman Voting Assemblies* (Ann Arbor: University of Michigan Press, 1966).

Thevenot, E., *Divinités et sanctuaires de la Gaule* (Paris: Fayard, 1968).

———, "L'Interprétation gauloise des divinités romaines," in M. Renard, ed., *Hommages à Albert Grenier* (Brussels: Collection Latomus, 1962), vol. 1, pp. 1476–1490.

Thornton, M. K. and R. L., *Julio-Claudian Building Programs: A Quantitative Study in Political Management* (Wauconda, Ill.: Bolchazy-Carducci, 1989).

Thuillier, J.-P., *Les Jeux athlétiques dans la civilisation étrusque* (Rome: École française de Rome, 1985).

Thurneysen, R., *Die irische Helden- und Königsage bis zum siebzehnten Jahrhundert* (Halle: M. Niemeyer, 1921).

Tierney, J. J., "The Celtic Ethnography of Posidonius," *Proceedings of the Royal Irish Academy*, 60 (1960): 189–275.

Tierney, P., *The Highest Altar: The Story of Human Sacrifice* (New York: Viking, 1989).

Touchefeu, O., "Aias," in *LIMC*, vol. 1.1, pp. 312–336.

Toutain, J., *Les Cultes païens dans l'empire romain, III* (Paris: Leroux, 1920).

———, "Sacrificium-Rome," in Ch. Daremberg and E. Saglio, eds., *Dictionnaire des antiquités grecques et romaines* (Paris: Hachette et Cie, 1877–1919), vol. 4:2, pp. 976–977.

Trendall, A. D., *Vasi antichi dipinti del Vaticano: Vasi italioti ed etruschi a figure rosse I* (Rome: Citta del Vaticano, 1953–1955).

Tristram, H. L. C., "La razzia des vaches de Cuailnge et les archéologues," *Études celtiques*, 29 (1991): 403–414.

Turcan, R., "L'Autel de Rome et d'Auguste 'ad confluentem'," *ANRW* II.12.1 (1982): 607–644.

Turner, V., *The Anthropology of Performance* (New York: PAJ Publications, 1986).

———, *The Ritual Process* (Chicago: Aldine Publishing Company, 1969).

van der Veen, M., "Native Communities in the Frontier Zone: Uniformity or Diversity?" in V. A. Maxfield and M. J. Dobson, eds., *Roman Frontier Studies*

1989: Proceedings of the XVth International Congress of Roman Frontier Studies (Exeter: University of Exeter Press, 1991), pp. 446–450.

van Gennep, A., *Rites of Passage* (Chicago: University of Chicago Press, 1960).

Vanderbroek, P. J. J., *Popular Leadership and Collective Behavior in the Late Roman Republic* (Amsterdam: J. C. Gieben, 1987).

Versnel, H. S., *Triumphus* (Leiden: Brill, 1970).

Veyne, P., *Bread and Circuses: Historical Sociology and Political Pluralism* (London: Penguin, 1990).

Ville, G., *La Gladiature en Occident des origines à la mort de Domitien* (Rome: École française de Rome, 1981).

———, "Les Jeux de gladiateurs dans l'empire chrétien," *MEFRA*, 72 (1960): 273–335.

Volkmann, H., "Studien zum Nemesiskult," *Archiv für Religionswissenschaft*, 26 (1928): 295–321.

von Petrikovits, H., *Das römische Rheinland: archäologische Forschungen seit 1945* (Cologne: Westdeutscher Verlag, 1960).

von Premerstein, A., "Nemesis und ihre Bedeutung für die Agone," *Philologus*, 53 (1894): 400–415.

Wacher, J., *The Towns of Roman Britain* (London: B. T. Batsford, Ltd., 1995).

Wagenvoort, H., *Roman Dynamism: Studies in Ancient Roman Thought, Language and Custom* (Oxford: B. Blackwell, 1947).

Wait, G. A., *Ritual and Religion in Iron Age Britain* (Oxford: British Archaeological Reports, 1986).

Walbank, F. W., *A Historical Commentary on Polybius* (Oxford: Oxford University Press, 1957).

Waley, A., ed., *Shih Ching: The Book of Songs* (New York: Grove Press, 1960).

Wallace, A. F. C., *Religion: An Anthropological View* (New York: Random House, 1966).

Ward-Perkins, J. B., *Roman Architecture* (New York: H. N. Abrams, 1977).

Warde Fowler, W., *The Religious Experience of the Roman People* (London: MacMillan and Co. Ltd., 1911).

———, *The Roman Festivals of the Period of the Republic: An Introduction to the Study of the Religion of the Romans* (London: MacMillan, 1899).

Wardman, A., *Religion and Statecraft among the Romans* (London: Granada, 1982).

Warmington, E. H., ed., *Remains of Old Latin* (Cambridge, Mass.: Harvard University Press, 1935).

Webster, G., *The British Celts and Their Gods under Rome* (London: B. T. Batsford, Ltd., 1986).

Webster, J., "Sanctuaries and Sacred Places" in M. Green, ed., *The Celtic World* (London: Routledge, 1995), pp. 445–464.

Weeber, K. W., "Troiae lusus," *Ancient Society*, 5 (1974): 171–196.

Weege, F., "Oskische Grabmalerei," *JDAI*, 24 (1909): 99–162.

Weinfeld, M., "The Worship of Molech and of the Queen of Heaven and Its Background," *Ugarit-Forschungen*, 4 (1972): 133–154.

Welch, K., "The Roman Arena in Late-Republican Italy: A New Interpretation," *JRA*, 7 (1994): 59–80.

Wells, P. S., *Culture Contact and Culture Change* (Cambridge: Cambridge University Press, 1981).

Westermann, W. L., "Sklaverei," *RE* Sup. 6, cols. 1035–1036.

———, *The Slave Systems of Greek and Roman Antiquity* (Philadelphia: American Philosophical Society, 1955).

Wheeler, R. E. M., and T. V. Wheeler, "The Roman Amphitheatre at Caerleon, Monmouthshire," *Archaeologia*, 78 (1928): 111–218.

Whittaker, C. R., *Frontiers of the Roman Empire* (Baltimore: Johns Hopkins University Press, 1994).

———, "Rural Labour in Three Roman Provinces," in P. Garnsey, ed., *Non-Slave Labour in the Greco-Roman World* (Cambridge: Cambridge Philological Society, 1980), pp. 73–99.

Wiedemann, T., *Emperors and Gladiators* (New York: Routledge, 1992).

Wilkes, J. J., *Dalmatia* (London: Routledge and K. Paul, 1969).

Wiseman, T. P., *Remus: A Roman Myth* (Cambridge: Cambridge University Press, 1995).

Wissowa, G., *Religion und Kultus der Römer* (Munich: Beck, 1912).

Wistrand, M., *Entertainment and Violence in Ancient Rome* (Göteborg: Ekblads, 1992).

Woolley, L., *Excavations at Ur* (London: E. Benn, 1954).

Woolley, L., with P. R. S. Moorey, ed., *Ur "of the Chaldees"* (London: Herbert Press, 1982).

Wright, R. P., "Roman Britain in 1966: The Inscriptions," *JRS*, 57 (1967): 203–210.

Wünsch, R., "Roman Human Sacrifice," in J. Hastings, ed., *The Encyclopedia of Religion and Ethics* (New York: Charles Scribner's Sons, 1914), vol. 6, pp. 858–862.

Yavetz, Z., *Plebs and Princeps* (Oxford: Clarendon Press, 1969).

Zanker, P., *The Power of Images in the Age of Augustus* (Ann Arbor: University of Michigan Press, 1988).

Zuidema, R. T., "Bureaucracy and Systematic Knowledge in Andean Civilization," in G. A. Collier, R. Rosaldo, and J. D. Wirth, eds., *Inca and Aztec States 1400–1800: Anthropology and History* (New York: Academic Press, 1982), pp. 419–458.

———, "Shafttombs and the Inca Empire," *Journal of the Steward Anthropological Society*, 9 (1978): 133–178.

INDEX

Italicized page numbers refer to illustrations.